Scientists Making a Difference is a fascinating collection of first-person narratives from the top psychological scientists of the modern era. These readable essays highlight the most important contributions to theory and research in psychological science, show how the greatest psychological scientists formulate and think about their work, and illustrate how their ideas develop over time. In particular, the authors address what they consider their most important scientific contribution: how they got the idea, how the idea matters for the world beyond academic psychology, and what they would like to see as the next steps in research. The contributors, who were chosen from an objectively compiled list of the most eminent psychological scientists of the modern era, provide a broad range of insightful perspectives. This book is essential reading for students, researchers, and professionals interested in learning about the development of the biggest ideas in modern psychological science, described first-hand by the scientists themselves.

Robert J. Sternberg is Professor of Human Development at Cornell University. Formerly, he was IBM Professor of Psychology and Education at Yale. He won the 1999 James McKeen Cattell Fellow Award and the 2017 William James Fellow Award from the Association for Psychological Science. He is editor of *Perspectives on Psychological Science*. His main fields of interest are intelligence, creativity, wisdom, ethics, love, and hate. His PhD is from Stanford and he has 13 honorary doctorates. He is a member of the National Academy of Education and the American Academy of Arts and Sciences. Sternberg is the author of roughly 1,600 publications and has been cited over 112,000 times, with an h index of 160 and an i10 index of 790. He has been a university professor, dean, provost, and president, and is past-president of the American Psychological Association and the Federation of Associations in Behavioral and Brain Sciences.

Susan T. Fiske is Eugene Higgins Professor, Psychology and Public Affairs, Princeton University. She investigates cognitive stereotypes and emotional prejudices, culturally, interpersonally, and neuro-scientifically. Her books include *The Human Brand: How We Relate to People, Products, and Companies* (with Chris Malone, 2013); *Envy Up, Scorn Down: How Status Divides Us* (2011); and *Social Cognition* (with Shelley Taylor,

2013). She edits *Annual Review of Psychology*, *PNAS*, and *Policy Insights from Behavioral and Brain Sciences*. She is past president of the Federation of Associations in Behavioral and Brain Sciences, was elected to the National Academy of Sciences, and won Princeton University's as well as APS's Graduate Mentoring Award.

Donald J. Foss is Professor of Psychology at the University of Houston and has served on the faculties of the University of Texas at Austin and Florida State University. He has served as a department chair, dean, and provost. His publications have focused on language processing, memory, and student success, including a recent book for college students, *Your Complete Guide to College Success: How to Study Smart, Achieve Your Goals, and Enjoy Campus Life*. He has been editor, associate editor, and board member of numerous publications, including *American Psychologist*, *Annual Review of Psychology*, and *Contemporary Psychology*. He is Vice President of the Federation of Associations in Behavioral and Brain Sciences. Foss received an all-University Outstanding Teaching Award at the University of Texas at Austin, and an Outstanding Achievement Award from the University of Minnesota.

Advance Praise for Scientists Making a Difference

"In 100 autobiographical essays, psychology's preeminent contributors reveal the roots and fruits of their famed contributions. Here are stories for posterity, from the funding barriers that challenged Thomas Bouchard's study of reared-apart twins, to Michael Gazzaniga's exhilaration on discovering the wonders of human split-brains, to Carol Dweck's "me-search" on how she and others could find a thriving mindset when facing obstacles. This is living history—and a great read for both psychological scientists and students."

> – David G. Myers, Professor of Psychology, Hope College

"Reading this book is like spending an afternoon chatting with some of psychology's most prominent scholars. They talk about the significance of their work, describe how they honed their creative ideas, and offer advice for dealing with failures, adversity, and success. The authors invite us inside their laboratories and provide a rare insight into the process of making a difference."

> – Diane Halpern, Dean of Social Sciences, Emerita,
> Minerva Schools at KGI and Professor of Psychology,
> Emerita, Claremont McKenna College

"Asking a couple 'How did you two meet?' inevitably elicits an interesting story, and this is essentially what the editors of this volume have done by asking a group of eminent psychological scientists to talk about their love affairs with their work. The result is a set of brief but fascinating stories that not only inspire admiration of these brilliant authors but will surely lead some of today's best students to dream of following in their footsteps."

> – Douglas A. Bernstein, Professor of Psychology,
> University of South Florida

"A wonderful book and an instant classic. In this remarkable series of essays bookended by two thought-provoking summaries, 100 eminent psychological scholars offer readers an insider's glimpse of how to achieve scientific excellence. This superb book is a powerful reminder of the value of serendipity in scientific discovery. Psychology lovers will find the often surprising insights from our field's premier scholars invaluable, and will have a difficult time putting the book down. Great fun and highly recommended."

> – Scott O. Lilienfeld, Ph.D., Samuel Candler Dobbs
> Professor of Psychology, Emory University & Editor,
> Clinical Psychological Science

"In engaging and highly personal essays, the most eminent psychologists of our time show the human side of their life's work. Anyone with an interest in the influences behind the key theories and findings of the discipline will be captivated by this volume."

> – Robert S. Feldman, Professor of Psychological
> and Brain Sciences and Deputy Chancellor,
> University of Massachusetts Amherst

"Surely every psychological researcher or professor will want to read this insightful book. Moreover, every student should be *required* to read it. Most undergraduate psychology majors and even many graduate students can name hundreds of athletes, singers, and actors, but they struggle to name any living psychologist other than their professors and "Dr. Phil." It's about time we call attention to our research rock stars!

– James Kalat, Professor Emeritus, N. C. State University

"Even beyond the Who's Who of Psychological Scientists represented by the authors and editors of this volume (and talk about an impossible task to begin with!), the sum of the topics contained throughout these chapters makes the indisputable case for Psychological Science as the way forward in understanding so much of what is important in our world."

– Alan Kraut, Association for Psychological Science,
Executive Director Emeritus

"A wonderful collection of essays from psychology's A-listers. We quickly learn that they are engaging writers, as their stories bring their important discoveries to life. Every aspiring psychological scientist will want to read these essays, hoping to emulate at least some of the qualities that these eminent scientists share."

– Todd F. Heatherton, Lincoln Filene Professor
in Human Relations, Dartmouth College

Scientists Making a Difference

One Hundred Eminent Behavioral and Brain Scientists Talk about Their Most Important Contributions

---

Edited by

Robert J. Sternberg
Cornell University

Susan T. Fiske
Princeton University

Donald J. Foss
University of Houston

CAMBRIDGE
UNIVERSITY PRESS

CAMBRIDGE
UNIVERSITY PRESS

One Liberty Plaza, 20th Floor, New York NY 10006, USA

Cambridge University Press is part of the University of Cambridge.

It furthers the University's mission by disseminating knowledge in the pursuit of education, learning, and research at the highest international levels of excellence.

www.cambridge.org
Information on this title: www.cambridge.org/9781107566378

© Cambridge University Press 2016

First published 2016

Printed in the United States of America by Sheridan Books, Inc.

A catalogue record for this publication is available from the British Library.

Library of Congress Cataloguing-in-Publication Data
Sternberg, Robert J., editor. | Fiske, Susan T., editor. | Foss, Donald J., 1940–, editor.
Scientists making a difference : one hundred eminent behavioral and brain scientists talk about their most important contributions / edited by Robert J. Sternberg, Susan T. Fiske, Donald J. Foss.
New York NY : Cambridge University Press, 2016. | Includes bibliographical references.
LCCN 2016016315| ISBN 9781107127135 (hardback) | ISBN 9781107566378 (paperback)
| MESH: Behavioral Sciences | Neurosciences | Personal Narratives
LCC BF76.5 | NLM BF 76.5 | DDC 150.72–dc23
LC record available at https://lccn.loc.gov/2016016315

ISBN 978-1-107-12713-5 Hardback
ISBN 978-1-107-56637-8 Paperback

Contents

Part VI   Social and Personality Processes: Who We Are and How We Interact

Contributors

Amabile, Teresa M.
Anderson, Craig A.
Anderson, John R.
Aronson, Elliot.
Atkinson, Richard C.
Baddeley, Alan.
Bandura, Albert.
Bargh, John A.
Barlow, David H.
Baumeister, Roy R.
Belsky, Jay.
Berkowitz, Leonard.
Berscheid, Ellen.
Bouchard, Thomas J., Jr.
Bower, Gordon H.
Brewer, Marilynn.
Brooks-Gunn, Jeanne.
Buss, David M.
Cacioppo, John T.
Cantor, Nancy.
Carey, Susan.
Carver, Charles S.
Caspi, Avshalom.
Ceci, Stephen J.
Clore, Gerald L.
Cohen, Sheldon.
Craik, Fergus I. M.
Csikszentmihalyi, Mihaly.
Damasio, Antonio.
Davis, Michael.
Deci, Edward L.
Deutsch, Morton.

Pinker, Steven.
Plomin, Robert.
Posner, Michael I.
Prochaska, James O.
Robbins, Trevor W.
Roediger, Henry L. III.
Ross, Lee.
Ryan, Richard M.
Salovey, Peter.
Salthouse, Timothy A.
Schacter, Daniel L.
Schaie, K. Warner.
Scheier, Michael F.
Schneider, Walter.
Seligman, Martin.
Shepard, Roger N.
Shiffrin, Richard M.
Siegler, Robert S.
Slovic, Paul.
Spelke, Elizabeth.
Squire, Larry R.
Sternberg, Robert J.
Taylor, Shelley E.
Treisman, Anne.
Triandis, Harry C.
Tulving, Endel.
Wagner, Allan R.
Watson, David.
Wilson, Timothy.

Foreword
Making a Creative Difference = Person × Environment

Salovey, Peter

Obviously this volume is a *Who's Who* of contemporary behavioral and neuroscience. In my teaching days, I believe I could have organized an entire Introduction to Psychology course just by describing the work of the individuals listed in the Table of Contents. And it is easy to focus on these names: they represent some of the smartest and most creative individuals in the world, resilient scholars not afraid of hard work or failure.

But as a social psychologist (and one with clinical training), I am also aware of the context in which these individuals carried out this wonderful work – the settings in which these ideas were developed, experiments designed, and findings communicated. Social psychologists place great importance on context – situations and environments that shape behavior. The father of modern social psychology, Kurt Lewin, famously articulated the first principle of this emerging field of study: $B = f (P, E)$. Behavior is a function of the person, his or her environment, and the interaction between the two. This simple formula may seem like a truism to any student of psychology, but it serves to remind us that behavior is not motivated in a vacuum. We may believe we are the architects of our actions – especially our accomplishments – but, in fact, the environments in which we find ourselves, and the manner in which we as individuals respond to those environments, can create huge differences in outcomes that we often assign "merely" to individual agency or internal attributes such as "grit" or determination.

So, let me tell a little story and then circle back to this amazing volume. On a trip to Sweden a few years ago, my wife and I visited the Nobel Museum, a wonderful place located in what was once the Stockholm Stock Exchange. We appreciated a presentation designed to coincide with the 100th anniversary of the Nobel Prize. Remarkably, at what anyone would expect to be the ultimate glorification of the individual person and self-directed accomplishment, the theme of the Museum's Centennial Exhibition was *Cultures of Creativity*. It would be reasonable to expect the Nobel Museum to bask in the glory of personal achievement, but, no, the

xxi

Centennial Exhibition was not about Lewin's P but about his E – the importance of environment in promoting the courage to think in entirely new directions, dare to question established ideas, and innovatively combine insights from different fields of study.

The Nobel Museum's theme was that special places, and the unplanned conversations and interactions that arise within them, spur creativity. Spectacular examples from all over the world were presented in amusing ways. Visitors could travel to Calcutta and find themselves in a progressive school inspired in 1901 by the poet Rabindranath Tagore. Then it is on to the cafes of Paris in the 1920s to feel the atmosphere of creative revolt as experienced by Ernest Hemingway and Samuel Beckett. The exhibition asked us to appreciate next the endless conversations and "Copenhagen spirit" that characterized the theoretical physics institute of Niels Bohr in the 1920s and 1930s. Guests were transported to Cambridge University's Cavendish Laboratories, where young James Watson and Francis Crick worked out the double-helical structure of the DNA molecule. Visitors could enjoy the Basel Institute of Immunology, described as a scientist's paradise, distinguished during the 1970s and 1980s by its lavish resources, egalitarian spirit, lively parties, and, of course, prize-winning science. These and other work environments fostered spontaneity, collegiality, intellectual intensity, and, most importantly, the opportunity for the unfettered exchange of insights and ideas, some bizarre and others amazing. The point was that whatever brilliance we have been able to attain is in part a function of the environments in which we find ourselves.

I was so impressed by this exhibition that I spoke about it at Yale's matriculation ceremony for new graduate students that year, and again in a welcoming address for freshmen in Yale College. And I think it is relevant to the present volume as well: take a look at the places where these great behavioral and brain scientists have conducted their most important work – this is not a list of randomly sampled departments and universities! Rather, they constitute the kinds of cultures of creativity celebrated by the Nobel Museum. Of course the scholars represented in this book bring to their laboratories admirable wisdom, deep insight, and the capacity for persistence in the face of setbacks. But they also are immersed in social environments where they are allowed to flourish and, I suspect, are actively encouraged and supported.

The authors of the chapters of this volume – these scientists making a difference – work in environments where students, postdoctoral scholars, and colleagues influence them, and vice versa. Perhaps they explicitly created environments where ingenuity and imagination can flourish, where tenacity and determination are reinforced. There is no doubt that what they bring to these environments, as well as the nature of these environments themselves, interact in the way Lewin's formula suggests to motivate inquiry in psychology and the brain sciences. To appreciate the precise way in which that interaction unfolds requires one to read these chapters: Each of the authors describes relevant psychological processes at various levels of analysis, from the biological to the cognitive to the developmental to the social and cultural, and all may matter in motivating work that makes a difference. To their explications of these processes, I might add that emotional intelligence (which Jack Mayer and I defined as the set of abilities that allows one to identify, understand, and manage one's own and others' emotions in order to use this information to organize thinking and motivate behavior) would seem like a good candidate for an attribute that enables scientists to select or create environments that will contribute positively toward their successes or to obtain the most from those environments in which they find themselves.

But I do not want to end this foreword on a self-referential note. Rather, I would like to conclude with a bit of gratitude. These chapters were written by my heroes. Whatever role I may now play at my university, my identity is as a researcher and educator in psychology first, and these are the individuals who have contributed enormously to my understanding of human behavior. They are also role models as investigators and as teachers. I can imagine no better introduction to the major issues in our field, broadly speaking, than the thoughts of these individuals. By reading about their most important contributions, one will be inspired to join them in making a difference.

Preface

What do research psychologists do? How do they think about their work? What does psychological science look like as it goes on in the heads of top psychological scientists? How do these scientists develop their ideas over time?

The purpose of this book is to hear, in the first person, from some of the most eminent psychologists of the modern era regarding what they view as their single most important contribution to the behavioral and brain sciences. The list of invitees was based on rankings compiled by Diener, Shigehiro, and Park (2014), using criteria such as number of major awards, total number of citations, and pages of textbooks devoted to the scholars' work. Such lists, of course, would have different members depending on the criteria used, but the list seemed to us as good a basis for recognition as any we could find.

We invited all living members of the list of 200 individuals (many were deceased at the time we were preparing the book) for whom we could find contact information. The overwhelming majority of individuals still living and able to write, 100 scientists in all, agreed to write either singly or jointly, yielding 101 chapters, including the introduction and conclusion. (Some individuals were still alive but no longer in sufficiently good health to be able to write a chapter.) In each case, they were given the option of either writing a sole-authored piece (which the large majority did), writing with another member of the list (which happened in two cases, in which the individuals became famous for their collaborative work), or writing with someone outside the list (which happened in one case, in which the junior author of the chapter was instrumental to the accomplishment of the work described). After asking each member of the list to write, we asked two additional extremely distinguished psychologists who are also academic leaders and administrators – a university president and a university chancellor – to write the foreword and afterword, and both agreed to do so.

Each essay addresses just five questions:

1. What do you consider to be your most important scientific contribution?
2. Why do you consider it to be your most important contribution?

3. How did you get the idea for the contribution?
4. How does the idea matter for the world beyond academic psychology?
5. What would you like to see as the next steps in theory and/or research?

We asked the scientists to write for a first-year undergraduate taking a course in introductory psychology. The goal of the book is to present to students and possible future scientists the excitement of the field and how some of its best people think about their science. We hope that the book will be inspirational as well as informative to you. It attempts to inform readers not just about the great contributions, but also about how behavioral and brain scientists think about their contributions, where these contributions come from, and where they are going. We have tried to capture personal stories of the authors' involvement in, and excitement about, the scientific process.[1]

When students read about the contributions of great behavioral and brain scientists, they usually read them in one of two forms. The first is through textbooks. Such presentations lack the voice of the originators of the ideas and often give students little sense of the science that was involved – where the idea came from, why the scientist thought it was important, and where the scientists wanted to go with it. The second is through articles in journals – the place where much of original science is presented to the world. Such articles purposely lose the autobiographical element and are "formulaically" written. The articles are often so detailed that students at entry levels cannot understand them or see why they are important in a larger context. Our book is intended to convey to you the excitement of the science and the depth of thinking that characterizes the great scientists of the era.

The primary intended audience of the book is undergraduate and graduate students in psychology. We believe the book could serve as a supplementary text in many different courses in psychology and psychological sciences in general. For example, it might serve as a supplement in history of psychology and in methods courses, as well as in first-year graduate proseminars. The secondary intended audience for this book is active behavioral and brain scientists. Many of these scientists will want to learn how some of the greatest scientists in the field go about getting ideas, doing their research, and promoting their theories and findings.

This book is divided into eight parts: Each part corresponds roughly to a part of a course in introductory psychology. Moreover, each part is

---

[1] A few words about the list: its inclusion criteria were broad and multiple, but no selection rules are perfect. In addition, because of the era in which these scientists achieved eminence, you will not find many women or members of minority groups writing for this collection. Times are steadily changing, however, and we hope this book inspires all kind of students to consider a career in our stimulating field.

further divided into sections corresponding to topics in introductory psychology courses, so the book can easily be used in conjunction with a course in introductory psychology.

This book was written under the auspices of FABBS—the Federation of Associations in Behavioral and Brain Sciences. We, as editors, are all officers of FABBS (at the time that the book is being prepared). The goal of FABBS is to educate people, and especially the public, legislators, and policy analysts, about the contributions the behavioral and brain sciences have to make to science as a whole and to society. All royalties from the book are being donated to FABBS.

We hope you enjoy our book. It was written for *you!*

ROBERT J. STERNBERG
SUSAN T. FISKE
DONALD J. FOSS

REFERENCE

Diener, E., Shigehiro, O., & Park. J.-Y. (2014). An incomplete list of eminent psychologists of the modern era. *Archives of Scientific Psychology*, 2, 20–32 (http://psycnet.apa.org/journals/arc/2/1/20.html).

Part I

Introduction

1   What Makes a Psychological Scientist "Eminent"?

Sternberg, Robert J.

The chapters in this book represent the contributions of more than 100 eminent psychological scientists, but they also represent the work of countless other individuals who have supported these scientists in their work. Almost any time one speaks of eminence, one really is speaking of the work of a team of people – not only the great psychological scientists, but also the collaborators and support staff who made their work possible. Almost all – perhaps all of the eminent psychological scientists represented in this book – would view the success of their students as among their greatest accomplishments. At the same time, they would recognize that they could serve only as mentors – that it was the students themselves who, to a large extent, lifted themselves up by their own bootstraps. If you are a student reading this book, you have the opportunity to come to represent the next generation of eminent psychological scientists.

When I was a graduate student, I often wondered how I could get from where I was as an unknown quantity to where eminent scientists like my advisors (Gordon Bower and Endel Tulving, both of whom authored chapters in this book) were. I was not even sure, at that point, what it was that the field of psychological science looked for to recognize a scientist as "eminent." The final chapter of this book discusses some of the *characteristics of scientists* in this book who have achieved eminence. This chapter, in contrast, discusses the *characteristics of the work of these scientists* that have led the scientists to achieve eminence. So, if you are a student, these are some of the goals you may have for the work you do, if indeed your goal is to achieve eminence in the field. Put another way, these are some of the goals to seek if you might want to be in the next generation of eminent scientists like those in this book. Of course, these goals could apply to any field, but this essay considers goals as they apply in psychological science.

Impact

Impact refers to the influence a scientist's ideas have on a field of endeavor – essentially, the force of the ideas in terms of changing the ways

3

people think or the things people do. Impactful work changes a field (hopefully for the better!). Many scientific articles are published in a given year, but the large majority of them change the field little, if at all.

There are different ways to have impact. My colleagues James Kaufman, Jean Pretz, and I have categorized some of the ways in which impact can be achieved. Some scientists have impact by moving current paradigms forward in leaps and bounds. Other scientists change the direction in which a field is moving. And still other scientists propose that in the future the field has to start over – that currently it is moving in the wrong direction. For example, the cognitive psychologists of the late 1950s and early 1960s – individuals such as Herbert Simon, Jerome Bruner, and George Miller – suggested that psychology had to start over in the way it conceived of thinking, moving from the Skinnerian emphasis on contingencies of reinforcement to an emphasis on the mental processes that go on inside the head when an individual is learning, remembering, or thinking.

Low-impact work is not work people disagree with; it is work that people do not even bother to cite because they do not believe it of sufficient importance to talk about it. Sometimes, scientists can get so caught up in the desire to publish that they forget that it is important not just to publish, but also to publish work that will somehow influence the field.

Quality

Quality refers to the excellence of scientific work, usually relative to other work being done in the field. Although one can think of some kind of "absolute" rather than "relative" quality, it is hard to know what "absolute" quality would mean. For example, what we could expect in terms of quality of work done in 1816 would be different from what we could expect in terms of quality in 2016. The techniques and lab equipment available in 1816 simply were not up to the standards of 2016, so one could not judge the quality of work done then by the same standard as might be used today.

Quality involves many different components. Perhaps the most important ones are the size, scope, and importance of the problem one is studying. Does one seek to study big important problems or just tiny unimportant ones? A second component is how well one studies the problems one chooses – does one study them in a rigorous and elegant fashion, or in a sloppy ill-considered way that makes it difficult to draw conclusions? A third component is how well one communicates one's data. Does one recognize what is important in one's data, and present it so people can understand it, or does one communicate in a way that no one can or wants to understand, with the result that the work never achieves its potential?

Why separate quality from impact? Because not all work of excellent quality is extremely high impact. The impact of work will depend in part upon how many scientists work in a given field. If a particular scientist is working in a field with many other scientists in it, it will be easier to achieve impact than if that scientist is working in a smaller field where there simply are not as many other scientists likely to cite the work. A scientist could do elegant, innovative, and top-quality work that just happens to be on problems different from those of interest to many other scientists, and we would not want such scientists to be viewed as inferior because they choose to explore problems less studied by others.

Quantity

Quantity refers simply to the amount of work that a scientist has produced. More eminent scientists, on average, have produced a greater volume of work than less eminent scientists. They are not "one-idea" scholars who have a great idea, only then to disappear into obscurity. Rather, they keep coming up with new ideas that keep them productive.

Some scientists cast a skeptical eye on the idea of quantity, believing that highly productive scientists, at least in terms of quantity of work, often turn out lots of articles or books that are of lesser quality. But Dean Simonton, one of the foremost scientists of all time in the field of creativity, has shown this folk conception of quantity to be a myth. In fact, there is a high correlation between quality and quantity in scientific work. They are not the same, of course. But the idea that there are marvelously deep thinkers out there who produce only a small quantity of profound work does not hold up to empirical analysis. Certainly there are some low-quantity producers who do work of top quality. And there are mass producers who turn out junk. But for the most part, the two characteristics – quality and quantity – are highly correlated, and eminent people have lots of ideas rather than just a few. On the whole, eminence tends to result from many excellent ideas, not just one or two.

Visibility

Visibility refers to the extent to which scientists other than oneself are aware of one's work. Scientists achieve visibility by publishing in widely read (and usually high-quality) journals, by giving conference presentations or posters, by giving colloquia in a variety of settings, by sometimes having their work picked up by the media, and so forth. Visibility is different from quality or impact. Someone can be highly visible for doing inferior work. For example, a medical researcher, Andrew Wakefield, achieved great visibility by falsely claiming to have shown that childhood vaccinations are linked to autism. But, for the most part, visibility is correlated with eminence. More eminent researchers tend to be ones that scientists, and sometimes laypeople, have heard about. And to achieve impact, one often needs visibility so that other scientists are aware of one's work and thus are in a position to cite it.

Measurement of Eminence

Eminence can be measured in a variety of ways. Diener and his colleagues, whose work formed the basis of selecting authors for the chapters of this book, used certain measures. Other scientists might have chosen other measures. There is no one set of universally agreed-upon measures of eminence.

The most common measure is simply the number of times the work of a scientist is cited. Are other scientists recognizing the work? Are they using it in their own work? Number of citations does not signify that individual scientists agree with the ideas or findings in the research. They may disagree with the work, perhaps strongly. Rather, it indicates that the scientists believe the work is worthy of notice and of being referenced.

There are other measures of eminence besides number of citations. One is a measure called the *h*-index, which refers to the number, *h*, of publications of a scientist that have been cited at least *h* times. So, a scientist with an *h*-index of fifteen would have fifteen publications that have been cited at least fifteen times. A second is a measure called the *i-10* index, which is the number of publications that have been cited at least ten times. Another way to measure eminence is to assess the extent of coverage of a scientist's work in textbooks – the vehicles for transmitting scientific ideas and research to the next generation. There are many other measures as well.

All measures of eminence are imperfect. A scientist may be cited because his work is bad ("Don't do what Professor X did!") or because his views are controversial ("It's hard to believe that Professor X can hold to these beliefs!"). But for the most part, if one views the measures only as advisory and uses several of them in conjunction (e.g., total number of citations, *h*-index, and *i-10* index), one can get some idea of a scientist's impact. In the end, what matters is not one particular index or another, but something harder to pin down: just how much a scientist's work has changed the way people think and act in a field.

It is important also to realize that none of the measures of eminence are completely "fair." Scientists have had lesser citation rates at various times in history (perhaps including the present) because of their gender, religion, race, nationality, or ethnicity, or because they were at less widely recognized institutions. In assessing the eminence of an individual scientist, one must realize that indices such as the h or i-10 are no substitutes for considered judgment.

Do you want to become an eminent scientist like the ones in this book (and also like the many eminent scientists not represented in the book)? If so, think about some of the characteristics that make scientists in this book eminent. Think about impact, quality, quantity, and visibility. And think about one other thing: scientific ethics. Nothing destroys a career, even an eminent one, faster than unethical behavior in scientific work. So, accomplish your goals whilst always adhering to the highest standards of scientific ethics.

REFERENCES

Diener, E., Shigehiro, O., & Park. J.-Y. (2014). An incomplete list of eminent psychologists of the modern era. *Archives of Scientific Psychology*, *2*, 20–32 (http://psycnet.apa.org/journals/arc/2/1/20.html).

Simonton, D. K. (1994). *Greatness: Who makes history and why*. New York: Guilford Press.

Simonton, D. K. (2004). *Discovery in science: Chance, logic, genius, and Zeitgeist*. New York: Cambridge University Press.

Sternberg, R. J., & Fiske, S. E. (eds.) (2015). *Ethical challenges in the behavioral and brain sciences: Case studies and commentaries*. New York: Cambridge University Press.

Sternberg, R. J., Kaufman, J. C., & Pretz, J. E. (2002). *The creativity conundrum: A propulsion model of kinds of creative contributions*. New York: Psychology Press.

2   Feelings and Decisions

Damasio, Antonio

Writing about one's work is embarrassing, but the editors of this book have made the assignment easier by providing the authors with guiding questions. I will address them in the original order, as if I were answering questions in an imaginary interview.

1.   What Do You Consider to Be Your Most Important Scientific Contribution?

I believe my best contribution has been the attempt to elucidate the nature of affective phenomena, in particular the collection of processes known as feelings and emotions. I have tried to understand these phenomena in psychological as well as neural terms, by placing them in the context of their likely evolutionary origin, immediate functional consequences, and ultimate implications.

Part of my contribution has to do with achieving some clarity regarding the definition of these phenomena, an indispensable part of scientific progress. This has not been easy because problematic definitions have hampered affect research beginning with William James, the genius creator of the field. For example, feelings and emotions are often thought to be one and the same thing, by specialists and by lay public alike, but they clearly are not.

Feelings are mental accounts of the state of life within the organism in whose mind the feeling occurs. In other words, feelings are mental portrayals of the myriad actions required to perform life's management as it proceeds, moment by moment, within an organism. The range of "portrayed" actions includes the contraction or distention of muscle fibers required for visceral functions (cardiac, respiratory, digestive), as well as the release of endocrine and neuromodulator molecules. Thus, the language used in the portrayal is not that of the external senses – such as vision or audition – but rather the language of internal sensation, also known as interoception.

The regulatory operations that we experience as feelings can be quite simple or fairly complex. Examples of the former include the physical states of hunger, thirst, pain, and pleasure. The corresponding feelings are called *homeostatic*. Examples of the latter – the complex regulatory operations – include emotive reactions such as panic, desire, caring and compassion, joy, fear, and anger. The corresponding feelings are called *emotional*. The action programs of such emotions are engaged either by internal drives and motivations or by certain external conditions. For instance, powerful mammalian drives such as "attachment" and "play" generate emotive organism states felt as caring and joy; the perception of a potentially destructive stimulus generates fear, and so forth. Ultimately, all of these reactions are life-regulatory.

In sum, feelings are mental experiences of *any* homeostatic-related actions, simple or complex, while emotions, in the most typical instances, are the actual sets of actions. To confuse feelings with emotions is to confuse mental experiences – mind states – with actions.

We also must distinguish feelings from other mental experiences because the source of feelings is the living body, and the contents of feelings are the variable states of life's functions. Other mental experiences can be about anything out in the world, present or past, concrete or abstract. Feelings reflect automated *value assessments* of internal life states in mental terms. The values may be positive, conducive to the continuation of life, in which case the mental experience is pleasant; or they may be negative, reflect dysfunction, and point to disease and death, in which case they are unpleasant. Feelings have valence; they are not indifferent mental experiences.

The remarkable consequence of the physiological status of feelings is as follows: when feelings are juxtaposed to other mental experiences, they automatically *qualify* those experiences. I have written that the valence of feelings lets them act as a passionate commentator to the otherwise cold procession of other mental experiences. I believe the metaphor is apt. Feelings compel behavior.

Seen in this light, the merit of feelings is obvious. Feelings provide a *conscious*-level report on the state of life. By so doing they introduce a new layer into the biological machinery of life regulation. Life regulation proceeds in great part under the radar of consciousness, at chemical and neural levels unbeknownst to the owner of these processes. When life regulation gives rise to feelings, the situation changes. Now the mind of a given organism actually *knows* of the state of life underneath. What the mind of each organism will do with the information depends on how rich that mind is in intellectual terms – how intelligent, how knowledgeable about the world around and within.

One critical issue regarding the feeling process concerns its system-level neural basis. Contrary to traditional thinking, we do not see the cerebral cortex as the primary or even single source of feelings. Nuclei in the upper brain stem play a critical role here. The process also depends on contributions from peripheral nerves and from molecules acting directly on central nervous system structures devoid of blood-brain barrier.

2.   Why Do You Consider It to Be Your Most Important Contribution?

My view of feelings helps elucidate the possible evolution of homeostasis. It addresses the transition from non-conscious homeostasis occurring in organisms without nervous systems (or with very simple nervous systems) to the sort of homeostasis that occurs in organisms that generate feelings and in which, as a result, the efficiency of the homeostatic process is vastly improved and extended to sociocultural levels of operation.

My perspective on the feeling process addresses seemingly intractable aspects of the hard problem of consciousness, which consists of explaining how mental experiences – subjective mental states imbued by feelingness, i.e., qualia – arise from biological tissue. I regard subjectivity – which requires a unique organism perspective on percepts, recalled memories, and reasoning processes – as a by-product of feelings. As for feelingness, it is a direct consequence of the ability to feel.

3.   How Did You Get the Idea for the Contribution?

When I began my professional career I was interested in the workings of the mind and in discovering the neural mechanisms behind those workings. Language was my main topic, along with other aspects of the intellectual machinery – perception, memory, reasoning. In retrospect this was odd, because my general interests included music, poetry, the novel, and film – art forms dominated by an emotive and feeling sensibility. Yet, I kept my pastimes and my work in separate compartments, as it were.

All of this was to change when I had the chance to study patients with a striking dissociation newly acquired as a result of focal brain damage. The patients had the smarts necessary to act intelligently – the requisite knowledge and the ability to manipulate it – and yet they acted poorly. I tried to explain this most striking dissociation in terms of a primary intellectual flaw, but to no avail.

As my colleagues and I investigated these cases further, it became clear that the causes of the problems did not reside primarily within their intellectual processes, but, rather, within the processes of emotion and feeling. I still remember the very first such patient I saw. It had been noted already that there was a certain flatness in his affect, but the problem was worse than mere flatness. He was unable to react emotively to the ongoing contents of his mind. This personality feature was new. In this patient, and in others like him, this feature had followed the onset of damage to a specific sector of their brains – namely, their frontal association cortices, especially in the ventromedial region.

In line with what I explained earlier, I reasoned that when these patients needed to select a course of action rapidly among several options, their failure to react emotively and thus differentially to each option, based on their prior experience, made them approach all options as equally meritorious. They did not feel especially well or especially poorly about any of the options. In practice, the decision-making field of such patients was now flat. The selection of a response was assigned to a lengthy and time-consuming intellectual analysis, unaided by the quick sorting system that differential feelings naturally provided. In normal individuals, on the contrary, differential emotive responses would cause differentiating feelings and thus quickly favor a particular option. Note that I was not suggesting that feelings make the decision. Feelings simply assisted the reasoning process. And note that the helpful emotion/feeling was a result of prior emotive experiences with comparable situations, rather than being extraneous to the decision problem.

Because the contents of feelings always refer to the body – that is, the soma – I called those feelings *somatic markers*. The name has stuck, attached to the description of this framework as the *somatic marker hypothesis*.

4.   How Does the Idea Matter for Psychological Science and Also for the World Beyond Academia?

Understanding affect in the context of psychology and neurobiology is relevant, for example, to the elucidation of decision-making processes and to the treatment of illnesses such as depression and the addictions. As noted, I regard it as critical to reorienting thinking and research on the problem of consciousness.

5.   What Would You Like to See as Next Steps in Theory and/or Research?

We need to have a detailed investigation of the relationship between non-nervous and nervous system structures – literally, the relationship between body and brain – at molecular, cellular, and system levels. When we study the physiology of the autonomic nervous systems, or the relationships between glia and neurons, we are beginning to approach the problem.

REFERENCES

Damasio, A. (1999/2000). *The feeling of what happens: body and emotion in the making of consciousness.* New York: Harcourt.

Damasio, A. (2005). *Descartes' error* (10th anniversary edn.). New York: Penguin Books [First edition Putnam, 1994].

Damasio, A. (2010/2011). *Self comes to mind: Constructing the conscious brain.* New York: Pantheon/Vintage.

3   My Career in Fear

Davis, Michael

As with most important things in life (who your parents were, where you were born, how you met your spouse), my adoption of the acoustic startle reflex as a way to study fear happened by chance. When I entered graduate school in the Yale Psychology Department in 1965, Allan Wagner and others were trying to duplicate studies which reported that rats injected with RNA, extracted from the brain of rats trained to avoid a shock, could actually avoid the shock without being trained themselves. One of these experiments used habituation of the startle reflex. When rats are presented with a loud noise they startle, just like we do when we hear a firecracker or clap of thunder. If the loud noise is presented repeatedly they eventually startle less (habituation of the startle reflex). The study reported that rats injected with RNA from habituated rats did not startle very much – that is, they were already habituated. This did not happen in rats given RNA from non-habituated rats.

My task was to try to reproduce this study. Loving to build things, I made a device to elicit startle by dropping a heavy weight onto an aluminum plate and figured out how to measure startle magnitude in four rats at a time. This system generated reliable "habituation curves" (regular decreases in startle magnitude with repeated presentations of the loud sound), but we saw no transfer of habituation by injecting RNA from habituated rats to naïve rats. However, we all realized this was an efficient and rapid way to collect data on habituation. Allan Wagner and I did several novel habituation studies that were well received by our colleagues, a wonderful reinforcement for a graduate student.

In 1969 I moved to the Yale Psychiatry Department, again by chance. My wife was working there and told me they were investigating the effects of hallucinogens such as LSD on startle habituation in rats. It sounded like a good fit so I interviewed, got a job offer, and spent the next twenty-nine years on the faculty until I moved to Emory University in 1998. Amazing how life goes.

The acoustic startle reflex has an extraordinarily short latency. Electrical activity in the hind leg begins 8 msec after the onset of the auditory

16

stimulus. This is the fastest reflex we have and means it must be mediated by a simple neural pathway. I reasoned if I could delineate this neural pathway, I should be able to determine where various treatments act along that pathway to alter startle. The circuit has three central synapses (connections between cells). Axons from the inner ear connect to neurons (nerve cells) embedded in the auditory nerve called cochlear root neurons. These cells connect to large neurons in the brainstem that project to the spinal cord. By eliciting startle electrically via tiny electrodes implanted into different parts of the pathway, we learned that habituation occurred in the brainstem, whereas sensitization occurred in the spinal cord. Some drugs that altered startle acted on cochlear root neurons, others in the brainstem, and others in the spinal cord.

Being in a psychiatry department, I soon learned that excessive fear and anxiety were central to many types of psychiatric disorders, so I began using the startle reflex to study fear. Rats first are trained to be afraid of a signal (e.g., a light) by pairing it with a shock (this is fear conditioning). Later they are startled with a loud noise. "Fear-potentiated startle" is defined by a greater startle magnitude, elicited by the loud noise, in the presence versus the absence of the light. Medications that block fear and anxiety in humans decrease fear-potentiated startle in rats, but have no effect on startle alone. This has practical implications. We set up the identical *fear-potentiated startle test* in humans, which now is used widely to measure fear and anxiety in psychiatric patients as well as college students.

But how does fear increase the startle reflex? Many studies in animals had shown a taming effect when a brain area called the amygdala (Latin for "almond," which it resembles in the human brain) was removed. In people, electrical stimulation of the amygdala produced feelings of fear (e.g., "I feel like someone is standing behind me"). The amygdala sends direct anatomical connections to brainstem targets involved in different aspects of the fear response. As predicted, removal of the amygdala totally and selectively blocked fear-potentiated startle, whereas removal of many other brain areas did not. Low-level electrical stimulation of the amygdala increased startle via a direct connection from the amygdala to the startle pathway in the brainstem.

How does a light (e.g., the fear stimulus), which initially has no effect on startle, increase startle after being paired with a shock? Sensory inputs, elicited by lights and shocks involved in fear conditioning, converge on specific cells in the amygdala, an ideal condition for associating two events in time. Inactivation of a protein called the NMDA receptor, implicated in associative learning in other brain areas, completely blocked fear learning but had no effect on conditioned fear that had already been acquired. So, it blocked learning, but not fear itself. Infusion into the amygdala of a virus genetically engineered to produce a protein critical for learning in invertebrates facilitated fear learning. These studies, as well as those by many other investigators, have now explained how fear conditioning works at a highly detailed cellular level. David Walker and I found that another part of the brain, closely related to the amygdala, is more involved in anxiety versus stimulus specific fear. Human studies are beginning to support this distinction.

However, the pressing issue faced by clinicians is that patients who become fearful, such as following trauma, have great difficulty getting over being afraid, even in situations that are safe. Some Vietnam veterans still dive for cover when they hear a gunshot or a car backfiring, decades after the war. Women who have been raped may feel uneasy in bed with their husbands. Can we use our knowledge of fear conditioning to help these individuals? If, after fear conditioning, the fear stimulus is presented over and over again, without further shock, fear-potentiated startle is reduced. This is called experimental extinction. However, the term "extinction" is actually a bad choice because, unlike the dinosaurs, fear can return after a stressor, over time, or when presented in a new place.

So, extinction is an active form of learning that inhibits fear, and we found it also was dependent on the NMDA receptor in the amygdala, the same protein mentioned above involved in fear conditioning. It turns out this protein is in lots of different types of neurons, including those that inhibit amygdala output and hence inhibit fear. Blocking the NMDA receptor in the amygdala, when the fear stimulus was presented repeatedly without shock, blocked extinction. A drug called D-cycloserine was known to make this protein work better by changing its shape, and we found it enhanced extinction when given either systemically or directly into the amygdala. Thus, presenting the fear stimulus only a few times after giving D-cycloserine was enough to produce full extinction. Giving D-cycloserine by itself had no effect. So, it was improving the learning that occurs during extinction without reducing fear itself.

To test whether D-cycloserine would help patients get over their fears, we teamed up with Barbara Rothbaum, who pioneered the use of virtual reality to expose patients to their feared situations in the absence of any negative outcomes. This form of extinction-based psychotherapy is very effective in treating phobias and was an ideal system to test whether D-cycloserine would improve psychotherapy. Height-phobics were given either D-cycloserine or a placebo and then exposed to successively higher floors in a virtual glass elevator. Patients given D-cycloserine had a much greater reduction of fear in the virtual reality environment one week and then again three months later, compared with those given the placebo.

Importantly, the results transferred outside the clinic because the group given D-cycloserine plus psychotherapy reported significant reductions in their avoidance of high places (e.g., driving over high bridges, flying in planes). By itself D-cycloserine did not reduce fear ratings, but instead improved extinction of fear, just as we found in rats. This work has now been replicated for all of the major anxiety disorders. Unfortunately, because D-cycloserine is only given before a relatively small number of therapy sessions, drug companies did not see enough profit to commercialize it. Hopefully, better medications that improve psychotherapy will be patented by drug companies to help patients get over their debilitating fears, which are so painful and disruptive to them.

So, the lowly startle reflex, which I began to study quite by chance, has been my window into the brain. It has allowed us to understand processes such as drug effects on behavior, habituation, sensitization, fear conditioning, and fear extinction. It also has become an ideal translational tool because exactly the same response measure can be used in humans, monkeys, and rodents. Who would have known so long ago?

REFERENCES

Davis, M., & Whalen, P. J. (2001). The amygdala: vigilance and emotion. *Mol Psychiatry*, 6, 13–34.

Myers, K. M., Carlezon, W. A., Jr., & Davis, M. (2011). Glutamate receptors in extinction and extinction-based therapies for psychiatric illness. *Neuropsychopharmacology*, 36, 274–293.

Ressler, K. J., Rothbaum, B. O., Tannenbaum, L., Anderson, P., Graap, K., Zimand, E., ... & Davis, M. (2004). Cognitive enhancers as adjuncts to psychotherapy: use of D-cycloserine in phobic individuals to facilitate extinction of fear. *Arch Gen Psychiatry*, 61, 1136–1144.

4   Child Poverty and Brain Development

Farah, Martha J.

What's a nice cognitive neuroscientist doing in a field like child poverty? Why would anybody work with ill-defined concepts such as socioeconomic status (SES) when they could be manipulating binocular cues to depth perception with precision? Allow me to explain, by way of presenting my current work and how I came to it.

The first decades of my career were spent working to understand the neural bases of vision and visual cognition, using behavioral research methods with normal participants and brain-damaged patients, as well as by using event-related potentials (ERPs) and functional magnetic resonance imaging (fMRI) to study normal brain function more directly. The 1980s and 1990s were rewarding times to be involved in such research, as neuroscience first grappled with fundamental questions about how humans perceive the world.

Being a cognitive neuroscientist in the early days of the field satisfied many of my intellectual needs and wants. I could engage with age-old questions of mind and brain in a productive new way, asking how we come to know the visual world and how our brains implement or enable our minds. Of course, the deepest philosophical readings of these questions will never be settled with experiments, but to me it was nevertheless exciting to work on various empirical issues concerning mind–brain relations.

Perverse as it may sound, I also enjoyed the conceptual messiness of early cognitive neuroscience. In a mature science, there is a theoretical framework that guides us to the next questions to ask and provides models of the kinds of explanations that could count as answers. There is also a stable of methods recognized as able to deliver relevant evidence. With a framework, questions, and methods in place, the path of scientific progress is relatively clear. But, at the risk of sounding flippant, where's the fun in that? The cognitive neuroscience of the 1980s offered few of the conveniences of a mature science, but plenty of messy intellectual fun. Coming up with questions, deciding what kinds of data were relevant to answering them, parsing the array of possible answers, and examining the theoretical assumptions that underlay these decisions – these were necessary everyday thought processes for us.

But, for all the intellectual joy of grappling with issues of mind and brain in a developing science, I did feel that one thing was missing from my work life: social relevance. So, as the field of cognitive neuroscience matured, I began to wonder whether it might it now be applicable to real-world problems. I had a particular real-world problem in mind: childhood SES and its association with cognitive development and life chances.

Thus began my current research program. It was born shortly after my daughter, the connection between the two being my daughter's babysitters. The women I hired were of low SES status, having grown up on welfare. They were themselves receiving state assistance, and worked part-time as cleaners and babysitters to better support their own children. I got to know them and their families well, and became very fond of them.

I was also shocked by what I learned of their lives. One shock was the incredibly high level of stress and the frequent, uncontrollable misfortunes in their lives. I have middle-class friends who have suffered tragedies, and of course people from any social class can be their own worst enemies and create ongoing problems for themselves. But what I saw in my small foray into the world of low SES was different – there was an unrelenting cascade of problems, many related to living in bad neighborhoods, sending their children to bad schools, and having no financial cushion, often compounded by ignorance about health; fear or mistrust of doctors, teachers, and police; and a hopelessness (not hard to understand) that hampered their efforts to avoid future problems.

Another shock came from getting to know their children. Their daughters and sons and nieces and nephews began life with the same evident promise as my daughter and her friends. Yet, as the years went on, I saw their paths diverge. This led me to do some reading. From the psychology and epidemiology literatures I learned that childhood SES predicts many important life-long traits, including mental health, cognitive ability, and academic achievement. As these are all related to brain function, and I was a cognitive neuroscientist, it gave me a handle to try to understand the long-term effects of poverty on children: I could study how the brain develops in poverty.

In early work, with then graduate student Kim Noble and colleague Hallam Hurt, we investigated the neurocognitive profile of poverty in children. That is, we asked: Does poverty affect all cognitive systems of the brain evenly, across the board, or do certain systems bear the brunt of poverty while others are relatively spared? The answer to this question would helpfully constrain the kinds of causal, mechanistic explanations

we might look for, as well as the kinds of targeted interventions we might consider. The answer we found, across several studies of children from kindergarten age to adolescence, was that poverty has distinctly uneven effects on neurocognitive function. The executive functions of prefrontal cortex, language functions of left perisylvian cortex, and declarative memory processes of the medial temporal lobe all tend to show pronounced disparities between poor children and middle-SES children, controlling for potential confounders such as race, ethnicity, and birth weight.

In connection with the subject of confounding variables, or "confounders," let me mention that this new research direction certainly put me back in the middle of conceptual messiness. The word "confounder" seems to label a clear category, distinct from the variable of interest. But when the variable of interest is SES, which we know is associated with all kinds of differences, from nutrition to child-rearing practices, how do we decide which of these associated factors is a confounding variable (so we should try to measure effects of SES above and beyond effects of nutrition and child-rearing practices, for example) and which is part and parcel of SES, as an influence of child development? My belief is that there are no blanket right answers to this question, and that any of a number of reasonable decisions will be defensible, so long as one is clear about the decision in the reporting of the results. By and large, we have considered race and ethnicity to be confounders, but have viewed nutrition and child-rearing practices as part and parcel of SES for both practical (difficult to measure) and theoretical (these are more consistently associated with SES than are race and ethnicity) reasons. But the effects of these factors on development, in the context of SES and more generally, are of great interest and importance.

Having established at least a preliminary determination of the neurocognitive profile of poverty, we could begin to inquire into its antecedent causes and its structural brain correlates. To illustrate this process I will recount one strand of research emanating from the early finding that most surprised us: the relation of learning and memory to SES. Initially, I expected declarative learning (learning *that* something happened, as opposed to the kind of how-to learning that underlies skill formation, for example) to be unaffected by SES. I had no rationale for this expectation except that, as a cognitive ability, acquiring new declarative memories seemed too "nuts and bolts" to be subject to the complex influences of SES. But we soon learned that this was not true, and that memory testing and imaging of the medial temporal structures required for declarative memory showed SES gradients, with better performance and larger regional brain volumes in higher SES children. Why would this be?

Research with animals provided a promising explanation, which then found converging support from research with human children. Starting with pioneering research in rodents, it has been shown that early life stress adversely affects the development of the hippocampus, a key structure for learning and memory, located within the medial temporal lobe. It has also been found that certain kinds of early maternal nurturance can buffer the rat pups' hippocampi from these effects. Stress, as noted at the outset of this essay, is much more common in low-SES families. And maternal availability and related behaviors are themselves affected by stress and by other features of SES. In sum, we had a promising hypothesis based on experimental animal research that, on the face of things, seemed extendable to human childhood and SES.

Our own early work then confirmed that, in human children, early life parental nurturance predicted declarative learning ability in later childhood, and also predicted differences in hippocampal volume. Several excellent studies by other research groups, with larger samples of children, showed SES effects on hippocampal volume. One study even tied things up with a beautiful bow, showing that SES predicts hippocampal volume and that this effect is entirely accounted for by differences in stress levels and maternal behavior, just as the original rat studies would have predicted!

This emerging area of research remains a kind of "basic science" – that is, science aimed at understanding what, how, and why things are the way they are. It would be premature to dictate child policy solely on the basis of a dozen good studies of SES and medial temporal memory processes. But already it buttresses existing arguments about the importance of reducing the stress experienced by young children and parents of low SES. Considering that the earliest studies on the subject were published just ten years ago, and most of the research has been published in the last five years, I think we can look forward to substantive help from cognitive neuroscience in improving the life chances of poor children.

REFERENCES

Evans, G. W., & Kim, P. (2013). Childhood poverty, chronic stress, self-regulation, and coping. *Child Development Perspectives, 7*(1), 43–48.

Farah, M. J., Shera, D. M., Savage, J. H., Betancourt, L., Giannetta, J. M., Brodsky, N. L., ... & Hurt, H. (2006). Childhood poverty: Specific associations with neurocognitive development. *Brain Research, 1110*(1), 166–174.

Hackman, D. A., & Farah, M. J. (2009). Socioeconomic status and the developing brain. *Trends in Cognitive Sciences, 13*(2), 65–73.

5   Try It and Assume Nothing

Gazzaniga, Michael S.

For the last 100 years, neuroscience has been in its Dodge City stage: chock full of unruly and unfettered "shoot 'em up" cowboys and outlaws. Why has neuroscience been so unruly? No sheriffs. Unlike many other fields, it has not been disciplined by an agreed-upon set of next questions to be answered. As a result, neuroscience, with its unrestrained and unfettered researchers at large poking about in whatever has interested them, has accumulated information about nervous systems (from insects to humans) at an astonishing rate. As I have related before, so much information is stacking up, however, that if one adopted the intellectual style of first learning all there is to know about a topic before studying new dimensions of it, then future progress would be stopped dead in its tracks, like so many cowboys on the streets of Dodge.

No place was as unfettered and unrestrained as Roger W. Sperry's lab at Caltech. Perhaps the premier brain scientist of the last century, he must have told me a hundred times, "Try it. And don't read the literature until after you have made your observations. Otherwise you can be blinded by pre-existing dogma." This is how we operated in those delicious free-ranging days in his lab exploring the unknown. If we had an idea, we "tried it." We were also spurred on by other greats wandering the halls. Linus Pauling (recipient of two Nobel Prizes) once stumbled across me in the midst of an experiment, which resulted in the take-away lesson "Assume nothing."

As an undergrad, I was interested in neural specificity. In 1960, I lucked out, getting a summer NSF fellowship to study with Sperry, but soon was captivated by all the experiments being done in his lab on "split-brain" animals, primarily cats and monkeys. The results were almost unbelievable: If one side of the brain was trained to do a sensory task, the other side of the brain didn't have a clue about it. I jumped in with both feet, went to work on rabbits, and was hooked.

In cats and monkeys, in order to train one half of the brain only, two things had to be done. First, the optic chiasm was divided down the middle. Thus, information exposed to one eye was only projected to the

24

ipsilateral half brain. These animals learned a task quickly and were easily able to perform it through both the trained and the untrained eye. If, in addition, the corpus callosum and anterior commissure were also sectioned, the split-brain phenomenon presented itself. With this additional sectioning, the untrained hemisphere remained ignorant of the task learned by the other half brain. The learned information appeared to be communicated through the second set of fibers that had been cut. Incredibly, it seemed as if there were two mental systems cohabitating side by side in one head. Riveting as these findings were in monkeys and cats, when considered in the context of human behavior, they didn't seem relevant. Could a left hand not know what the right hand is holding? Totally ridiculous.

I was captivated: captivated by Caltech, by Sperry, by research, and by all the questions that split-brain research had engendered. Before I knew it, I was back at Caltech, starting graduate school the following summer. Sperry gave me my marching orders: I was to design and prepare a set of studies for a human patient, W.J., who was being worked up by a neurosurgical resident, Joseph E. Bogen. W.J. was a World War II veteran, who, disabled from a parachute jump, had been knocked out by a blow from the butt of a German rifle. He was left with intractable epilepsy, suffering several grand mal seizures a week. Bogen's research had suggested that sectioning his corpus callosum might decrease his seizures. W.J. was desperate and willing to try desperate measures. He'd already proved he was brave.

With all that we now know, it may not seem like it, but at the time our project was beyond daring. This was wild and crazy stuff. No one seriously entertained the notion that the mind could be split, nor that we would actually find evidence that it could be. Weeks earlier, a patient with agenesis of the corpus callosum (a rare congenital condition in which there is a complete or partial absence of the corpus callosum) had come through the lab, and testing showed nothing out of the ordinary. Nothing out of the ordinary been found in a series of "split-brain" patients in New York, who had been tested twenty years earlier by Andrew Akelaitis, a talented neurologist. Neither Sperry, one of the world's greatest neurobiologists, nor definitely I, a greenhorn graduate student, had any significant experience examining patients. Who did we think we were? On paper, it might have seemed to be a fool's game and a waste of time. But at Caltech it wasn't, because the attitude was "try it" and "assume nothing."

The adventure began slowly enough. The pre-operative testing held no surprises. W.J.'s two hemispheres were normally connected: Each hand knew what was in the other, and each visual cortex seamlessly connected to the other. The very thought it could be otherwise was stupefying and could barely be considered. After all the studies were completed, we put the work aside, focused on other projects, and waited until W.J. had had his surgery. A few months later, W.J. had recovered nicely from his operation and his seizures were under control. He was ready and eager to be tested again. That made two of us: I was equally eager.

The day arrived for the first post-surgical testing. Pasadena was bright and sunny as W.J.'s wife rolled him up to the entrance of the biology building on San Pasquale Avenue. He still wore a helmet for protection (in case he had a seizure) and was using a wheelchair to get around. I wondered, "Will this World War II veteran reveal a deep secret?" It didn't seem likely, and no one else thought so: The Triumphal March from Aida didn't kick in as we walked down the hall to the lab. In fact, I, the greenhorn, was left alone to do the testing, which started out routinely, as I have recently described:

MSG: *Fixate on the dot.*
W.J.: *Do you mean the little piece of paper stuck on the screen?*
MSG: *Yes, that is a dot . . . . Look right at it.*
W.J.: *Okay.*

I make sure he is looking straight at the dot and flash him a picture of a simple object, a square, which is placed to the right of the dot for exactly 100 milliseconds. By being placed there the image is directed to his left half brain, his speaking brain. (This is the test I had designed that had not been given to Dr. Akelaitis's patients.)

MSG: *What did you see?*
W.J.: *A box.*
MSG: *Good, let's do it again. Fixate on the dot.*
W.J.: *Do you mean the little piece of tape?*
MSG: *Yes, I do. Now fixate.*

Soon, however, things got more interesting:
Again I flash a picture of another square but this time to the left of his fixated point, and this image is transmitted exclusively to his right brain, a half brain that does not speak. Because of the special surgery W.J. had undergone, his right brain, with its connecting fibers to the left hemisphere severed, could no longer communicate with his left brain. This was the telling moment. Heart pounding, mouth dry, I asked,

MSG: *What did you see?*
W.J.: *Nothing.*
MSG: *Nothing? You saw nothing?*
W.J.: *Nothing.*

My heart races. I begin to sweat. Have I just seen two brains, that is to say, two minds working separately in one head? One could speak, one couldn't. Was that what was happening?

W.J.: *Anything else you want me to do?*
MSG: *Yes, just a minute.*

I quickly find some even more simple slides that only project single small circles onto the screen. Each slide projects one circle but in different places on each trial. What would happen if he were just asked to point to anything he saw?
And this is when things became mind-boggling:

MSG: *Bill, just point to what stuff you see.*
W.J.: *On the screen?*
MSG: *Yes and use either hand that seems fit.*
W.J.: *Okay.*
MSG: *Fixate the dot.*

A circle is flashed to the right of fixation, allowing his left brain to see it. His right hand rises from the table and points to where the circle has been on the screen. We do this for a number of trials where the flashed circle appears on one side of the screen or the other. It doesn't matter. When the circle is to the right of fixation, the right hand, controlled by the left hemisphere, points to it. When the circle is to the left of fixation, it is the left hand, controlled by the right hemisphere, that points to it. One hand or the other will point to the correct place on the screen. That means that each hemisphere does see a circle when it is in the opposite visual field, and each, separate from the other, could guide the arm/hand it controlled, to make a response. Only the left hemisphere, however, can talk about it. Oh, the sweetness of discovery.

Thus begins a line of research that, twenty years later, almost to the day, will be awarded the Nobel Prize.

I could barely contain myself, and I doubt that Christopher Columbus felt any more exhilarated by his discovery than I felt by mine. Fifty years of intense research commenced on that day, probing the underlying brain mechanisms for human conscious experience.

REFERENCES

Gazzaniga, Michael S. (2015). *Tales from both sides of the brain*. New York: Harper Collins.

Gazzaniga, M. S. (2015). The split-brain: Rooting consciousness in Biology. *PNAS 111*(51), 18093–18094.

Myers, R. E., & Sperry, R. W. (1958). Interhemispheric communication through the corpus callosum. *Archives of Neurology and Psychiatry, 80*, 298–303.

6   Coming Full Circle: From Psychology to Neuroscience and Back

LeDoux, Joseph

I got interested in psychology while studying business administration in the late 1960s and early 1970s at Louisiana State University. I was particularly taken with the rigors of behaviorism and wrote to B. F. Skinner asking him to help me create a behaviorist model of consumer behavior. He wrote back and declined my offer on ethical grounds. I was actually pursuing this work for the purpose of consumer protection, not exploitation, but I was so moved by his letter that I abandoned my weak commitment to business and turned more and more toward psychology. I ended up working with a professor who was studying the neural basis of learning and motivation, and decided to pursue graduate work in biological psychology. I ended up doing my PhD at SUNY Stony Brook with Mike Gazzaniga.

In the mid-1970s, it was clear that cognitive science was dethroning behaviorism and bringing the mind back to psychology. But the mind being brought back was not the mind the behaviorists got rid of. The cognitive mind was an information-processing system that basically worked non-consciously, with only the late stages giving rise to reportable subjective experience. Early cognitive science was behavioristic in terms of its methods and rigors, but more ecumenical psychologically in that it made room for internal processes in the control of behavior. But subjective experience was not the focus.

For my PhD studies with Gazzaniga, I explored how the left hemisphere dealt with behaviors produced by the right hemisphere. From the point of view of the left, anything done by the right was done non-consciously. We were fascinated with how the left hemisphere, when observing the responses of the right, confabulated an explanation of why those responses occurred. If the right caused the person to laugh or stand up, the left explained the response as being due to the humor of the situation (for the laugh) or the need to stretch (in the case of standing up). We drew upon the emerging field of cognitive social science, explaining the left hemisphere's confabulations as efforts to reduce cognitive conflict by attributing cause to non-consciously controlled processes. Gazzaniga and I summarized this work in our 1978 book, *The Integrated Mind*, in which we argued that the interpretation of experience in such a way as to maintain a coherent sense of self was an important role of conscious experience.

My career has, ever since, been dedicated to understanding how systems that operate non-consciously provide fodder for the construction of conscious experiences. I was especially interested in how so-called emotion systems generate signals that are consciously interpreted as feelings. There was little work on emotion and the brain at the time, and this seemed to be a topic begging to be researched. But I decided that the way to go was not the obvious one of studying emotion in humans. There were no good techniques for exploring the detailed mechanisms of the human brain at the time, so I turned to rats to make progress on how the emotion systems work.

I decided to use the paradigm called Pavlovian fear conditioning, in which a neutral stimulus (a tone) that has previously been paired with an aversive stimulus (a shock) elicits autonomic nervous system responses and freezing behavior. At the time, the field of neuroscience was coming of age, and I and others took advantage of the new technical approaches available to map the circuits involved. In brief, we found that the tone traveled through auditory pathways to the amygdala, and from there to motor pathways that control the responses. The auditory inputs to the amygdala were from the thalamus and cortex, and both inputs terminated in the lateral nucleus of the amygdala. Interestingly, the thalamic inputs were sufficient on their own to allow learning and response expression. This meant that the amygdala could detect and respond to the stimulus either simultaneously with, or even before, the cortex knew the stimulus was present. This, I proposed, was a way that non-conscious subcortical processing could trigger responses independent of conscious awareness. It turns out that even the cortical sensory inputs activate the amygdala non-consciously in humans, but the point is the same – that the amygdala can initiate so-called emotional responses independent of conscious awareness of the stimulus. The non-conscious nature of amygdala processing has been confirmed by studies of healthy humans using masking and other consciousness-preventing procedures, and in blind sight patients (those who have no conscious awareness of seeing, yet can make appropriate responses to visual stimuli).

Work on the neurobiology of fear conditioning grew rapidly and is now one of the most successful and productive areas of research in behavioral neuroscience. We know much about not only the systems, but also the cells, synapses, molecules, and genes involved. But we are at a crossroads conceptually.

Our understanding of the brain bases of behavior and cognition can only be as good as our understanding of the behavioral and cognitive process in question. Neuroscientists today can study the brain with amazing techniques that would have been considered science fiction a decade or so ago. But we are not attending to the psychology of the experiments with the same clarity and precision as we do the neuroscience components. Our neuroscience is twenty-first-century science at its best, but in my field, our behavioral concepts are stuck in the 1950s.

For example, when "fear" in rats began to be studied by behaviorists in the first half of the twentieth century, they viewed fear as an intervening variable that linked stimuli with responses, rather than as a real psychological or physiological state. By mid-century, fear became a physiological theoretical construct: a hypothetical physiological state that was said to connect stimuli and responses. The amygdala came to be the home of that physiological state of fear. It was a short leap to the equation of that physiological state in the amygdala with the conscious experience of fear, the feeling of being afraid. Today, it is common to talk this way. Researchers talk about how threats elicit fear in the amygdala and the fear causes the "the frightened rat" to freeze. The amygdala is often described by scientists and lay people as the brain's fear center.

But the fact is that fear does not live in the amygdala. Humans can be conditioned in the same way as rats and will express responses to threats even if the stimuli are masked. The person does not know the stimulus is there and does not feel fear, but the amygdala is activated and the body responds appropriately. The job of the amygdala in such situations is to detect and respond to the threat. All of this happens non-consciously. The feeling of fear is not a product of the amygdala.

Although I have been working on neurobiological mechanisms in rats for all these years, I never really left behind the ideas I got hooked on in graduate school: that much of our behavior is generated non-consciously, and one of the jobs of consciousness is to explain or interpret those responses by monitoring the detectable components of non-conscious responses (e.g., the myriad responses in the brain and body controlled by amygdala activation). I thus view conscious fear not as something inherited from animals that is resting in the amygdala and waiting to be unleashed by a threat, but instead as an interpretation, a cognitive construction, by cortical processes. In my PhD dissertation, I emphasized the role of language in these processes, which I still do.

I also never got over the letter I received from B. F. Skinner. While I'm not a radical behaviorist (I believe we need to understand consciousness to understand human nature), I am a stickler about calling upon subjective states to explain behavior. Several decades into the cognitive revolution, we are now experiencing a wave of unconstrained mentalism. By this I mean that today processes are often assumed to be conscious until proven otherwise; no justification is required. This free use of mental-state terms in explaining animal and human behavior needs to be checked. Just because something seems like it might have been consciously controlled does not mean that it was. In order to demonstrate that some behavior depended on a conscious state, one has to provide evidence that the behavior can be explained by a conscious account, as well as evidence that a non-conscious account won't do the trick. There are ways to do this in humans; verbal self-report is not foolproof but is still useful because it can help distinguish non-verbal behaviors that are reportable from those that are not. In animals, though, there is no response mode to distinguish when a non-verbal behavior is a result of a conscious versus a non-conscious process.

Non-conscious states are presumably the default states of the nervous system, evolutionarily speaking, and should not be dismissed simply because a conscious account seems plausible in humans or animals. For example, in humans, the feeling of fear is tightly correlated with body responses when we are threatened, and the feeling is assumed to be the cause of the responses. And since the circuits that control the responses are similar in humans and animals, studies of the circuits in animals are assumed to tell us where fear lives in the brain. But since, as we've seen, these are products of different systems in humans, it is a mistake to treat such introspective observations of a correlation between responses and feelings as meaning that the responses are caused by the feelings in humans – and, in my opinion, an even bigger mistake to make this assumption in non-human animals.

I spent a lot of my youth trying to become a neuroscientist. Now I spend a lot of time trying to be a better psychologist.

7   Hormones, Epigenetics, the Brain, and Behavior

McEwen, Bruce S.

Trained in chemistry and cell biology, and following post-doctoral work in the new field of "neuroscience," I became a junior faculty member in the laboratory of Neal Miller at The Rockefeller University in 1966 and was inspired by his integrative view of brain–body interactions and his pioneering work in defining the field of behavioral medicine. Together with my interest in hormone action on gene expression and the fact that very little was known about how and where hormones act in the brain, this led to a serendipitous discovery. In 1968, I discovered that the stress hormone, cortisol, secreted by our adrenal glands, is taken up from the blood and binds to receptors in the brain region known as the hippocampus. We now know that cortisol regulates gene expression and other cellular processes related to cognitive function and mood, acting in the hippocampus as well as elsewhere in the brain by epigenetic mechanisms. Epigenetics is the emerging science of how genes are seamlessly regulated by the environment, and it plays an important role in the emerging collaborations between the social and biological sciences. Here is the story of how this all happened.

1.   What Is This Discovery?

The discovery: that stress hormones affect a brain region that we now know is involved in episodic, spatial, and contextual memory and mood regulation, rather than just affecting the hypothalamus and vegetative functions such as hunger, thirst, and sex. This discovery has triggered many studies on rats and mice, with increasing translation to human stress-related disorders, such as depression and anxiety, accelerated aging, and Alzheimer's disease. We discovered that the effects of acute and chronic stress involve not brain damage, but, rather, a remodeling of neural architecture – turnover of synaptic connections, shrinkage and growth of dendrites, and the suppression of neurogenesis (i.e., the generation of new neurons in the dentate gyrus of the hippocampus). This discovery has also engendered a broader view of brain–body interactions that has led me and colleagues to develop the concepts of allostasis and allostatic load and overload (i.e., how the body as well as the brain can be altered by too much stress so as to cause disease, as explained further below).

The hippocampus has been a gateway for discovery of stress effects upon remodeling of architecture in other brain regions and their relationship to anxiety, depression, working memory, and the ability to regulate one's impulses and mood. An interesting twist is that the same chronic stress that causes dendrites to shrink in the hippocampus causes dendrites to expand in other brain regions such as the amygdala, a brain region involved in fear, leading to increased anxiety and vigilance. This can be adaptive in a dangerous environment, but is maladaptive if these changes persist when safety returns.

This gateway has also led to the finding that the hippocampus, and, indeed, the entire brain, has receptors for sex hormones that act via a variety of cellular mechanisms and cause the generation of new synaptic connections as well as other consequences. This is leading to the discovery of subtle sex differences in brain structure and function in many brain regions that help to explain why men and women use different "strategies" in their thinking and behavior while showing equal overall ability.

Another discovery growing out of our cortisol receptor finding is that the brain, and especially the hippocampus, is also a target for metabolic hormones such as insulin, which influence cognitive function and neuronal architecture and normally protect against brain damage. In Type 2 diabetes, however, these protective actions are impaired and there is increased risk for Alzheimer's disease as well as depression.

2.   Why Do You Consider It to Be Your Most Important Contribution?

This work is important because it has broadened the scope and altered the definition of neuroendocrinology, which was originally confined to understanding how the hypothalamus and pituitary gland regulate hormone production. This broadened scope has led to a multilevel approach to questions, ranging from molecular mechanisms to human behavior, and this has stimulated research in fields as disparate as molecular biology and public policy. This latter point is exemplified by my role in the development of the allostatic load concept as part of two MacArthur Foundation research networks. Allostasis is the active process of adapting to stressors via cortisol and the autonomic, metabolic, and immune systems that act together to maintain homeostasis (the stability of the body that keeps us alive). Allostatic load refers to the cumulative effects of multiple stressors as well as the unbalancing of the adaptive process (e.g., too much or too little cortisol, or adrenalin or inflammation in response to a challenge). Allostatic overload refers to the cumulative damage that can result not only from stress but also from health-damaging behaviors, such as eating too much, smoking, drinking alcohol, inadequate sleep, and lack of exercise.

3.   How Did You Get the Idea for the Contribution?

I have been fortunate to have had mentors and serendipitous experiences that have shaped my career, all the way from a science teacher in high school in Ann Arbor, Michigan, to chemistry and psychology teachers at Oberlin College, as well as my PhD mentors at The Rockefeller University and my introduction to neurobiology in Sweden as a post-doctoral fellow. Then, while starting in Minnesota as a junior faculty member, I was, unexpectedly, recruited back to Rockefeller to become part of the Behavioral Sciences Program as a junior faculty member with Neal Miller, gaining experience in behavioral science from Peter Marler, Donald Griffin, George Miller, William Estes, and Carl Pfaffman, and my contemporaries, Donald Pfaff and Fernando Nottebohm.

Besides Neal Miller and the Behavioral Sciences Program, another major influence for this contribution was the PhD mentorship of Alfred Mirsky and Vincent Allfrey, who pioneered in elucidating cellular mechanisms of what is now called "epigenetics," referring to environmental regulation of gene expression. This influence turned me on to the study of how genes are regulated in the nervous system and led me to look for steroid hormone receptors in the brain that act via such epigenetic mechanisms.

My career at Rockefeller has been complemented and enriched by membership in two MacArthur Research Networks: one on Health and Behavior, with Judith Rodin as chair, and the other a Research Network on Socioeconomic Status and Health, with Nancy Adler as chair. Eliot Stellar from the University of Pennsylvania, whose textbook with Morgan I used as an undergraduate at Oberlin College, recruited me into these networks. As a result of these experiences, I now participate in the National Scientific Council on the Developing Child, led by Jack Shonkoff at Harvard University, where I have come to appreciate even more the contributions of other disciplines in the social sciences, economics, and biomedicine, and where I have been able to contribute further to the concepts of allostasis and allostatic load.

4.   How Does the Idea Matter for Psychological Science and Also for the World Beyond Academia?

The new view of reciprocal brain–body communication and the plasticity and vulnerability of the brain, with its central role in perceiving and reacting to experiences that we call "stressors," puts a new meaning to the statement "It's all in your head." Memories of "lived experiences," both good and bad, have a profound impact on the life course of health and disease, as unfortunately exemplified by the embedding of memories of early life abuse and neglect and by post-traumatic stress disorder. Furthermore, the realization that the social and physical environment influences the expression of the genes ("epigenetics") via a host of remarkably complex mechanisms counteracts the common view among some in the social sciences that "biology" (and especially "genetics") is "destiny." We now realize that we can do a lot to direct and redirect our biology and behavior!

The new view makes it imperative that psychologists and other social scientists embrace the new view of biology and the plasticity of the brain, and that they contribute their unique skills, tools, and insights, as has been my experience in the MacArthur Networks and other interdisciplinary groups. Only an interdisciplinary perspective and effort will effectively address the most important issues facing humanity, dealing with the impact of social organization and the social environment on mental and physical health in the broadest sense. In particular, this perspective tells us that there are no "magic bullets" for the non-communicable diseases (e.g., antidepressants such as Prozac do not by themselves "cure" depression) that are increasing in prevalence and cost. Only a combination of social and behavioral interventions, sometimes aided by pharmacological agents, can be effective. These interventions should also involve improving policies of the government in relation to such things as education, health, taxation, and housing, and by the private sector in relation to such things as flexible working hours, pensions, and health insurance. Every such policy is a health policy!

5.   What Are the Next Steps?

Besides the cumulative effects of life experiences, embodied in the concept of allostatic load and overload, early life experiences that lead to "biological embedding" (i.e., the memories and other long-lasting effects of early life experiences that epigenetically change gene expression) have a lasting influence on the body through the brain and enhance development of allostatic overload. This results in greater incidence of various diseases over the life course, including cardiovascular disease, depression, and substance abuse. The increased numbers of individuals with adverse early life experiences who need continuing health care should be a motivation to reduce these numbers by increasing programs that enhance early life experiences by improving nutrition, parental and extra-family (e.g., day-) care, and educational opportunities, and reducing adverse life events in the family. At present, the greatest expenditures in our society are for prolonging life, due to health problems later in the life course. The next highest expense is for prevention in mid-life, and the least expenditures are for prevention of adverse early life experiences, when prevention can do the most good. This spending pattern must be reversed!

REFERENCES

Davidson, R. J., & McEwen, B. S. (2012). Social influences on neuroplasticity: stress and interventions to promote well-being. *Nat. Neurosci. 15*:689–695.

McEwen, B. S. (2006). Protective and damaging effects of stress mediators: central role of the brain. *Dial. Clin. Neurosci. 8*:367–381.

McEwen, B. S., & McEwen, Craig A. (2015). Social, psychological, and physiological reactions to stress. In *Emerging trends in the social and behavioral sciences.* Robert Scott and Stephan Kosslyn (eds). John Wiley & Sons, New York. http://onlinelibrary.wiley.com/doi/10.1002/9781118900772.etrds0311/abstract.

8   Brain Plasticity, Science, and Medicine

Merzenich, Michael

My motivation for pursuing studies in integrative neuroscience stemmed from a juvenile interest in the "great issues" of philosophy and psychology. As a student, it seemed obvious to me that the "rules" that underlie our psychology are discoverable brain rules, and that the disputes of historic philosophy would be trumped by neurological science. Alas, in the early period of my own studies, scientists had not gotten very far in addressing these great issues of philosophy and psychology in direct neurological terms. A dramatic change was to occur over the subsequent five decades of my scientific life.

Our own contributions to a progressive change in an understanding of our humanity initially stemmed from two principal sources. First, I led a team that created one of the first commercialized multiple-channel cochlear implants. These hearing recovery devices deliver patterned electrical stimuli to the auditory nerve in deaf individuals, thereby restoring aural speech understanding. Our ability to simulate the highly detailed representation of aural speech inputs normally delivered from the ear to the brain was, to say the least, crude. I've described it as akin to playing a Chopin sonata with your forearms. Not surprisingly, this new and radically degraded representational form of encoded speech was initially incomprehensible.

Several months later, our patients understood everything.

In the same era, research teams in Melbourne and Vienna created other multichannel cochlear implant models, applying very different speech encoding schemes. To our great surprise, several months later, even with their very different "front end" encoding, their patients *also* understood everything. The brain just didn't care. Moreover, both our patients and their patients said that their recovered speech sounded "just like it did before [they had lost their hearing]."

We realized that, especially given these three very different forms of artificial speech coding, a remarkable level of adaptive brain change – plasticity – must be contributing to the recovery of their speech understanding and the seamless cognitive extensions in the uses of aural language observed in cochlear implant patients. Contrary to the predominant neuroscientific view in this era, *the adult human brain must be continuously plastic*, on a grand scale.

Serendipitously, across the same scientific era, our research team was also working on the documentation of what we termed "the functional organization" of the great sensory-perceptual systems in the brain – in our models, the somatosensory and auditory systems – as a scientific prerequisite for our later study of "higher brain function." In those studies, we generated highly detailed reconstructions of how the brain "mapped" acoustic and tactual information at every somatosensory and auditory system level. It was soon obvious to us that the system organization that we witnessed in carnivores and primates made little sense *unless* one were to assume that the brain was plastic throughout life. To cite one observation among many, each individual animal expressed idiosyncratic responding and mapping variations that almost certainly reflected variations in adult-acquired behavioral abilities.

In one set of studies conducted in collaboration with Dr. Jon Kaas and colleagues at Vanderbilt University, we manipulated inputs from the hand, showing that cortical representations were rapidly remodeled after any modification or loss of input. Those studies led to experiments in which we trained primates and rodents at tactual or listening tasks – repeatedly showing that skill acquisition or improvement was accounted for by neurological remodeling. Because we were reconstructing changes driven by simple forms of training in exquisite detail, we saw that the cortical machinery (e.g., cortical columns' sizes and boundaries, representational topographies, spatial distributions of axonal arbors and dendrites, myelination, properties of excitatory and inhibitory neurons) was itself revised, far beyond mere synaptogenesis or synaptic strengthening, in parallel with the advance of behavioral abilities. This remarkable capacity for physical and functional brain change was recorded in animals of every age.

It might be noted that physiological psychologists had already collectively generated powerful evidence that the adult brain was "plastic." Still, rather astonishingly, their view was not accepted by the neuroscientific or neurological/psychiatric medical mainstreams. Our studies, coming *from* that mainstream, provided an experimentally and politically important validation of their longer-held position.

The cochlear implant is a kind of medical miracle for an individual who has acquired profound deafness. Our demonstration of adult plasticity underlying operant training and our studies directed toward understanding how to control brain change for human benefit were significant scientific contributions. Still, the primary important finding in our studies was the discovery that *the expressions of plasticity are achieved by processes that are fundamentally reversible.* I view this as the single most important discovery by our team, in my scientific lifetime.

In early studies of plasticity, we realized that changes followed a Hebb-like rule ("What fires together is co-strengthened/wired together"). By that one logical stroke, we understood that the brain's representations were time-based; that stimulus coding, recognition, and cognitive control operations in the brain were continuously reversible; and that all these (and other) aspects of our coding and representation must be relational. Importantly, we also understood that we could drive "positive" or "negative" representational changes at will (e.g., slow down or speed up, differentiate or de-degrade feature representation, degrade or refine cortical network operations) by simply changing the spatiotemporal forms of input delivered into any given brain system or cortical area.

As we were conducting these studies (and considering a massive body of related scientific evidence) we realized, again, that MANY physical and chemical aspects of engaged cortical neurons and networks were altered by training. In learning, we saw ALL of them advance – or *ALL regress* – TOGETHER. Perhaps the most compelling way this was documented was by determining the status of about twenty operational characteristics of the "primary auditory cortex" (A-1) in a rat model. Differences in these many features – known to arise via the expressions of hundreds of genes controlling more than a thousand known cellular/molecular processes – were examined in animals near the prime of life versus near the end of life. Cortical neuronal response selectivity, time constants governing cortical processes, successive signal responding, processes governing selective attention and prediction, local response coordination, receptor sub-units governing inhibitory and excitatory processes, local and long-range myelination, trophic factor expression, modulatory neurotransmitter transporters and receptors, cross-system coordination, physical status of specific inhibitory neuronal populations, representational orderliness, cortical column sizes and boundaries, network process noise, attention modulation, distractor suppression power, adaptation to continuous or repetitive background stimulation, responses to an unexpected stimulus, cortical expression of immune regulators – among other indices of cortical functions – were all on our study list.

How many of these physical/chemical/functional properties differed in prime-of-life vs. end-of-life animals? The answer: All of them.

How many advantaged the older brain? The answer: None of them.

The real question: *How many of these aspects of those old rodent brains are "rejuvenated" (reversed) by appropriate forms of brain training?* The answer: All of them.

Most were reversed all the way back, to achieve equivalency to the physical and functional status of a brain in the prime of life. In other words, *plasticity changes physical/chemical/functional aspects of our neurology in a fundamentally reversible way*. Scientists have long viewed the processes by which the brain establishes "mature" processing by the third or fourth decade in life as a post-natal extension of development. In fact, exactly the same progressive changes that account for the young brain achieving that "maturity" were recorded when we drove an old brain backward "out of that old age" to the same refined prime-of-life state, by training. To further explore this two-way plasticity, we also showed that we could accelerate normal aging by simply exposing a brain system in the rodent to continuous high neuronal noise ("chatter") for 2–3 weeks. The brain in such rats was indistinguishable from that of a rat near the end of life – or, for that matter, from that of a rat that had had almost no experience, in their very early life.

Collectively, these studies provided a demonstration of the fact that the operational person that we are arises from the progressive spatiotemporal organization of responding in our brains, refined from that initial state of near-chaos on a massive scale by our experiences across the course of our lives on Earth. In those lives, complex, coupled neurological processes changing positively (or negatively) *together* account for our "highs" (and "lows") – on the upside, accounting for the remarkable genesis of our beautifully specialized and individuated personhood expressed most powerfully in the prime of life – then often, on the downside, for its collapse into mental illness, or an inexorable decline in our again-noisier older brains.

Harnessing the genie: The emergence of brain plasticity-based medicine. It has long been obvious that "negative" plasticity underlies most aspects of the expressions of human impairments and illnesses. Our plastic brains provide a direct avenue for neurological correction. We've deployed these brain-plasticity-guided strategies to more holistically treat impairments and illnesses in more than six million children and adults with problems ranging from dyslexia and ADHD to Schizophrenia to Alzheimer's. Positive outcomes are being achieved in more than twenty of these treatment and resilience training populations.

What is completely clear from our neurological science at this time is that any hope for a "cure" (true neurological renormalization) for clinical indications such as these shall *require* our engaging the power of each patient's brain to repair itself, by exploiting its powerful, intrinsically reversible, brain-plasticity capabilities. Over the next decade, this new approach to treatment, exploiting advanced technologies, can be expected to sweep across neurological and psychiatric medicine, improving the health and altering the fates of many millions of individuals whose lives are limited and often degraded by neurological impairment or disease, or by psychiatric illness.

REFERENCES

Merzenich, M. (2014). *Soft-Wired*. San Francisco: Parnassus Publishing.

Merzenich, M. (2015). Early UCSF contributions to the development of multiple-channel cochlear implants. *Hearing Res. 322*:39–46. doi:10.1016/j.heares.2014.12.008.

Nahum, M., Lee H., & Merzenich, M. M. (2013). Principles of neuroplasticity-based rehabilitation. *Prog. Brain Res. 207*:141–171. doi:10.1016/B978-0-444-63327-9.00009-6.

Section B

Cognitive and Social Neuroscience

9   Social Neuroscience

Cacioppo, John T.

Social species by definition create organizations and processes beyond the individual. These superorganismal structures and processes can differ across species, but typically evolved hand in hand with neural, hormonal, cellular, and genetic mechanisms because the consequent structures and behaviors helped these organisms survive, reproduce, and leave a genetic legacy. Humans, born to a long period of utter dependency and dependent on conspecifics across the lifespan to survive and prosper, are an ultra-social species. Attachment, attraction, attitudes, aggression, altruism, affiliation, attribution, conformity, contagion, cooperation, competition, communication, culture, and empathy are just a few behavioral processes that are fundamentally social.

I attended graduate school at Ohio State University, where I studied both social and biological approaches to behavior. When I proposed a dissertation that sought to bring these perspectives together to better understand the factors and mechanisms underlying social behavior, however, I received pushback from both sides. From the biological perspective, social factors were thought to be a recent evolutionary development, and therefore to have few (if any) implications for the basic development, structure, or function of the nervous system. And even if they did, the notion was that they were too complex to study effectively in our lifespan. From the social perspective, the twentieth century had seen two world wars, a great depression, generations of social injustice, and the development of nuclear warfare. Even if the brain and biology were relevant, the pushback was that it would take far too long to develop a sufficient understanding of the brain to contribute anything to our understanding of social processes or behavior, much less to the solution of the social ills that threatened society.

If not for the encouragement of my roommate – a fellow graduate student and now life-long friend, Richard Petty – to pursue my passion, my career might have taken a very different course. And if not for the good fortune of joining the faculty at Ohio State University in 1989 in both social psychology and biopsychology, and striking up a collaboration with yet another great friend and colleague, Gary Berntson, we likely would never have proposed the interdisciplinary field of social neuroscience with the goal of identifying the neural, hormonal, cellular, and genetic mechanisms underlying social structures and processes, and identifying the specific influences and pathways linking social and neural structures and processes. We noted that specifying these mechanisms required the integration of multiple levels, and that mapping across systems and levels (from genome to social groups and cultures) would benefit from inter-disciplinary expertise, comparative studies, an integration of human research and animal models, innovative methods, and integrative con-ceptual analysis.

Scientific research on the brain and the biological processes underlying social behavior can be traced back to the late nineteenth century and saw important contributions from many scholars throughout the twentieth century, but work in the field was largely fragmented. When we published our first paper on social neuroscience in 1992 – prior to the ready avail-ability of functional neuroimaging, prior to the discovery of mirror neurons, and prior to the recognition of the importance of epigenetics – we felt the need to address why "social neuroscience" was *not* an oxymoron.

The study of the structure and function of the brain is so complex that it requires disparate basic, clinical, and applied disciplines to cover the terrain. Although scientific investigations of structure and function go hand in hand, differences in emphasis exist in this scientific frontier. The emphasis in some fields is on identifying constituent structures at different levels of organization, such as neuroanatomy, neurobiology, cellular and molecular neuroscience, genetics, and biochemistry. The emphasis on others is weighted more toward understanding the function of the brain and nervous system. Among the latter are the complementary fields of behavioral, cognitive, and social neuroscience. Behavioral neuroscience generally views the nervous system and brain as instruments of sensation and response, with representative topics of study including learning, motivation, homeostasis, biological rhythms, and reproduction. Cognitive neuroscience generally views the brain as a computer, with representative topics of study including attention, representations, memory systems, reasoning, and executive functioning.

Social neuroscience represents yet another broad perspective in which, rather than viewing the brain as a solitary computer, it is viewed as a mobile, broadband-connected computing device closer metaphorically to a cell phone than to a desktop computer that is connected only to an electrical outlet. The brain functions that imme-diately come into focus, given this perspective, are very different from those highlighted by the perspective of behavioral or cognitive neuroscience. Rather than language being viewed as a representational system for the comprehension, manipulation, storage, and retrieval of information, language is viewed as a system for information exchange between brains, a system that promotes communication and coordination across discrete and sometimes distant organisms. In sum, the perspectives of behavioral, cognitive, and social neuroscience are distinct, and each has something valuable to offer in our quests to understand the structure and function of the nervous system and to understand human behavior.

To investigate the effects of the social environment on neural, hormonal, cellular, and genetic mechanisms, I used an approach that is common in the neurosciences – the subtractive or deletion method for functional analysis. If one seeks to investigate the function of a gene, for instance, one can measure the differences in responses from genetically intact mice and mice in which that gene is inactivated (knocked out). If one seeks to investigate the function of the orbitofrontal cortex, one can determine the differences in responses of a gentleman, now deceased, named Phineas Gage, both prior to and following the accident that destroyed his orbitofrontal cortex. In each case, the biological function of some element (a gene, a nucleus in the brain) is determined by comparing the function in an organism or individual with this element against the function observed in an organism or individual without this element. Thus, to investigate the importance of normal social bonds and relationships for brain and biology, we compared people who varied in terms of their perceived social isolation.

The focus in social epidemiology had been on objective social isolation and health behavior, but if the brain is the key organ for forming, monitoring, maintaining, repairing, and replacing salutary connections with others, then we reasoned that perceived social isolation should be associated with health and longevity through biological rather than solely behavioral mechanisms. Perceived social isolation had been termed "loneliness" in the literature, so I began studying the effects of loneliness. When I moved to the University of Chicago in 1999, I began a population-based, longitudinal study to investigate loneliness, controlling for standard risk factors and various alternative mediators. We discovered that loneliness is not only associated with early morbidity and mortality above and beyond objective isolation, but it is also associated with increased sleep fragmentation, increased hypothalamic pituitary adrenocortical (HPA) activity, altered gene expression indicative of decreased inflammatory control and protection from viral infection, elevated vascular resistance and blood pressure, and diminished immunity.

Not surprisingly, we also found that loneliness is associated with a host of neural effects, including differences in the regional activation of the brain in response to social stimuli, and ongoing work suggests it is associated with differences in functional connectivity even when the brain is at rest.

The perspective and metaphor of social neuroscience seem to have been important because it helped bring together so many different scientific fields, scales of analysis, methods, samples (e.g., insects, rodents, non-human primates, patients, and healthy people across the lifespan), and important behavioral processes and problems. Contemporary social neuroscience has grown into a broad and interdisciplinary field, with some researchers focused on social insects to understand the genetics of social behavior, others focused on non-human animal models to probe the epigenetics and neurobiology of social behavior, others focused on human brain imaging in an attempt to elucidate social cognition, and still others focused on the interplay of social and biological factors underlying human distress associated with atypical social behavior or disease, and so on. Although some of the fragmentation that characterized research in the field throughout most of the twentieth century can still be found, there is also emerging evidence of increased communication and collaborations among what had long been distinct research areas. Social neuroscience is still young, but the growth of and developments in the field are encouraging.

REFERENCES

Cacioppo, J. T., Amaral, D. G., Blanchard, J. J., Cameron, J. L., Carter, C. S., Crews, D., ... & Quinn, K. J. (2007). Social neuroscience: Progress and implications for mental health. *Perspectives on Psychological Science, 2,* 99–123.

Cacioppo, J. T., Cacioppo, S., Capitanio, J. P., & Cole, S. W. (2015). The neuroendocrinology of social isolation. *Annual Review of Psychology, 66,* 733–767.

Cacioppo, S., Capitanio, J. P., & Cacioppo, J. T. (2014). Toward a neurology of loneliness. *Psychological Bulletin, 140,* 1464–1504.

10   Modulating Memory Consolidation

McGaugh, James L.

Why do we remember some of our experiences but forget most of them? One important reason for this was suggested by the philosopher Francis Bacon in 1620, when he noted that *"memory is assisted by anything that makes an impression on a powerful passion."* My major research contributions focused on two issues related to Bacon's observation: (1) drug enhancement of memory consolidation, and (2) physiological regulation of memory consolidation involving stress hormone release and amygdala activation. Both issues help explain how the emotional significance of events regulates our memory.

Drug Enhancement of Memory Consolidation

When I was a graduate student at the University of California, Berkeley, in the mid-1950s, I initiated experiments investigating the effects of central nervous system (CNS) stimulant drugs on learning in rats. I chose this project for two reasons. First, I thought that understanding the drugs' effects on learning would provide some insights into the neurobiology of memory. Second, I discovered a 1917 paper published by Karl Lashley (the dominant physiological psychologist/behavioral neuroscientist of the last century) reporting that the stimulant drug strychnine administered to rats, each day before training in a maze, enhanced learning. I repeated Lashley's experiment and replicated his findings. Although this was an exciting finding for me, it offered only the conclusion that the drug enhanced learning performance. As the drug was administered before training, it may have influenced learning simply by influencing the animals' performance in some way, rather than by influencing the neural processes underlying learning. Thus, it was clear to me that some other approach to the problem was required to understand how the drug acted to enhance learning.

I was aware of a finding, reported a few years earlier, that electroconvulsive shock – delivered to rats each day within a few minutes after they received training – impaired their learning. Those findings provided novel

49

experimental evidence supporting the hypothesis (proposed by Mueller and Pilzecker in 1900) that newly acquired information is initially fragile and becomes consolidated over time after learning.

The consolidation hypothesis suggested that it might be possible to enhance memory by administering stimulant drugs after learning. I investigated this possibility and obtained the first evidence that administration of stimulant drugs shortly after training enhanced learning performance. Many subsequent experiments in my laboratory, as well as other laboratories, using a variety of training tasks and stimulant drugs, provided extensive evidence that stimulant drugs administered shortly after training can enhance memory. These findings provided compelling evidence that the drugs acted by influencing memory consolidation.

Endogenous Modulation of Memory Consolidation

These experiments raised an interesting and important question that my laboratory subsequently addressed. Why do memories consolidate slowly after learning experiences? Perhaps the consolidation is slow in order to allow physiological processes activated by experiences to modulate the consolidation of memories. And, we thought, perhaps stress hormones activated by experiences might play that role. It is well known that emotionally arousing experiences initiate the release of stress hormones. And remembering emotionally arousing experiences is important for adapting and surviving. As the philosopher Decartes noted in 1650, *"The usefulness of the passions (e.g., emotions) consists in their strengthening and prolonging in the soul thoughts which are good for it to preserve."*

Experiments in my laboratory investigated this issue. In several experiments using different kinds of learning tasks, we found that the stress hormone epinephrine (adrenaline), which is normally released from the adrenals by arousing stimulation, enhanced memory when administered shortly after training. In many subsequent studies, we found that other stress-activated hormones, including corticosterone (cortisol in humans), which is also released from the adrenals by emotional arousal, enhanced memory consolidation. Additionally, we found that administration of propranolol, a drug that that prevents the actions of epinephrine (and noradrenaline), by blocking beta-adrenergic receptors, prevents the memory-enhancing effects of stress hormones, as well as those of stimulant drugs. These findings suggested that adrenergic activation is essential for memory modulation.

In other experiments we looked for a brain locus of these effects. We found that the amygdala (basolateral region), located bilaterally in the medial temporal lobe, is a critical site for adrenergic/noradrenergic regulation of memory consolidation. Noradrenergic activation of the amygdala (by microinfusions of norepinephrine administered directly into the amygdala) enhanced memory consolidation; inactivation (by microinfusions of propranolol) impaired consolidation. Additionally, in experiments in which we measured the release of norepinephrine within the amygdala, we found that retention performance, assessed one day after training, varied directly with the amount that was released shortly after training. And, importantly, findings of other experiments indicate that noradrenergic activation of the amygdala influences the consolidation of different forms of memory through its projections to other brain regions involved in consolidating memory, including the caudate nucleus and hippocampus.

Comparable findings were obtained in studies of memory in human subjects. Administration of propranolol blocked the enhancing effect of emotional arousal on memory. Viewing of emotionally arousing films induced activation of the amygdala, as assessed by positron emission tomography (PET) brain imaging, and memory of the films tested weeks later correlated highly with the degree of amygdala activation induced by viewing the films. Additionally, findings of PET and fMRI studies indicated, consistent with those of studies using rats, that the enhanced memory involved amygdala activation of the hippocampus.

Significance of These Findings

Why do we remember some experiences and forget others? There is considerable evidence from both human and animal studies that emotionally arousing experiences are well remembered. This idea is, of course, not new. The findings from my laboratory strongly support Bacon's and Decartes' observations that emotion assists memory. They provide neurobiological understanding of how emotional arousal assists the preservation of our significant experiences. But, they also indicate that intense emotional arousal and the release of high levels of stress hormones are not required for modulating memory. Our memories of highly significant personal or public events tend to be lasting. However, many of our memories of relatively insignificant events can be enhanced by even mild emotional arousal occurring after the events. Thus, the modulation of memory consolidation appears to be an ongoing process that ensures that the emotional significance of experiences regulates their remembrance. These findings are important because they increase our understanding of the neurobiological processes underlying our most precious ability: memory. They may ultimately provide clues to our understanding of, as well as treatment for, disorders of memory, including those found with post-traumatic stress disorder (PTSD) and dementia.

Future Investigations

These findings raise many questions that will require many kinds of investigations. Stimulant drugs and stress hormones enhance consolidation when administered in low doses, but impair memory when administered in high doses. But, it is not known whether endogeneously released stress hormones impair the consolidation of memory of recent experiences when released in high levels. Such information is needed to provide an increased understanding of the influence of emotion on memory.

There is extensive evidence that different brain systems are involved in the learning of motor skills and cognitive information. Our findings indicate that stress hormones can enhance memory for many kinds of training. Such findings suggest that amygdala activity influences processing in many "downstream" brain systems that mediate different forms of memory. Our studies have found that adrenergic activation of the amygdala influences processes in the hippocampus, a region known to be involved in spatial memory. But such studies have only begun to investigate the interactions of the amygdala with other brain systems as well as the molecular processes influenced in those brain systems. The findings of such studies will significantly increase our understanding of how our brains acquire and retain information.

REFERENCES

McGaugh, J. L. (1990). Significance and remembrance: The role of neuromodulatory systems. *Psychological Science, 1*, 15–25.

McGaugh, J. L. (2003). *Memory and emotion: The making of lasting memories.* London: Weidenfeld and Nicolson The Orion House Group Ltd. and New York: Columbia University Press.

McGaugh, J. L. (2015). Consolidating memories. *Annual Review of Psychology, 66*, 1–24.

11 Memory Consolidation and Transformation: The Hippocampus and Mental Time Travel

Moscovitch, Morris

Background

Older adults with failing memories often state that they have difficulty remembering what happened to them yesterday, yet they can remember very well events that occurred when they were in high school or college. These impressions were probably noted from time immemorial, but they were given scientific credibility by Ribot, a nineteenth-century French neurologist, who proposed that following brain damage, recent memories are more likely to be lost than remote ones. Even relatively mild damage, such as a concussion sustained during sport or in a car accident, will cause similar effects. The reason given for this pattern of lost and preserved memories is that remote memories were consolidated (made relatively permanent) in the brain before the onset of damage (or deterioration, in the case of older adults), whereas the damage hindered the consolidation of more recent memories and left them vulnerable to decay or interference.

In the 1950s, Brenda Milner and her collaborators, William Scoville and Wilder Penfield, reported that damage to the hippocampus, a region on the inside surface of the medial temporal lobes, which lie next to your temples, leads to a profound amnesia that conformed to Ribot's Law. Henry Molaison (H.M.), the most celebrated of the neurosurgical patients, could acquire few, if any, memories of which he was consciously aware from the time of his surgery in 1953 to his death in 2008. Initial, casual observation indicated, however, that he remembered events that occurred prior to his surgery very well. Based on this evidence, and that of similar cases, investigators concluded that the hippocampus is a temporary memory structure that helps retain and retrieve memories until they are consolidated in other parts of the brain. Once consolidated, the hippocampus is no longer needed for their retention or recovery; these functions would now be mediated by other parts of the brain. This was the standard consolidation theory accepted by most neuroscientists and enshrined in most textbooks.

My Contribution

Fifty years after the report on H.M. was published, the standard consolidation theory reigned supreme. Lynn Nadel, Gordon Winocur, and I, with the help of our students and collaborators, dethroned this theory and replaced it with an alternative, which has evolved into the "Multiple Trace Theory and Trace Transformation." According to this theory, every time you consciously experience a new event or think of an old one, the hippocampus automatically lays down a memory trace. Old memories, which you may have retrieved many times, would therefore have multiple traces. Not all memories, however, are encoded in this way by the hippocampus. The hippocampus is implicated in retention and retrieval only of detailed memories, the sort that allow you to re-experience the past in great detail as if you were mentally traveling back in time and reliving the event, such as your first passionate kiss. It's a process called "recollection," and it depends on the hippocampus no matter how long ago the memory was formed. Contrary to Ribot's Law, and to the standard theory, memory of this type is impoverished in people with hippocampal damage or deterioration, and the deficit extends to the very first memories of this sort that were formed. A re-examination of evidence collected from H.M. by Suzanne Corkin indicates that he, too, had this dense and temporally extended retrograde (for the past) amnesia. In fact, he seems to have possessed only one truly episodic memory of his entire lifetime. By contrast, his memory for facts about the world (Where is Paris? Who is Louis Armstrong?) and about himself (who his parents were, where he went to school) and for vocabulary – what psychologists call semantic memory – was preserved if these memories had been acquired prior to his surgery, indicating that the hippocampus is not needed for their retention and retrieval. With time and experience, the vast majority of episodic memories are *transformed* and lose much of their detail, retaining only their gist – the memories become schematic. As memories become transformed from detailed, contextually rich memories to gist-like, schematic representations, they become increasingly less dependent on the hippocampus, and rely on other brain regions in the cortex (and possibly other areas) for their retention and retrieval.

Arriving at the Theory and Testing It

Being raised in Montreal, I attended McGill University (1962–1966), where Brenda Milner, Wilder Penfield, and Donald Hebb were on the faculty, and whose research and theories on the neural basis of memory were featured prominently in my courses. Among the graduate students who TA'd my course was Lynn Nadel, who wrote an influential book with John O'Keefe, the 2014 recipient of the Nobel Prize, on the hippocampus. For my honors thesis, I worked with Peter Milner, the co-discoverer of rewarding electrical brain stimulation in rats. I conducted a project on memory consolidation using electroconvulsive shock to disrupt consolidation in rats. I did not return to the topic, however, until 1996 when I was invited by Lynn Nadel to spend a sabbatical at the University of Arizona.

During that year, Nadel and I received a preprint of a paper by Larry Squire and his collaborators on anterograde and retrograde amnesia in three people with hippocampal lesions. Two aspects of their data caught our attention. First, amnesia for autobiographical memories seemed more severe, and stretched further back in time, than memory for public events and personalities. Second, the retrograde amnesia for autobiographical memories extended for about thirty years, which seemed far too long for memories to consolidate. Mindful of the distinction between episodic and semantic memory, Lynn Nadel and I hypothesized, contrary to the standard model, that the hippocampus must always be necessary for retention and retrieval of rich, detailed episodic memories, of which autobiographical events are an example, no matter how long ago the memories were formed. By contrast, semantic memories are dependent on the hippocampus only temporarily, until they are consolidated in the neocortex, where they are assimilated to semantic networks and schemas that are represented there. With this hypothesis in mind, we reviewed the literature and found that the evidence favored our view over the standard theory.

Would a similar pattern be found in non-human animals? We adopted the working assumption that memories that are context-dependent would be the animal homologue of episodic memory. A preprint of a paper by Robert Sutherland confirmed our prediction: Rats with hippocampal lesions had an extensive retrograde amnesia for context-dependent memories. No such extensive retrograde amnesia was found for memories that were not context-dependent.

Armed with this evidence, we presented our Multiple Trace Theory and, together with Wincour and others, tested it in humans and rodents with lesions to the hippocampus, and in healthy humans using functional neuroimaging to see which structures are activated during memory retrieval. The results confirmed our model and led to the development of the complementary Trace Transformation component of it.

Implications for Psychological Science

The vast majority of research on memory in humans is concerned with memories acquired in the laboratory and tested within an hour or two of acquisition, yet in life outside the laboratory our activities and thoughts are governed as much by remote as by recent memories. Showing that the hippocampus is equally involved in representing detailed, episodic memories in the same way, regardless of when they were acquired, allows for greater integration of real life with laboratory-based memories. The theory we advanced – that the hippocampus is equally involved in representing detailed episodic memories, no matter how recently or remotely they were formed – fundamentally altered our view of the hippocampus from that of a temporary to a permanent memory structure.

The idea that the hippocampal representations enable mental time travel suggested that it should not matter whether mental travel is backward or forward in time. Indeed, investigators have now confirmed this prediction and shown that the hippocampus is implicated as much in imagining the future in rich detail as it is in recollecting a detailed past. From here, it was a short step to showing that the hippocampus is implicated in imagining any rich fictitious scene or episode.

The World Beyond Academia

What use are these rich and detailed episodic memories, other than to impress your family and friends with your life stories? Over the last few years, research has shown that these rich episodic memories contribute to a growing variety of functions, from problem-solving to decision-making, from language to empathy, and even from perception and creativity to eating.

How well you can solve open-ended problems, such as how to make friends when moving to a new neighborhood, depends on how richly you can imagine scenarios that bring you closer to that goal. The same is true for performance on tests of creativity, such as naming multiple uses for common objects such as a brick. Interestingly, how empathic you are and how willing you are to help someone in distress will also depend on how well you remember details of the person's predicament and how detailed your imagination is in devising ways to help the person.

Even your ability to regulate your food intake depends crucially on remembering what you ate. Researchers have shown that being inattentive or distracted while eating increases your intake in proportion to how good your memory is of the meal you had. Conversely, richly imagining eating different foods will reduce your intake of that food when it is offered later. These ideas were inspired by finding that people with hippocampal lesions who are severely amnesic, H.M. among them, will finish a meal, and, if distracted for a few minutes so that they forgot they ate, will judge themselves to be just as hungry as before the meal and eat a second and even a third meal when it was offered to them.

These examples show the power of these rich episodes, whether recollected, or imagined and invented, to influence behavior in real life. There is no telling the great worth that this newly tapped vein of research will yield.

REFERENCES

Nadel, L., & Moscovitch, M. (1997). Memory consolidation, retrograde amnesia and the hippocampal complex. *Current Opinion in Neurobiology, 7*, 217–227.

Winocur, G., Moscovitch, M., & Bontempi, B. (2010). Memory formation and long-term retention in humans and animals: Convergence towards a transformation account of hippocampal-neocortical interactions. *Neuropsychologia, 48*, 2339–2356.

Moscovitch, M., Cabeza, R., Winocur, G., & Nadel, L. (2016). Episodic memory and beyond: The hippocampus and neocortex in transformation. *Annual Review of Psychology, 67*, 105–134.

12   Imaging the Human Brain

Posner, Michael I.

I had a role in making it possible to visualize the working of the human brain while it is engaged in thought. The development of neuroimaging has made it possible to connect the abstract mental operations or computations studied by cognitive psychology with the brain areas studied by neuroscience and helped to establish cognitive neuroscience as a field within psychology. Here, I tell the history of how my role in visualizing the human brain came about.

Vernon Mountcastle was one of the pioneers of modern brain research. His work with animals showed that the basic functional unit of the brain was the cortical column. In 1978, I read a paper of his describing attention cells in the posterior part of the parietal cortex of alert monkeys. He suggested that these attention cells might be critically involved in orienting attention toward visual events. A Tuesday night meeting of our research group was assigned to read these papers. Our group had shown that reaction time to respond to a target was enhanced when a cue directed attention to the target location. We interpreted this to mean that attention had been oriented covertly to the location of the target, without any overt change in eye position or behavior. I asked the students whether the reaction time improvements were the results of the attention cells observed by Mountcastle. I thought that if the covert shifts of attention in humans could be connected with the monkey work, it might contribute to linking cognitive psychology to brain mechanisms. I don't think there was much enthusiasm for this idea at the time. After all, the slogan in cognitive psychology was that it was about software, and what did that have to do with the parts of the brain in which cells were found in the monkey?

In 1979, I met Oscar Marin, an outstanding behavioral neurologist, at a meeting in New York City. He was about to move to Portland, Oregon, to set up a clinical and research effort at Good Samaritan Hospital, and he invited me to set up a neuropsychology laboratory in conjunction with the hospital. It was a perfect time for me because I had spent six months of 1979 in New York working with Michael Gazzaniga, one of the originators of work with split-brain patients, and my brother Jerry Posner, a well-known neurologist, both of whom helped me test patients with parietal lesions. I pursued these questions in the new laboratory in Portland. In the end, I commuted from Eugene to Portland once a week for seven years. It was such a pleasure to work with Dr. Marin that the long drive was worthwhile.

The results seemed to me to be a revelation. Patients with different lesion locations in the cerebral cortex and in areas below the cortex all tended to ignore information on the side of space opposite the lesion. However, using our reaction-time task it was clear that according to the lesion location, they differed in showing deficits in specific mental operations of disengaging, moving, and engaging attention. As I saw it at the time, we had found a new form of brain "localization." Different brain areas executed individual mental operations or computations, such as disengaging from the current focus of attention (parietal lobe), moving or changing the index of attention (colliculus), and engaging the subsequent target (pulvinar). No wonder Lashley had thought the whole brain was involved in mental tasks. It was not the whole brain, but a widely dispersed network of quite localized neural areas. Even looking back from the perspective of thirty-five years, I can again feel the excitement I had surrounding this idea at the time. However, the patients had brain lesions; what was found in the case of lesions might not really explain normal function. Thus, I knew something more needed to be done to investigate my idea.

I read an article from Sweden in *Scientific American* indicating changes in cerebral blood flow when reading silently. In cognitive psychology, reading had been studied quite a lot, and we knew something about the orthographic, phonological, and semantic operations that must take place while reading, but they would be combined in the overall blood flow comparing reading with rest. Even more compelling for the possible anatomy of mental operations was a paper appearing in 1985 by Per Roland, indicating that different parts of the cortex were active during tasks of navigating from place to place, of performing mental arithmetic, and of still others when executing a verbal task. However, even in this paper, there was no effort to uncover the mental operations that might be performed by the brain areas involved.

About this time, Washington University School of Medicine started a national search for a psychologist who might work in conjunction with a developing brain imaging center led by Marcus Raichle. It might be surprising how reluctant psychologists were to take a chance on brain imaging. For me, this was an opportunity to test the idea that arose from the patient studies that individual mental operations would be localized in separate brain tissue. James S. McDonnell had wanted to develop an institute that would study extrasensory perception, but the powers that be at Washington University were not going to do that. Instead, they agreed to a Center on Higher Brain Function. A psychologist who studied brain function was about as mystical as they wanted to go, and Marc Raichle and his colleagues at Washington University recognized the importance of being able to use positron emission tomography (PET) to illuminate questions of higher mental function that could not be studied in animals. I had gone to St. Louis in the hopes of pursuing work on attention. When I talked to neurologists about covert shifts of attention (without eye movements) and then proposed to break the invisible shift into component mental operations such as disengaging and moving, I saw eyes glaze over. Language studies have the advantage that the operations were more concrete and that neurosurgeons valued knowledge about the localization of language areas to aid them in avoiding these areas during surgery. Language studies, summarized in my book with Marc Raichle, *Images of Mind*, had an important influence on the field, fostering many studies of language and other cognitive processes.

The development of functional magnetic resonance imaging (fMRI) allowed studies that were much less invasive than studies with PET, which used radioactivity to trace blood flow. This opened the floodgates for literally thousands of studies of brain areas active in many human tasks. Maurizio Corbetta and Gordon Shulman showed that it was possible to image many of the brain areas I had studied in patients during tasks involving attention. Moreover, imaging was not limited to the study of cognitive processes, but also could be used in studies of developmental, social, personality, and clinical psychology.

However, our studies and those of others were often criticized as "mere localization." While it seemed to me that "mere localization," if accurate, was a step forward, it was important to determine how these brain areas were brought together into a brain network that could actually carry out tasks. Our imaging work and the subsequent studies using magnetic resonance imaging made it possible to examine when each area of the brain came on in real time. One method for doing so was to use scalp electrodes that give detailed knowledge of when things occur. Using information from fMRI studies, it is possible to localize where in the brain the information arose. Developmental studies provided evidence on how some of these brain networks developed during infancy and childhood. Thus, imaging the brain has allowed a greatly enlarged picture of the role of mental operation in the development of the human mind.

My experience may hold a few general lessons for students. A half-century ago it seemed almost impossible to study the human brain in a way that would illuminate psychological problems. We have learned that it is often the boundaries between academic disciplines that offer important opportunities for advances. The limitations of current methods may change with the development of new techniques. Exploitation of new techniques may also open up new questions, and thus new opportunities to advance the field.

REFERENCES

Abdullaev, Y. G., & Posner, M. I. (1998). Event-related brain potential imaging of semantic encoding during processing single words. *Neuroimage, 7*:1–13.

Mountcastle, V. M. (1978). The world around us: Neural command functions for selective attention. *Neuroscience Research Progress Bulletin, 14*:1–47.

Posner, M. I., & Raichle, M. E. (1994). *Images of mind*. New York: Scientific American Books.

13 Different Mechanisms of Cognitive Flexibility Within the Prefrontal Cortex

Robbins, Trevor W.

My significant contribution arose from a simple and perhaps naïve question about localization of function within the primate prefrontal cortex (PFC). Ever since Brenda Milner's seminal discovery about the problems of patients with frontal lobe damage in performing a "test of cognitive flexibility" (Grant and Berg's Wisconsin Card-Sorting Test; WCST), my colleagues and I had debated WCST's precise neural basis. Following analysis of effects of variable lesions suffered by frontal patients, Milner thought that the dorsolateral PFC was the key zone, whereas lots of extant theory about the role of the PFC in behavioral inhibition favored a more ventral region: the orbitofrontal cortex (OFC).

We can classify the WCST either as a test of concept formation or as a trial-and-error rule-learning task. A clinical neuropsychologist tests patients with a pack of 128 cards, each of which varies with respect to three perceptual dimensions: color, shape, and number (of shapes). The neuropsychologist provides spoken feedback for card-sorting according to three possible "rules": color, shape, or number. Once a patient has learned the rule, the rule changes without warning, and they have to suppress the just-learned "rule" and learn another instead. Patients with frontal lobe damage perseverate with the former rule, even though they are apparently aware that it is wrong.

To address the issue of neural localization we modified the task for non-human primates, as the WCST essentially exemplified a paradigm well known in animal learning theory and developmental psychology. For complex ("compound") stimuli comprising multiple dimensions, we make a distinction between learning to generalize a rule across different exemplars of a dimension, such as circles to squares (intra-dimensional shift [ids]; also known as "learning set"), and extra-dimensional shifts (eds) where the subject learns to respond to an alternative perceptual dimension, e.g., color, after attending to shape – similar to the shift in WCST rules. This distinction was important to learning theory in the 1970s, developed by Mackintosh and Sutherland, because a comparison of learning these two shifts predicts that the former, within-dimensional shift, will be easier according to their theory of attentional learning.

However, our non-human primate, the New World marmoset, could not be expected to sort cards (or indeed reliably perceive colors or numbers), so we adapted the test for use on a touch-sensitive screen with computer-controlled stimuli, using perceptual dimensions of lines and shapes. The test also had several inbuilt controls: marmosets learned initially to discriminate, say, "shapes," and then compound stimuli in which irrelevant "lines" were superimposed. In order to entrain the dimension (i.e., shape) rather than the particular exemplar (e.g., polygon), we also arranged for occasional reversals, in which the reward contingency was swapped from one stimulus to the other, formerly punished, stimulus of the same dimension, and vice versa – another, perhaps even more basic form of flexible responding. Such reversals were known to be important for entraining attention to a particular dimension, supporting Mackintosh and Sutherland's two-factor theory of attentional learning.

As a "translational agenda" funded our research, we also devised a set of discrimination tasks for human patients with dementia and Parkinson's disease, as well as localized brain lesions, using the same touch-screen modality and exactly the same stimuli and procedure, except that we rewarded humans with computer-generated green checkmarks and verbal feedback, whereas we gave marmosets cool banana juice. (We punished errors with reward omission and red crosses or a loud noise, respectively). We began the sequence of discrimination tasks with a simple discrimination, then simple reversal within a single perceptual dimension, before the compound stimuli were introduced with a further reversal and an ids (and subsequent reversal) before an eds (and subsequent reversal). This suite, together with many other cognitive tasks based on a similar philosophy, became part of what became known as CANTAB (Cambridge Neuropsychological Test Automated Battery), now used internationally (even on iPads) in many research institutions and clinics.

For the convenience of rapid testing in these studies, we used a hand-based version for the monkeys. After preliminary training, marmosets received infusions of the neurotoxin quinolinic acid into either the OFC or lateral PFC to remove most of the cells in those regions, whilst sparing fibers of passage. Results were clear-cut: Animals with lateral PFC lesions had difficulties with eds but no other stage of discrimination learning, including reversal; by contrast, those with OFC lesions were impaired on reversal learning (i.e., in learning to shift responding to the alternative, previously punished option and away from the previously rewarded object), again with no other deficits. There was thus a logical "double dissociation" of effects, implying that these different

PFC regions have different functions and that the findings cannot be attributed to differences in sensitivity of the eds and reversal tests to brain-damage-induced impairments. Such findings are crucial for indicating specific functions for particular brain regions and strongly suggest some specialization of control mechanisms within the PFC.

This was one of the first such double dissociations shown for PFC function in the primate brain – a significant observation at the time, as it has often been claimed that the PFC contributes in a rather general manner to "executive functions" – for example, mediating general intelligence ("g"). Hence, it was still controversial whether such location of function was possible within this structure. Theoretical implications were considerable; the findings mapped onto the Mackintosh–Sutherland theory of attention in defining two somewhat independent factors. A computational modeling approach (by Krushke) also showed two independent factors were necessary. The findings were also compatible with modern hypotheses of hierarchical organization of function within the PFC, with exemplar-specific reward learning subsidiary to dimensional "rule" learning.

Earlier work in non-human primates, before the age of human neuroimaging, had strongly hinted at the possibility of fractionating and localizing executive functions in this way. "Working memory" performance had been shown to depend on the dorsolateral PFC in the rhesus brain. However, our findings could not easily be explained by problems of "working memory" and related more strongly to everyday problems of rigidity of thinking and behavior evident in a number of neuropsychiatric disorders.

Using the human CANTAB version of the same task with the same visual stimuli, we showed that patients with frontal lobe damage had similar deficits to those seen in the monkeys; the same lateral to orbitofrontal dissociation apparently held. (A recent functional imaging study in healthy volunteers using the same logic also confirmed the anatomical dissociation of eds and reversal within the PFC). Moreover, we also applied the task to patients with psychiatric or neurological disorders to define the nature of their cognitive problems. Thus, we demonstrated eds problems in patients with obsessive-compulsive disorder and their relatives, suggesting that some form of cognitive rigidity was core to the disorder, despite patients' highly specific symptoms. Patients with schizophrenia also showed considerable problems with both reversal and eds. Patients with gene-positive Huntington's disease exhibited problems in eds even before the onset of clinical symptoms; later in the disease, they showed profound problems in reversal learning, greater than those shown in early Alzheimer's disease, and consistent with what was known about the spread of pathology with disease progression.

The basic findings have since ramified in several directions. Other researchers developed an ingenious modification of the id/ed/reversal paradigm for rats with smell and touch as the main perceptual dimensions; eds and reversal were again shown to depend on distinct PFC regions in the rat and mouse brain: medial PFC and OFC, respectively. These findings address a continuing evolutionary controversy about relationships between the rodent and the primate PFC; these functions may be basic "building blocks" of more sophisticated "executive" functions in humans. Pragmatically, the rodent findings have been applied to the problems of pharmacological screening of drugs for cognitive deficits in humans, and also for detecting genetic influences on these basic "executive" functions.

The twin functions of eds and reversal are also apparently modulated by different chemical neurotransmitter systems. We found that manipulations of the chemical transmitter pathways that innervate the PFC from subcortical regions, the catecholamine (dopamine and noradrenaline) and serotonin pathways, had doubly dissociable effects. Thus, serotonin depletion specifically impaired reversal and not eds, and dopamine and noradrenaline manipulations more readily affected ids and eds. We are still contemplating the significance of this striking confirmation of a fundamental difference between eds and reversal in terms of the wider neural networks underlying these functions. Further work across all the species is addressing this issue – we and others have shown that structures such as the parietal cortex and, subcortically, the striatum and amygdala are important. We need to determine when and how these functional networks overlap and are coordinated at a neural level, as both depend on similar rewarding (or punishing) feedback.

This challenge may lead to the crucial, yet largely unexplored question of how PFC sub-regions communicate and cooperate during complex cognitive operations, and how these computations produce cognitive and behavioral outputs. Tackling such questions will probably require the development of sophisticated neuroimaging procedures across species in a number of modalities, including electrophysiology and magnetic resonance imaging, as well as appropriate theoretical advances in psychology.

REFERENCES

Milner, B. (1963). Effects of different brain lesions on card-sorting. *Archives of Neurology*, *9*, 90–100.
Dias, R., Robbins, T. W., & Roberts A. C. (1996). Dissociation in prefrontal cortex of affective and attentional shifts. *Nature*, *380*, 69–72.

Squire, Larry R.

My first studies focused on the pharmacology of memory in rats and then on protein synthesis and memory in mice. What propelled me to human work was a 1971 publication on retrograde amnesia in memory-impaired patients. Retrograde amnesia refers to memory loss for information acquired before the onset of amnesia. The patients in that study had memory loss extending decades into the past, and its severity was similar at all past time periods. This result completely perplexed me. It did not fit what I had come to understand from the animal literature, where retrograde amnesia was typically limited and also temporally graded, affecting recent memory more than remote memory. Indeed, retrograde amnesia in animals was thought to provide evidence for memory consolidation: the idea that memory becomes more fixed and less vulnerable to disruption as time passes after learning.

I had been in graduate school at MIT at the time when the noted amnesic patient H.M. was being studied there. We were all familiar with his story and the neurosurgery that he had undergone to relieve severe epilepsy. So, it was not a big jump for me to begin studying memory and amnesia in humans, initially with psychiatric patients who were prescribed electroconvulsive therapy (ECT) for depression. (ECT was known to cause transient memory impairment). What was needed, I thought, was a test of past memory that could sample past time periods equivalently – that is, assess information from different time periods which had originally been learned to the same extent. We ended up with a memory test for the names of television programs that had broadcast for only one season during the past seventeen years. The popularity of the programs was similar across time periods. ECT resulted in temporally graded retrograde amnesia, sparing older memories but impairing memories acquired up to three years before treatment. This work provided the first evidence that memory consolidation in humans can occur across a lengthy time period (a few years) and that consolidation depends on reorganization within long-term memory. This led us to many more studies of retrograde amnesia, remote memory, and to what is referred to as the standard model of consolidation (not my term). We now understand that retrograde amnesia can sometimes be quite extensive – even as extensive as reported in 1971 – depending on the neuropathology and on whether the damage extends into the neocortex of the lateral temporal lobe.

In 1978, another publication appeared that had a big influence on my work. This paper emphasized how little we understood about the brain structures important for memory. We knew that the medial temporal lobe was important because this was the region that had been removed bilaterally in patient H.M. However, the medial aspect of the temporal lobe includes a number of different brain structures, and in 1978 it was unclear which structure or group of structures was important. Was damage to the hippocampus sufficient to account for H.M.'s memory impairment? Was the amygdala important? What about the adjacent cortex, which was also included in the resection? It was clear that these questions could be addressed most directly in the experimental animal. The approach would be to systematically damage or remove structures within the medial temporal region and evaluate memory performance.

One might have supposed that the most appropriate animal for such a project would be the rat. However, early efforts with rats had foundered, largely due to uncertainty about what tasks were the appropriate ones for demonstrating memory impairment in the experimental animal. As it turned out, the best tasks for assessing memory impairment in animals were developed first for the monkey, and monkeys with large H.M.-like lesions were known to fail these tasks. It was the right time to take on this problem. The work involved a long series of studies, across twelve years, but in the end Stuart Zola and I successfully identified the anatomical components of what is now termed the medial temporal lobe memory system. The important structures are the hippocampus and the adjacent entorhinal, perirhinal, and parahippocampal cortices, which lie along the parahippocampal gyrus. The amygdala, which was a candidate structure, is not part of this system. Damage to the hippocampus itself causes a moderately severe memory impairment, but profound memory impairment, as in H.M., occurs only when the damage includes the hippocampus as well as adjacent cortex.

Our study of human memory and memory impairment continued all through this period. I had been fascinated by reports that patients could sometimes benefit from recent experience, despite their severe memory impairment. For example, across successive learning trials patients improved the speed at which they performed a maze task, even though they did not learn the path through the maze. Why should patients begin performing more quickly if they cannot remember what they have just done? Did this imply that some kinds of memory could be acquired successfully by patients such as these? The earliest experimental work on this matter (in the 1960s) demonstrated that H.M. could learn a hand-eye coordination skill over a period of days despite not remembering having practiced the task before. However, discussion at the time tended to set motor skills aside as a special case of a less cognitive form of memory. The view then was that all of memory (except motor skills) is of one piece and that all of memory is impaired in patients like H.M.

Motor skills proved to be the tip of the iceberg. In 1980, Neal Cohen and I found that amnesic patients could acquire a perceptual skill (reading mirror-reversed text) at a normal rate, despite poor memory for the words that had been read. On the basis of this finding, we proposed that a fundamental distinction should be drawn between different forms of memory, reminiscent of the philosophical distinction between knowing how and knowing that. We distinguished declarative memory from procedural memory (terms used originally in the artificial intelligence literature). Roughly, declarative memory referred to conscious memory for facts and events (knowing that), and is dependent on the medial temporal lobe structures damaged in amnesia. Procedural memory (knowing how) referred to skill-based knowledge and is spared in amnesia.

In subsequent work we found additional kinds of spared abilities in memory-impaired patients: the phenomenon of priming, classical eyeblink conditioning, and habit learning. Yet, as these examples accumulated, it became difficult to fit them into a two-part dichotomy. So, in 1988 I suggested the term "nondeclarative," with the idea that declarative memory refers to one memory system and that nondeclarative memory is an umbrella term referring to additional kinds of memory. These nondeclarative forms of memory, I suggested, correspond to unconscious forms of memory and are supported separately by the basal ganglia (habit learning), the amygdala (emotional learning), and the cerebellum (conditioning of skeletal musculature), as well as abilities intrinsic to the neocortex such as priming and perceptual learning.

The empirical work thus provided the foundation for a new way of thinking about the organization of memory and its biological foundations. Declarative and nondeclarative memory can be distinguished in terms of the different kinds of information they process and the principles by which they operate. Declarative, conscious memory provides a way to model the external world. It is representational and is either true or false. Nondeclarative memory is neither true nor false. It refers to the habits, skills, attitudes, and dispositions that determine how we behave. Declarative memory is expressed though recollection and depends on the medial temporal lobe structures damaged in H.M. and other amnesic patients. Nondeclarative memory is expressed through performance. Performance changes as the result of experience and in that sense deserves the term "memory," but performance changes without requiring any conscious memory content or even the experience that memory is being used.

We are very fortunate to have been able to carry out post-mortem neurohistological studies of the brains of several of our memory-impaired study patients. Such studies are quite rare because of the multiple procedures and personnel that must be in place in the event of a patient's death. Yet, detailed anatomical information is invaluable for relating cognition to biology, and for interpreting qualitative and quantitative differences in how patients perform. Here, I must mention patient R.B., who had a bilateral lesion limited to the CA1 field of the hippocampus. This was the first reported case of memory impairment following a lesion limited to the hippocampus in which extensive neuropsychological and neuropathological analyses had been carried out. Another notable patient (E.P.) had a large, bilateral post-encephalitic lesion of the medial temporal lobe similar to H.M.'s surgical lesion. E.P. had been studied for fourteen years, and his anatomical findings illuminated a number of issues about memory and cognition and about the function of the medial and lateral temporal lobes.

In 2000, I initiated a new program of studies with rats. This work, directed by Robert Clark, allows for parametric studies of brain and behavior on a scale not practical with monkeys, and it complements our continuing studies of human memory. I believe that the best and most satisfying answers to questions about memory will come from hybrid approaches such as this that involve more than one species, multiple tools, and different levels of analysis.

REFERENCES

Squire, L. R. (1992). Memory and the hippocampus: A synthesis from findings with rats, monkeys, and humans. *Psychological Review*, *99*, 195–231.

Squire, L. R., & Kandel, E. (2009). *Memory: From mind to molecules, 2nd edition*. Greenwood Village: Roberts & Company.

Squire, L. R., & Wixted, J. (2011). The cognitive neuroscience of human memory since H.M. *Annual Review of Neuroscience*, *34*, 259–288.

Section C

Behavioral and Molecular Genetics

15   Genes and Behavior: Nature via Nurture

Bouchard, Jr., Thomas J.

My most important scientific contribution was the research program on human individual differences, namely the Minnesota Study of Twins Reared Apart (MISTRA). A detailed report of the study and its findings up to 2012 can be found in work by Nancy Segal, but we continue to publish findings from this data set. MISTRA was a comprehensive psychological and medical assessment of monozygotic and dizygotic twins reared apart. It also included spouses of twins and additional participants such as partners and various relatives who were invited when it facilitated the participation of the twins. Launched in 1979, the program lasted for twenty years. MISTRA was funded almost entirely by private grants (with one exception: a small NSF grant, which the agency refused to renew). Federal funds were provided only for medical research, and only after the program was well established. Segal provides a history of the funding stream. We never had funds to carry us over for more than a year or so, and at times we were in considerable debt. Numerous grant applications were submitted to federal agencies, but all were rejected as many of the reviewers were hostile to the research program. The program was run on a shoestring and all my colleagues (medical and psychological) contributed their time and energy, and that of their laboratories, gratis.

There were two major findings from the study: (1) virtually all medical and psychological traits are to a notable degree heritable; and (2) shared environment was a much less important contribution to similarity between relatives in psychological traits than previously believed. These results have now been fully confirmed by a meta-analysis of fifty years of behavioral genetic research. MISTRA did lead to large-scale funding of ordinary twin research at the University of Minnesota. That psychology department now houses a leading research center for quantitative and molecular behavior-genetic research.

Our interpretation of the results of MISTRA was very straightforward. We expected that with regard to psychological traits, monozygotic twins reared apart were similar because their effective environments were similar. This was because their environments were self-selected and that selection was guided by their genotype. This idea has been operationalized as Experience Producing Drive Theory (EPD theory). According to EPD theory, genes influence the mind indirectly by influencing the choices and, consequently, the effective experiences that individuals undergo. This theory explains both the heritability and modifiability of psychological traits and makes it clear that phenotypic outcomes depend in an important way on the environment, but not in the manner assumed by social scientists in the past (i.e., direct effects). The content of the minds of twins reared apart, if they were reared in the middle ages, would be quite different from the content of the minds of similarly reared apart twins today, as their environments would differ dramatically. Nevertheless, given that they were raised in the average expected environment for their time (an important boundary condition), they would most likely be quite similar across many traits. The correct developmental formula is *nature via nurture*.

The idea for this research program has a straightforward history. I did most of my undergraduate and all of my graduate work in the Psychology Department at the University of California, Berkeley. During my graduate career, my advisors were Harrison Gough and Donald Mackinnon. As a consequence, I spent a great deal of time at the Institute of Personality Assessment and Research (IPAR, now called the Institute of Personality and Social Research). Donald MacKinnon had worked with Henry Murray in the Office of Strategic Services (OSS), selecting secret agents during World War II. Mackinnon was the director of "Station S," where over 2,000 prospective spies were subjected to intense assessment (personality and situational), and later was the founder of IPAR. Gough received his PhD in 1949 at the University of Minnesota and was invited by MacKinnon to join IPAR at the time he joined the Berkeley faculty. There were no assessments being conducted at IPAR while I was there, but I become familiar with the assessment method and the work of the IPAR staff at the time (Jack Block, Frank Barron, and Ravenna Helson). IPAR assessments had focused on samples of outstanding individuals (with controls) in a variety of domains (e.g., architecture, mathematics, and literature). I should also mention that I was a teaching assistant in Introductory Psychology for Robert Tryon (also of OSS fame), whom I got to know, and spent a number of hours discussing scientific methodology with him. He explained in straightforward terms why social classes differed genetically in terms of IQ. This issue was discussed in the *Bell Curve* by Herrnstein and Murray, and is still controversial. In any event, I became familiar with the famous studies of the inheritance of maze-learning ability in rats. This background was reinforced by my being required (by Harrison Gough, for my preliminary doctoral exams) to read the first textbook on behavioral genetics by Fuller and Thompson. After joining the faculty at Minnesota I was mentored in behavior genetics by my colleague Irving Gottesman. This background prepared me to carry out a comprehensive, genetically informative medical and psychological assessment project.

During my time in graduate school I was heavily influenced by Karl Popper's view of science – namely, that theories should be falsifiable. At that time I also discovered that psychologists are constantly seduced by their biases and find it difficult to comprehend that correlation does not imply causation. I will never forget a course in psychopathology in which I challenged the prevailing wisdom that parental behavior was the cause of schizophrenia and argued that genetics was a plausible alternative causal mechanism. The studies supporting environmental causation were almost all correlational, and the extant twin studies were simply mocked by the students and faculty rather than carefully examined and given their due. Metaphorically speaking, I left the seminar a bloody pulp. I recall thinking "so much for rigorous evidence, causal analysis, and falsifiability!" Interestingly, MISTRA was able to show that self-reports of family environmental rearing style are significantly heritable and have minimal influence on most individual differences. These findings are consistent with a large body of evidence demonstrating that purported environmental measures, when gathered from biological families (the standard source of such data), are contaminated with genetic variance. Two such measures – educational attainment and socioeconomic status – are often used as covariates in social science research on IQ. When this is done, genetic variance is improperly partialled out as IQ is a partial cause of each of these outcomes. Psychological science will have to implement much more sophisticated research designs and models before we can even begin to partially understand the causal pathways, both genetic and environmental, that give rise to human individual differences. The goal of science is to explain how things work, not to confirm pre-existing biases. Genes play an important role in the genesis of human individual differences and they have to be incorporated into our research strategies; otherwise, we are engaging in what Feynman called "Cargo cult science" and do not deserve to be taken seriously as scientists. The bottom line is that, as a research enterprise, psychological science is not a stand-alone discipline. To be successful, its practitioners must collaborate closely with its many sister disciplines (genetics, psychiatry, neuroscience, evolutionary biology, sociology, anthropology, epidemiology, economics, etc.).

Our research program was conducted as a branch of quantitative genetics. A major assumption of quantitative genetics is that complex traits of the sort that we studied are influenced by a very large number genes, each having a very small effect (Ronald Fisher's "infinitesimal model"). This model works well in predicting the outcome of selection studies. The findings from modern molecular genetics (the use of high-density genetic markers) using quite large samples are strongly consistent with this model. This means that future research designed to trace the causal pathways (both genetic and environmental) that underlie human individual differences will require very large samples and large collaborative teams in multiple locations. In addition, the research should begin when participants are born and continue across the lifespan, as different genes come into play at different times during development. These studies should also make use of a wide range of well-developed measures (psychological, medical, and biological), include intensive observation, and be designed to pit multiple theories (EPD theory and others) against each other, using various types of collaboration (e.g., adversarial collaborative techniques or agreement among adversaries, decided ahead of time, regarding what outcomes qualify as a refutation). Adversarial collaboration – collaboration by researchers with opposing points of view – should be required by the relevant funding agencies.

REFERENCES

Bouchard, T. J., Jr. (2016). Experience producing drive theory: personality "writ large." *Personality and Individual Differences*, *90*, 302–314. doi:10.1016/j.paid.2015.11.007.

Polderman, T. J. C., Benyamin, B., De Leeuw, C. A., Sullivan, P. F., van Bochoven, A., Visscher, P. M., & Posthuma, D. (2015). Meta-analysis of the heritability of human traits based on fifty years of twin studies. *Nature*. doi:10.1038/ng.3285.

Segal, N. L. (2012). *Born together-reared apart: The landmark Minnesota Twin Study*. Cambridge: Harvard University Press.

16 The View from the Center of the Triangle: Psychology, Psychiatry, and Genetics

Gottesman, Irving I.

In retrospect, after reaching my eighty-fifth birthday and still thinking/writing/editing, I can retrace the paths that resulted in some of my most prominent successes as a behavioral genetics researcher. My childhood curiosity about Nature took the form of collecting leaves, birds' eggs, and pond water, and really escalated with birthday and Hanukkah gifts of junior microscopes and expansions of starter chemistry sets, supplemented by "innocent" trips to the pharmacy. Before completing elementary school, my mother had to constrain my expertise due to bad smells emanating from the basement as well as the potential self-harm from homemade fireworks.

Fast forward to my undergraduate days at the Illinois Institute of Technology (the MIT of the Midwest), courtesy of an NROTC scholarship during the Korean War, where my curriculum was slightly constrained by a mandatory minor in Naval Science. It took only one course in abnormal psychology for me to switch my major from physics to focus on psychopathology as a way to reconcile my interests. After a three-year interlude as a naval officer during the Korean War, and courtesy of the new G. I. Bill, I was fortunate to be accepted into the scientist-practitioner-model training program in clinical child psychology at the University of Minnesota. Core courses on the psychology of individual differences, taught by Donald G. Paterson and James J. Jenkins, exposed me to the classical twin studies of schizophrenia and other psychoses, with their unambiguous conclusions that hereditary factors play major roles in their distal etiologies (or causes) – unambiguous, that is, to those not bitten by the psychodynamic bug endemic in post-World War II behavioral-science discourse.

Paterson, an eminent psychologist who had shaped cognitive testing for illiterate draftees during World War I and who was an avid civil libertarian, introduced me to his friend in the Department of Zoology, Sheldon C. Reed. The latter was a fruit-fly geneticist whose interests had shifted to humans with mental retardation or psychoses, conceptualized as

77

continuously distributed traits. He had coined the term "genetic counseling," and it was one of the skills I acquired. Conversations with him and members of the clinical program gave rise to the design of my dissertation, initiated in 1957: I would somehow collect a representative sample of adolescent identical and fraternal twins from the high schools of the Twin Cities, administer the true–false Minnesota Multiphasic Personality Inventory (MMPI) to assess their personality traits, and then delve into the "psychogenetics of personality" – not a popular topic at that time.

The objective results were very reinforcing to a would-be behavioral geneticist. Such findings, especially when replicated a few years later in a sample twice the size and in a different locale, helped to usher in a paradigm shift in the study of psychopathology and personality two decades later, wherein genetic factors, including genes and SNPs (single-nucleotide polymorphisms, which are DNA sequence variations), would become targets of large-scale research using new tools from molecular genetics and medicine.

My earlier twin studies of normal adolescents (an oxymoron?) were to become milestones on the path to my major accomplishments in the study of the genetics of schizophrenia, conducted in the United Kingdom with my British colleague James Shields.

The task of assembling a decent-sized sample of both identical and fraternal twins meeting the criteria is facilitated by having national population and twin birth registries such as those in Australia, the Netherlands, and the Scandinavian countries, or by having special records of twin status in large teaching hospitals in countries with a form of national health insurance that records treatment for mental disorders in both inpatients and outpatients.

When James Shields and I, under the guidance of Eliot Slater, commenced our 1962 London-based study of schizophrenia in twins consecutively admitted to the Bethlem Royal Hospital and the Maudsley Hospital (Joint Hospital), we could identify all same-gender twin pairs from some 45,000 patients admitted between 1948 and 1965. After personal and record follow-up of the 479 patients who were twins to determine their most valid diagnoses, we accumulated a sample of sixty-two individual twins with a diagnosis of schizophrenia, ascertained independently of one another in our hospital from fifty-seven pairs equally divided by gender. Further research showed that we had twenty-four pairs of MZ (identical) twins and thirty-three pairs of DZ (fraternal twins) – a small sample by contemporary standards, but intensively studied with personal interviews. Our prize-winning book was published in 1972. Our results have been replicated in more than a dozen studies across the globe. What were those results?

In the course of writing our book, we needed a concept that would bridge the explanatory gap in the genes-to-behavior pathway. We had noticed that an article on the geographic distribution of grasshoppers in Australia had been published in *Science Magazine* by John and Lewis in 1966 and had used the term "endophenotype" to define a concept that served their purpose, as neither the known genotype (collections of genes) nor the manifest phenotype (the set of observable traits) matched the distribution. A microscopic examination of the chromosomes themselves provided the solution. We seized upon the term and adapted it as an explanatory construct for psychopathology, in this instance for schizophrenia, providing initial defining characteristics or "rules" to make the term operational. I had been attuned to the importance of the insect world for providing animal models for behavior during my graduate student days at Minnesota, thanks to the Drosophilist Sheldon C. Reed. In introducing the concept of endophenotype, we sought to address two pressing needs in psychopathology research. First, clinical phenotypes are typically highly heterogeneous with complex etiologies (causal mechanisms). In being more proximal (closer) to the primary gene products than the observable phenotype, it was thought (hoped) that endophenotypes would have a less complex genetic structure that would more readily allow for the identification of the specific genetic factors underlying the risk for psychopathology. Second, by being intermediate between direct gene effects and the observed phenotype, endophenotypes would aid in clarifying the specific etiological mechanisms that underlie psychopathology risk.

Now, on to the final lap in my story, leading to the receipt of both the Lieber Prize for Schizophrenia Research and the Grawemeyer Award for Psychology based on the combination of ideas generated by empirical twin research. I can summarize what I found with the following headline: the multifactorial threshold model of complex phenotypes mediated by endophenotype strategies.

If my research partner, James Shields, had not died in 1978 at the age of sixty, he would have been a co-nominee for the above-mentioned awards. Our thinking about a multifactorial threshold model (MFTM) for understanding the genetic and non-genetic contributors to the etiology of schizophrenia emerged from our joint labors beginning in 1962. I have continued to use and to develop the ideas further, emphasizing endophenotype strategies, in the direction of molecular genetics in the years since his death.

Research into both the distal and the proximal contributors to the etiology of schizophrenia had ground to a halt by 1960. Data from common, qualitative traits/disorders were not easily susceptible to genetic analyses until D. Falconer explicated a new model in 1965 that permitted the conversion of such data into the framework of continuous variation already used in agricultural genetics (plant and animal breeding).

In brief outline, the model allows for the variable contributions of specific and general genetic liabilities, general environmental liabilities, genetic assets, and environmental assets contributing idiosyncratically to the chances of developing schizophrenia over time. When the combined chances reach a theoretical threshold, they result in 1 percent of the general population manifesting clinical schizophrenia. The model readily permits calculation of the risks to relatives with various degrees of genetic relatedness to a particular case. The endophenotypes, which are closer to the implicated genes in the polygenic system, permit research to move forward with the much larger samples of clinically unaffected relatives who share many of the genes, but not enough to be above the threshold marking disease. Finally, the closely related idea/concept of "reaction surface/reaction range" emerged to convey the notion of the plasticity of susceptibility over time, driven by interactions of genes with environments. The trio of concepts/ideas has defused the useless Nature versus Nurture battles (i.e., the argument over how much behavior is determined by nature and how much by nurture) for a majority of life-science researchers and students, furthering an integrative neuroscience-systems approach that combines the empirical facts gathered across the spectrum from sociology through psychology to the molecular genetics of complex traits and disorders. This "trio" has had a major influence in shaping research on psychopathology since 1972.

No one has ever been as bold or uninformed as to believe that understanding why one human differs from another across behaviors would be easy. Even formulating the best questions to ask requires a talented, judicious, and multidisciplinary task force.

I can only hope that I have whet your appetite for complexity with this brief essay and the clues it has provided along the pathway from my own interests to examples of some of the research I have pursued for the past fifty-nine years. Those clues and the suggested readings may lead some of you to a non-traditional career in psychology, one that has permeable borders without departmental "silos," and one that prepares you for working collaboratively for the betterment of our species on projects akin to those that led to the Manhattan Project and putting an astronaut on the moon.

REFERENCES

Gottesman, I. I., & Gould, T. D. (2003). The endophenotype concept in psychiatry: Etymology and strategic intentions. *American Journal of Psychiatry, 160,* 636–645.

Gottesman, I. I., & Shields, J. (1972). *Schizophrenia and genetics: A twin study vantage point.* New York: Academic Press.

McGuffin, P., Owen, M. J., & Gottesman, I. I. (eds.) (2004). *Psychiatric genetics and genomics* (rev. edn.). Oxford: Oxford University Press.

17 Bringing Genetics into the Mainstream of Psychology

Plomin, Robert

Three formative experiences in my life primed me for what I like to think is my most important scientific contribution: bringing genetics into the mainstream of psychology. First, when I was in fourth grade in an elementary Catholic school in Chicago, I was suspended from school because of a book I innocently brought to class for a show-and-tell assignment. The book was about Darwin's voyage on the *Beagle*; at that time, evolution was not mentioned in Catholic schools because it was considered to be a mortal sin to believe in evolution. To my mind, evolution seemed an idea that was beautiful and obviously true. The religious opposition, coupled with my stubbornness, planted a genetics seed in my mind.

Second, when I was a philosophy major at DePaul University in Chicago, I kept trying to think of testable hypotheses to solve disputes in philosophy, until I realized that if you can come up with a testable hypothesis, it's no longer philosophy – it's psychology. This realization made me switch my major to psychology, and it primed me to stay close to data. (My most overused phrase is "it's empirical.")

The third experience occurred when I went to graduate school in psychology at the University of Texas at Austin in 1970, which, unknown to me when I accepted their offer, had the only graduate program in behavioral genetics in the world. I was completely bowled over by a required course in behavioral genetics about early animal and human studies that suggested substantial genetic influence on many aspects of psychology. Genetics had not been mentioned in my other classes until then, and I was excited to get a first glimpse of the potential impact of this new way of thinking about psychology and society.

As I learned more about psychology, I saw that genetics was generally ignored or even abhorred. The environment was thought to be completely responsible for individual differences in psychological traits – for example, why some children are shy, why some find it difficult to read, and why some are autistic. During the past few decades, my research, and the research of others in the small field of behavioral genetics, has shown that genetics can no longer be ignored. Its influence is significant and substantial for all areas of psychology.

Bringing genetics into the mainstream of psychology involved more than merely demonstrating the importance of genetics. I will mention five examples of specific discoveries that helped to propel genetics into the psychological mainstream. These discoveries came about because I was able to use genetically sensitive methods that make it possible to investigate nature (genetics) together with nurture (environment). Two of the most widely used genetically sensitive methods are the twin method that compares the resemblance of identical (monozygotic) and fraternal (dizygotic) twins, and the adoption method that compares the resemblance of genetically related individuals such as parents and their offspring who have been separated by adoption. If genetics is important for a trait, identical twins should be more similar than fraternal twins, and parents and their offspring should be similar even if they were separated at birth by adoption.

The first two findings are especially interesting because they are as much about the environment as they are about genetics and could only have been discovered by studying nurture together with nature. The first is that the way the environment works is to make two children growing up in the same family as different from one another as children in different families, which I dubbed *non-shared environment*. This finding is important because it contradicts the widespread belief among developmental theorists from Freud onwards that growing up in the same family makes brothers and sisters similar. The message is not that family experiences are unimportant but, rather, that the salient experiences that affect children's psychological development are specific to each child in the family, not general to all children in the family.

The second finding is that "environmental" measures widely used in psychological research – such as parenting, social support, and life events – show substantial genetic influence. Genetic factors also contribute to correlations between environmental measures and developmental outcomes. This discovery leads to a new way of thinking about how our behavior shapes our experiences. Rather than the traditional passive model in which the environment "out there" is imposed on us, this finding suggests an active model of experience in which we select, modify, and create our own environments, driven in part by our genetic tendencies, known as *genotype-environment correlation*.

The third finding is the dramatic increase in genetic influence on intelligence across the lifespan. Heritability, the proportion of observed differences between individuals that can be ascribed to genetic differences, increases from 20 percent in infancy to 60 percent in adulthood.

The fourth finding is that the same set of genes influences most cognitive and learning abilities and disabilities. For example, the same genes are largely responsible for the heritability of cognitive abilities such as verbal and spatial abilities and learning abilities such as reading and mathematics.

The fifth finding is that common psychological disorders are merely the extremes of the normal distribution of genetic and environmental influences. In other words, psychological disorders are only quantitatively, not qualitatively, different from the normal range of variation. For example, reading disability (or its "diagnosis" as dyslexia) is influenced by the same set of genes as those that contribute to the normal distribution of reading ability; hyperactivity (or its "diagnosis" as attention-deficit hyperactivity disorder) is influenced by genes that affect the normal range of individual differences in attention and activity. These latter two findings are having an impact on the diagnosis and prediction of psychological disorders.

Since that graduate course in 1971, I have happily spent my life studying behavioral genetics, at first using mice (until I developed a severe allergy to mice), then using twin and adoption studies, and now with DNA. Everywhere I looked, I found converging evidence for significant and substantial genetic influence in psychology, even including genetic influence on "environmental" measures. There are two things I especially love about behavioral genetics research. First, it has come up with some "big" findings – "big" both in the sense of effect size and of the potential impact on psychology and society. Bringing genetics into the mainstream of psychology has changed the way psychologists, teachers, and parents think about our children and about ourselves. Second, standing out from the current crisis in science about failures to replicate classic findings, these behavioral genetics findings have been replicated over the years using different designs, samples, and measures. Recently, it has been very satisfying to see that new techniques for assessing DNA differences directly in large samples of unrelated individuals are now also confirming results from twin and adoption studies.

Scientifically, acceptance of genetics poises psychology to take advantage of the amazing advances in DNA technology, especially whole-genome sequencing that can identify all 3 billion base pairs of DNA (the spiral steps in the double helix) of each individual's DNA. People are beginning to have their DNA sequenced, and it is likely that eventually everyone's DNA will be sequenced as the cost of sequencing continues to plummet. This will be a game-changer for psychologists because having the entire genetic code already available will mean that psychologists can use DNA in their research without collecting it. Some of the genes responsible for heritability are beginning to be identified, and these can be used in psychological research. Geneticists will be faced with the daunting task of understanding how these genes affect behavior from the bottom up – from DNA to brain to behavior. In contrast, psychologists can take a top-down approach: using genes shown to be associated with psychological traits as a genetic index in their research without knowing how the genes have their effects on behavior.

The most important next step is to identify more of the genes responsible for genetic influence. This has proven far more difficult than anyone expected because what we have learned so far is that the biggest effect sizes are extremely small, which means that genetic influence is likely to be caused by many genes – perhaps thousands – of very small effect size. Nonetheless, it is possible to aggregate these genes into genetic indices called *polygenic scores* and use them in psychological research. Another critical next step is to equip future generations of psychologists to take advantage of the DNA revolution. For this reason, I would like to see behavioral genetics taught in every undergraduate and graduate psychology program.

REFERENCES

Plomin, R. (2013). Child development and molecular genetics: 14 years later. *Child Development, 84,* 104–120. doi:10.1111/j.1467-8624.2012.01757.x.

Plomin, R., DeFries, J. C., Knopik, V. S., & Neiderhiser, J. M. (2013). *Behavioral genetics* (6th edn.). New York: Worth.

Plomin, R., DeFries, J. C., Knopik, V. S., & Neiderhiser, J. M. Top 10 replicated findings from behavioral genetics. *Perspectives on Psychological Science.* 2016, 11, 3–23.

Part III

Cognition: Getting Information from the World and Dealing with It

Section A

Attention and Perception

18   Gaining Control

Jonides, John

When I was a child (oh, let me be honest: until the age of about seventeen), I was overweight. I was not clinically obese (often defined as 30 percent higher than recommended body mass index), but I was clearly overweight. My parents were not overweight; my siblings were not overweight; indeed, no one in my extended family was overweight. So, why was I? The answer is straightforward: I found the sight, taste, and smell of high-calorie foods appealing, I thought about high-calorie foods even when they weren't in front of me, and I could not resist grabbing whatever high-calorie food was available. In short, I liked to eat. What I didn't like was controlling my eating behavior: I didn't avoid being in the company of food, I didn't avoid thinking about food, and I certainly didn't resist the temptation to reach for food when it was available.

Psychologists often call this a failure of cognitive control, and it is a complex phenomenon. It involves controlling distractions from the environment (e.g., the sight of an ice cream cone), controlling how irrelevant thoughts intrude on ongoing behaviors (e.g., thoughts of ice cream cones), and controlling responses when temptation hits (e.g., not reaching for the cone when it is offered). Indeed, much of the research in my laboratory concerned with cognitive control has been motivated by this tripartite division of control processes: preventing distraction during perception, preventing distraction from internal thoughts, and preventing unintended and irrelevant behavior. Behaviorally, it is possible to distinguish among these three kinds of cognitive control using well-designed experimental tasks in the laboratory.

The distinction among these processes is underscored by neuroimaging research that reveals different patterns of brain activation that accompany each kind of cognitive control. Together, largely with former students Tor Wager, Derek Nee, and Marc Berman, we have amassed a good deal of evidence indicating that cognitive control is not monolithic; it depends on multiple processing systems, but it also depends on some common mechanisms that are enlisted by all these systems. An important contribution to understanding the commonalities and differences among mechanisms of cognitive control comes from brain imaging evidence. Documenting the structures that are activated in various parts of the brain (e.g., prefrontal cortex) and how the activation of these structures differs depending on the type of cognitive control that is enlisted has made major contributions to our understanding of which brain systems underlie cognitive control.

The importance of keeping irrelevant thoughts out of mind can't be overestimated as a critical component of cognitive control. Our ongoing behavior is often governed by what's in mind right now, which psychologists call what's in "working memory." The centrality of working memory to cognitive control has led many scientists, myself included, to spend large portions of their careers investigating the characteristics of working memory. Together with collaborators and former students (notably my former close collaborator Ed Smith, along with many others, notably Patti Reuter-Lorenz, Ed Awh, Tor Wager, and Moshe Naveh-Benjamin), we have uncovered some of the psychological characteristics of working memory (e.g., that you hold in mind no more than about four thoughts at a time) as well as the neural mechanisms that allow you to successfully use working memory (e.g., that the parietal and frontal cortices play a very important role in these processes). These characteristics have served as important foundations for porting our basic knowledge of working memory to problems that people face in the wild.

So, where does all this research on basic cognitive processes take us? One truism that you'll find evident in many of the essays in this book is that as psychologists mature in their fields, they become increasingly interested in applying their knowledge to problems that are faced by the man or woman on the street. This has certainly been true of my own career. Here are but four examples that illustrate how what we have learned about cognitive control and its failure can be applied to real-world problems.

Major Depressive Disorder

One of the symptoms of Major Depressive Disorder is rumination, the tendency to recycle negative thoughts about life events and current symptoms. As we (Patty Deldin, Ian Gotlib, Jutta Joormann, Ethan Kross, Marc Berman, Derek Nee, and others) contemplated this phenomenon, we observed that rumination might cash out as a failure to rid oneself of negatively valenced thoughts from working memory. Indeed, we discovered just that: Healthy and depressed individuals were comparable in controlling what is in working memory and what can be removed from it when that information is neutral in tone. But when it is negative in tone, depressed individuals show a deficit. Importantly, we were able to identify brain signatures that reveal the systems that might be compromised in cognitive control of negatively valenced thoughts.

Delaying Gratification

Among the more interesting investigations of brain mechanisms linked to cognitive control and its failure is a sequel to a longstanding and seminal research project begun by Walter Mischel and his colleagues. They famously studied the ability of four-year-olds to delay gratification in favor of a larger reward later (say, two cookies later rather than one now). In recent years, we again studied some of those then four-year-olds, now in their forties. Using functional magnetic resonance imaging, we discovered brain activation differences between those who could delay gratification as children and those who could not. These differences arose in a test of being able to withhold a response and a test of being able to rid information from working memory – in other words, two of the classic tests of response impulsivity and cognitive control. What is stunning about this research is that performance on a simple test of delaying gratification as children was predictive of patterns of performance and brain activation some forty years later, suggesting that there is perhaps some lifetime stability to these patterns.

Controlling Weight

One problem that has interested me in recent years takes me back to my weight problem: Can we characterize the kinds of difficulties that overweight individuals have that might lead them to make poor food choices? For example, compared to normal-weight individuals, are they selectively more sensitive to the sight of distracting foods, or to the thought of distracting foods – two of the problems in cognitive control, the basic mechanisms of which we have studied in the laboratory? Together with Lynn Ossher, we have documented increased susceptibility to interference in both perception and memory, but with somewhat different profiles. Distracting information in memory that is food-related seems to dominate for overweight individuals compared to people who are lean; but for perception, obese individuals are more distractible regardless of the content of the distraction. So, there are emerging issues in cognitive control among the overweight that deserve deeper understanding.

Training Cognition

Let me add just one more example to tie basic research on cognitive control to real-world outcomes. For several years now, my colleagues Susanne

Jaeggi, Martin Buschkuehl, Priti Shah, and I have been studying whether training on certain basic cognitive tasks that heavily engage processes of cognitive control can lead to improvements in other cognitive skills, among the most interesting being fluid intelligence (the ability to reason about novel problems). We have amassed a good deal of evidence that there may be interesting possibilities here, although the jury is still out on just how effective cognitive training is, how long it lasts, and what individual differences among people influence its success. One can think of this line of research as an extension of the very basic principle that education matters. After all, the hope of sending children to school for twelve or more years is that they will acquire skills that will go beyond the specifics that they learned from those hours in the classroom. Our research has extended this rationale by asking whether training on an elementary set of cognitive processes (including, importantly, processes of cognitive control) can lead to more successful cognition for more complex problems. This rationale, of course, is at the heart of the various commercial enterprises that attempt to engage their clients in "brain training." As I say, the jury is out on how effective this sort of training is and under what circumstances. But there is enough promise in this line of research, just as there is promise in the basic principle of education, to look into it much more deeply.

These examples show that there are important consequences of understanding basic cognitive processes. Understanding mechanisms of mind and brain as they apply to cognitive control opens up lines of investigation about a host of natural problems that people face in daily life. And, by citing various collaborators above (as well as many others that space constraints prevent me from citing), I have tried to make clear that it takes large teams of scientists to gain this sort of understanding. It is these scientists who deserve great credit for working at the "bench" and transitioning from the "bench to the bedside."

REFERENCES

Jonides, J., Jaeggi, S. M., Buschkuehl, M., & Shah, P. (2012). Building better brains. *Scientific American Mind, 23*, 59–63.

Jonides, J., Lewis, R. L., Nee, D. E., Lustig, C. A., Berman, M. G., & Moore K. S. (2008). The mind and brain of short-term memory. *Annual Review of Psychology, 59*, 193–224.

Mischel, W., Ayduk, O., Berman, M. G., Casey, B. J., Gotlib, I., Jonides, J., ... & Shoda, Y. (2011). "Willpower" over the life span: Decomposing self-regulation. *Social, Cognitive, and Affective Neuroscience, 6*, 252–256.

The Essential Dave Meyer: Some Musings
on "Scholarly Eminence" and Important
Scientific Contributions

Meyer, David E.

Introduction

While accompanied by considerable satisfaction, writing this chapter has
also caused some noteworthy reservation, embarrassment, and trepidation in me. Specifically, the basis for this book is Diener, Oishi, and Park's
"incomplete list of 200 eminent modern psychologists." In my opinion,
though, certain enormously distinguished scientists fall much lower down
the list than their true eminence merits. For example, there's R. Duncan
Luce, who revolutionized research on psychological measurement theory,
individual choice behavior, and much else of Mathematical Psychology.
In 2003, he received the National Medal of Science, the United States'
highest scientific honor. His seminal contributions have inspired multiple
individuals in the nominal top twenty-five "eminent modern psychologists." Yet Luce ranks only 170th on Diener et al.'s list. Several other
extremely eminent psychological scientists aren't even on the list. I feel
embarrassed to get ranked above them, and I'm also embarrassed that our
scholarly field would have profound contributors such as Luce ranked
much lower than they deserve.

So what went awry here? "Eminent" ordinarily means "highly successful, famous, *and respected* (also distinguished, authoritative, and excellent)
in a particular sphere or profession." Apparently, however, Diener et al.'s
operational definition of "eminent" emphasized fame far more than
respect. Especially dubious in this imbalanced regard was their heavy
(33 percent) weighting of page counts from introductory psychology
texts in the composite "eminence" scores.

I fear that Diener et al.'s resultant ranking of putative "eminent"
modern psychologists may further encourage research aimed at achieving

Inspiration for this title came from an *Afterword* by the great mathematician and Nobel
Laureate economist, John Forbes Nash, Jr. (cf. *The Essential John Nash*; H. W. Kuhn &
S. Nasar, eds., 2007).

rapid fame rather than rigorous, long-lasting, fundamental scientific findings. Indeed, there's already such an undesirable trend underway. Pressures to gain quick recognition in highly visible journals that publish "short-form" articles with "sexy" titles and minimal, perfunctorily reported studies have escalated. Questionable, fragile, difficult-to-replicate findings have also increased dramatically. These worrisome developments are exactly what our field does *not* need. I'd therefore urge young psychological scientists to eschew rapid superficial fame, mass production of "sexy" but shallow research, and efforts toward maximizing nominal "eminence" scores.

Important Scientific Contributions

Accompanying these preceding considerations, I have what may seem like an idiosyncratic take on my own "important" scientific contributions. For me, true importance is multi-dimensional. So, here I'll briefly mention three types of contribution that are especially important to me, without designating any one as "the most important."

Perpetuation of Intellectual Virtues

My first important contribution has been endeavoring to perpetuate the intellectual virtues of several scholarly role models who inspired my style of research. Among them were Clyde Coombs, Saul Sternberg, J. E. Keith Smith, and Paul Fitts. Following their lead, I have tried to manifest (1) love of mathematics and enthusiasm for new unorthodox ideas in Psychology; (2) theoretical creativity, careful experimentation, and the power of mental chronometry, i.e., interpretation of people's reaction times to make inferences about the durations of mental processes; (3) use of sophisticated statistical techniques for testing precise psychological models; and (4) interest in practical real-world applications of psychological science. My appreciation for each of these virtues arose from being mindfully observant in the presence of my several role models; and subsequently, I've made myself similarly available to my own students as best I could.

Training Young Psychological Scientists

I consider my training of young investigators to be a second important scientific contribution. Consistent with my aspirations to promote research versatility, investigations conducted by the dozens of doctoral students who worked with me have spanned cognitive, developmental, social, personality, and clinical psychology, as well as kinesiology, computer science, and human-factors engineering. None would I trade to keep any citation classic or honorific award on my curriculum vitae.

Elucidating Basic Mental Processes and Brain Mechanisms

My students and senior collaborators (e.g., Roger Schvaneveldt, Keith Smith, Sylvan Kornblum, and David Kieras) have helped me pursue various research projects for understanding and explaining numerous basic mental processes and brain mechanisms. I consider this accomplishment in toto to be my third important scientific contribution. Among these projects have been ones concerning human speech perception and production, short-term "working" memory (i.e., the memory system responsible for temporarily holding new and previously acquired information for current processing), long-term semantic memory, visual word recognition, sentence comprehension, motor control of limb movements, executive mental functions, multitasking, cognitive aging, and individual differences in cognitive style. Pursuing many different projects, despite repeated start-up costs, has let me enjoy great fun, explore lots of new ideas, and make at least a few significant scientific discoveries.

At the outset, for example, there was my doctoral dissertation, the results of which were published in 1970 in *Cognitive Psychology*. My goal back then was to generalize findings by Saul Sternberg about rapid short-term memory search (i.e., mentally searching through lists of recently stored items). After several attempts that didn't pan out, this project evolved to focus on structures and processes of semantic memory (i.e., knowledge about meanings of words and concepts referenced by them). Through experiments with mental chronometry and novel tasks that required participants to quickly indicate whether various sentences are true or false, I found that people rely on two distinct stages of memory retrieval involving different types of stored semantic information. In essence, this discovery constituted some of the most compelling evidence to date for what later became called "Systems 1 and 2" in Daniel Kahneman's popular book, *Thinking, Fast and Slow*, where Kahneman hypothesized that System 1 leads to fast intuitive responses, and System 2 leads to slower, more deliberate reflective ones.

Pursuing my dissertation project yielded additional payoffs as well. It taught me about the value of "if at first you don't succeed, try, try again." I also came to understand that one successful step may quickly, but unexpectedly, lead to a next.

An immediate case of such occurred soon after I finished my PhD at the University of Michigan and, through fortuitous circumstances, next obtained a technical position at Bell Laboratories in Murray Hill, New Jersey, which perhaps saved my life, and definitely allowed me more time for productive science instead of fighting the war in Vietnam. Upon arriving at "the Labs," it became clear that continuing my research on semantic memory would require simplifying the experimental methods that I had used previously. This was because many fewer test participants (no huge cohorts of undergraduate conscripts) were available there. Also, to maintain adequate statistical power in data analyses, I needed larger inventories of linguistic stimulus materials than had been feasible for my Michigan dissertation. These mundane necessities – not deep methodological or theoretical inspiration – led me to introduce the dual lexical-decision task: a simple procedure where participants are rapidly presented with successive strings of letters (e.g., "mafer" after "shoe") while having to accurately respond "yes" or "no" about whether or not each letter string is an English word.

Through this procedure, I soon discovered that words such as "nurse," when immediately preceded by related words like "doctor," yield significantly (about 10–20 percent) shorter reaction times than when preceded by other unrelated words, such as "butter." My discovery of this basic facilitation effect, subsequently called "semantic priming," was rather serendipitous. Nevertheless, it triggered an enormous "priming revolution" in future studies by many other cognitive, social, developmental, and personality psychologists.

Moreover, another benefit from my discovery of semantic priming was that I met Roger Schvaneveldt, one of our generation's best cognitive psychologists. Our first meeting happened at the 1970 Psychonomic Society meeting in San Antonio, Texas. Right after I gave a talk there about word recognition – but *not* semantic priming – Roger, a native of Utah, approached me in his cowboy boots, blue jeans, and leather vest. Stretching out his right hand for a shake, he blithely said something like "Hey dude, guess what; I've just found a really cool effect that'll blow your mind." Then he blew my mind by telling me that he had discovered the same priming phenomenon pretty much exactly like I did! This was at a time when I, without telling anybody else, had myself found semantic priming only a few months earlier. So I replied "Well, guess what, partner; I've already found exactly that same effect too!" Finally, to cut a long story short, we both looked at each other in amazement, shook hands again, and agreed to co-author an article on our complementary data, which appeared ten months later in the *Journal of Experimental Psychology*, and initiated an active collaboration that lasted several years more (Meyer and Schvaneveldt, 1976).

However, my stay at Bell Labs and study of semantic priming didn't last forever. After eight years there, my professional path took me back to Michigan as a member of the faculty, where I've remained ever since. This return to a diverse vibrant university community enabled me to work on many different projects (Meyer, 2002). For example, partly due to a life-long interest in sports, I began exploring how rapid aimed limb movements are produced. As a result, one of the most exciting "aha!" moments of my career later occurred. I had an abrupt insight that such movements, which involve a fundamental speed-accuracy trade-off called "Fitts' Law," may stem from people coping optimally with random neural "noise" in their movement-production systems.

Furthermore, because of Professor David Kieras's presence at Michigan, I eventually began combining many strands of my research into a single integrated theoretical package (Meyer and Kieras, 1999). This collaboration, like several others, started serendipitously; as they say, "chance favors the prepared mind." Kieras, a prominent expert on human–computer interaction, was approached by agents for the US Navy, who wanted to establish a research project on human multi-tasking in practical (i.e., military) contexts. To pursue this project, he invited me, a nominal expert on speeded human performance under many task conditions, to join him. The rest is history: we created EPIC (Executive-Process Interactive Control), a computational cognitive framework on whose basis many useful models of complex multitasking (e.g., in aircraft cockpits) have been developed.

Epilogue

Whether the products from any of this research will have lasting significance in the long-term future remains to be seen. But regardless of how this all eventually turns out, it's been an exciting and rewarding adventure.

REFERENCES

Diener, E., Oishi, S., & Park, J. Y. (2014). An incomplete list of eminent psychologists of the modern era. *Archives of Scientific Psychology*, *2*, 20–32.

Meyer, D. E. (2002). Professional Biography. *American Psychologist*. [A further brief synopsis of my career and scientific contributions, published on receipt of the APA Distinguished Scientific Contribution Award: see http://www.umich.edu/~bcalab/Meyer_Biography.html.]

Meyer, D. E., & Kieras, D. E. (1999). Précis to a practical unified theory of cognition and action: Some lessons from computational modeling of human multiple-task performance. In D. Gopher & A. Koriat (eds.), *Attention and performance XVII* (pp. 17–88). Cambridge, MA: MIT Press. [A review that summarizes much of my later research with David Kieras on computational modeling of multitasking and the human cognitive architecture.]

Meyer, D. E., & Schvaneveldt, R. W. (1976). Meaning, memory structure, and mental processes. *Science, 192*, 27–33. [A concise survey of my early research on semantic memory and priming in visual word recognition.]

20 Just Turn It Over in Your Mind

Shepard, Roger N.

An Atypical Background for a Psychologist

As a child I was, like my engineer father, fascinated by mechanical devices. I would happily spend hours alone building elaborate Tinkertoy structures. I would take apart discarded clocks and other gadgets, to study their mechanical works. Later, I went on to build various electro-mechanical devices: one would electrically transmit the motions of a pen at one location, causing a pen at a distant location to duplicate in ink what was being hand-written at the first location; another was a robot, animated by motors and mechanical parts, built from abandoned appliances in my grandparent's barn. I also constructed a variety of three-dimensional regular polyhedra by gluing together carefully cut and folded pieces of cardboard. But, while pursuing these solitary extracurricular projects, I neglected many homework assignments. I was far more interested in books I found in the public library, on technology, astrophysics, relativity, and cosmology.

As an undergraduate at Stanford, I had difficulty choosing a major. I feared that I lacked sufficient mathematical training for a career in engineering or physics. Moreover, the likelihood of my making an outstanding contribution to such already highly developed fields seemed negligibly small. Then, having reluctantly signed up for an introductory course in philosophy (to satisfy an annoying distribution requirement), I was surprised to find the subject so intriguing that I began taking all the philosophy courses available to me. But the young assistant professor who had first sparked my interest in philosophy was now telling me of his own discouragement with the field. His academic appointment was not renewed, and I was subsequently saddened to learn that he had committed suicide.

What had most enthralled me about theoretical physics was how laws statable in beautifully succinct mathematical formulas (as in Newton's laws of gravitation and motion, Maxwell's laws of electromagnetism, and Einstein's laws of special and general relativity) govern physical phenomena throughout the universe. But these elegant, far-reaching physical laws did not address issues of an entirely different class of phenomena that also fascinated me – namely, the mental phenomena of imagery, dreams, and thought experiments. And yet, these more subjective phenomena may have played a significant role in the discoveries of the very laws of physics I so admired. I began to wonder: could such purely mental phenomena themselves be governed by universal laws?

At this point my father, now a professor in Stanford's School of Engineering, surprised me by asking "Have you considered majoring in psychology?" I began to think: yes, psychology might be at least worth considering. Among the empirical sciences, psychology was perhaps closest to philosophy. Surely, it must be the one field suited to investigating mental phenomena such as dreams, mental imagery, and creative thinking. Moreover, as a relatively new field among the sciences, it might turn out to be governed by yet-to-be-discovered but mathematically formalizable laws.

So, I signed up for Psychology 1, to be taught by a Professor Donald Taylor. But, during that course, I failed to see anything susceptible to the formulation of quantitative laws like those that so appealed to me in physics. Professor Taylor, however, offered to admit me as the only undergraduate student in his graduate-level course on "Sensation and Perception." In that course, he said, I did as well as any of the graduate students. Moreover, I learned of some phenomena that seemed potentially susceptible to mathematical formulation. As time was running out, I finally settled on psychology as my major, and then went on to Yale for graduate study in experimental psychology. (Much later, Donald Taylor moved to Yale, first to head the Department of Psychology and then to serve as Dean of the Graduate School.)

After receiving my Yale PhD, I devoted much of my subsequent research (at the Bell Telephone Laboratories, at Harvard, and finally back at Stanford) to seeking "universal psychological laws" – specifically, quantitative laws of perception, learning, generalization, memory, cognition, and mental imagery. In the limited space available here, I focus exclusively on my investigations of mental processes of the last-listed type – namely, "mental transformations."

The Phenomenon of "Mental Rotation"

As I was beginning to awaken in the early morning of November 16, 1968, with eyes still closed, I had the vivid visual experience of two polyhedral objects majestically rotating around their vertical axes in three-dimensional space. As soon as I became fully awake, I was inspired to start working out, in my head, the design of an experiment for studying

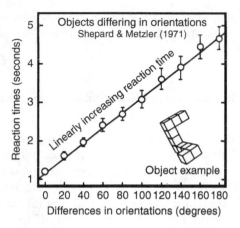

Figure 20.1: Reaction time as a function of differences in orientation of figures

the phenomenon of mental rotation. The results of the first such experiment (carried out in collaboration with my new Stanford graduate student, Jaqueline Metzler) was published in 1971 as the cover article in the American Association for the Advancement of Science journal *Science*. The accompanying figure presents the essential results.

Participants were visually presented with pairs of computer-generated images of three-dimensional objects (like the "Object Example" in Figure 20.1). The two images of such objects in each presented pair were either of identical or of mirror-image shapes, but usually portrayed in different spatial orientations. Participants were instructed to pull a left- or a right-hand lever as soon as possible to indicate whether the two objects, regardless of their relative orientations, were the same or different shapes. The mean times to correctly determine that the two objects were of the same shape increased remarkably linearly – from 1 to almost 5 seconds, as the difference in their orientations increased from 0 to 180 degrees – as shown by the small circles in the figure. The linearity of the reaction-time function is consistent with the subsequent reports of many of the participants that to compare the shapes of two objects, they first "mentally rotated" one object into the orientation of the other. The slope of the linear reaction-time function implies that they could carry out this mental transformation at a maximum rotation rate of somewhere between 50 and 60 degrees per second.

Space limitations preclude description of many important further findings on mental rotation by my former students and coworkers. Some of the most definitive results were obtained by Lynn Cooper. She and I reviewed most of the work up until 1982 in our book *Mental Images and Their Transformations.*

The Related Phenomenon of Rotational "Apparent Motion"

Later experiments with other of my collaborators investigated a related phenomenon of visual "apparent motion." Two images portraying the same object in different orientations were alternately presented at different rates of alternation. The critical onset-to-onset times were determined at which a participants' experience changed from seeing (at faster alternations) two stationary objects just flickering on and off to seeing (at slower alternations) a single object smoothly rotating back and forth between the two orientations. These critical times also increased strictly linearly with the angular difference between the two presented orientations. But, unlike the earlier measured rate of actively imagined mental rotation of 50 or 60 degrees per second, this newly measured rate of passively experienced rotational motion proceeded at the 18-fold faster rate of about 1000 degrees per second.

In the general case – in which the motion (whether actively imagined or passively experienced) is between two arbitrarily different positions of an object in space – the motion traverses the simplest, helically curved path prescribed by kinematic geometry. Through natural selection we may have internalized universal principles of three-dimensional kinematics. We would thereby be afforded the quickest possible identification of two successive glimpses as of the same potentially significant object (e.g., a dangerous predator or a desirable prey), and of the motion of that object relative to one's self.

Significance of this Research on Mental Transformations

(1) It contributed to psychology's shift from strictly behavioristic studies of non-verbal animals (such as rats, pigeons, and monkeys) to experimental investigations of human cognition.

(2) It raised the possibility of universal psychological laws governing the mental capabilities of cognitively advanced beings, wherever they may have evolved in our space–time universe.

(3) It provided evidence that some mental processes consist not of digital language-like symbol manipulations, but of analog simulations of physical processes in the three-dimensional world.

(4) It revealed how unseen mental processes conform to precise quantitative laws, in the absence of any knowledge about how these processes are neurologically implemented in the brain.

(5) It illustrated how the conception of a new line of research can arise (as did many other of my most creative ideas) from spontaneous mental imagery of objects and their transformations.

REFERENCES

Shepard, R. N., & Cooper. L. A. (1982). *Mental images and their transformations.* Cambridge, MA: MIT Press.

21　Attention and Automatism

Shiffrin, Richard M., and Schneider, Walter

Attention is the foundation of cognition. We use it to control everything we do: to focus perception, store information in and retrieve information from memory, make decisions, and direct action. A key to understanding attention is understanding its limitations. For a large class of the situations we face, the resources we have to deploy attention are limited – we can choose to attend to some things but not everything. When we start to learn how to drive, we can focus on steering, or braking, or accelerating, or the traffic in front of us, but not all at once. Yet practice and learning can cause such perceptions, decisions, and actions to become increasingly automatic, bypassing the initial limitations and allowing the implementation of ever-increasing expert behavior. The transition from resource-limited behavior to automaticity (also termed automatism), the processes involved in each, the mechanisms that produce learning, and a model framework in which to explain each of these were the foci of two articles we published back to back in *Psychological Review* in 1977. The titles were informative: *Controlled and automatic human information processing: I. Detection, search, and attention*; and *II. Perceptual learning, automatic attending, and a general theory.*

There are many ways attention is employed and assessed. To various degrees it can be focused narrowly, spread widely, maintained over time, and interrupted by distraction. All of these are made difficult because attentional capacity is highly limited, largely through its implementation in short-term memory, also called working memory. The short-term memory system has limited capacity. It can hold a limited amount of information, and can employ a limited number of processes that control cognition – not only attention, but also memory storage and retrieval (as discussed in the 1968 chapter by Atkinson and Shiffrin titled "Human memory: A proposed system and its control processes."). It would be extremely difficult for us to operate in our daily lives if we had to employ limited attention to control all our activities. Thus, it is essential and fortunate that we have a means to overcome such limitations: Learning can produce automatic behavior that bypasses such cognitive limitations. Responses gradually come to be made by rote in response to consistently occurring environmental situations. The driving example is one case familiar to all of us: Once we learn to drive, the many and various processes required come to occur automatically in response to the changing driving demands and situations.

Thus, in our articles we chose to organize a vast literature by distinguishing processes that can be controlled on a momentary basis (e.g., decisions about what to say in conversation with a stranger on an airplane) and those so well-learned that they operate autonomously (e.g., a startle response to an unexpected loud noise; adjustments in posture to keep a bicycle upright; stepping on the brakes when the tail lights of the car in front turn red). These are of course end points of a continuum, because most automatic processes are learned through experience, and develop gradually. We needed a paradigm in which the transition from controlled to automatic processing could be clearly assessed and studied. This led us to use memory search and visual search. This experimental paradigm is particularly useful for assessing the transition from attentional control to automatic responding because the learning component is easy to distinguish from other sorts of performance changes.

In each trial, the subject is given a small set of items (e.g., letters) to hold in memory and decide whether any of those items appear in a small display of items presented next – that is, a set of more letters is displayed; zero, one, or more of these might have been in the memory set. A memory set item in a display is called a target, and the non-target items in the display are termed foils; usually half the displays contain only foils, and half contain one or more targets. At the start of training, search is highly constrained by resource limitations and is well described by serial comparisons – for example, a memory set item is chosen and compared one at a time to the display items; then another memory set item is chosen, and so on. Alternatively, a display item is chosen and compared to the memory set held in short-term memory, then another display item chosen, and so on. Search stops when a target is found, and a negative response is given if all comparisons fail to locate a target. Resource limitations are indicated by the rate at which comparisons are carried out. In serial search, the rate is determined by the time to carry out one comparison. If one comparison takes time t then comparing n items until a target is found would take time nt. This linear increase in time is usually identified with and diagnostic of capacity-limited serial search.

The key conditions involve the ability to learn: In "consistent mapping," the targets and foils are the same in every trial, and appropriate responses to them are learned – in fact, perfect responding can eventually occur without attending to the memory set. Suppose, for example, that 3, 6, and 7 are always targets and 2, 5, and 9 are always foils. One can learn to press one key for 3, 6, or 7 and another for 2, 5, or 9, and do so consistently on every trial. As learning takes place the task becomes very easy and requires no significant effort or use of scarce attentional resources. In "varied mapping," the targets and foils are chosen randomly from a single group, so targets for one trial can be foils in the next, and vice versa. One must pay attention in each trial to the memory set. This condition is difficult and attention-demanding.

We were particularly interested in showing how learning altered the process of attending. In consistent mapping, search changes character as learning proceeds. Attention comes to be drawn automatically and in parallel to a target (if the display contains one): e.g., if there is a target among eight display items, attention may be drawn to the target so it is compared first – it is as if there is just one item in the display and the rate of search is speeded considerably. We used several versions of the basic paradigm: In some, multiple displays were presented rapidly (termed RSVP) – too rapidly for each display to be searched with high accuracy. However, in RSVP conditions using consistent mapping, learning to attend automatically to targets again takes place, and accuracy climbs with the degree of automaticity attained.

Other types of learning take place as well. For example, sufficient consistent training causes the memory set to cohere as a group and be identified by a single higher-order abstraction; this process is similar to the way that experience in life causes individual numerals to be coded as "digits" or "numbers," individual letters to be identified as "letters," and particular letter combinations to be identified as a single "word." When a particular memory set is trained consistently as a group, even if it switches roles as target or foil from trial to trial, it comes to be learned as a single entity: e.g. if 3, 6, and 7 are always together, in some trials used as memory set items, and in other trials appearing in display as foils, then they can be coded with a higher-order label, in the same way that letters come to be coded as a word. The effective memory set size drops to one and each display item can be compared in one comparison, in the same way that one can search a word display one word at a time, not one letter at a time. This learning of a higher-order code is how we showed how higher-order abstractions come to be learned through consistent experience.

Our two articles laid out a general theory of attention and automaticity based on original studies using variants of the memory and visual search paradigm, models of the findings, and partial reviews of a large literature on the subject (a more thorough review appeared in a chapter titled *Attention* in a 1988 edition of the Stevens Handbook of Experimental Psychology.) Our experiments introduced many original findings that later became objects of fields of study in their own right, sometimes under different terminology (e.g., the "attentional blink," by which a second target in a rapid sequence tends to be missed). The framework was taken further by many theorists and investigators, such as Gordon Logan, who taught participants to carry out arithmetic with letters rather than numbers (each number is consistently assigned the same letter). Some of the ideas were employed by Daniel Kahneman in his excellent and popular book *Thinking, Fast and Slow*.

Richard Shiffrin has remained at Indiana to the present day, continuing research on attention and automatism, among other research topics in cognition. Walter Schneider took a postdoctoral research position at Berkeley with an emphasis on neuroscience, followed by a position at the University of Illinois and then a professorship at the University of Pittsburgh. He has also continued research on attention, including a great deal rooted in neuroscience (his main research at present is on technology of brain measurement and clinical applications).

What was the inspiration for this research? One source was research on attention and automatism that was carried out at Indiana University in the early years of experimental psychology in the United States. William Lowe Bryan (later to be a long-serving president of the university) studied the way reception of telegraphy was learned, and published the results in *Psychological Review* in 1899. The ideas we put forth may therefore be said to have fleshed out ideas present since the start of research in psychology, but did so on the basis of extensive empirical research coupled with a general theory.

The ideas, the methods, the results, and the theory have become standard in the field; have generated additional research, both behavioral and neural; have been the basis for clinical treatments; and have led to further progress in both theory and findings.

REFERENCES

Schneider, W., & Shiffrin, R. M. (1977). Controlled and automatic human information processing: I. Detection, search, and attention. *Psychological Review, 84*, 1–66.

Shiffrin, R. M. (1988). Attention. In R. C. Atkinson, R. J. Herrnstein, G. Lindzey & R. D. Luce (eds.), *Stevens' handbook of experimental psychology, 2nd edition*, 739–811. New York: Wiley.

Shiffrin, R. M., & Schneider, W. (1977). Controlled and automatic human information processing: II. Perceptual learning, automatic attending, and a general theory. *Psychological Review, 84*, 127–190.

22 How the Brain Constructs Objects

Treisman, Anne

Scientists sometimes have an idea, then spend years before they fully understand it or appreciate its importance. So it was with the idea that defined much of my career. I believed for many years that I had that idea sometime in 1973 or 1974, and that I immediately embarked on a program of research to explore and test it. Decades later, however, a colleague showed me that the idea was stated quite clearly in an article I had published in 1969; I was very surprised.

There was in the air at the time a notion that perception involves the separate analysis of different features, including shape, color, orientation, and motion, which could be separately attended to. The notion of separate analyzers raised a question, which is now known as the "binding problem": how are the separate features recombined into representations of the objects that we perceive and recognize? For example, imagine a display consisting of a red T and a green X. The color analyzers register the presence of two colors and the shape analyzers register two shapes. How does the observer know which color goes with which shape?

The solution that occurred to me was that a spotlight of attention travels over the visual field, binding together the features that it finds in each location as it passes through it. The features that are present in that location are perceived as belonging to the same object. The features are known to be present even before the spotlight visits their location, but they are free-floating, not localized in space. If the scene contains yellow objects and squares, for example, I immediately know that there is yellow somewhere and a square somewhere, but I can only know that there is a particular yellow square in a particular place by bringing the spotlight of attention to that place.

Many psychological ideas can be understood by referring to our subjective experience, and psychologists often develop hypotheses by examining their mental life. This was not the case for my solution to the binding problem, which involved events that occur without any awareness and that are not directly represented in mental life. You are surely not aware of your attention scanning the visual scene at a very rapid rate, much faster than the rate at which you can move your eyes. Nor are you conscious of a difference between objects in the scene that your attention has already bound together and other objects whose features are free-floating. Rapid scanning and free-floating features cannot be observed directly even by the subject. Their existence can only be confirmed indirectly, by testing distinctive hypotheses that the theory implies.

I remember conducting an early test of the theory on my children, sitting on our lawn in Oxford one day in the summer of 1975. I made up a set of cards, each containing several red Ts, several green Xs, and a target item that my young "observers" had to find. The targets were of two kinds:

(1) A new feature: "is there an O on the card, or any blue letter?"
(2) A new conjunction of existing features: "is there a red X?"

The result was quite striking. On a background of red Ts and green Xs, my children found it much harder to detect a new conjunction than a new feature.

This was the result that my developing theory predicted. Search for a feature should be easy, because the theory assumes that the presence of a feature is detected without having to know where it is. In contrast, a specified conjunction of features ("red X" among many "red T's" and "green X's") can only be recognized when the spotlight of attention happens to land on its location while scanning the display. The contrast between the two search tasks was a new finding. I spent the better part of the next thirty years following it up.

I conducted many experiments with a more rigorous version of the search task that my children had performed. A standard psychological technique requires participants to search for a specified target in successive displays, and to indicate whether or not they found it by pressing a "yes" key or a "no" key. Participants are told to respond as quickly as they can, and their reaction time is measured.

My theory implies highly specific predictions about search for conjunctions and for features. In particular, it implies that varying the number of items in the display will have different effects on the two kinds of search.

For an example, compare two displays: one contains three letters, the other contains eleven. The background items are red Ts and green Xs. Consider first the task of searching for a feature: "is there a blue letter?" My theory predicts that if the display contains a blue letter the feature "blue" will declare itself immediately, regardless of whether the display contains two or ten non-targets. Similarly, the observer is expected to know almost immediately if the "blue" feature did not declare its presence, in which case the correct response is "no." Here again, display size is not expected to influence reaction time.

Next, consider the conjunction task: "is there a red X?" First, imagine a "yes" trial with three items in the display (a red X and two background letters). The target will be found when the spotlight of attention lands on it. Reaction time will vary depending on whether the target happens to be the first letter that the spotlight visits, or the second, or the third. On average, the target will be the second letter to be scanned. Now suppose the display consists of eleven items. Here again, the target is equally likely to be the first letter scanned, or the second ... or the eleventh. On average, the target will be found on the sixth letter that is scanned. Unlike finding a feature, finding a conjunction takes longer when the display is large than when it is small. The theory also predicts that the observer will only press the "no" key when *all* the items have been scanned without finding a target – three scans for the smaller display, eleven scans in the larger one. Note that the effect of display size in the "no" case (11 minus 3) is twice as large as the difference in the "yes" case (6 minus 2).

A substantial experiment I conducted with Oxford students confirmed these detailed predictions quite precisely, encouraging me to conduct many other tests of "feature-integration theory," as I later called it, and to explore alternative versions and refinements of it.

The main goal for a theory, of course, is to be true. But another measure is whether the theory suggests new and interesting questions that would not have come to mind without it. By that measure, feature-integration theory was a success. It led us to many questions, including the following:

- Do complex shapes consist of features? The answer is "yes": the letter R shares a feature with Q and other features with P.
- How difficult is it to search for the absence of a feature? The answer is "quite difficult": it is much harder to find an O in a field of Qs than to find a Q in a field of Os.
- Objects that share a feature can define a shape, as when you see a disk of blue letters on a background of red letters. Can you do the same with conjunctions? The answer is "no": If you divide an array into two parts, arranging red Xs and green Ts in a disk, with green Xs and red Ts in the background, the disk will not emerge in the same way.
- If features are free-floating, can they combine at random? For example, will you occasionally see a red X when you present a red O and a green X? The answer, to everyone's surprise, is "yes." People often see illusory conjunctions of features, and are not aware of their error. Lynn Robertson and I studied a patient who appeared unable to move the spotlight of attention over a representation of space, and found that the patient was exceptionally vulnerable to illusory conjunctions. When shown two colored letters, even for a long time, he could not reliably

see the correct combination of shape and color. This unfortunate man seemed to be a poster case for feature-integration theory.

A long time has passed since I first tested my children in the garden. Feature-integration theory attracted a fair amount of attention, because the binding problem is significant not only to psychologists but also to neuroscientists, students of computer vision, and even some philosophers. As expected, there were numerous challenges to the theory, including counter-examples that required refinements of the basic concepts of the theory: object, feature, spotlight, and space representation. The questions that I raised are still the subject of much active research, and that is a source of great satisfaction.

REFERENCES

Treisman, A. M., & Gelade, G. (1980). A feature-integration theory of attention. *Cognitive Psychology*, *12*, 97–136.

Section B

Learning and Memory

23 Human Memory: A Proposed System and Its Control Processes

Atkinson, Richard C., and Shiffrin, Richard M.

It is hard to imagine how understanding memory could not be important for the field and for humanity generally: Memory is what we are, and what defines us as individuals. Despite an ever-increasing reliance on external aids to memory (e.g., looking up forgotten material on the web), we rely on our memory for almost all decisions and interactions in our daily lives. Everyone is particularly aware of the tragedy of memory failure due to diseases such as Alzheimer's. With memory so fundamental, with such a broad scope, and with such great complexity, it is essential that its components be delineated carefully, and it helps enormously if such delineation is made precise with the use of formal theorizing and especially quantitative modeling.

Such delineation was what we put forth in our 1968 chapter, and is the primary reason we regard it as our most important contribution, despite its age and the fact that one of us was a graduate student at the time of its publication. This chapter has served as a template and inspiration for about fifty years of research since.

Our theory has been called the "modal model" of memory and it remains so: Almost all of its insights into memory can be found in contemporary publications. It represented a turning point in the evolution of memory theory because it took many of the concepts proposed since the field of psychology began, as exemplified by William James in his 1890 book *Principles of Psychology*, and formalized them in a comprehensive framework that was backed up by empirical research (much of it original) and quantitative modeling. The theory has undergone many elaborations over the years, in our hands and those of students and colleagues, and has served as a starting point for the development of alternative models, though most of them instantiated the same basic concepts in alternative verbal and computational machinery.

What are these core concepts? We divided the concepts into structural components of the memory system and processes that controlled memory storage and retrieval. It was primarily the second of these that led us to the theory's formulation and its general acceptance: It seemed obvious to us that the control of memorial processes such as storage, retrieval, and

115

decision was responsible for much of the observed phenomena of memory, and such control processes were in need of exposition, delineation, and formal modeling. These control processes acted upon and resided in the three structural components: the short-lived sensory memories, the short-term store(s), and the relatively permanent long-term memory. We used the term "working memory" to describe the control processes that primarily reside in the short-term component of the system; this theme persists today. The various memories were construed to consist of separate traces, a common theme that is also prevalent in categorization research in the form of exemplar theories.

Both the basic structures and the concepts of control processes have remained core concepts as the field has evolved, as empirical studies have grown in huge numbers, as models have proliferated, and as neural measurements have become ever more important and tied to behavioral data. In the 1968 model, we focused on rehearsal as the most apparent and easily modeled of the control processes, but made it clear that this was just one example and that there were a host of other control processes that were in use in working memory, particularly including those used in memory retrieval via memory search.

The chapter was replete with new empirical studies and mathematical modeling of the results. Now it is almost fifty years since its appearance and few scientists have read it or are aware of its contents, other than through a few core ideas that have appeared in secondary and tertiary sources such as textbooks. Yet the chapter and the theory in it would never have achieved the reputation it did without the scientific validation conferred by those studies and their predictions by the models.

The theory presented has become the basis for further research and modeling ever since. In various publications in the 1970s we elaborated on the role and uses of short-term store, working memory, and control processes. Raaijmakers and Shiffrin elaborated the theory by focusing on the role of various kinds of context in storage and retrieval. They showed how a vast array of recall results, both successes and failures (memory loss), could be explained in a simple and coherent fashion, within the framework established by the original theory. This focus on context was a key to further development and has appeared in different guises, but with similar concepts, in recent years (e.g., in modeling by Mike Kahana and his students and colleagues). In 1984, Gillund and Shiffrin extended the model to include recognition; that approach has become the standard way to model recognition decisions based on "familiarity." What is familiarity? A test item and its context are used to probe memory. Traces are activated due to similarity to the memory probe (these are the same activations that are sampled in recall tasks). The activated trace strengths are in effect summed to produce a measure of familiarity, and strong enough familiarity is used to produce a positive recognition decision. In 1997 and 1998, Steyvers and Shiffrin placed the whole system on a more firm probabilistic footing. Traces were implemented as collections of features. Bayesian modeling was used to define trace activation strengths in terms of the probability that a given trace could have been produced by the memory probe. In 2001 Huber and Shiffrin showed how short-term priming operates: A prime (or primes) presented prior to a test word adds features to short-term memory; these features join with features of the test word, and both are used to probe memory. The theory explained how both positive and negative priming comes about based on the way the evidence returned from memory is evaluated. In 2013, Angela Nelson and Shiffrin extended the model of storage in and retrieval from long-term store by showing how event traces could accumulate to form knowledge, and how knowledge is used to encode events. Among other things, this recent research elaborated on the point we made in 1968 that storage produces a long-term memory trace, that further storage adds to and changes that trace, and that later retrievals of a trace changes the trace yet again. This theme presaged much recent research on malleability of memory and development of false memories (e.g., the research of Elizabeth Loftus).

One reason the theory has withstood the test of time is the way its components match "common sense" and are easy to understand. As many theorists have noted, all models and theories are wrong, but are nonetheless useful in various ways (the statistician Box is well known for this observation). Theories lead to future experimentation, alternative theorizing, and critical tests. Perhaps most importantly, they lead to increases in understanding and a concomitant increase in ability to communicate that understanding to others. The importance of our chapter and our theory was certainly enhanced by the way it incorporated many prior concepts and put them together in an easy to understand conceptual framework. That chapter had no lack of technical rigor, presenting new experimental data analyzed in sophisticated ways to validate formal models that were formulated to fit the conceptual framework. Yet the chapter would not have achieved its renown had it not been accessible and understandable.

This characterization helps explain the origin of the idea behind the research. It took concepts prevalent and common in the field since its inception, organized and formalized them, and applied them to a wide range of old and new findings. Both of us began working on these ideas simultaneously, and initially independently. In his first year of graduate study Shiffrin started working with Gordon Bower, developing a model of free recall based on short- and long-term memory, with a strong emphasis on control processes. At the same time Atkinson was working across the Stanford campus on development of short-term memory models with similar themes. When Gordon left to take a sabbatical in England, he sent Shiffrin to work with Atkinson. There was a seamless and natural convergence of our ideas and approach, leading to a number of publications in addition to the 1968 chapter, but the chapter represented a synthesis of all the ideas together in a broad and comprehensive framework.

The successes of the Atkinson and Shiffrin framework, its continued development over the years since, the incorporation of similar concepts in neural modeling, and all the experimentation that has bolstered this approach have hardly exhausted our understanding of memory. We have uncovered only the tip of the iceberg, and we expect many new insights to emerge in the future. Only time will tell if the Atkinson and Shiffrin general theoretical framework will remain the best functional approach to understanding the enormously complex system we describe with the term "memory."

REFERENCES

Atkinson, R. C., & Shiffrin, R. M. (1968). Human memory: A proposed system and its control processes. In K. W. Spence and J. T. Spence (eds.), *The psychology of learning and motivation: Advances in research and theory* (vol. 2, pp. 89–195). New York: Academic Press.

Nelson, A. B., & Shiffrin, R. M. (2013). The co-evolution of knowledge and event memory. *Psychological Review, 120*(2): 356–394.

Raaijmakers, J. G. W., & Shiffrin, R. M. (1980). SAM: A theory of probabilistic search of associative memory. In G. H. Bower (ed.), *The psychology of learning and motivation* (vol. 14, pp. 207–262). New York: Academic Press.

24   Working Memory

Baddeley, Alan

My principal contribution comes from the proposal, with my colleague Graham Hitch, that the capacity to think, to learn, and to plan for the future all depend on a temporary memory system that can be divided into a small number of separate components. It was important to us that the resulting theoretical model could then be applied outside the laboratory to help understand a range of issues of practical importance. Our original idea has been more successful than we dared hope, with the term "working memory" having occurred in the title of over 170,000 papers – not all, of course, accepting our own theory, although our initial paper has been quoted more than 10,000 times. The idea of working memory combines two essential features – temporary memory, and its attentional control – both of which are limited in their capacity. Theorists vary in their emphasis on memory or attention, but all accept the need for both.

My own approach began with an emphasis on temporary storage and was strongly influenced by the controversy during the 1960s as to whether human memory involved separate short-term and long-term memory systems, or whether a single system could explain everything.

I began my research career in long-term memory, researching the way in which postal codes could be constructed so that people would find them easy to remember. I was working at the Medical Research Council Applied Psychology Unit in Cambridge, which specialized in linking the development of theory with its practical application. Having worked on postal codes, I was next given the task of attempting to improve methods of measuring the quality of telephone lines. The standard method was simply having people listen to potentially confusable words.

I proposed that having both to discriminate and to remember the words might make the task more sensitive, particularly since my boss, Conrad, had shown that similarity of sound made sequences much harder to recall. For example, a sequence such as *b g c t d* would be harder to remember in the right order than *k w y q x*. I decided to use words since this also allowed me to incorporate similarity of meaning, contrasting sequences such as *man mat cat cap map* or *huge big wide long tall*. I expected adding noise would make similar items much more difficult to remember in the right order. It did not. I was, however, very impressed by the difference simi-larity of sound made and added another experiment in which I doubled the length of the lists and allowed several learning trials. The pattern changed completely, with similarity of meaning becoming crucial. I found myself in the middle of the long-term versus short-term controversy, arguing for two systems based on separate codes: a short-term acoustic system, and a long-term semantic.

At about this time I moved to the University of Sussex to my first teaching job, and obtained my first grant to work on the link between long- and short-term memory, with Graham Hitch as a post-doctoral fellow. Unfortunately, as we arrived, the whole field was moving from being highly fashionable to becoming increasingly unfashionable. It had become cluttered with different experimental methods and different explanatory models, and evidence began to grow that the assumption that simply holding information in short-term memory would lead to long-term memory was false. What was important was not how long you held the material, but what you did with it, with better learning coming from deeper and more elaborate processing. Furthermore, patients with a tiny short-term memory system did not seem to be handi-capped in long-term memory. Everyone was turning to other problems.

We decided that the best way ahead was to test the idea that short-term memory did indeed act as a working memory, helping people perform complex tasks. We had our volunteer participants perform a range of tasks that were assumed to depend on the short-term system, such as solving simple reasoning problems, learning new material, and comprehending prose, at the same time as they were holding sequences of numbers in their short-term memory. We predicted that the longer the number sequence, the more of the system would be taken up, resulting in ever poorer performance on reasoning, learning, and comprehending. The results surprised us since, although there was an effect, it was much smaller than we had anticipated. Existing theories seemed inadequate to explain how people could still do so well – for example, performing a reasoning task while reciting what was in effect an eight-digit telephone number. We went on to propose the three-part system shown in Figure 24.1. This involves an attentional controller – the *central executive* – and two subsystems: one holding verbal and acoustic information – the *phonological loop* – and the other its visual equivalent – the *visuo-spatial sketchpad*. One way of getting the feel of your own working memory is to close your eyes, think about the house or apartment you live in, and work out how many windows there are.

Most people form a visual image of the house in their "mind's eye," then go around and count the windows. The central executive creates and

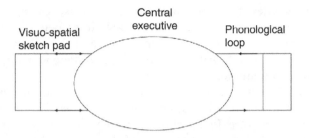

Figure 24.1 The original model of working memory

runs the strategy, the sketchpad holds the image, and the phonological loop does the counting. We have since had to add a fourth component – the *episodic buffer* – which can be regarded as a storage system capable of holding both visual and verbal features, rather like a television screen combining spoken and related visual information. We think the episodic buffer underpins our capacity for conscious awareness. Our original paper came from an invitation to contribute to an influential book. We were in some doubt given that the theory was far from complete, but eventually agreed. It is this paper that, some forty years later, is still being heavily quoted.

Why has it survived? The first reason is that it gives a broad account of a system that provides a link between our perception of the world, our access to long-term memory, and our capacity to use attention to understand the world and to interact with it. It is therefore an important system. It later proved to be the case that people with a good working memory perform better on a wide range of tasks, including understanding complex prose, performance on intelligence tests, and capacity to do well at school. As a result, there is considerable interest in understanding it at a theoretical level from both psychologists and neuroscientists interested in the way in which the system is represented in the brain.

Because it has just four components, each of which is relatively easy to understand, it can be applied to practical issues and has had an increasing influence on areas such as education, second language learning, developmental problems in children (such as dyslexia), and understanding the effects of brain injury. The use of the model is helped by the fact that we have developed a range of methods for teasing apart the different components, many of them relying on different forms of similarity, and on the method of using a concurrent additional task as used in our original studies. The model was intentionally loosely specified, allowing the detail to be built in gradually, rather like beginning with a sketch map of a new country that includes its main mountains and rivers, leaving detailed surveying to later. This has resulted in clearer links between working memory and long-term memory, and in the case of the subsystems, to the processes involved in hearing and speaking, on the one hand, and in vision and spatial orientation, on the other.

In the future, I am sure that detail will continue to build up, perhaps gradually modifying the original framework, but hopefully keeping the broad interactive structure. In due course, I have no doubt that this will be linked to a more detailed understanding of the way in which the brain performs these functions. However, one area that particularly intrigues me is the relatively unexplored link between working memory and emotion. This has led to a concern with motivation. Why do we do anything? A major negative feature of much illness is the lack of energy. More generally, people's achievement seems to depend very heavily on how energetic they are, but we currently lack a good theoretical grasp on mental energy. Working memory is about controlling our mental life. It would be good to have a better idea of just what drives it.

25   Emotionally Colored Cognition

Bower, Gordon H.

Intellectual curiosity can take you to unexpected places. Scientists often do not anticipate the future applications of their research. My research into emotional influences on memory is a good example. I did not expect it to deepen our understanding of personal and interpersonal relationships. This essay describes my work in this field as well as that of many others who built on those early findings.

Mood-Dependent Memory Retrieval

In 1979 I became curious about odd effects that psychotropic drugs and multiple-personality disorders have on memory. I wondered if strong emotions could effectively color-code memories that then get stored in separate cerebral storage bins. In other words, do people store memories of what occurs when they are sad in one "compartment," while relegating into separate storage bins the memories that they form when they are happy, or angry, or frightened, and so on? And, if this is true, could a memory formed when someone felt sad best be retrieved later if the person re-entered a sad emotional state? I called this idea the "mood-dependent retrieval" hypothesis. That basic idea, like a loyal old bird dog, has been retrieving meaty research findings ever since.

In early tests of this hypothesis, my graduate students and I induced college-student volunteers to experience several minutes of happiness or sadness. We did this by asking them to judge the artistry of upbeat or bummer films or music, or by asking them to imagine or recall a happy or sad experience and rate its vividness. Variants of these mood-priming tricks have been used in countless experiments since. Typically, after the mood induction, subjects would be tested on the cognitive task of primary interest to us. This task was usually presented as a separate experiment in order to circumvent subjects consciously enacting the role of a "happy" or "sad" person.

In our first experiment using such mood-inductions, we asked participants to memorize two lists of words. They learned one list in a happy mood and another in a sad mood. Later they were returned to one or the other mood and asked to recall both word lists. Regardless of whether they were happy or sad, participants recalled many more words if the mood in which they first learned the words *matched* their mood when they recalled them later on.

Mood-dependent retrieval also affected people's ability to recall brief stories or photographic scenes. Furthermore, happy- or sad-induced students revealed mood-congruent biases when we asked them to recall events from their childhood or recent events that they had recorded in an "emotional diary." Clinical psychologists often notice this same emotional bias in their clients' autobiographical descriptions. Depressed patients often recall an unhappy, deprived childhood. After recovery, however, they frequently recount much rosier childhoods. The same depressed people who selectively retrieve negative childhood memories will retrieve fonder memories when their mood improves.

Mood-Congruent Memory

Our experiments uncovered a second effect that I called "mood-congruent memory." We found that people's emotional state can prompt them to selectively focus on information that agrees (or is "congruent") with their mood. People focus on mood-congruent information more than other material, thereby evoking richer and more memorable associations to it.

In one experiment, students induced to be happy, sad, or angry read a series of brief stories that alternated between happy, sad, and anger-provoking narratives. In a neutral mood later, the students recalled more of those episodes that matched their mood when they read the stories. Students reported really "getting into" the imagery of the stories that mirrored their own mood. Those vivid images boosted their subsequent recall of the mood-congruent stories.

Subjects in another experiment formed impressions of a stranger by reading descriptions of his behaviors in different settings. Happy-induced people focused more on the stranger's socially acceptable, positive behaviors, while sad-induced people dwelt on his antisocial, negative behaviors. Happy-induced readers later recalled more of his sociable behaviors and liked the stranger, whereas sad-induced readers disliked him. Similar outcomes occur when mood-induced subjects "interview" stooge candidates for a job. Happy interviewers recall more of the candidate's favorable replies and usually hire him; sad interviewers recall more of his unfavorable replies and show him the door.

Emotionally Biased Thinking

Mood-congruent processing suggests that an aroused emotion selectively evokes words and ideas that reinforce a person's overarching emotion. By giving these ideas a head start, moody people lead themselves to perceive, interpret, or judge their surroundings to practically confirm, justify, and perpetuate their feelings.

Consider some examples. When researchers ask students to respond to cue words with quick free associations, happy students provide mostly happy associations, with mood-congruent cue words triggering richer images for them. When researchers ask students to make up stories about pictures of emotional scenes, happy-induced students tend to recount stories of success or romance. Viewing the same picture, sad-induced people concoct stories about impending defeat and failure. The stories people concoct are deeply colored by their feelings.

Liking Like-Minded Individuals

Sad-induced students report little interest in socializing with others, preferring solitary activities, while happy-induced students opt for enjoyable social activities. People's moods alter the costs versus benefits that they expect to get from social interactions. Emotions thus influence when we feel like "dropping in" socially or "dropping out."

Emotions also influence who we choose to associate with. Most people are either mildly happy, or at least neutral, most of the time and prefer to hang out with happy people. Yet this preference can be reversed when they are induced to feel sad. Sad-induced subjects seek out more information about unfortunate people and prefer to be with others who feel blue. In one experiment, pairs of students who did not know one another were introduced and encouraged to exchange views about themselves for twenty minutes. If a duo shared the same initial mood – be it mildly depressed or non-depressed – over the course of the conversation they reported an increased liking for one another. In contrast, students of opposing moods usually developed a dislike for their partners. Thus, people appear to seek out like-minded companions who share their prevailing mood.

Mood-Congruent Evaluations

Mood-priming implies that our prevailing good or bad mood enhances positive or negative aspects of our knowledge about people, things, or ideas, thereby biasing our expressed evaluations of them. Indeed, happy-induced people rate their cars, televisions, or other possessions more favorably than do sad people. In one study, subjects who had just viewed a comedy or tearjerker film answered a brief survey in the lobby afterwards. Those who had watched happy films reported much more satisfaction with their lives, careers, spouses, future prospects, and even with politicians than did those who had watched sad films.

Moods bias our evaluations of our health. Researchers induced students suffering from cold and flu symptoms into happy or sad moods and then asked them to complete a health questionnaire. Sad-induced students rated their cold symptoms as more painful and miserable and more likely to continue than did happy-induced students.

Mood also influences how people characterize their successes and failures. Happy-induced students ascribe their academic successes ("acing" an exam) to their high ability but redirect blame for their failures ("an unfair test"). By contrast, sad-induced students blame their low ability for failures ("I'm stupid") but deflect their successes ("just dumb luck"). Such explanations serve to perpetuate a person's good or bad mood.

Moods Influence Life Decisions

Moods bias how we forecast the future, influencing our planning and decision-making. Happy- and sad-induced students estimated the likelihood of future events. These included such "blessings" as finding a cancer cure or receiving academic honors, as well as such "disasters" as getting maimed in an automobile accident. Happy subjects increased the likelihood of future blessings while downplaying future disasters. In contrast, sad subjects made far more pessimistic prognostications. Similarly, happy-induced students were more confident about their abilities to succeed at athletic, intellectual, and interpersonal tasks than were their sad counterparts. Such judgments influence what challenges people undertake and how long they persist in the face of difficulties.

Concluding Comment

Happily, the overall drift of this research is easy to summarize. Positive or negative moods inject commensurate biases in all manner of cognitive processes, from memory to personal and social judgments. In one experiment after another, moods heavily colored our subjects' memories of the past, their current judgments, and even their expectations about their future. These findings contradict the common assumption that people are rational agents who can set aside their passions in order to engage in objective evaluations of situations, people, and events. Many of our subjects who subscribed to this delusion were unaware of how their judgments were shaped by their moods. Nevertheless, their moods infused and cast a bright light or dark shadow over practically everything they did.

Some 240 years ago Thomas Jefferson wrote in the Declaration of Independence that each of us has an inalienable right to the pursuit of happiness. Psychologists have now shown that when we pursue happiness with optimism, we can make ourselves not only happier but also more successful. So, let's all get to it!

REFERENCES

Bower, G. H. (1981). Mood and memory. *American Psychologist*, *36*, 129–148.
Bower, G. H., & Forgas, J. P. (2000). Affect, memory, and social cognition. In E. Eich et al. (eds.), *Cognition and emotion*. Oxford: Oxford University Press, chapter 3, pp. 87–169.
Bower, G. H., & Forgas, J. P. (2001). Mood and social memory. In Forgas, J. P. (ed.), *Affect and social cognition*. Mahwah: Lawrence Erlbaum Associates, chapter 5, pp. 95–120.

26   Levels of Processing in Human Memory

Craik, Fergus I. M.

Throughout my professional career as a cognitive psychologist, I have been interested in the topics of memory, attention, perception, and thinking – how best to characterize them, how they relate to each other, and how they change over a person's lifespan. In everyday life, these mental activities are usually considered to be rather different from each other – remembering meeting someone a month ago seems different from seeing the person in front of you – and this separation is often echoed in psychology textbooks, in which perception, memory, and decision-making are treated in different chapters. Much of the current thinking in cognitive psychology has reacted against this commonsense view, however, suggesting instead that these areas of study are better regarded as closely related and interacting aspects of one general processing system.

This latter position was one starting point for the formulation of the levels of processing (LOP) framework for memory research proposed by Robert Lockhart and myself in 1972. The LOP article with Lockhart, plus a later empirical article with Endel Tulving in 1975, are my most-cited pieces of published research, and may therefore be regarded as my best-known scientific contributions to cognitive psychology. Additionally, the general ideas in which the LOP framework was embedded – for example, that remembering should be regarded as an activity of mind rather than a collection of structural "memory traces" waiting to be revived – have always been central to my thinking about memory. Thus, the LOP paper and its spinoffs have been the starting point for much of the work that my lab has produced over the years.

In the 1960s, ideas about learning and memory were changing from the belief that the formation of associations between two mental events was the crucial element, to concepts derived from information-processing theories. From this latter point of view, the brain/mind was regarded as a highly sophisticated computer, processing sensory information from the environment, performing computations on that information, and finally translating the products into relevant actions. To accomplish these operations efficiently, the proposed system

128

needed a variety of memory stores, holding information of different qualitative types either temporarily, while it was processed, or relatively permanently, in the case of learned knowledge. The stores were also postulated to have different capacities, running from a limited capacity but very accessible short-term memory (STM) for recent memories, to long-term memory (LTM), a store of very large (unlimited?) capacity for older memories and accumulated knowledge. This model gave a good account of many experimental findings, but the notions of capacity and representation were vague and often contradictory. As one example, the capacity limits of the various stores appeared to vary with the type of material: the short-term store can hold only 4–6 unrelated words, but if the words form a coherent sentence it is relatively easy to reproduce strings of 20–25 words. It seems that meaningfulness somehow enlarges the capacity of the store.

As a young faculty member at the University of London in the late 1960s, I had been very influenced by the theories and experiments on attention proposed and performed by Donald Broadbent and Anne Treisman. Broadbent's "filter theory" of attention embodied an all-or-none switch at early stages of processing – attention could be switched to hearing, as opposed to vision, or to one ear relative to the other ear. However, Treisman and others showed that if a stimulus was expected or was highly meaningful – like your own name – it was perceived consciously, regardless of where attention was directed. Other experiments showed that when participants heard a prose passage played to one ear while wearing a headset, and were asked to repeat back the passage as it came in, they could say little about changes in material coming in the unattended ear – they often did not realize that the speaker had switched to a different language, for example. However, participants *did* always notice if the "unattended" voice changed from a male speaker to a female speaker. On the basis of these and other similar findings, Treisman proposed that incoming information was processed by a series of levels of analysis, running from early "shallow" analyses of such attributes as voice quality, color, loudness, shape, and taste, to such "deeper" attributes as meaning and implication. She further suggested that each level of analysis functioned like a pass–fail test, in which passing was determined both by the incoming strength of the signal and by how expected or meaningful the stimulus was to that person. In the second case, high levels of expectation or meaningfulness set the "pass mark" at a more lenient level, so that such stimuli would be passed on to deeper levels of analysis. So, Treisman replaced Broadbent's on–off view of an attentional switch with a view in which attention functioned throughout all stages of processing.

Although Treisman's "levels of analysis" view was an account of attention and perception, it occurred to me that it could also serve as a framework to understand memory. The basic idea was that deeper (more complete and meaningful) processing might be associated with richer and longer-lasting memories of the event. Attention and memory are intimately related in this scheme. First, paying attention to external events facilitates deeper processing and thus better subsequent memory; but Lockhart and I also proposed that continual attention to incoming material maintains the information "in mind" or in conscious awareness. In this way, we kept the distinction between STM and LTM, but neither is a "memory store" in this formulation. Rather, STM is equivalent to continued attention and conscious processing of information that may vary widely in its qualitative type (e.g., verbal, visual, auditory, pictorial, semantic), whereas material "stored in LTM" presumably depends on some structural changes in brain networks that persist after the material has been dropped from attention and awareness. The characterization of STM as continued attention and processing is very similar to current notions of "working memory" proposed by a number of researchers. Additionally, I think of retrieving the memory of a past event from LTM not as "finding" its record, as in locating a book in a library, but more like reconstituting the same pattern of neural activity that took place when the event was originally experienced. In this sense, remembering is an activity of the brain/mind that is very similar indeed to perceiving: "Memory encoding" is nothing more than the normal processes of perceiving and understanding, and "memory retrieval" consists essentially in recapitulating these same mental operations at a later date; but neither is a "memory store" in this formulation.

Robert Lockhart and I published a version of these ideas in 1972, greatly helped by Endel Tulving, who was at that time the editor of the relevant journal. Tulving and I then went on to conduct a series of experiments to illustrate the ideas of depth and elaboration in memory; these studies were published in 1975. The experiments explored the prediction that if single words are processed to deeper levels, they will be recalled and recognized better in a subsequent test. The basic design was to precede each word in the learning phase with a question that required processing the word to either shallow or deeper levels. The main result was that both recall and recognition followed the predicted pattern. As one example, recognition memory following questions about typescript was 15 percent, whereas the performance level was 81 percent following questions involving meaning. This result was found despite the fact that the same words appeared in the different conditions for different participants; only the type of processing was varied, yet this led to a five-fold increase in later recognition performance. The LOP manipulation thus appears to be a very strong determinant of memory performance.

At this point, forty-five years later, I would say that the legacy of the LOP work has been to help shift the thinking about memory from a structural view of memory traces as "things in the head" to a more dynamic view of remembering as an activity of the brain/mind that is highly related to perceiving, and strongly influenced by attending and thinking. The ideas have also had some practical implications. They have been taken up, for instance, by some educational researchers who have been impressed by the laboratory results showing that memory for words can be increased substantially by processing the material to a deeper level – that is, by engaging attention and meaningfulness.

Some outstanding questions include puzzles at the level of cognitive descriptions – for example, why exactly does deeper meaningful perceiving result in such good memory? Speculative answers include the notion that semantic analysis results in a more distinctive representation, which is then easier to specify at the time of retrieval. Such deeper processing may also embed the encoded representation in an organized schematic network, which in turn may be used to facilitate retrieval. Further questions at the level of brain correlates include specification of the processing networks associated with different levels of processing, exploration of the neural activities associated with short-term retention as opposed to those associated with LTM, and corroboration of the essential similarity between encoding and retrieval processing. There is still a lot to learn!

REFERENCES

Craik, F. I. M. (2002). Levels of processing: Past, present ... and future? *Memory*, *10*, 305–318.

Craik, F. I. M., & Lockhart, R. S. (1972). Levels of processing: A framework for memory research. *Journal of Verbal Learning and Verbal Behavior*, *11*, 671–684.

Craik, F. I. M., & Tulving, E. (1975). Depth of processing and the retention of words in episodic memory. *Journal of Experimental Psychology: General*, *104*, 268–294.

27   Falling Down the Duck/Rabbit Hole

Johnson, Marcia K.

I saw the ambiguous duck/rabbit figure in an introductory psychology textbook the summer I graduated from high school (1960). Perhaps I'd seen it before, but this time the message seemed profound – there are alternative ways of seeing the world, affecting our very perceptions. This is the origin of all human conflict – misunderstandings between friends, disagreements with parents, racism, the Cold War – we were seeing the duck, and the Russians were seeing the rabbit. Is there anything more important for understanding the human condition than this idea that our experience is determined by the mind as well as the external world? Then, during my freshman year of college, another startling experience: I invited some friends to my parents' house and, over dinner, I recounted an elaborate childhood memory, only to have my parents point out that the memory wasn't true. It was suddenly clear that, as a child, I'd concocted an embellished version of an actual event and was now failing to discriminate the real from the imagined elements. These personal examples that perceptions and memories are mental constructions made the classic question of our relation to reality vivid and fascinating.

At the University of California, Berkeley, I learned from talented mentors (especially Geoff Keppel and Leo Postman) that one could systematically study mental processes. From the first experiment I generated myself as an undergraduate (investigating how participants describe shapes affects how easily participants later perceive the shapes embedded among other shapes) through various studies in graduate school (e.g., the impact of organizational processes on memory), I was hooked on the possibility of studying the mind empirically. I arrived at Stony Brook as a new faculty member in 1970, the same year John Bransford joined the faculty as a new PhD from the University of Minnesota. We began collaborating on our mutual interest in the role of constructive processes in memory. For example, we had people listen to stories such as "It was late at night when the phone rang and a voice gave a frantic cry. The spy threw the secret document into the fireplace just in time since 30 seconds longer would have been too late." Subsequently, they often falsely recognized sentences that included implications – such as "the spy burned the secret document" – claiming to have heard information based on inferences they made (e.g., the spy intended to destroy the document) that were not necessarily true (e.g., the spy may have been hiding the document behind wood in a cold fireplace). As part of normal comprehension, people construct representations of situations, drawing on prior knowledge about objects, intentions, actions, and so forth. This runs the risk of importing information that was not part of the actual perceptual event – that is, of producing false memories.

To avoid such false memories, one cannot simply turn off one's schemas or prior knowledge. When you make it difficult for people to use prior knowledge, comprehension and memory suffer (e.g., "The haystack was important because the cloth ripped" is more comprehensible and memorable if preceded by the word *parachute*). In short, despite the fact that organizational processes that depend on prior knowledge (e.g., schemas, concepts) might produce false memories, they are essential for accurate memory. In addition to theoretical implications about the nature of comprehension and memory, there are clear implications for education, and John went off to do important work in that domain.

I was drawn in another direction – deeper into the duck/rabbit hole. If what we see and remember depends on what we already know or how we interpret what we see, and includes inferences that may not be true . . . what ties our beliefs to reality? It may be all right for you to remember a duck and me to remember a rabbit, but certainly there was no elephant! How do we discriminate between reasonable alternative constructions of reality and fabrication? Are there differences in the memories created by perceptual processes and those created by inference, imagination, fantasy, and dreams? How do we determine if autobiographical memories are false? Where do minor distortions end and major distortions (hallucinations or delusions) begin?

I began exploring the psychological processes by which people discriminate real from imagined events. Carol Raye (then on the faculty of Barnard College) and I mapped out a set of empirical questions and a strategy for studying the problem of what we called "reality monitoring." Our 1981 *Psychological Review* paper proposing a theoretical framework for reality monitoring is perhaps the paper that has been the most consequential for me. It clarified the nature of the fundamental question that attracted me to experimental psychology to begin with and that frames how I've thought about many domains involving human cognition. Shahin Hashtroudi, Steve Lindsay, and I extended this reality monitoring approach to the general problem of identifying the origin of mental experience (calling it the "source monitoring framework"). Our 1993 *Psychological Bulletin* paper is my lab's most highly cited paper, and thus had the broadest impact. There are now many studies from our lab and other labs exploring reality/source monitoring, investigating the factors that affect whether people confuse memories of what they perceived with memories of what they imagined, what they saw with what they heard, and so forth. Some of our findings and theoretical ideas have influenced work on eyewitness testimony, interpreting reports of recovery of repressed memories, understanding hallucinations and delusions in psychopathology and confabulations in brain-damaged patients, and episodic memory in general, and have influenced studies of the cognitive neuroscience of memory.

Thinking about reality monitoring was also the impetus for trying to generate a more general model of cognition. Memory models of the '70s and early '80s did not focus on potential differences in the processes of perception and thought and the representations they might generate, or the conditions under which they were discriminated and confused. What kind of memory system could be exquisitely sensitive and faithful in some instances and wildly creative and/or inaccurate in others? In 1983 I summarized what I thought were the main findings at the time about memory and cognition in a Multiple-Entry, Modular Memory framework (MEM, for short). In my years at Princeton (where I moved in 1985) and Yale (where I moved in 2000), students, colleagues, and I expanded this framework and used it to consider issues such as disruption of cognitive function (for example in aging, or psychopathology), the nature of consciousness and attention, and the relation between cognition and emotion.

The MEM architecture organizes component processes of cognition into functional subsystems: two *perceptual* systems (consisting of perceptual component processes) and two *reflective* subsystems (consisting of component processes of what we generally call "thought" and "imagination"). The persisting consequences of these component processes are memories. Reflective processes permit us to foreground, sustain, organize, manipulate, and revive information – mental activities that not only contribute to a sense of remembering, but also give us a sense of control, and allow us to anticipate future events, and imagine possible alternative pasts and futures.

Working on MEM prompted me to read more widely; it was a challenge to try to fit facts together, and a treasure hunt for findings in the literature that would provide a test of ideas arising from MEM. This attempt at synthesis drew me into cognitive neuroscience – a direction I would not have expected earlier in my career – in order to test predictions from MEM and to further explore its component processes. Pursuing these goals prompted my lab to conduct studies of brain-damaged patients, age-related changes in memory, and neuroimaging in order to investigate reality/source monitoring and component processes of cognition, often in collaboration with Karen Mitchell. For example, our lab has used neuroimaging to compare activity in different brain areas arising from perception and reflection (e.g., seeing vs. imagining photos of scenes), and differences between young and older adults in how brain activity is associated with subjective vividness. There is still a lot to be learned about the cognitive processes and neural mechanisms that underlie the subjective experience of remembering and the component processes of cognition more generally.

The field is rapidly developing new methods for analyzing patterns of neural activity and correlating activity among brain regions across time – methods that should further clarify the component processes of cognition, their relation to subjective experience and behavior, and how they break down. Such findings should provide targets for remediation in cases of cognitive disruption. This translational goal – connecting basic research to clinical applications – is a major challenge for the field, with huge potential payoffs, given the high personal and social cost of cognitive deficits associated with aging, traumatic brain injury, and psychopathology.

Beyond the individual level of analysis outlined above, there is an analogous and equally intriguing set of questions about reality monitoring at the social/cultural level. Reality/source monitoring occurs when individuals interact (e.g., as when my parents challenged my childhood memory), when groups interact (e.g., different histories generated by different ethnic groups), and when institutions interact (e.g., when the press investigates public officials or governments regulate corporations). I've raised some issues about social/cultural reality monitoring in a few papers, but not focused on it. However, I think that social/cultural reality monitoring, especially inter-institutional reality monitoring, is a major challenge of our time. Understanding social/cultural reality monitoring processes, and avoiding their breakdown, seems increasingly critical; otherwise, we risk collectively getting stuck in a duck/rabbit hole.

REFERENCES

Johnson, M. K. (2006). Memory and reality. *American Psychologist, 61*, 760–771.
Johnson, M. K. (2007). Reality monitoring and the media. *Applied Cognitive Psychology, 21*, 981–993.
Johnson, M. K., Raye, C. L., Mitchell, K. J., & Ankudowich, E. (2012). The cognitive neuroscience of true and false memories. In R. F. Belli (ed.), *True and false recovered memories: Toward a reconciliation of the debate.* Vol. 58: Nebraska Symposium on Motivation (pp. 15–52). New York: Springer.

28   Memory Matters

Loftus, Elizabeth F.

In December 2004, the *New York Times* reported on that year's winners of the Grawemeyer Awards. The Grawemeyer Awards are given in Psychology and also several other fields (e.g., education, religion, improving world order). That year they were accompanied by a $200,000 prize – amongst the largest for an award in a field that does not have a Nobel Prize. It was with enormous pride that I learned that I had won the award in Psychology. Another news outlet reported that I was the most controversial researcher ever to win the prize, and the most controversial winner since former Soviet President Mikhail Gorbachev won the 1994 prize for improving world order. The award is for a big, important idea in Psychology. So what was my big, important idea?

A staff member sent me an email about that time, letting me know what the external awards committee had said when summarizing my "idea." Their summary practically made me weep. The committee said that I had "changed the way that both scientists and lay citizens think about the nature of human memory," and had "made it clear that human memory is not a literal and faithful recorder of experience." Of course, we've known for some time that memory is fallible, and just how easy it is for us to forget things. But what my work has shown is that we can also falsely remember things differently from the way they happened, and can remember entire events that never happened.

This work teaches us about the malleable nature of memory. Information suggested to an individual about an event can be integrated with the memory for the event itself, so that what actually occurred, and what was discussed later about what may have occurred, become inextricably interwoven, allowing distortion, elaboration, and even total fabrication from suggestions.

People often ask me how I came up with this idea, and to answer I have to take us back to the 1970s. Back then I was interested in what happened when witnesses were questioned about events they had experienced, important events such as crimes or accidents. I did several studies in which I showed that leading questions could bias what people claimed to have seen. For example: "How fast were the cars going when they

136

smashed into each other?" led to higher estimates of speed than the same question asked with the verb "hit." "Did you see *the* broken headlight?" led to more reports of seeing non-existent objects than the same question asked with the indefinite article, as in "Did you see *a* broken headlight?" But eventually I began to see the leading questions as a form of post-event misinformation, one of many forms of post-event information that had the potential to contaminate memory. Witnesses pick up misinformation not only from biased or leading questions, but also when they talk with other people who (consciously or inadvertently) give an erroneous version of a past event, or when they see news coverage about some event that they may have previously witnessed. I began to explore the myriad ways in which our memories could be contaminated as we encounter new information. My collaborators and I showed that distorted memories could be created not only in the minds of young children, or college students in laboratory experiments, but in the minds of all sorts of individuals. For example, we readily distorted the memories of people who had highly exceptional personal memories. We even distorted the memories of highly trained soldiers who were attending a survival school where they learned what it would be like if they were ever captured as prisoners of war. Without much effort at all, they could be led to believe that they had seen a telephone or a weapon in the interrogation room where they had spent a half hour. These objects were not there.

What I love about this research program is that not only does it tell us a great deal about the malleable nature of human memory, but it also has important implications for society. Precise memory, even for minute details, is often provided in court cases involving crimes and accidents and other legally relevant events. My research showed that we cannot always trust this testimony. We cannot assume that the degree of conviction expressed by an eyewitness is a reliable indicator of the accuracy of that testimony. Even when witnesses are trying to be as accurate as possible, they may not be describing what really happened. The testimony is honest in the sense that the witness fervently believes it to be valid and yet it can be partly or completely wrong.

Another real-world setting where memory has been important is psychotherapy. Often in therapy, patients are pressed for details about their childhood or an earlier phase of life experience. Sometimes even talking about a possible past can create a false sense of recollection that the event actually did occur. My collaborators and I established clearly that this can happen, showing that after a few discussions, a fabricated experience takes on a sense of verisimilitude that can fool someone into thinking that they remember the event as if it really did occur. The implications for how we should probe a person's memory, or for the advisability of engaging them in hypothetical thinking about possible past events, are enormous. Not only do these observations have implications for law and for psychotherapy, but they also have ramifications for one's sense of one's own past.

This is where the "controversial" part comes in. Some patients were producing false memories in psychotherapy and innocent lives were being destroyed in the process. Some of my critics did not like facing this truth.

These ideas about our malleable memory did not come out of nowhere. Current psychological science often builds on past work done by many others in the field. In the case of the malleable nature of memory, there certainly were some past giants. For example, the British psychologist F. C. Bartlett had shown in the 1930s that recollections of a story often contain distortions and additions that were not part of the material that was original read. The American psychologist Ulrich Neisser had described, in the 1960s, remembering as a reconstructive process, working a bit more like the paleontologist who constructs a skeleton of a dinosaur from a few bone fragments. Much later, I would liken memory to a Wikipedia page – something that is created with bits of information that can come from different times and places. You can change it, but so can other people.

After hundreds of studies showing how memory could be contaminated by post-event misinformation, my collaborators and I would wonder just how far you can go with people in terms of distorting memory. We showed that you could plant entirely false memories in the minds of people for events that never happened, false memories of events that would have been pretty traumatic had they actually happened. These include false memories of getting lost, or being bullied, or being harmed in a serious way. And these false memories had repercussions – they affected people's later thoughts, intentions, and behaviors. So, when we planted a false memory that as a child a person got sick eating eggs, pickles, or strawberry ice-cream, they didn't want to eat these foods as much. When we planted a warm fuzzy memory about a healthy food, they wanted to eat the foods more.

In the future, we will get even more skilled at tampering with memory. The techniques might include behavioral interventions (as we have done), perhaps enhanced by pharmaceutical elements. The work will show that falsely planted memories can affect people long after the distortions have taken hold. And with this power to contaminate memory and control behavior, some serious ethical considerations rise to the fore. When should we use this kind of mind technology? And should we ever ban its use? Future generations will grapple with these concerns.

In the meantime, my hope is that I have left the world with a deeper appreciation of the constructive and destructive ways in which memory can work. We would all do well to keep in mind a lesson I've learned over the decades: that just because someone tells you something with confidence, with details, and with emotion, it doesn't mean that it really happened.

REFERENCES

Costandi, M. (2013). Corrupted memory. *Nature, 500,* 268–270.

Loftus, E. F. (2007). Elizabeth F. Loftus (Autobiography). In G. Lindzey & M. Runyan (eds.). *History of psychology in autobiography* (vol. IX, pp. 198–227). Washington, D.C.: American Psychological Association Press.

Loftus, E. F., & Palmer, J. C. (1974). Reconstruction of automobile destruction: An example of the inter-action between language and memory. *Journal of Verbal Learning and Verbal Behavior, 13,* 585–589.

29 What Do You Know, and How Do You Know It? It's All in Your Connections!

McClelland, James L.

I entered the field of psychology around 1968, initially studying behavior, neurophysiology, and perception as an undergraduate at Columbia University. I was first exposed to the study of human thought and language in 1970 – a field then called "cognitive psychology" – after entering the PhD program in the Psychology Department at the University of Pennsylvania.

At that time, the field was dominated by a way of thinking that essentially went like this. Knowledge was a set of propositions (structured lists of items), stored in "long term memory." Some of these propositions were rules that guided thought; others were statements characterizing properties and relations among items. The result of a cognitive act was the creation of new propositions, through a series of discrete steps. For example, William Chase and Herbert Clark considered how we mentally represent a visual display like this:

*

+

The idea was that we would translate the display into a proposition, such as "the star is above the plus." We could then compare that to the proposition derived from a sentence, such as "the plus is not above the star."

I couldn't deny that people could construct propositions from looking at displays, but I wasn't completely satisfied with these ideas. I had learned that a neuron fires at a rate that depends on how closely an input corresponds to its preferred stimulus. I had learned that the rate at which a rat or a pigeon would respond to a stimulus was a continuous function of the similarity of the stimulus to previously rewarded stimuli. As I studied cognition, I learned that the probability of success in recognizing a visually presented word was a continuous function of its frequency of occurrence and of its brightness, clarity, and duration.

So I started to ask myself whether it could make sense to think of knowledge and cognition in continuous terms. Although I started down this path based on my own search for a new framework, the eventual

140

result was the collective product of the work of many, some of whom I've been lucky enough to have as collaborators. In what follows, I'll describe the development of three key ideas as I experienced them.

Units and Activations. For the first idea, I worked more independently as I made the transition from graduate student to assistant professor. I asked: What if an item's involvement in one's current state of mind could be a matter of degree? I tried to think about this in a purely abstract way, but it proved nearly impossible to make progress in that way. Then I had the idea that I could think of each item being represented by a unit corresponding to a neuron or set of neurons. Then the *activation* of the unit – how fast the neuron was firing at a certain time – could correspond to the degree of the item's participation at a given moment. I started building computer simulation models that contained units with continuous activation values that could change as a function of the activations of other units. For example, the activation of the unit for the word *cat* might depend on the degree of activation of units for the letters C, A, and T. The activation of the units for these letters, in turn, might depend on the degree of activation of units for the physical features that make up these letters. In developing these ideas, I was strongly influenced by hearing a talk by James Anderson, an electrical engineer turned cognitive modeler. Drawing on Jim's work, I studied a little math to learn how to write equations for these activations, to explore how the process might unfold over time. The result was my 1979 paper describing a model of the time course cognition called the *cascade* model, which described how activation could build up over time through a series of processing stages, such that once it reached a sufficient level, it could trigger a response, such as, "It's the word 'CAT.'"

Knowledge in the Connections. What I have described so far led to the second idea, a start toward an answer to the knowledge question: What is the knowledge that I have that underlies the activations produced by an incoming stimulus? For example, when the units for the letters C, A, and T are active, what is the knowledge that allows them to activate the unit for the word CAT? This knowledge could be in a list of words and their spellings – something psychologists and psycholinguists describe as "the mental lexicon" – but this idea began to seem problematic. To account for the build-up of activation in the cascade model, it seemed to require an extremely rapid search through all of the words on the list thousands of times each second. A simple alternative was to let the units for the letters activate the units for the words by way of direct connections that propagate activation, just as neurons influence each other via connections called synapses. This idea was embodied in the cascade model and in a model of word recognition David Rumelhart and I developed in

1981. In this work, the connections could be treated as simply being "present" or "absent." The unit for the letter C activates CAT, but doesn't activate MAT or DOG, so there is a connection from C to CAT, but not to the units for these other words. But once you have connections, their strengths can be matters of degree. The frequency of exposure to the spelling of the word CAT, for example, might determine the strength of the connections from the units for the letters to the units for the word. Like degree of activation, degree of knowledge becomes a continuous variable in this framework.

Connection Learning and Letting Go of Dedicated Units. We now come to the third idea – the most difficult and the most controversial. Up to now, I could still think of the items that we know (the word CAT, the letters C, A, and T) as discrete mental entities – for each one, there is a separate unit. While I don't have a set of items written down in a list, I still have a separate unit for each item, just as I could have a separate entry in a list. The third stage is the realization that it is not necessary to hold onto the idea that each item is represented by its own dedicated unit. I was first exposed to this idea, too, in the work of James Anderson, and its further development depended critically on the work of David Rumelhart, Geoffrey Hinton, and Ronald Williams, who developed a general method for training connection weights without assigning dedicated units to each item.

Let's consider learning to produce the pronunciation of a word ("cat") from an input specifying the spelling of the word (CAT) – something everyone nowadays is expected to learn how to do. It is possible to build a neural network with a unit for each known word, linking units for the appropriate letters to it, and then linking the word unit to units for speech gestures we make in pronouncing the word (we touch the tongue just behind the teeth, for example, to make a "t" when we pronounce the word "cat"). But it is not clear that experience can reach into the mind and directly assign units to correspond to particular words. What if you simply had a procedure that allowed you to adjust the strengths of the connections from a set of input units corresponding to line-segments that make up printed words to a set of output units corresponding to aspects of the gestures we make with when we speak? David Rumelhart and I began to explore this idea in the early 1980s as we and others began work to articulate our new framework in our 1986 book. This network starts with small random weights. Each time it sees an item, it adjusts the weights just a little, to increase the tendency for the units in the input to activate the units corresponding to the correct output (and not to activate incorrect units). Even with just direct connections from the units for the line-segments to the units for aspects of speech gestures, this system worked remarkably well, and in later work we did even better when we included "hidden" units between the inputs and the outputs, creating what is now called a "deep network." Mark Seidenberg, David Plaut, Karalyn Patterson, and I were able to account for human ability to read words aloud. The model could read words such as HINT, whose pronunciation is consistent with other words (MINT, LINT, SPLIT, etc.) and words such as PINT, whose pronunciation is not consistent with others. The model even learned to generalize to new items: As humans do, it pronounced ZINT with a short 'ih' sound, as in HINT, MINT, etc. This work remains controversial because it suggests that the units (words) and propositions (rules) that other scientists attribute to the human mind may only be in the mind of the scientist, not the mind of the human learner the scientist is trying to explain. In our models, the knowledge of words and rules is in the connections.

The work I've described above was part of the *second wave* of neural network research, cresting around 1990. A third wave has recently emerged. Neural networks based on the ideas I have described are now used in intelligent machines; when your mobile device understands a spoken query, it uses a neural network. Are there aspects of intelligence that still depend on propositional reasoning? Perhaps so, but I'm betting we'll better understand even advanced forms of thinking such as mathematical reasoning if we see thinking as activation propagating among neuron-like units and think of knowledge as being stored in the connections.

REFERENCES

McClelland, J. L. (1979). On the time relations of mental processes: An examination of systems of processes in cascade. *Psychological Review, 86,* 287–330.

Plaut, D. C., McClelland, J. L., Seidenberg, M. S., & Patterson, K. (1996). Understanding normal and impaired word reading: Computational principles in quasi-regular domains. *Psychological Review, 103,* 56–115.

Rumelhart, D. E., McClelland, J. L., & the PDP research group. (1986). *Parallel distributed processing: Explorations in the microstructure of cognition. Volumes I & II.* Cambridge, MA: MIT Press.

30 Serendipity in Research: Origins of the DRM False Memory Paradigm

Roediger, III, Henry L.

The editors have given the authors a difficult task: Pick out one of our "most important contributions to research" and write about it. Just the first part had me stumped: Most important in what way? I decided to subvert the question into telling about my most-cited article (which may or may not be the most important). Citations at least indicate whether others have found the work useful, one possible meaning of importance.

I write about what has come to be called the Deese–Roediger–McDermott (DRM) paradigm, owing to a suggestion by Endel Tulving. And Tulving is responsible in more ways than one. I had introduced him for a talk at Rice University in 1993 while I was on the faculty. The talk was on "the brain's proclivity for primacy" or why first (and new) events are well remembered. After my introduction, I sat off to the side. The talk was exciting, and the audience stayed long afterwards, asking questions. As moderator, I thought maybe they were going on too long, so I was about to pull the plug. Happily, I waited. Someone asked Tulving a question (the person and the question are lost to me), and during his reply Tulving said: "Your comment reminds me of an experiment by James Deese from years ago in which he presented lists of words, asked people to recall them in any order, and found they often intruded a related word in their recall" (my reconstruction of his answer, of course, not his exact words).

I wrote down "Deese experiment" on a note card. Later, I asked Tulving what year it might have been. He said "probably 1959." He and I talked about how unusual that finding was, because free recall of words is often surprisingly error free.

The note got buried in a pile on my desk. A couple of months later I found it while cleaning up. This was before all the journals were online, so sometime later I trekked to the library and copied two Deese papers from 1959. One was the correct one (it had rarely been cited). I discovered that Deese had created lists of related words, words that were associates to a key, seed word. For example, he took the top associates to the word *sleep* (bed, rest, awake, tired, dream, etc.) for one of his lists. Deese presented twelve words for immediate free recall and, for some of the lists, found that the word used to generate the list was often included in recall even though it had not been presented. (This outcome did not occur for other lists even though they were created the same way). The paper was about associative factors in recall.

The 1990s was a decade in which false memories were being discussed in various public arenas. I wondered if Deese's materials might provide a straightforward way to study false memories. Most of my research in this era was on implicit memory phenomena, but I decided to try to replicate Deese's finding in a classroom demonstration experiment to see if it were really true. He provided enough detail in his paper that I was able to pick out six lists that had produced reasonable levels of intrusions. I created lists, recall sheets, and a recognition test (one that included studied words, unrelated lure words, and then the critical seed words that had generated the lists). The recognition test was printed the night before class by my own hand and copied the next morning. I was teaching an undergraduate class on Human Memory, and told the students they would be participating in an experiment and writing about it later. I read the lists one by one and had students recall for two minutes after hearing each list. After six lists, they took the recognition test covering all the lists.

After they finished, I asked students to raise their hands if they had recognized the words I was about to read out. I then slowly read out the six words like *sleep* that had generated the lists. Many students happily raised their hands to the words (some to all of them). When I told them that none of the words I had just spoken had been in the lists, they appeared surprised and flummoxed. A lively discussion ensued; I knew the phenomenon was real.

This informal classroom study became Experiment 1 of a paper by Roediger and McDermott in 1995; it was a demonstration experiment, but it was carefully carried out and established the phenomenon. I tried to give this project to a new graduate student at Rice in the fall of 1993. He fiddled around and then, in December, announced that he was dropping out of graduate school and going on in Philosophy. Happily, Kathleen McDermott, then a more advanced student, had expressed interest in this project, and she jumped at the chance to work on it.

Together, in the spring of 1994, we designed and conducted a much more careful experiment along the same lines. We created twenty-four associated lists, guided by nothing more than intuition and word association norms, and hoped they would create false recall and false recognition. We rotated sets of eight lists through three conditions: lists that were studied and recalled; lists that were studied but not recalled; and lists that were not presented.

False recall across the studied lists was high; probability of recalling the critical items such as *sleep* was 0.55, whereas the probability of recalling items in list positions 4–11 (i.e., ignoring primacy and recency effects) was 0.47. Later replications confirmed that recall of the critical items was about the same as or slightly higher than the middle list items. Further, this outcome occurred on an immediate recall test when subjects had been instructed to be sure to write down only words they heard on the list.

Recognition results confirmed the DRM memory illusion. On the recognition test, subjects were to say yes or no to test words (*yes*, for studied); if they responded *yes*, they were also asked to make a remember/ know judgment. Briefly, they were to report *remember* if they could recall the moment of presentation of the word in the list or some detail about the presentation. If they were sure it was in the list – they knew it – but did not remember the moment of occurrence, they should say *know*.

Correct recognition of studied words was high for the lists that had been recalled, with a hit rate of 0.79. The false alarm rate to lures from unrelated lists was 0.11, showing good discrimination. However, false recognition of critical lures (the seed words) was 0.81, the same level as for studied words. In addition, subjects said they *remembered* the moment of occurrence of critical lures at the same level (0.58) as they did for studied words (0.57). This was surprising, because the critical lures had not even been presented. Subjects experienced remembering non-presented words during retrieval at the same level as presented words – a powerful illusion. We had trouble believing these results, so we replicated them while writing up the first two experiments. The field also had trouble believing the results, so many replications and extensions followed soon after publication. The effect is robust, and everyone gets it.

We provided several possible theories of the DRM effect in the 1995 paper, but advocated there and later for an associative theory. Briefly, words in the list such as *bed, rest, awake*, etc., trigger associations (either conscious or unconscious) to the critical non-presented word, and thus it is activated during study and recalled or recognized later during the test. This theory has been debated for various reasons, but still stands today.

Our paper appeared in July 1995, twenty years ago as I write now, and the DRM paradigm has been widely used (and occasionally abused) over the years. There is much more to say on the topic, but not much room to say it. Let me end with some reflections.

Given all the papers I have published, it seems odd that my most-cited paper (as I write, but probably forever) came about completely serendipitously. The genesis came from an offhand remark by Tulving after a talk. I had no grant funding for this research, and none would have been possible (but it was cheap). For Experiment 1, I used no equipment – I read the lists aloud, I tested students in class, and the recognition test was handwritten. Then I was lucky to find a great collaborator who carried the project forward with me. Experiment 2 was a bit more involved, but not much. The scoring and analyses were all done by hand. The statistics were straightforward. I still have the data sheets.

Yes, in retrospect, it does seem odd that what is my most famous paper (using citations as a metric) involved no complicated, sophisticated experimentation with elaborate equipment. The lesson for students reading this book: Keep your eyes open, don't think all research has to be expensive and complicated, and pay attention during the question and answer period of talks.

REFERENCES

Gallo, D. A. (2006). *Associative illusions of memory: False memory research in DRM and related tasks*. New York: Psychology Press.

McDermott, K. B. (2007). Inducing false memories through associated lists: A window onto everyday false memories? In J. S. Nairne (ed.), *The foundations of remembering: Essays in honor of Henry L. Roediger, III*. New York: Psychology Press, 2007.

Roediger, H. L., & McDermott, K. B. (1995). Creating false memories: Remembering words not presented in lists. *Journal of Experimental Psychology: Learning, Memory and Cognition, 21*, 803–814.

31 Memory: Beyond Remembering

Schacter, Daniel L.

When I completed my undergraduate studies as a psychology major at the University of North Carolina at Chapel Hill in May 1974, I knew that I wanted to continue in the field, but I didn't know exactly how. After graduation, I worked as a research assistant in the laboratory of Herbert Crovitz, a cognitive psychologist at Duke University. There I tested brain-damaged amnesic patients, whose dramatic memory loss sparked my interest in the workings of human memory. I went on to graduate school at the University of Toronto and studied with Endel Tulving, a leading memory researcher. At Toronto I learned how to conduct experiments that probed individuals' abilities to remember past experiences.

It may therefore seem odd when I say that I think that my most important scientific contribution has been to highlight this point: Much of what is most interesting and significant about memory either does not involve, or even goes beyond, simply remembering past experiences. I think that this is an important contribution because it has helped to expand our conception of what memory is and how it influences cognitive functioning. I've made contributions to two areas of research that highlight this point: (1) implicit memory, and (2) imagining future experiences.

Implicit Memory

In the standard laboratory procedure for investigating human memory, researchers show participants to-be-remembered information, such as words or pictures, and later give a test that requires them to recall or recognize the previously studied information. During the early 1980s, however, memory researchers began taking a different approach. They tested participants with tasks that did not require them to try to remember previously studied materials, tasks such as identifying a briefly flashed picture or completing a word stem (e.g., MOT__) with the first word that comes to mind. Numerous experiments, including several by my colleagues and me, showed that exposure to an item in a study list increased the likelihood of subsequently identifying or producing that item on a later test (e.g., participants were more likely to complete GAR__ with GARDEN when GARDEN appeared on the study list than when it did not). We and other researchers referred to this phenomenon as *priming*. Importantly, priming seemed to behave quite differently from standard measures of memory. Priming could occur in the absence of recall or recognition, and experimental manipulations that had large effects on recall and recognition tests (e.g., deep vs. shallow encoding) often had little effect, or even opposite effects, on priming. Indeed, studies of brain-damaged amnesic patients revealed that these patients often showed normal priming effects despite impaired recall and recognition.

How were we to think about these intriguing findings? Many theories were proposed, with some researchers claiming that differences between priming and remembering reflect the operation of fundamentally different memory systems, and others claiming that the differences could be understood without proposing more than one memory system. We needed a way to talk about the new findings without having to decide the question of one versus many memory systems. In a 1985 paper that reported new evidence for differences between priming and remembering in both healthy adults and amnesic patients, Peter Graf and I proposed using the descriptive terms *explicit memory* and *implicit memory*: explicit memory refers to conscious, intentional recall and recognition of past experiences, whereas implicit memory refers to a facilitation or change in task performance that is attributable to information acquired during a previous study episode, even though the task does not require remembering that episode. We left open for debate the question of whether differences between explicit and implicit memory reflect the operation of one or many memory systems.

Interest in priming and implicit memory continued to grow rapidly. I also saw connections to older psychological research on unconscious forms of memory. I thought that the time had come to link together new and old observations about implicit memory from diverse areas of psychology, and I did so in a 1987 review/theoretical paper that helped to organize this emerging area. The paper had a large impact, and was eventually named a "citation classic" by the Institute for Scientific Information. I think that the main value of this paper was to drive home the point that memory can have a powerful influence on thought and behavior even in the absence of any subjective experience of remembering, and to highlight that the tools of experimental psychology can help to understand the nature of that influence.

Imagining Future Experiences

Much of my research during the early 1980s focused on patients suffering from memory loss. In a testing session during that time that I still recall clearly today, Endel Tulving and I interviewed a head-injured patient known by the initials K.C. Patient K.C. had a severe case of amnesia that resulted in a total loss of what Tulving called *episodic memory*: K.C. could not recollect a single episode from his past; nonetheless, he showed robust priming on various implicit memory tests. During this session, Tulving asked K.C. a simple but revealing question: "What will you be doing tomorrow?" K.C. drew a total blank, the same kind of blank that occurred when he was asked to remember what he did yesterday, thus suggesting an important link between remembering past episodes and imagining future episodes: K.C. seemed incapable of doing either.

That striking observation stuck with me, and I began to think about ways to study the role of episodic memory in imagining the future. However, other projects always got in the way, and despite maintaining interest in the topic for many years, my plans to study future imagining kept getting put on the back burner. That all changed in 2005, as a result of a couple of developments. A new post-doctoral researcher arrived in my lab, Donna Rose Addis, who had been doing research using functional MRI to study the brain processes that are associated with episodic memories of everyday autobiographical events. I thought that some of the approaches that Donna had taken to studying episodic memory could be extended to studying how people imagine future episodes. Donna was eager to pursue that direction, and so we designed a new functional MRI study that directly compared remembering past episodes and imagining future episodes. The experiment provided strong evidence that both depend on a common network of brain regions.

At the same time, I began to see possible connections between future imagining and another idea that had been the focus of my research for much of the preceding decade: the notion that memory is a constructive process prone to error and distortion. I had written numerous articles and a couple of books on this theme, including a 2001 book titled *The Seven Sins of Memory: How the Mind Forgets and Remembers.* There, I proposed that memory errors could be divided into seven basic categories, and argued further that these so-called sins of memory were not really defects or flaws, but could be better thought of as costs associated with adaptive features of memory that normally contribute to its efficient functioning.

This is where I saw a possible conceptual link to future imagining. Several kinds of evidence, including Tulving's observations concerning K.C. and our functional MRI evidence, supported the idea that episodic memory plays a key role in imagining future experiences. This arrangement is adaptive because episodic memory is a constructive system that enables past experiences to be used flexibly to imagine novel future scenarios: We can recombine bits and pieces of past experiences into simulations of what might happen in the future. However, although a flexible episodic memory system is adaptive for imagining the future, this flexibility may come at a cost of vulnerability to errors and distortions that result from mistakenly combining elements of imagination and memory. In a 2007 paper, Addis and I called this idea the "constructive episodic simulation hypothesis." We and other researchers have since published numerous experiments that have explored various aspects of the hypothesis. Indeed, since 2007 there has been an explosion of research into the role of memory in imagination and future thinking.

This research might seem quite different from research on implicit memory, but I see a connection: Both lines of work highlight that there is much more to memory than simple remembering of past experiences. Memory influences cognition and behavior in subtle ways of which we can be entirely unaware, and also plays a key role in shaping our thoughts about what might happen in the future.

These ideas are relevant to life outside the laboratory because many of our everyday judgments, decisions, predictions, and plans may be powerfully influenced by memory. For example, when we are shopping and decide to buy a particular brand, memory for an ad we saw recently might influence that decision even if we don't explicitly recall the ad. When we think about next summer's vacation, memories of what we did during previous vacations likely impact the future plans that we construct. I think that an intriguing next step for this research would be to try to connect studies of implicit memory and future imagining, which have for the most part been investigated separately. The results of such research would hopefully shed further light on the idea that much of what is most interesting and important about memory goes well beyond remembering.

REFERENCES

Schacter, D. L. (1987). Implicit memory: History and current status. *Journal of Experimental Psychology: Learning, Memory, and Cognition, 13*, 501–518.

Schacter, D. L. (2012). Adaptive constructive processes and the future of memory. *American Psychologist, 67*, 603–613.

Schacter, D. L., & Addis, D. R. (2007). The cognitive neuroscience of constructive memory: Remembering the past and imagining the future. *Philosophical Transactions of the Royal Society (B), 362*, 773–786.

32   Episodic Memory

Tulving, Endel

You know what memory is. Everybody does. You know facts from life, or learn them from a textbook, and they are in your memory – for example, "grass is green," or "Paris is the capital of France." You take a trip to Paris, visit the Eiffel Tower, and when you get back home the event is still with you, in your memory (like, "In Paris we climbed the Eiffel Tower; it was amazing!") Pretty easy. Remembering requires no effort, it comes perfectly naturally to all healthy people, and nobody makes anything of it. Except some psychologists and other students of the brain/mind.

I have studied memory all my life. I have done experiments, had thoughts about memory's nature, proposed new theories, created new concepts, and made up fresh terms to go with the concepts. I have also read a lot of what other students of memory have written. It all has been fruitful and fun, and made for a satisfying life.

In the science of memory, as in other branches of science, every now and then something interesting is discovered. By "interesting" I mean that when the discoverers tell others about it, the others do not believe them. I discovered a new kind of memory that turned out to be "interesting," and have spent much of the rest of my life trying to explain it to those who resisted the idea.

I cannot relate the complete story about how the discovery happened. But its thumbnail summary goes like this: Many years ago, a colleague of mine, at a university far away from Toronto, invited me to organize a conference in his research center, on the theme of "organization of memory." I asked a group of respected specialists to come and give talks. After the conference all speakers wrote a chapter for the book based on the conference proceedings. I had not given a talk because I was no longer interested in organization of memory, but I edited the book along with a young colleague. Among the submitted chapters there were three that claimed to discuss "semantic" memory. Try as I might, I could not understand what the authors were talking about. It was very different from what I knew of memory. I relieved my frustration by writing a chapter for the book about a new idea I had about memory. The year was 1972.

152

The title of my chapter, "Episodic and Semantic Memory," was strange. No one knew what it meant. The term "episodic memory" had never seen the light of day before; "semantic memory" was familiar only to a handful of experts. In the chapter I proposed that, contrary to the traditional view, there may be two different kinds or categories of long-term memory. This hypothesis made sense to very few people. Two different kinds of memory? Isn't it like saying that there are two kinds of air, or two kinds of intelligence, or two kinds of supreme beings? Memory is memory is memory. Surely everybody – psychologists and the thinking people in the street – knew that. You do not have to have a PhD to know the plain fact that memory is unitary. Up to the time that I wrote the article I also had not had any doubt about this simple obvious truth.

Now, it is true that by 1972 it had already been proposed that there are important differences between short-term and long-term memory. Spirited debates about this heretical thought were still going on, with the dualists winning. But, in my article, the two new kinds of memory – episodic and semantic – had to do with long-term memory.

So, my suggestion was that long-term memory can be one of two kinds. One of them, semantic memory, had to do with the learning and remembering of general *facts*. Facts are propositions about the states of the world, expressions about something being such and such, or just general knowledge. For example "snow is cold," "my house had a red door," "the chemical formula for table salt is NaCl," or "Paris is the capital of France." These facts are, or could be, part of common, "timeless" knowledge, potentially shared by many people. And semantic memory can be independent of any personally remembered event or experience.

Episodic memory, on the other hand, I said, has to do with remembering one's own personally experienced *events*. For example, while walking your dog in the park, your mind goes back to yesterday when you and your friend managed to get tickets for seats in the top row of the ball park where you had to watch your team lose the game in the last inning. Another example could be how you remember flying to Paris several years ago, what you did there, and what a breath-taking view of the city you had from the observation platform of the Eiffel Tower. Still another example could be when you, as a subject for a memory experiment, have been shown certain words to remember and a few minutes later are asked to write them down "from memory." In each of these examples you are remembering events that occurred in your past. In that sense, these memories are personal. They happened in a particular place and at a particular time, even if you might not know exactly when. Re-experiencing the ballgame, or the trip to Paris, or the words in a presented list, is like instantaneous "mental time travel" to another place and another time, with you as the traveler into your own past. In contrast, thinking about facts – the color of your front door, or capitals of states, or a huge number of other facts like these – involves no such mental time travel into your past. The most essential difference between episodic remembering and semantic knowing lies in your own ability to tell whether you are retrieving a general fact or remembering a personal event.

In my 1972 chapter the distinction I drew between the two new kinds of memory was necessarily rather fuzzy, because I did not have it any clearer in my own mind. Also, I could not offer any hard facts in support of what I was proposing. It was just the idea. But I myself liked what I had come up with, and began playing with the theme in my mind. Over the following years I, with my students and like-minded colleagues, spent a good deal of time thinking about and working out the similarities and differences between the two "new" kinds of memory.

As I hinted already, my idea about episodic memory was not kindly received by my colleagues. Some took my proposal in stride, as a worthwhile issue to explore, but there were many others who did not like it one bit. It did not make sense to them. And they did not understand how I could make the silly claim without having any evidence for it. Sure, science involves making hypothetical guesses about unknown regularities of the world, but it also involves testing them for empirical facts. And in 1972 I did not have any. My critics also told me that my hypothesis about two kinds of long-term memory was not needed. They could explain phenomena of memory without postulating any imaginary memory systems. To this day there are still students of memory who do not like to use the term "episodic memory."

Over the years I studied the concept of episodic memory with even more passion. Episodic memory began to gain general attention as an important entity in memory research. A number of developments contributed to the change.

First, in cognitive psychology, some findings of experiments done with people with normal memory abilities made better sense if one assumed a distinction between episodic and semantic memory.

Second, in neuropsychology, brain-damaged people were discovered who exhibited a sharp "dissociation" (lack of association) between episodic and semantic memory. They would remember general facts that they had learned before the onset of their amnesia (i.e., their semantic memory seemed fine), but could not recall personally experienced events. That is, their retrograde amnesia was not "global," it applied only to episodic memory.

Third, developmental psychologists began to note that young children, up to four years or so, did not have adult-like episodic memory. And yet children are world champions in picking up information and knowledge about their world. It looked as if episodic memory was not necessary for semantic memory, although it was very clear that semantic memory was necessary for episodic.

Fourth, functional brain imaging techniques, which allowed investigators to identify brain regions associated with mental tasks, began to reveal differences in brain activity between tasks that required episodic memory and comparable tasks for which episodic memory ability was not needed.

Finally, perfectly healthy, intelligent, and professionally successful people were identified who admitted that they did not remember any personally experienced events. They lacked episodic memory, or at least had poorly developed episodic memory abilities. I even began wondering whether researchers who resisted the proposed distinction between episodic and semantic memory had poor episodic memory themselves!

***

In science, a foremost value of a new discovery, concept, or idea lies in the fact that it allows scientists to generate meaningful and potentially fruitful questions that they would be unlikely to pose otherwise. Because all science begins with questions, and that without questions science simply would not be, this value is inestimable. I hope that the concept of episodic memory will serve the same purpose.

REFERENCES

Tulving, E. (1972). Episodic and semantic memory. In E. Tulving & W. Donaldson (eds.), *Organization of memory* (pp. 381–403). New York: Academic Press.

33 What We Learn Depends on What We Are Remembering

Wagner, Allan R.

In 1968 there was a symposium at Dalhousie University, the proceedings of which were published with the title *Fundamental Issues in Associative Learning*. There may have been some exaggeration in the title, but there was an extraordinary shared vision among the participants about what was deemed challenging at the time, and how to approach the challenge through an invigorated investigation of Pavlovian conditioning. Especially congruent were the presentations by Leon Kamin, Robert Rescorla, and myself. An important result of the research and theorizing that followed has been the appreciation of how "expectations" shape the basic regularities of associative learning as they play out even in the simplest instances of animal behavior.

Associative learning refers to the process by which one stimulus comes to recall the memory of another with which it has been paired There are numerous ways in which this fundamental memory process can be studied. In the procedure introduced by Ivan Pavlov with dogs, an arbitrary stimulus such as a tone or a light (referred to as a conditioned stimulus, or CS) was presented prior to providing the animal access to food (referred to as an unconditioned stimulus, or US). The indication that such pairing of CS and US caused the animal to associate the two stimuli was that the animal would come to make a conditioned response (or CR) of salivation to the CS, prior to the delivery of the US that would normally provoke such response. In my laboratory, with rabbits, we frequently used similar CSs, but employed tactile stimulation to the skin near the eye as the US, and recorded eye blinks that developed to the CS as an indication of its acquired association with the US.

An interpretive speculation by Kamin concerning one of his studies had a special impact upon my subsequent theorizing. In his study all animals were trained with a compound of two CSs (call them "A" and "X") followed by a US (i.e., involved the sequence, AX→US), and were subsequently tested for their CRs to one of the two CSs (X) alone. If the animals received no other training, there were substantial CRs to X. The important comparative observation was that if the animals received pre-training with A paired with the US (i.e., A→US) *before* the AX→US training, there were few or no CRs to X alone. Although X was paired with the US exactly the same in the two cases, it appeared that pre-training with A→US prior to the training with AX→US blocked the acquisition of the association between X and the US that would otherwise have occurred. There were a number of familiar interpretations of this effect, but what Kamin proposed was novel: Assume that the A→US pre-training caused the US to be *expected* on the subsequent occasions of AX→US, and that this caused the US to be less effective than it otherwise would be in producing an association with X. Perhaps an effective US must not only be of sufficient intensity or biological strength, but must also be "surprising," to be able to produce associative learning. As it turned out, there was a substantial constellation of additional data reported from my laboratory and that of Robert Rescorla that encouraged us to take this interpretation seriously and to offer a congruent learning rule that came to be called the Rescorla–Wagner rule.

The Rescorla–Wagner rule involved a simple variation on a rule that was implied in various associative accounts. Suppose that the degree of association between some CS and US can be expressed by the value V. It was common to assume that each pairing of CS followed by US would cause a change in this value, ΔV, that is, some fraction, θ, of the difference between the current value of V and the maximum that the US would support, designated λ. That is, it was assumed that: $\Delta V = \theta(\lambda - V)$.

Rescorla and I recognized that the difference term $(\lambda - V)$ in this equation could be described as a measure of the degree to which the US was not fully expected (i.e., V had not attained λ, on the basis of the eliciting CS). The essential modification that we proposed to capture the notion suggested by Kamin is that the associative strength that determines the discrepancy from λ on any training trial is *the total associative strength of all of the CSs present on that trial, ΣV_i*. Thus, for a case with two CS components, A and X, trained in compound, such as that investigated by Kamin, the associative changes to the separate CSs, A and X, would be calculated as follows: $\Delta V_a = \theta(\lambda - \Sigma V_i)$, and $\Delta V_x = \theta(\lambda - \Sigma V_i)$, where $\Sigma V_i = V_a + V_x$. This rule could well account for the aforementioned data of Kamin: When V_a was increased by the A→US pre-training, it is presumed to have increased the ΣV_i and thereby decreased the $(\lambda - \Sigma V_i)$ that determined the subsequent increment in *both* V_x and V_a on AX→US trials.

We proposed that the same rule applies to the consequences of CS-alone trials as to CS–US trials, but with λ being zero when there is no US, to produce a decrement in association. By this reasoning, the greater the total associative strength of all of the CSs on a trial, the less their individual associations with the US will be incremented by CS–US trials, but the greater will the same associations be decremented by CS-alone trials. In practice, the rule made unambiguous predictions about many theoretically telling ways to facilitate or decrease associative learning, many of which would not otherwise have been anticipated.

The success of the Rescorla–Wagner rule encouraged me to offer a more inclusive theoretical formulation, referred to as "Priming Theory," and expressed in the language of information-processing accounts. The basic supposition of Priming Theory is that an "expected" stimulus, as referred to by Kamin, Rescorla, and Wagner, is one that is active in short-term memory (currently being remembered) at the time of its presentation. In this case, it was reasonable to conjecture that a stimulus would be equally rendered less surprising if it were "remembered" not only as a result of associative retrieval from long-term memory, but also as a result of persistence from a recent exposure to the stimulus itself (so-called self-generated priming). One of many implied empirical consequences is that recent exposure to either the CS or the US shortly prior to a CS–US pairing would lead to diminished associative learning from the pairing. This has now been supported by considerable direct evidence, and provides one of the explanations for the well-known fact that spaced training, which widely separates each CS–US experience from the last, produces more effective learning than does more massed training.

The quantitative formalization of Priming Theory required a much more complex characterization than did the Rescorla–Wagner rule, beyond the space allotted for its exposition here. It required detailed descriptions of the stimulus representations that are initiated by CSs and USs and how these change over time to produce learning and performance, either when presented alone or in conjunction with associatively generated or self-generated pre-representations. Because memorial pre-representation is assumed sometimes to support measures of immediate performance (as in eliciting a CR), as well as to oppose new learning, the model was called a Sometimes Opponent Process model (SOP).

In an article reviewing the contributions of the Rescorla–Wagner rule, Sheppard Siegel and Lorraine Allan concluded that its core assumption has come to be included in nearly all treatments of Pavlovian conditioning and, equally important, has inspired many useful theoretical extensions (such as those mentioned here). The authors note the widespread influence of the rule upon numerous fields of investigation beyond animal learning, including studies of human verbal leaning, category learning, causal attribution, inferential reasoning, interpersonal attraction, perceptual aftereffects, and homeostatic regulation. One of the most important influences has been in guiding the search for the physiological basis for associative learning.

Dopamine neurons in several brain structures, as well as the circuit functioning of the deep nuclei of the cerebellum that are implicated in eye blink conditioning, respond to prediction errors $(\lambda - \Sigma V_i)$ as they are treated in the Rescorla–Wagner rule.

Priming Theory and its formalization in SOP were attempts to broaden the scope of the essential reasoning. That attempt continues. For example, a significant void throughout the history of learning theory has been any compelling treatment of the response decrement with repeated exposure to a stimulus known as "habituation." When I studied the then current theories of learning as a graduate student, habituation was generally ignored. Indeed, Gregory Kimble's revision of the authoritative text *Hilgard and Marquis' Conditioning and Learning* denied that the phenomenon qualified as a form of learning. Today there is substantial evidence that one of the contributors to habituation is that the stimulus comes to be expected in the environmental context, à la Priming Theory and SOP. One critical form of evidence is that the effectiveness of the habituated stimulus is recovered, if the context is changed so as to remove its priming function. A current challenge to our understanding is that some studies that have concurrently recorded multiple responses to the same stimulus have found exactly such recovery of some habituated responses but not of others. The explanation may be in some differential associative learning involving different features of the habituating stimulus, related to what Susan Brandon and I proposed in an Affective Extension of SOP (AESOP). Or it may inspire a different theoretical advance.

REFERENCES

Rescorla, R. A., & Wagner, A. R. (1972). A theory of Pavlovian conditioning: Variations in the effectiveness of reinforcement and non-reinforcement. In A. H. Black & W. F. Prokesy (eds.), *Classical Conditioning II: Current research and theory* (pp. 64–99). New York: Appelton-Century Crofts.
Siegel, S., & Allan, L. G. (1996). The widespread influence of the Rescorla–Wagner model. *Psychonomic Bulletin & Review, 3,* 314–321.
Wagner, A. R. (1981). SOP: A model of automatic memory processing in animal behavior. In N. E. Spear & R. R. Miller (eds.), *Information processing in animals: Memory mechanisms* (pp. 5–47). Hillsdale: Ehlbaum.

Section C

Complex Processes

34   A Unified Theory of Mind

Anderson, John R.

I came to graduate school intent on becoming a mathematical psychologist and was going to work with Gordon Bower, one of the authors of a prominent textbook on mathematical psychology. On my first visit to his office he informed me that mathematical psychology was dead (a greatly exaggerated demise) and that I should go into artificial intelligence. The AI courses I took at Stanford presented an inspiring image of AI as pursuing the goal of a unified characterization of intelligence. While much of AI has abandoned this goal of unification, I imprinted on a similar but different goal of trying to achieve a more unified understanding of human cognition. My major accomplishment is what I have been able to contribute to this goal, currently realized in a cognitive architecture called ACT-R.

The first major step in this effort was the development with Gordon Bower of the HAM (Human Associative Memory) theory of human memory. We showed that many of the then fashionable effects in the study of human memory could be simulated by a computer system that just followed the links in memory. It did not take us long after completing the HAM theory, however, to recognize its major shortcoming. Just as Guthrie had criticized Tolman for leaving his rat buried in thought, we left the human buried in its memories with no course of action.

Allen Newell had been working on production systems to provide a principled theory of how human knowledge resulted in action. A production system is composed of many statements similar to: IF one's memory is in state x, THEN do y. Such a system essentially organizes set of cognitive reflexes into coherent cognitive behavior. The first published version of an ACT (Adaptive Control of Thought) theory was essentially a production system that responded to the declarative memories of HAM. Newell's work drew me to Carnegie Mellon, where I have spent over half my adult life. From Newell I learned about his conception of a cognitive architecture and realized that this was what I had been striving for with ACT. Borrowing heavily from the ideas in my environment, I developed a version of the ACT* theory, which I thought was "the final major

163

reformulation within the ACT framework." This was an incorrect projection to match Gordon Bower's from fifteen years earlier.

Believing that there was no more work for me to do on the ACT theory, I decided to apply the theory and to try to break it – that is, to test its limits. The major application of that theory was to the development of intelligent tutoring systems for mathematics. In these systems, ACT models were embedded as components that simulated student thinking and guided computer-based instructional decisions. We called these systems cognitive tutors and they were surprisingly successful. In another effort to break the theory, I pursued what seemed a radical idea – that mechanistic models of human cognition might be unnecessary and that we might understand human cognition as a statistical adaptation to the structure of the environment. I called this approach to understanding human cognition "rational analysis." I was eventually pulled away from my work both on cognitive tutors and on rational analysis. It is interesting to reflect on the fact that both fields have blossomed after my departure.

I was drawn back to work on ACT by two major lessons that I had taken from my work on rational analysis and cognitive tutors. From rational analysis, I came away with the insight that human cognition is not an arbitrary black box that we had to reverse engineer totally from our laboratory studies. Rather, it was constrained by the need to adapt to what the environment presented to it, and we could use this information from the environment to design core pieces of the architecture. The contribution of the rational analysis is reflected in the fundamental principles of ACT-R's (ACT-Rational) declarative and procedural memories.

The second lesson came from getting production-systems models to run in real classrooms: I came to realize a whole new level of standards for what it meant to have a robust running model rather than the kinds of systems I had cobbled together under earlier ACT labels. Thanks to the contributions of my collaborator, Christian Lebiere, we achieved a robust, general-purpose system.

Reflecting the newly achieved robustness, the first ACT-R system was described in a 1993 book that included a computer disk of the ACT-R system. That disk allowed others to run that system on any computer and develop models of phenomena that they were interested in. This led to the development of a user community. Nowadays the current system, manuals, and tutorials are constantly updated and available by downloading at the ACT-R web site (http://act-r.psy.cmu.edu/). Upon reflection, it became apparent that one cannot begin to achieve unification by a theory that is one's private domain. It has to be available for use by anyone who wants to apply it to a relevant task. Many members of the community have made fundamental contributions to the basic ACT-R architecture.

Since our early efforts to develop a robust cognitive architecture we have made major progress on three fronts. Human cognition involves more than the declarative and procedural systems, and thus modules were added to ACT-R to simulate critical aspects of the perceptual and motor systems. This allowed us to provide detailed accounts of what was occupying time as a person performed complex tasks. Our ACT-R models can now interact with the software that runs our experimental tasks. It can also interact in a human way with other pieces of software such as video games.

Second, because these new modules provided an end-to-end analysis of human performance, we were able precisely to model the fMRI neural data that was becoming so readily available. The brain has to do all of the perceptual and motor components of a task as well as the more central components. Modern ACT-R models make predictions (not just post-dictions, i.e., model fitting) for the patterns of activity that come from fMRI and ERP studies. This provides much denser data than just behavioral measures, sometimes confirming the architecture and sometimes pointing us in directions for improvement of it.

Third, we have made major progress toward eliminating the modeler from the design of ACT-R models. There are now many models that are capable of learning from instructions, examples, or discovery and transferring this knowledge. Improving these learning capabilities is one of the major dimensions of research within the ACT-R community.

Allen Newell, knowing that he had only about one year left to live, gave an inspiring talk about how cognitive architectures provide the answer to the question of how the human mind can occur in the physical universe. He said that that this was a question of such a depth that it would hold you for your entire life and you would be a "just a little ways into it." This is certainly true of my work on ACT-R, where much more needs to be done. While I am not looking at any such firm deadline as Newell, I can ask what it is that ACT-R has become at this point in time. Through the work of many in the ACT-R community, ACT-R has come to provide us with two things: First, it is a running hypothesis of how, in the words of Newell, "the gears clank and the pistons go" in a way that human cognition can emerge. Second, it is a theoretical tool that researchers can use to explore their interests in human cognition.

REFERENCES

Anderson, J. R. (1983). *The architecture of cognition.* Cambridge, MA: Harvard University Press.

Anderson, J. R. (1993). *Rules of the mind.* Hillsdale: Erlbaum.

Anderson, J. R. (2007). *How can the human mind occur in the physical universe?* New York: Oxford University Press.

35 Multiple Intelligences: Prelude, Theory, and Aftermath

Gardner, Howard

Beyond question, the contribution to psychology for which I am best known is the theory of multiple intelligences. Before turning to that theory, it's important for me to describe my own background and the ways in which I think about the scholarly work that I carry out.

Before going to graduate school in developmental psychology, I had never taken a conventional psychology course. My background was in the broader social sciences, with an emphasis on interpretive social science rather than on experiments or quantitative work. When I began to study developmental psychology, I became fascinated by the work of the great Swiss psychologist Jean Piaget. Piaget considered scientific thinking as the high point of cognitive development. That's one plausible "end state." But, as a trained musician and a lover of the arts, I wondered how one would construe human development – including cognitive development – if one were to think of "artistic thinking" as the apogee of human cognition.

As a budding scholar interested in the arts – an interest shared at the time by few psychologists – I was uncertain about my next career step. Uncertainty gave way to an unexpected career move when I encountered the literature on damage to the human brain. Without minimizing the tragedy of stroke, trauma, or tumor, any brain damage constitutes an "experiment in nature." One identifies the type and site of the lesion and ascertains how that lesion affects human cognition. As just one example, damage to the language areas spares the capacity to sing, while damage to the musical areas leaves linguistic capacities unaffected.

I had found a way to study human cognition in the arts. And indeed, for the next twenty years I divided my research time between the Boston Veterans Administration Medical Center, where I studied the effects on artistry of various kinds of brain damage, and Harvard Project Zero, a research center of which I was a founding member, where I studied the development in children of artistic capacities.

In studying the effects of brain damage, I made what I consider to be my most important discovery in scientific psychology. The classical teaching is that, in right-handed persons, language is housed in the left hemisphere; brain damage there produces aphasia (language disability). Neurologists had occasionally observed that, in right-handed persons, damage to the right side of the brain produces an odd set of symptoms. In particular, such patients exhibit a strange sense of humor, sometimes called "Witzel-sucht." With a number of colleagues, most notably Ellen Winner and Hiram Brownell, I began to study the language capacities and deficiencies of individuals with unilateral damage to the brain. While replicating the onset of aphasia after damage to the left hemisphere, my colleagues and I made an unexpected discovery. Patients with right-hemisphere damage understood language literally but *only literally*. When we probed their capacities to understand figurative language – metaphor, irony, proverbs, non-literal speech acts – these patients proved deficient. Indeed, despite their problems with ordinary language, patients with left-hemisphere damage sometimes outperformed those with right-hemisphere damage on tasks that probed their understanding of non-literal speech acts. These findings were reported in numerous scientific papers in the 1970s and 1980s, including one entitled "On going beyond the literal."

If I had continued in this vein, I would likely have become best known for this work and would have advanced our conceptions about human linguistic capacities. But it had become clear to me that many psychologists could perform experiments as well or better than I could (and they proceeded to do so with respect to the various linguistic capacities in the brain!); I had a talent for carrying out syntheses and writing about them. And so, unlike most of my fellow psychologists, I turned my energies to making sense of research carried out by scholars and to writing books about my conclusions.

Enter the theory of multiple intelligences. In the late 1970s, colleagues and I at the Harvard Graduate School of Education received a large grant. My assignment on the "human potential project" was to synthesize what is known about the nature and organization of human cognitive capacities. I used this once-in-a-lifetime opportunity to review a vast literature from psychology, anthropology, brain studies, education, and other fields – and to organize these findings in a simple yet powerful way.

As early as the mid-1970s, I had already sketched out a book called *Kinds of Minds*, in which I proposed to chronicle my studies in developmental psychology and neuropsychology. Receipt of the grant allowed me to go well beyond my own observations and experiments.

What was distinctive about this effort? Many writers – both scholarly and lay – had written about the diversity of human talents. My work stood out in four ways:

1. With help from a team of researchers, I reviewed and organized all the literature pertinent to my assignment.
2. I termed the resulting categories "intelligences" rather than talents. In so doing I challenged those psychologists who believed that they owned the word "intelligence" and had a monopoly on its definition and measurement. If I had written about human talents, rather than intelligences, I probably would not have been asked to contribute to this volume.
3. I proposed a definition of an intelligence – the biopsychological potential to process information in certain ways in order to solve problems or create products that are valued in at least one culture.
4. I proposed eight criteria for what counts as an intelligence (the criteria arising from a range of disciplines and sources of data) and discussed candidate intelligences in terms of the extent to which they met these criteria. In so doing, I made it possible for others to evaluate my initial list of seven intelligences and also to determine whether other "candidate intelligences" met these criteria.

I began to write about these ideas in the early 1980s, and in 1983 I published my most well-known book, *Frames of Mind: The Theory of Multiple Intelligences*. With its publication, I received the proverbial "15 minutes of fame." Nothing I've done before or since has achieved the same amount of attention. Whether or not I consider this to be my signal achievement, it appears that the world does!

A word about life after that quarter hour in the limelight. I had expected the work to be discussed chiefly by psychologists. But, in truth, most psychologists, and particularly most psychometricians, have never warmed to the theory. I think that psychologists are wedded to the creation and administration of short-answer tests, and particularly ones that resemble the IQ test. While such tests can probe linguistic and logical capacities, as well as certain spatial abilities, they are deficient in assessing other abilities, such as interpersonal intelligence (social intelligence), intrapersonal intelligence (akin to emotional intelligence), and other non-academic intelligences. I have not devoted significant effort to creating such tests.

Nor, indeed, have I carried out experiments designed to test the theory. This has led some critics to declare that my theory is not empirical. That charge is baloney! The theory is not experimental in the traditional sense (as was my earlier work with brain-damaged patients); but it is strictly empirical, drawing on hundreds of findings from half-a-dozen fields of science. (Please see the reference notes to *Frames of Mind* and succeeding works).

At the same time, I readily admit that the theory is no longer current. Several fields of knowledge have advanced significantly since the early

1980s. Any reinvigoration of the theory would require a survey similar to the one that colleagues and I carried out thirty-five years ago. Whether or not I ever carry out such an update, I encourage others to do so.

And that is because I am no longer wedded to the particular list of intelligences that I initially developed. What I – and others, most notably Daniel Goleman and Robert Sternberg – have done is to undermine the hegemony over the concept of *intelligence* that was maintained for a century by adherents to a Spearman–Binet–Piaget concept of intelligence. I have no idea where the study of intelligence(s) will be a century from now, but I am confident that the field will recognize a plurality of skills, talents, and intelligences.

In their introductory textbook, Richard Herrnstein and Roger Brown identify the two "great successes" of psychology in the twentieth century: the identification and measurement of intelligence, and the understanding of human motivation which enables advertising, marketing, and behavioral control. In the twenty-first century, I hope that psychology will direct its energies to the improvement of human life. In a globalized civilization, where human wit and grit are pivotal, how we conceptualize, measure, and nurture human intellect is crucial. I hope to have developed a more capacious conception of mind and to have encouraged the use of intelligences for constructive ends.

REFERENCES

Gardner, H. (1994). The stories of the right hemisphere. In W. D. Spaulding (ed.), *Integrative views of motivation, cognition, and emotion. The Nebraska Symposium on Motivation.* Lincoln, Nebraska: University of Nebraska Press.

Gardner, H. (1983/2011). *Frames of mind: The theory of multiple intelligences.* New York: Basic Books.

Gardner, H., Csikszentmihalyi, M., & Damon, W. (2001). *Good work: When excellence and ethics meet.* New York: Basic Books.

36   Heuristics and Biases

Kahneman, Daniel

My life changed when I invited my brilliant colleague Amos Tversky to give a guest lecture. Amos told my graduate seminar at the Hebrew University of Jerusalem about recent research at the University of Michigan, which had concluded that people are good intuitive statisticians. I thought that claim was completely wrong (Israelis tend not to mince words), and we had an intense and enjoyable conversation. Over the next few days we sketched an idea – perhaps the most productive either of us ever had – and decided to collaborate in the study of intuitive statistical thinking.

Our goal was to understand how people answer questions such as "what GPA will this student achieve?" or "what proportion of professors at our university have been divorced at least once?" We knew that people come up quickly with intuitive answers to such questions, without consulting statistical principles. How do they do it, and why are these intuitions so often wrong? In 1969 these were new questions. We reported our main conclusions five years later: "people rely on a limited number of heuristic principles which reduce the complex tasks of assessing probabilities and predicting values to simpler judgmental operations. In general, these heuristics are quite useful, but sometimes they lead to severe and systematic errors" (Tversky and Kahneman, 1974). We borrowed the term "heuristic" from the literature on problem solving, where it refers to computational short-cuts that are quick and efficient, but not guaranteed to produce the correct answer.

For an example of how intuitive statistical thinking can be analyzed, consider this question:

Julie is a graduating senior at a University. All I will tell you about her is that she read fluently at age 4. What is her GPA?

I expect that a number quickly came to your mind, probably not very far from 3.7. You were probably not aware of how the number came up, but there it was. The research program that Amos and I started has established that you – your mind, your memory – carried out several operations to produce your intuitive estimate.

(1) The evidence "read fluently at age 4" was assessed for precocity, yielding something like a percentile. This percentile was high – say, 95.
(2) The GPA that corresponds to the 95th percentile was identified.
(3) The resulting number (say, 3.7) was the one that came to your mind when the question was asked.

Note that you were only aware of your intuitive guess, not of steps 1 and 2. This is characteristic of much intuitive thinking: you do not know how you got there. The heuristic answered a difficult question ("how extreme is Julie's GPA?") by substituting the answer to an easier one ("how precocious was her reading?"). The answer was wrong, because it selected a GPA that is just as impressive as Julie's reading prowess – a violation of the statistical principle that a prediction should be more moderate than the evidence on which it is based. An unbiased prediction would be much closer to the average GPA.

The answer to the Julie question illustrates the *representativeness heuristic*, in which the judgment is based on an assessment of matching or similarity. Other examples follow:

- Most people believe that the sequences of coin tosses H-H-H-T-T-T is much less likely than H-T-T-H-T-H, because the former does not fit our image of a random outcome and the latter does. The two sequences actually occur equally often.
- A man described as "an introvert with a passion for detail" is judged much more likely to be a librarian than a farmer, because the description fits a stereotypical librarian. This judgment ignores the relevant fact that there are twenty male farmers for every male librarian.
- "A person who hunts for a hobby" is judged more likely to be a Republican than a Democrat.

As the last example illustrates, the representativeness heuristic often yields true judgments. Our research, however, focused on cases in which the heuristic produces predictable errors, called *judgmental biases*.

A heuristic called *availability* often determines judgments of the frequency of categories, such as road accidents, hurricanes, or musical prodigies: judged frequency is matched to the ease with which instances of the category come to mind. The availability heuristic often yields good approximations, because frequent repetition facilitates retrieval. However, the availability of instances is also affected by other factors. For example, the sight of a burning car on the road causes a temporary increase in estimates of the risk of driving – a predictable bias. Research by Lichtenstein, Slovic, and Fischhoff demonstrated related biases in assessments of causes of death: most people greatly exaggerate the pre-valence of shark attacks and erroneously believe that homicides are more frequent than suicides. Shark attacks and murders are salient events that come more readily to mind than less dramatic causes of death.

Amos and I spent several years exploring the representativeness and availability heuristics. We also studied biases called *anchoring effects*. For example, imagine you see a wheel of chance stop at 95. After answering the simple question "Was Mahatma Gandhi's age at death more or less than 95?" you are asked for your best guess about Gandhi's age at death. Now ask yourself: would your estimate have been as high if the wheel had stopped at 31? Our experiments showed that estimates are anchored on any number that is considered as a solution, even when the anchor is obviously uninformative. This robust bias is exploited by negotiators, prosecutors and defense attor-neys, and fund-raisers for charities.

The summary report we published in 1974 described a baker's dozen of judgment biases and traced them to representativeness, availability, and anchoring. The title of our article was "Judgment under Uncertainty: Heuristics and Biases," and the label of "Heuristics and Biases" has stuck to our approach ever since. The findings we described held up and the article is still current, but some weaknesses are now apparent:

- **The term "heuristic" was misleading.** The word is commonly applied to approximations and short-cuts that people choose to use in solving problems. Applying it to intuitive thinking masked an important difference between problem-solving and intuitive judgment: Reasoning is controlled, but intuitive judgment is automatic (2+2), like the num-ber that just came to your mind. In terms that are frequently used today, your estimate of Julie's GPA was generated automatically by an intui-tive "System 1," and your deliberate System 2 probably endorsed it. Readers who are sophisticated in statistics are assumed to have the same intuition, but are able to override it and search for another solution. Amos and I did not appreciate the importance of the distinction between controlled and automatic thinking, which only became central to cognitive psychology a few years later.
- **The inclusion of anchoring as a heuristic was confusing.** Our research began with a study of representativeness and availability, both of which involve substitution of one assessment for another and both of which produce biases. We studied anchoring biases only later. Because we were determined to present our main results together in our 1974 article, Amos and I offered a definition of heuristics that was sufficiently vague to include anchoring and did not explicitly mention substitution. The only feature shared by our "heuristics" was that all

three produce predictable biases. Almost thirty years later, Shane Frederick and I proposed a modified view, in which substitution is the common mechanism of heuristic thinking and anchoring is a separate process.

- **The substitution mechanism is not restricted to uncertainty.** If asked "How happy are you these days?" many people will answer an easier question: "How good is your mood right now?" If asked "How much will you contribute to preserving dolphins?" many people will answer as if they had been asked "How much emotion do you feel about dying dolphins?" There is not a finite number of heuristics.
- **We missed a third crucial heuristic.** Representativeness and availability have special status as highly versatile heuristics, which suggest intuitive answers to many questions. A third general-purpose heuristic was introduced by Paul Slovic. This is the *affect heuristic*, in which judgments are made by matching the intensity of an emotion. Thus, the question "how large are the potential benefits of the fracking technology?" is answered by substituting "how do I feel about fracking?" and the question "how much travel insurance will you buy for this trip?" evokes "how afraid are you of dying on this trip?"

Our 1974 article carried two messages about intuitive judgment: it is mediated by heuristics, and it is riddled with biases. Both messages were quite influential – especially the latter. The discovery of predictable errors was seen as challenging the prevalent assumption that human thinking is basically rational and that errors are random, and the notion of bias was central to the thinking that eventually produced behavioral economics. It was fortunate that we did not anticipate this outcome. The quality of our work would have suffered if we had lost our narrow focus on the topic of judgment under uncertainty. Questions about the broad significance of your work are important, but are best left to the readers.

REFERENCES

Kahneman, D. (2011). *Thinking, fast and slow*. New York: Farrar, Straus Giroux.
Tversky, A., & Kahneman, D. (1974). Judgment under uncertainty: Heuristics and biases. *Science, 185*, 1124–1131.

37 Comprehension

Kintsch, Walter

My first publication appeared in 1956 when I still was a graduate student, while my most recent one came last year (2014), a decade after I retired from my position as a psychology professor and director of an Institute of Cognitive Science. That is a long time, and psychology has changed a great deal during that period, and so has my work. Nevertheless, much of my career has focused on the same problem: to study how people read and comprehend texts, both in the psychological laboratory and in educational settings. Today, the study of text and discourse comprehension, text memory, and learning from text is a flourishing branch of experimental psychology and cognitive science, and I had a small part in making this happen.

I came to text and discourse from the study of memory. Memory research was one of the big achievements of the new cognitive psychology. Indeed, it is not too much to say that the modern conception of memory was formulated in the 1960s. Of course, there has been significant progress since then, but the basic framework for our understanding of memory was worked out at that time. This achievement was made possible because the new research on memory adopted a principle that goes back to the earliest days of experimental psychology. Namely, the laboratory studies of memory avoided dealing with meaningful material, by adopting nonsense syllables in the tradition of Ebbinghaus, or by working with word lists. This was a brilliant move in that, by disregarding the complexities of meaning, much could be learned about basic memory processes. It was, however, no easy task to eliminate meaning. The subjects in our experiments found ways to introduce meaning even into lists of nonsense syllables, and meaning was always a major factor in how subjects remembered word lists. In trying to understand memory, we had to deal with meaning, whether we wanted to or not. Once I realized that, I decided to leave nonsense syllables and word lists to others and focus on meaning directly – that is, on how we understand and remember texts.

The Representation of Meaning in Memory

At some point, memory research comes down to this: you give your subjects a set of items – nonsense syllables, words, even sentences – to study and then count how many they have remembered. But if a text is to be remembered, what do you count? Obviously, the exact number of words reproduced from the text won't do. Researchers have used the number of idea units reproduced from the text, but what should count as an idea unit?

The first problem in the study of text memory was, therefore, to define a unit of meaning that could be used in laboratory experiments with texts. I looked to linguistics for help. Much of linguistics, and psycholinguistics, sidestepped the problem of meaning as much as psychologists did, but several suggestions by linguists could be adapted for our purposes. What I proposed was to represent the meaning of a text as a network of propositions. The term proposition is borrowed from logic but is used here in a different sense. For instance, the sentence *Mary watched an old movie* consists of two propositions *Mary watched a movie* and *old movie*, which are connected by the common term *movie*. Our research showed that comprehension difficulty depends on the number of propositions in a text and how many new terms are introduced per proposition. It also depends upon the coherence of a text: coherent texts are connected by common terms. If common terms are missing, inferences are required to bridge that gap. These can be trivial (as in *It rained. The streets were wet*), but often demand considerable mental effort.

The Process of Text Comprehension

How do readers construct these propositional representations? I investigated this question in collaboration with the Dutch linguist Teun van Dijk.

Texts are processed sentence by sentence or phrase by phrase, not all at once. Thus, to ensure a coherent representation, working memory must retain traces from the already processed text to connect with the current processing cycle. Furthermore, comprehension requires that readers not only understand the details of a text, but also its gist, especially in the case of longer texts. Some texts are well structured, so it is easy to determine their gist (often the first sentence of a paragraph states the main idea), but that is not always the case (e.g., a story may be about betrayal, but that is never spelled out).

Much of the time when we are reading, our goal is to acquire information about something. We use the text to construct a mental model about some phenomenon or event of interest, or to update an already existing model. If I read a chapter in a biology textbook, I am not so much interested in remembering the text itself, but what it teaches me about biology. If I read a description of a hiking route in the mountains, my goal is to construct a useful mental map of that route, not to remember the actual words and sentences. As psychologists, we often are not concerned with the text itself, but with what the text is about. Thus, we consider comprehension to be successful when a reader has constructed a situation model that becomes a more or less permanent part of his or her knowledge. This mental representation constructed from reading a text may take many forms other than a propositional network (e.g., the gist of a story), such as a visual image, an abstraction, a melodic theme, gestures and movement, and so on.

The Construction-Integration Model

How are the mental representations of a text, particularly the situation model, created during comprehension? The construction-integration (CI) model of comprehension, which I proposed in 1988, addresses this problem, as illustrated by the following example. One of the problems readers face is to find the right meaning of the words they are reading. Consider the word *bank* in the following two sentences: *Peter went to his bank to get some money for his trip* and *Peter camped on the bank of a rushing river that evening.* Readers effortlessly identify *bank* with one thing in the first sentence and another in the second. The CI-model proposes that all word senses as well as other associated knowledge become briefly activated when a word is encountered. That is, in the *construction* phase of the comprehension process, each word in the sentence activates all the knowledge it is associated with, resulting in a network of associations that are inconsistent and contradictory with each other. There is, however, a natural way to clean up this mess. The network quickly settles into a consistent, sensible structure if contextually related pieces are allowed to strengthen each other and inconsistent pieces are inhibited in the *integration* phase of comprehension.

Understanding a text is thus a constraint-satisfaction process, resembling perception: we make sense of a scene by focusing on related structural elements that fit together, and we neglect isolated details. Similarly, as we read a text, the unrelated pieces of knowledge that had been triggered (e.g., about *money bank*) become deactivated, while what fits into the common context (e.g., about a *river bank*) is retained.

Knowledge Structures

Understanding a text also involves the integration of new information from a text with what the reader already knows. Here the question is how to model the reader's knowledge. As a shortcut, one can hand-code portions of the reader's knowledge, but more objective, automatic procedures are needed. Recent advances in machine learning techniques are making it possible to model human knowledge without recourse to hand coding. An early version of such a computational technique is Latent Semantic Analysis (LSA), which was developed by my colleague Tom Landauer and his collaborators. LSA analyzes the meaning of a text by constructing a map of the word meanings it contains. It is a complicated map because the relations among words are quite intricate. Consider, for instance, that *bank* is closely related to both *river* and *money*, but the meanings of *river* and *money* are far apart. A large number of dimensions are needed to map such complexities.

The Future

I have focused my research on reading comprehension. Of course, comprehension is involved not only in reading and is not restricted to language. But I believe that the principal features of comprehension as they have been studied in the reading context apply to other types as well. In particular, the bottom-up, constraint-satisfaction process described by the CI-model may characterize human comprehension processes in general.

So what has been my contribution to our science? I would say we made a good beginning. Five decades of work have served to refine our questions, to identify some fundamental features of comprehension processes, and to develop some tentative models. I trust this work will help future researchers formulate a definitive theory of human comprehension.

REFERENCES

Kintsch, W. (1974/2014). *The representation of meaning in memory*. Hillsdale: Erlbaum. Psychology Library Editions, Routledge.
Kintsch, W. (1988). The role of knowledge in discourse comprehension: A construction-integration model. *Psychological Review, 95*,163–182.
Kintsch, W. (1998). *Comprehension: A paradigm for cognition*. New York: Cambridge University Press.

38 The Perception of Risk

Slovic, Paul

I believe that my most important scientific contribution has been to participate in a decades-long collaboration with many fine colleagues in a program of research exploring the perception of risk. I shall briefly review the path this research has taken, its main contributions, and its importance to science and society.

The origins of this research can be traced to 1959, my first year as a graduate student in psychology at the University of Michigan. I was assigned to work for Professor Clyde Coombs and became fascinated by a study Coombs was doing in which he examined people's preferences among gambles. I replicated and extended this study for my first-year project. The following year I began to work with Ward Edwards, who was also studying risk-taking and decision-making. In Edwards' laboratory I met Sarah Lichtenstein. After graduate school, Lichtenstein and I went our separate ways, but we were reunited in Eugene, Oregon, in 1966, and worked together for more than forty years.

In 1970, I was introduced to Gilbert White, a famed geographer and pioneer researcher in risk perception, who asked if the laboratory studies on decision-making that Lichtenstein and I had been doing could provide insight into some of the puzzling behaviors he had observed in studying human responses to natural hazards. Much to our embarrassment, we realized that our studies had been too narrowly focused on choices among simple gambles to tell us much about risk-taking behavior in the flood plain or on the earthquake fault.

White's questions were intriguing, however, and, with economist Howard Kunreuther, we turned our attention to natural hazards, attempting to relate behavior in the face of such hazards to principles that had been emerging from psychological studies of probabilistic judgments and risky choices. We found the work that Amos Tversky and Danny Kahneman had been doing on heuristics and biases in probabilistic thinking to be particularly valuable in explaining people's failures to take adequate precautions against the threats posed by natural hazards.

The mid-1970s was a time when concerns about pesticides and nuclear power were rapidly increasing, and we soon found our attention drawn to technological hazards. With Baruch Fischhoff, Sarah and I began a research program designed to study what we referred to as "cognitive processes and societal risk-taking." We conducted surveys in which we asked people to judge the risks and benefits from a wide range of activities, technologies, and natural hazards.

Borrowing from personality theory, we also asked people to characterize the "personalities" of these hazards by rating them on various qualities or characteristics (e.g., voluntariness, catastrophic potential, controllability, dread) that had been hypothesized to influence risk perception and acceptance.

Another distinguishing feature of our studies was the use of a variety of psychometric scaling methods to produce *quantitative* measures of perceived risk, perceived benefit, and other aspects of perceptions (e.g., estimated fatalities resulting from an activity). This general approach to studying perceived risk became known as the *psychometric paradigm*.

We found that perceived risks and acceptable levels of risks were systematic and predictable. Psychometric techniques seemed well suited for identifying similarities and differences among groups with regard to risk perceptions and attitudes. Our results also showed that the concept of "risk" meant different things to different people. When experts judged risk, their responses correlated highly with technical estimates of annual fatalities. Laypeople's judgments of "risk" were sensitive to other factors (e.g., catastrophic potential, controllability, threat to future generations) and, as a result, often differed considerably from experts' judgments.

We argued that the differences we observed between expert and lay judgment of risk were not due to public ignorance and irrationality. Rather, there appeared to be legitimate, value-laden issues underlying the multiple dimensions of public risk perceptions, and these values need to be considered in risk-policy decisions. For example, is risk from cancer (a dreaded disease) worse than risk from automobile accidents (not dreaded)? Is a risk imposed on a child more serious than a known risk accepted voluntarily by an adult? Are the deaths of fifty passengers in separate automobile accidents equivalent to the deaths of fifty passengers in one airplane crash? Is the risk from a polluted Superfund site worse if the site is located in a neighborhood that has a number of other hazardous facilities nearby?

One direction taken by early work within the psychometric paradigm was to examine the role of perceptions in determining the degree of impact resulting from an "unfortunate event" (e.g., an accident, a natural disaster, a discovery of pollution). Early theories equated the magnitude of impact to the number of people killed or injured, or to the amount of property damaged. However, our studies showed that there were other impacts as well, analogous to the ripples from a stone dropped into a pond. These higher-order impacts could be enormous and were found to depend upon risk perceptions stimulated by extensive media coverage.

With geographer Roger Kasperson and his colleagues, we developed a conceptual framework known as "the social amplification of risk" to describe how psychological, social, cultural, and political factors interact to amplify risk and produce ripple effects. An important element of this framework is the assumption that the perceived seriousness of an accident or other unfortunate event, the media coverage it gets, and the long-range costs and other higher-order impacts on the responsible company, industry, or agency are determined, in part, by what that event signals or portends. *Signal value* reflects the perception that the event provides new information about the likelihood of similar or more destructive future mishaps. A terrorist attack, for example, likely carries greater signal value than a routine accident that produces the same immediate damage, and such an attack would likely result in ripple effects far more costly than those the accident produces.

Two important findings from the earliest psychometric studies were not adequately appreciated and lay dormant for two decades, until additional findings led them to be recognized as key links in a theory about the role of affective processes in judgment, decision-making, and risk perception. We had observed that, although risks and benefits are positively correlated in the world (e.g., highly beneficial activities such as surgery often carry high risks), the judged risks and benefits of those activities tend to be strongly negatively correlated. We had also found that the characteristic most highly correlated with perceived risk was the degree to which a hazard evoked feelings of dread. We eventually learned that the inverse risk/benefit relationship occurred because people derive these judgments by consulting their feelings. For example, technologies we like (e.g., X-rays and medicines) are judged high in benefit and low in risk. Technologies that carry negative feelings (e.g., nuclear power and pesticides) are judged low in benefit and high in risk. Reliance on feelings as a guide to risk perception and, more generally, all manner of judgments and decisions was named "the affect heuristic."

This fast, intuitive, feeling-based mode of thinking is really quite sophisticated and rational, much like our visual system. But just as the visual system can be deceived by certain stimuli that create visual illusions, the feeling system also may play tricks on us, some of which may be costly or even deadly. For example, a rare event will seem much more likely when we are told it will occur to 1 out of 100 of people like us than when we are told we have a 1 percent chance of experiencing it. The "1 percent" likely makes us think of a small number. The frequency description creates images of "the one" with corresponding positive or negative feelings that amplify the feeling of benefit or risk. Another foible is that envisioning a scary consequence may feel as frightening when its probability is low as when it is high, leading to what some have called "probability neglect."

Dramatic consequences resulting from the affect heuristic are demonstrated by the way we value lives. We will spare no effort to protect or rescue one identified individual (the "singularity effect"), but that same life loses its value when others are also at risk. We will feel little different learning that eighty-eight persons are in danger rather than eighty-seven. The feeling system loses sensitivity and responsiveness when the scale of a problem increases, a phenomenon known as "psychic numbing." This insensitivity contributes significantly to societal under-reaction to mass threats from problems such as poverty, famine, disease, and genocide that are communicated to us through statistics. We need faces, and stories, and careful deliberation, to comprehend the realities underlying these statistics of scale and to build procedures, laws, and institutions that can counter the destructive anesthetizing illusions brought about by psychic numbing.

REFERENCES

Slovic, P. (ed.) (2000). *The perception of risk*. London: Earthscan.

Slovic, P. (ed.) (2010). *The feeling of risk: New perspectives on risk perception*. London: Earthscan.

Slovic, P., Zionts, D., Woods, A. K., Goodman, R., & Jinks, D. (2013). Psychic numbing and mass atrocity. In E. Shafir (ed.), *The behavioral foundations of public policy* (pp. 126–142). New Jersey: Princeton University Press.

39   What Does It Mean to Be Intelligent?

Sternberg, Robert J.

When I was a young child in early elementary school, I performed poorly on IQ tests, so my teachers and I had low expectations for me. In particular, my teachers thought I was stupid, and so I thought I was stupid; my teachers were happy that I acted stupid, and I was happy that they were happy. So everyone was pretty happy. It was not until I was in fourth grade, when I had Mrs. Alexa as a teacher, that I realized that I could do better and became an "A" student.

Things just chugged merrily along until I took introductory psychology as a freshman at Yale. I was determined to major in psychology because I wanted to understand why I had seemed so stupid as a child. But that was all in the past – or so I thought. The first test we took, I received a score of three out of ten. My professor, handing me my test paper, commented that there was a famous Sternberg (Saul) in psychology, and it looked like there wouldn't be another one. I ended up with a "C" in the course, which the professor referred to as a "gift." Seven years later, that same professor was chair of the search committee that hired me back to Yale as an assistant professor of psychology. How times change!

Experiences such as these led me to believe – or at least to hope – that there is something more to intelligence than IQ (my fourth-grade experience) and being able to memorize books (my freshman-year experience). By my last year as a graduate student in psychology at Stanford, I was convinced that the "something more" was an understanding of the mental processes (or, as I called them, components) underlying intelligence. So I started a research program looking at the mental processes used to solve IQ-test-like problems, such as analogies and series completions. The idea was that I would be able to detect, for example, if someone was solving a verbal analogy incorrectly because she did not reason well or, instead, simply did not know the meanings of the words constituting the analogy.

Eventually, though, I realized that my "componential" theory of intelligence was incomplete. It specified processes, sure enough, but only those involved in solving IQ-test-like problems. As director of graduate

183

studies in psychology at Yale, I was encountering students who were intelligent in ways differing from anything that intelligence tests measure. One student, whom I came to call Barbara, had many creative ideas but was not especially strong analytically. Another student, Celia, had unusual common sense and practical judgment but was neither particularly creative nor particularly analytical. And a third student, Alice, was strong analytically – and aced standardized tests – but seemed to have trouble coming up with her own original ideas. Eventually, my experiences with these students and others led me to the development of what I came to call a "triarchic theory of intelligence," which specified that intelligence has three interrelated aspects – creative intelligence to generate novel and powerful ideas; analytical intelligence to ascertain whether they are good ideas; and practical intelligence to apply the ideas in everyday life and to persuade others of the value of those ideas.

But after a while I came to realize that this theory, too, was incomplete, because intelligence did not seem to be merely some kind of linear combination of levels of analytical, creative, and practical intelligence. Rather, intelligence seemed to comprise the ability to succeed in life, according to one's own conception of success, within one's sociocultural context. And to succeed, people needed to recognize and capitalize on their strengths while at the same time compensating for or correcting their weaknesses. The new theory of successful intelligence, therefore, stressed the importance of understanding oneself and how to leverage one's abilities. In fact, our research showed that people often used strategies in solving problems that were suboptimal, given their patterns of abilities.

I thought I had reached the end of the line for my thinking about intelligence, but then I realized that there still was something missing from the theory. People, I discovered, could be intelligent but foolish. Some very smart people were unrealistically optimistic and egocentric (in always putting themselves first), and falsely believed themselves to be omniscient, omnipotent, and invulnerable. Often they became ethically disengaged (in believing that ethics were important for other people but not for them). So I added a fourth aspect to the theory of successful intelligence: wisdom, or the use of one's abilities and knowledge toward a common good, by balancing one's own with others' and higher interests, over the long and short terms, through the infusion of positive ethical values.

In addition to abilities, creativity and wisdom involve aspects of personality, attitudes, motivation, thinking styles, and environment. For example, creativity involves an attitude toward life – the realization that to be creative, one must be willing to defy the crowd, or, metaphorically, to buy low and sell high in the world of ideas. Creative people, like good investors, are willing to try out ideas that others shun or even fear, and they have the courage to take risks of failure that many people simply are not willing to take.

My research group at Yale and I spent some years doing research showing that it was possible statistically to separate out creative and practical intelligence, both from each other and from the more conventional (IQ-test-like) analytical intelligence. Moreover, measures of creative and practical intelligence enhanced prediction of various kinds of success, including academic and non-academic success in college, while at the same time reducing differences in performance among members of different ethnic groups.

Our assessment studies showed that it is possible to improve prediction not only of college performance, but also of job performance, using measures of creative and practical intelligence as well as of wise thinking. But is it possible also to teach students in a way that better fits with their patterns of strengths and weaknesses?

In a series of studies, we developed curricula for a variety of school subjects based on the notion that all subjects could be taught in ways that would promote analytical, creative, and practical thinking. The idea would be for students to learn in ways that enabled them both to capitalize on strengths and to correct or compensate for weaknesses. We found that students who were taught in ways that enabled them to leverage their strengths outperformed students taught in traditional, memory-oriented ways, even if the assessments used mostly emphasized memory. However, we found that upscaling our teaching methods to large numbers of teachers and schools was challenging, in part because teachers are so used to teaching in conventional ways, not just in the United States, but also abroad.

In research on five continents, my colleagues and I found that what constitutes "adaptive" behavior varies widely across cultures. Our notions of intelligence are often culture-bound. For example, in many parts of the world, practical intelligence in treating parasitic illnesses with natural herbal medications is much more important than advanced academic skills or knowledge for which there may be little use.

One would like to believe that a career is linear in direction and straightforward in its execution, but it never is. Mine certainly has not been.

First, with any degree of prominence, one acquires enemies. I certainly have acquired some. Indeed, my first book, based on my dissertation, received a scathing seventeen-page single-spaced review from someone with a competitive theory; it was published anyway and later became a citation classic. Other scholars have written caustic reviews of my work post-publication. Of course, people often have legitimate scientific disagreements, but I have been disappointed by the speed with which these disagreements can become personal. I have tried my best to avoid personalization and have even remained friends with some of my detractors.

Second, I have been less successful than I had hoped in the translation of my work into practice. As a university dean and then a provost, colleagues and I implemented some of my ideas about admissions, instruction, and assessment, but with the pressure of narrow state and federal measures of accountability (especially through the No Child Left Behind Act) and with the power of often very conservative testing organizations, new ideas about teaching and assessment (including my own) often have had trouble being adopted by schools. Clearly, I never figured out how to achieve successfully the impact I had hoped for.

Finally, I always have hoped that my work would live well beyond me. And there is a chance that parts of it may. At the same time, I recognize that life comprises more than just one's work. As a result, I feel fortunate to have a wonderful wife and five children. For me, long-term impact is not just through my work, but also through my children, and their children down the line.

REFERENCES

Sternberg, R. J. (1977). *Intelligence, information processing, and analogical reasoning: The componential analysis of human abilities*. Hillsdale: Erlbaum.

Sternberg, R. J. (2003). *Wisdom, intelligence, and creativity synthesized*. New York: Cambridge University Press.

Sternberg, R. J. (2010). *College admissions for the 21st century*. Cambridge, MA: Harvard University Press.

Part IV

Development: How We Change Over Time

Section A

Cognitive Development

40   Building a Unique Network of Scientific Enterprises

Carey, Susan

Quite reasonably, the editors' charge was describing our most important contribution to psychology. Here, I draw morals for young people contemplating a career in psychological research.

Each scientist builds, through continued hard work and attention to detail, unique expertise and networks that elucidate several threads in the fabric of nature. Over a lifetime, these add up to a body of work. The first challenge budding young scientists face is settling on mysteries that are *so* interesting to them they want to spend their lives trying to explain them. Beginning as an undergraduate, my work has aimed at explaining how abstract concepts, such as *infinity, life, matter, agent, cause,* and others arise in the human mind.

Accounting for the human conceptual repertoire formidably challenges psychological science. Our genetic make-up and brains are remarkably similar to those of our nearest animal cousins, the great apes. Yet, we are the only animals that can ponder the causes and cures of cancer or of global warming, that can conceive orders of infinity – indeed, that can think any thoughts beyond the representational capacity of non-human animals. **Moral 1. Find a scientific mystery that fascinates *you*.** The mystery of human conceptual development structured my life's work.

As a biology major, my sophomore tutorial was taught by a postdoc working on bodily mechanisms that underlie biological clocks. What fascinated me was how scientists knew animals *could tell time*. My tutor guided me in reading the ethological literature of 1961: how omnivores learn what food to eat, how animals navigate, how infants recognize their mothers. At year's end, my tutor said, "Ethology IS a branch of biology, so you can do this kind of work as a biologist, but the future of biology is molecular biology. I believe that the deeper work on these kinds of issues will come from the new discipline of cognitive science, and highly recommend that you check it out." **Moral 2: Seek out good teachers, and follow their advice; good teachers have *your* interests at heart.**

Junior year, I took a course on the nature of knowledge from three founders of cognitive science, George Miller, Jerome Bruner, and Noam Chomsky. My biology tutor was right; these were my issues. Barbel Inhelder, a long-time collaborator of Jean Piaget (founder of the cognitive development field), demonstrated non-conservation of amount before a lecture hall of 300 enthralled students. We watched as a five-year old carefully poured the same amount of liquid into two identical glasses, agreed that each had the same amount, and watched while the contents of one glass was poured into a thinner one. The child then insisted on "more to drink" in the thinner glass, because, "LOOK" (pointing to how much higher the liquid is in that glass)! I thought, give me a break; the child doesn't understand what question he is being asked. Give me five minutes with that child and I could clarify the question and of course he'd know the answer. I said as much to my discussion-section leader, who said experiments on this phenomenon were going on in Bruner's lab, and she could arrange for me to come see if I was right. **Moral 3: Test *your* ideas in the lab.**

Of course, I was both right and wrong: right that the child didn't understand what question was being asked, wrong that it would be easy to set him right. Six more years of hard work, and a PhD thesis called "Are Children Little Scientists with False Theories of the World?" and I had my first original insights into conceptual development. Piaget and Inhelder were right: five-year-old children do not have concepts of amount, weight, volume, or density. But they were also wrong: the problem lay not in their being qualitatively different kinds of *thinkers* from older children and adults, but, rather, from their holding qualitatively different *theories* of the world – in this case, theories of matter. Conceptual development constructs intuitive framework theories, theories of matter, theories of the biological world, and theories of the social world; these go through qualitative changes, just as do the explicit theories in formal science. Conceptual changes are hard, taking years as individuals grapple with mastering the theories and concepts constructed over centuries of cultural evolution, which is why five minutes with five-year-olds will not change them from being non-conservers to conservers.

These insights led me to establish collaborations with anthropologists and a historian of science to study cultural construction of knowledge; subsequent work confirmed that theory change in childhood is indeed structurally similar to theory change in the history of science, despite obvious and profound differences between professional scientists and children. Scientists explicitly know they are constructing theories, experimentally testing hypotheses, and engaging with other scientists, whereas children lack such explicit understanding of the processes involved in knowledge acquisition. **Moral 4. To develop your own unique network of enterprises, seek out collaborators with expertise you need to gain.**

Now a professor at MIT, I still engaged in case studies of the historical and ontogenetic origins of the concepts that articulate intuitive and scientific theories. In the late 1980s, an MIT graduate student, Karen Wynn, now a professor at Yale, ask me to supervise her case study of mathematical development, specifically the origin of representations of integers. I barely knew the literature on mathematical concepts, which began with Piaget's work on conservation of number. Just as five-year-olds do not have a concept of amount of matter conserved over transformations that change shape, so too they argue that a line of seven pennies, spread further apart but without adding any new ones, now has "more pennies" than before. Wynn's dissertation would fill important gaps in my network of enterprises. And, indeed, studies of numerical cognition have become a central case study in my thinking about the origins of abstract knowledge: **Moral 5. Be open to requests for collaboration that take you in new directions, for they will expand your network of enterprises. But keep your eye on the ball – all research is extremely time consuming and so be sure projects you engage in will further your understanding of the scientific issues you most care about.**

After Piaget's seminal work, others (most notably, Rochel Gelman) pointed out that even two-year-olds know how to count, which would seem to require that they have concepts at least of the integer values *1, 2, 3, 4, . . .* (for as high as they can count). But, do they know the numerical *meaning* of counting? Wynn's initial studies sought evidence they did. She asked two-year-olds and young three-year-olds, all of whom knew how to count to ten, to give her "one fish" from a pile, "two fish," or "three" fish. She discovered (and you can try this at home if you have a younger sibling or cousin) that many children could hand over one when asked for "one," but grab a handful, always more than one, when asked for any other number. That is, they knew that all these words were relevant to number, and they knew what "one" meant, but they did not know what set size the other numbers in their count meant. Children were in this state of number-word knowledge for *six* to *nine* months, until they figured out the meaning of the word "two": but took all other verbal numerals just to contrast with "one" and "two," without knowing their set sizes. That is, children are first "one"-knowers, and then they become "two"-knowers. Over the next months, they become "three"-knowers and then "four"-knowers. At around age 3.5–4 years, they figure out how counting represents number, and they know the numerical meaning of all of the words in their count list. These results again suggest a major discontinuity in development: if children had the *concepts* of the first ten integers, it should not be so hard to learn the meanings of the words.

How we account for the human conceptual repertoire was coming into focus – we must characterize infants' innate representational resources. Infants must be born with some innate (unlearned) capacities to make sense of their world; otherwise they could not learn. We must characterize in detail the *nature* of adult concepts, so we can then ask whether, and how, infants' representations differ from adults'. Finally, we must characterize mechanisms (learning processes, maturational processes) that transform the initial state into the adult state.

Over my career, I tackled these questions and collaborated with experts in infant cognition and animal cognition (living by Moral 4). In my infant lab, studies of causal and numerical representations have supported the conclusion that Piaget and others got it wrong. Young infants do not look out into the world and see only patches of color, shapes that as yet have no meaning to them, and so on, but, rather, are born with rich abstract representational capacities and powerful domain-specific learning mechanisms. Even newborns see the world in terms of objects separate from themselves, people likely to communicate with them, and the capacity to quantify over sets.

Despite this nativist conclusion, conceptual development involves radical discontinuities. How do we reconcile evidence for rich abstract knowledge in infancy, including of number, with the evidence for discontinuities in subsequent development? Conceptual development, both over the time course of the cultural construction of knowledge and the time course of single life spans, involves radical discontinuity: Characterizing learning mechanisms that achieve it has been my most important scientific contribution. And now we have gotten to the technical pay-off of a long career in science.

Discontinuities in conceptual development matter, both theoretically and practically. Theoretically, they challenge the dominant "building block" or "feature composition" models of conceptual structure. They demonstrate increases of conceptual systems' expressive power over cultural history and over ontogenesis. Also, education's conceptual goal is guiding students to construct the hard-won understanding achieved over centuries. My work on the nature of conceptual discontinuities gets to the heart of why students too often remember virtually nothing from math and science courses. Conceptual change is hard, and understanding the learning processes that underlie it has implications for curricular interventions – how to teach new theories and mathematical knowledge that differ radically from students' initial understanding. Work on the acquisition of human concepts necessarily proceeds case by case, and much work remains.

REFERENCES

Carey, S. (2009). *The origin of concepts*. Oxford: Oxford University Press.

Carey, S. (2011). The origin of concepts: A précis. *Behavioral and Brain Sciences*, *34*, 113–167.

Carey, S. (2015). Why theories of concepts should not ignore the problem of acquisition. In E. Margolis & S. Laurence (eds.), *Concepts: New directions* (pp. 415–454). Cambridge: MIT Press.

Ceci, Stephen J.

My most important scientific contribution concerns the development of "source misattributions." That's a fancy term to describe an event that is familiar, but not because we actually experienced it. Instead, it's familiar to us because in the past we either imagined it, or read about it, or saw something related to it on television, or overheard a conversation about it. These prior mental activities reside in memory but sometimes without their source: is this event familiar because I truly experienced it, or is the source of its familiarity having imagined it or heard someone talking about it? Although we all have a propensity for misattributing the source of why something is familiar, very young children are most vulnerable. It turns out that a lot of really important phenomena are related to it, including court cases involving child witnesses.

You may find the way I became interested in source misattributions interesting. In graduate school I studied children's memory. By the time I got my PhD I thought I knew a lot about how children remember. But I was jolted into reality one day when a judge from upstate New York called me at my office at Cornell. He had a case in his courtroom involving a child's recollection that puzzled him. He said someone gave him my name as an expert on children's memory. The gist of the case was as follows: a woman disappeared when her son was twenty-two months old. After several months had passed, and the mother did not return home, her husband took their son to his missing wife's sister and asked her to care for the child. The aunt and father had not had a good relationship, and they were known to have argued vehemently about his mistreatment of her sister. The aunt agreed to care for her nephew until her sister resurfaced. The father moved to Florida, and his contact with his son and sister-in-law was limited. He remarried eventually.

At the time of the judge's phone call, the boy had been living with his aunt for four years. The house in which the boy lived with his parents had been sold and resold, and the newest owners were adding an extension when the excavator discovered the skeletal remains of the missing mother.

The coroner's report indicated she had been killed by blunt force trauma to her head by a rounded object. I recall the judge telling me that when the aunt initially questioned her nephew about whether he saw his father hit his mother with a rounded object – a baseball bat or pipe – the boy said he had no such memory.

Over time, with repeated questioning by the aunt, the boy began to retrieve fragments of a scene that were disconnected from each other. In its final form, however, the fragments were fully woven into a persuasive narrative. The boy said he remembered one day watching his parents violently arguing, screaming at each other, his father hitting his mother with a baseball bat, blood on her face, and his father dragging his mother by her feet out the back kitchen door. The judge wanted to know if this was how children's memory works; if they initially profess to have no memory for an event, do they assemble it fragment-by-fragment? I had no clue, and I declined to serve as an expert witness. (I later found out that the father was convicted.)

So, despite thinking I knew a great deal about children's memory, I had no idea how to advise the judge. And this bothered me a lot because I had published numerous experiments on children's recollections! Within weeks of this call, I began designing experiments to capture some of this real-world complexity that was missing from my laboratory experiments. I am referring to factors such as a child's emotional arousal and the effect of repeated questioning over long intervals. I also organized a conference in which child memory researchers from the United States, Canada, and Europe came to Cornell to chart a program of research that could inform courts, schools, and law enforcement about children's remembering. That conference appears to have been hugely successful; when many of the researchers returned to their universities, they undertook studies that incorporated legally relevant aspects. A volume based on the conference became highly cited. I also served as a scientific advisor for a NATO conference around the same time, which added impetus to this line of research. Within a decade of receiving the judge's call, the field of memory development had largely moved outside the lab and into the real world!

In the ensuing thirty-five years since the judge's call, my students, colleagues, and I have attempted to chart the natural course of remembering in preschool children. To do this we have sometimes taken advantage of naturally occurring stressful experiences that would be unethical and impermissible to create in a laboratory experiment. For example, to examine the effect of arousal on the accuracy of children's memory, we have studied their recollection of painful medical procedures (inoculations or emergency room experiences). We have studied recollections spanning several years. And, most importantly, we have examined a variety of suggestive questioning techniques.

In one line of work we have done something that today may seem obvious, even trivial. But at the time we launched these experiments, they were anything but obvious. I am referring to a really simple procedure. We first ask parents of preschoolers to describe some actual experiences. They provided a list of both pleasant (e.g., a trip to Disneyworld) and unpleasant events (e.g., an emergency room visit for suturing). We next made up fake experiences that the parents assured us never happened (e.g., getting their fingers injured in a mousetrap and going to a hospital to get it off). The experiment was alluringly simple. Kids sat with an interviewer who held twelve index cards. On each card was an event, six of which were fake. She read the event description on each card and asked the child to think hard and say whether it really happened to them. For example, she would read: "Did you ever get your hand caught in a mousetrap and go to the hospital to get it off? Think hard. Did this happen to you?"

The first time children were asked about the six fake questions, they usually correctly denied experiencing them. Only 10 percent of the youngest children claimed to "remember" having experienced fake events. But this percent grew each week we brought them back and asked about them. By the tenth week, 55 percent of the youngest children claimed to remember having experienced fake events, as did 41 percent of the older children! So what began as a correct rejection of a false memory developed over time into a false belief that it occurred. Anyone watching the children "recollect" these fake experiences would be misled into thinking that they really experienced them. We showed videotapes of the children describing both true and fake events during the tenth week to thousands of experts (child psychiatrists, psychologists, judges, social workers, police). Their odds of telling if the child was describing a true or fake event were usually no better than chance.

In our subsequent work, we have probed this finding to better understand the mechanisms that are responsible. It turns out that the reason the children are so convincing to professionals is because by the tenth week they themselves have come to believe them. In other words, they are not lying when they give vivid accounts about fake events. They have come to believe them. Why? Because the first time they are asked if they remember them they search their memory for evidence and, finding none, they correctly say "I don't remember anything like that; I don't have a mousetrap in my house, and I have never been to a hospital." However, over time, when they are repeatedly questioned, they search memory and they *do* find details pertaining to the fake experiences – the result of having previously thought about them. They now say things like "I seem to remember something like that, a mousetrap snapped on my finger." By the tenth week, when they are asked about the fake events they quickly retrieve details from memory based on prior mental activities, and they report elaborate narratives about the fake experiences. In fact, these false narratives are as embellished and as convincing to judges and others as their narratives about true experiences.

My research team and I have now spent more than three decades studying children's true and false memories. There remains much to be learned, of course (e.g., next steps include charting children's progression from lying to actually believing their lies). However, we are gratified to have discovered that what was once thought by many in the law enforcement and advocacy communities to be unthinkable is actually common and fairly easy to produce. It is crucial for professionals with access to young children to be made aware of practices that can lead to source misattributions that are so elaborately described that they fool experts. We have tried to inform professionals by various means, including interviewer training, judicial workshops, and amicus briefs to the United States Supreme Court. As I just turned sixty-five, many of the next steps will fall to my students and their students.

REFERENCES

Ceci, S. J., & Bruck, M. (1995). *Jeopardy in the courtroom: The scientific analysis of children's testimony*. Washington, D.C.: American Psychological Association. (*Winner of the 2000 William James Book Award by APA*).

Ceci, S. J., Fitneva, S. A., & Williams, W. M. (2010). Representational constraints on the development of memory and metamemory: A developmental-representational theory. *Psychological Review, 117*, 464–495.

Ceci, S. J., Loftus, E. F., Leichtman, M., & Bruck, M. (1994). The possible role of source misattributions in the creation of false beliefs among preschoolers. *International Journal of Clinical and Experimental Hypnosis, 42*, 304–320.

42 Development of Children's Knowledge About the Mind

Flavell, John H.

I believe my most important scientific contributions have been in the area of the development of children's knowledge about the mind, often referred to by psychologists as theory-of-mind development or metacognitive development. As so often happens in science, my research on this topic had its origins in work on what seemed at the time to be a different topic, namely, the development of children's private, non-social, speech-for-self.

To study that topic, in the early 1960s, my students and I devised a task in which kindergarteners, second graders, and fifth graders wore a "space helmet" with an opaque visor that could, when lowered, prevent them from seeing a series of object pictures on the table in front of them. The pictures showed objects, the naming of which required rather large, distinctive, easily readable mouth movements (e.g., "pipe," "apple," "flag"). On each trial with the visor up, the experimenter pointed in a fixed order to a subset of the pictures and then asked children to point to the same pictures in the same order, either immediately or after a fifteen second delay during which the vision-obscuring visor was lowered.

We found a marked increase with age in children's spontaneous picture naming (which we either heard or lip-read). In particular, unlike the younger ones, most of the oldest children tended to name the objects when they first saw them, repeat the names to themselves while the visor was down, and then try to repeat them again while pointing to the pictures after the visor was lifted.

In this and subsequent studies it became apparent to us (slow learners, we!) that what we were really investigating was the development of tacit knowledge about what remembering was like and how best to accomplish memory goals (e.g., verbal rehearsal); we gave the name "metamemory" to this domain of naïve knowledge about memory. It was then but a short step to conceptualize (with the help of independent work by the late Ann Brown) the area more broadly as any kind of cognition about any kind of cognition – that is, as "metacognition." Thus it was that we began to trace the development of naïve knowledge about other forms of cognition.

198

Visual perception was one of these forms of metacognition. During the early preschool period, children already understand that a person will see an object if and only if the person's eyes are aimed in the general direction of the object, and if there are no vision-blocking obstacles interposed between the person and the object. With this understanding, they are able to do simple, non-egocentric visual perspective-taking: for example, they can infer that you may see something that they do not and vice versa. (We called this Level 1 knowledge about visual perception.) Later in the preschool period, they go on to recognize that the thing may present different visual appearances to two people if the people view it from different positions (called Level 2 knowledge). For example, older pre-schoolers realize that even though they and another person seated opposite them both see the same picture book, the pictures will appear upside down to the person if they appear right side up to them, and vice versa.

In another task involving Level 2-like understanding of dual mental representations, after pre-training on the appearance–reality distinction, children were presented with a sponge made to look like a rock or a little object that looks big when viewed through a magnifying glass. After discovering each object's true identity or property, children were asked how the object currently appears to their eyes (rock; big) and how or what it really and truly was (sponge; little). We found that three-year-olds tend to give the same answer to both questions, reporting either the appearance twice or the reality twice, as if they do not distinguish conceptually between the misleading perceptual appearance and the underlying reality. In contrast, children age four and older typically showed some command of the distinction.

A rough distinction can be made between more or less enduring, disposition-like mental states, such as knowledge, beliefs, and attitudes, and here-and-now-occurring, conscious mental experiences, such as having a sudden thought, memory, percept, or feeling. Much of the research on theory-of-mind development had focused on children's developing understanding of mental states, especially that of beliefs. In contrast, most of the research Frances Green, Eleanor Flavell, my students, and I have done more recently has dealt with the development of children's intuitions concerning ongoing mental experiences, especially thinking, attention, and consciousness. These studies have shown that such intuitions are present, but very limited in preschool children, and undergo considerable development during middle childhood. The overall objective of our research in this area can be variously phrased as trying to find out what children of different ages know about what the mind is like, what tends to happen in there and when, and what it is like, experientially, to be a person – in short, the nature of the inner world of mental experiences.

Consider the following, mundane intuition: When they are awake, people are experiencing a more or less continuous, essentially unstoppable flow of conscious mental content (William James' famous "stream of consciousness"), even when receiving no significant perceptual input and engaged in no cognitive task. We have shown in several studies that young children tend to be unaware of this fundamental intuition about the way our minds work. For example, in one study, three-year-olds, four-year-olds, six-year-olds, and seven-year-olds, and adults were first given some pre-training on the meaning of "having some thoughts and ideas" (while awake) versus not having any (while sound asleep and not dreaming). Next, one experimenter sat quietly in a chair facing a blank wall, "just waiting." The other experimenter then asked the participants: "How about her mind right now? Is she having some thoughts and ideas right now or is her mind empty of thoughts and ideas?" Empty and non-empty thought bubbles, previously used in the pre-training, were employed to illustrate each option. The percentages of participants saying that the first experimenter was having some thoughts and ideas while waiting were 15 percent, 35 percent, 80 percent, and 95 percent.

Why might preschoolers lack such seemingly obvious intuitions about mental experiences? In order to acquire them, they may need to be able to attend to their own internal goings-on. Consistent with this possibility, we have shown that preschoolers have very limited introspective abilities. In one such study, for example, the experimenter showed five-year-olds a little bell, and then hid it under the testing table. She said, "In just a few seconds I'll ring it." After a four-second delay, she rang the bell and said, "Okay, one more time. In just a few seconds I'll ring it again." This time she failed to ring the bell, and after 10–12 seconds of dead silence she asked whether the child "was wondering about or thinking about anything right now or not," and, if so, what about. One would have thought that all the children must have been wondering why the bell did not ring as expected, yet only 38 percent of the group reported having wondered that. In a subsequent study, this figure rose to a not-very-impressive 60 percent in a group of six-year-olds.

In another study, five-year-olds, eight-year-olds, and adults were asked to try to have no thoughts at all for a short period of time (20–25 sec.). When asked immediately afterwards whether they had had some thoughts anyway during this period, all of the adults and the majority of the eight-year-olds said they had, but only a few of the five-year-olds did. Although we cannot be sure, of course, we believe that the five-year-olds did have some thoughts during this period, but simply did not notice them or could not recall them. In contrast, the introspective sensitivity of many of the eight-year-olds was particularly impressive: They tried hard not to have any thoughts and (unlike adults) seemed to expect that they wouldn't; nevertheless, they did notice some of the mental content that inevitably occurred, often with expressions of surprise. Preschoolers' relative insensitivity to their own ongoing mentation is sometimes evident in their everyday interactions. An extremely bright four-and-a-half- year-old of my acquaintance was looking very pensive, so his father said, "What are you thinking about?" The answer: "Nothing. I never think. I just walk and talk."

The acquisition of introspective abilities and the intuitions about mental experiences these abilities may spawn are surely important developments. They help children learn what they and other people are like subjectively, and thus what it is like to be a human being. They also put children in a position to infer and influence their own mentation and behavior (e.g., when studying) and that of others.

REFERENCES

Flavell, J. H. (2000). Development of children's knowledge about the mental world. *International Journal of Behavioral Development*, *24*, 15–23.

Flavell, J. H., Miller, P. H., & Miller, S. A. (2000). *Cognitive development* (4th edn.). Upper Saddle River: Prentice-Hall.

43   Real Representations in Two Dimensions

Gelman, Rochel

The term "real" is extremely ambiguous. A trip to an art museum brings out one interpretation. For example, the French Impressionist Edgar Degas (1834–1917) painted ballet dancers practicing in mirrored rooms. Some dancers in Degas' paintings show dancers in front of, and reflected in a mirror; some show mirror images of dancers off to the side. Which, if any, is a reflection of a real person? Many other artists' paintings challenge viewers to ponder reality. Sometimes the work shows reflections in windows, outside open windows, or even reproductions within a painting inside the painting.

Our research provides a rather simple way to determine whether an artist assumed that the reflections or reproductions in their paintings were "real" or not. This is to ask observers to count the number of separate objects in a particular painting. If a mirror captures the reflection of an object in front of it, it cannot be counted, but an object shown outside an open window, can. Why? Our implicit counting knowledge prohibits the double counting of an item. So, if you do not count the reflection in the mirror, you do not think it is a real item. To explain, I need to cover a bit about your counting knowledge.

When we count, we must honor the one–one principle and, therefore, uniquely tag every object once and only once. If we double tag an item, we will use too many tags and get the wrong answer to a "how many?" question. All normal adults and many young children are good counters. Even four-year-olds will correct a puppet that counts an item twice. If one counts an exact mirror copy of a foregrounded item, one commits a principled violation. In our experiments with adults we took advantage of this fact.

Dana Chesney and I showed college students line drawings of frames that we dubbed a mirror, picture frame, or an open window. Within each there was a reproduction of the objects drawn in the foreground (e.g., two chairs). So, two chairs were shown in the mirror, two were outside the open window, and two smaller ones were in a painting on the wall. People simply were asked how many were present in each kind. The overwhelming answers were *two* and *four*, respectively for the mirror and window frames. Apparently, they did not think the drawings on the mirror were real, whereas those outside the window were. The items inside a picture frame were counted sometimes, perhaps because their change of size mattered.

We have yet to run preschoolers in the above counting studies because we do not know how they will respond to the different frames. Direct questions with the word "real" yield various answers, including *alive, not dead, non-alive, not pretend, just a picture*, and so on. Still, Kim Brenneman and I reached an idea that served to focus children on the animate versus inanimate meanings. We presented young children with photographs of novel pairs of look-alike living and copies of an animal. These were very similar on the surface and could not be named by graduate students. The experiment started with a warm-up where children looked at examples of look-alike photo pairs and we told them where we took each of the pictures. One of the pair was taken in a zoo, where animals move around, eat, and so on. The fabricated version was taken in a store were they sat still on a shelf. Then the experimenter put a "zoo" and "store" book on the table and prepared to show new pairs of examples for the children to sort into each book. Just as she was about to start, the pictures fell on the floor. The child agreed to help pick them up and went on to sort each of a pair into their respective book. Even many three-year-olds did the task reasonably well. This is a surprising result because many developmental theorists hold that preschool children cannot think abstractly.

Stage theorists hold that young children rely on the perceptual surface when comparing objects. This is especially so for Jean Piaget's account. But, this cannot always be true, given that the photos in our study were perceptually similar. Some children even said the animals were real and not-real. Further studies with three- to five-year-olds help support our conclusion.

Real animals can move themselves, including unfamiliar animals such as an echidna, tarantula, starfish, etc. If asked if a statue can do the same thing, the answer is "no way." It does not matter that it has legs and arms. Further, wheeled objects might roll down a hill, as if on their own. However, they certainly cannot go up a hill without the help of an agent. Christine Massey and I set up an experiment to determine if children reacted the same way to photographs. The children were shown a drawing of a hill and were asked: "Can this (object in the picture) go up/down a hill, or does it need help?" Exemplars included unfamiliar animals, wheeled objects, statues, and household items that looked like they had arms and legs. The children in all age groups did remarkably well. The seemingly perceptual surface features of statues did not fool them. One child said that a statue could not move itself "because it does not have feet." It actually did, and when Massey pointed to the feet, she replied "They are only pretend feet." Another child said a statue was only a "furniture-animal." These children seemed to have intuitions about the different materials in the composition of objects.

To determine if young children can think abstractly about the animate and inanimate distinction, we conducted studies without pictures. For example, we asked questions about a rock, a doll, and a person. These included: "What is on the inside and outside of a, b, c?"; "Can you play with a, b, c?"; "Can a, b, c play with you?"; "Can each of the objects talk/walk?"; and so on. Again the children did well. They assumed people had bones, blood, and food on their insides, and faces, eyes, mouths, and hair on their outsides. Dolls had nothing, stuff, batteries, or strings inside, and clothes on the outside. One can talk to a doll, but a doll cannot talk back; rocks had more of the same stuff inside and dirt on the outside. Follow-up studies revealed that young children assume that all living creatures can move themselves, and have bones, blood, and food inside – even if they have no knowledge of the particular animal. But what is inside different artifacts varies. For example, airplanes have seats, pilots, engines, and even people inside; plants have the same inside as outside, and dirt outside. Overall, these interviews provide evidence in favor of the idea that young children have some very abstract ideas and knowledge about real animate and inanimate objects in the world. This distinction is relevant to biology, but I prefer to say that the children are on a relevant learning path for studying biology.

It still remains to be determined what cues the children and adults used to succeed with pictures. A few clues as to what drew children's attention in the "hill" study come from their comments: A statue had a pattern on it or "was too shiny," whereas "an echidna had feet," even if these were not showing, and "a bug has these things (feelers)." These suggest abilities to make inferences about unknown animals and perceive clues about material. We have much to learn about children's knowledge about different materials and how they relate this to their ideas about animate and inanimate items.

It surprised us that young children think that real living things share common insides. After all, these are not visible. If they really are perception bound, how can they have abstract thoughts about a real and not-real copy? I suggest that the rapid learning about the differences between animate and inanimate objects is due to a biological disposition. The idea is that we are born to actively learn about some domains on the fly. I call these Core Domains. These include the animate–inanimate distinction, natural number, and sociality. Brain scientists are working on this hypothesis. The hypothesis could gain support if different brain areas responded to animate and inanimate stimuli, despite their surface similarity. If, on the other hand, the same areas light up for both items in the look-alike pairs, a general perception hypothesis would gain support. This contrast is more complicated than first meets the eye. But it demonstrates how a psychologist can guide brain exploration. The same is true for the development of a taste for art.

REFERENCES

Gelman, R. (1979). Preschool thought. *American Psychologist, 34*, 900–905.

Massey, C., & Gelman, R. (1988). Preschoolers' ability to decide whether a photographed unfamiliar object can move itself. *Developmental Psychology, 24*, 307–317.

Spelke, E. S. (2000). Core knowledge. *American Psychologist, 55*, 1233–1243.

44   Language and the Social Brain: The Power of Surprise in Science

Kuhl, Patricia K.

In 2003, I discovered that when nine-month-old infants are exposed to a new natural language for twelve sessions over a month's time, that interaction with another human being is essential for infants to learn. A beautiful DVD presentation of the exact same material to another group of babies produced no learning whatsoever, nor did an audio-only presentation.

The graduate students and post-doctoral fellows in my laboratory took bets after watching infants in the DVD condition – who stared at the monitor and even crawled up to it. Some touched it. They bet that the DVD would win over "live" because the DVD was so beautifully clear. There were fewer distractions and babies seemed riveted by the action on the screen.

But the results of brain and behavioral tests showed that only infants who experienced native Mandarin speakers "live" showed evidence of having learned. Those who watched the same native speakers on DVD, or heard them through loudspeakers, performed no differently on tests of Mandarin sounds than infants in a control group who heard only English from American native speakers in otherwise identical sessions. Learning was phenomenal: "live" infants matched Taiwanese infants who had ten months experience listening to the language.

The result was a huge surprise. It challenged existing theory, has affected educational practices, and jolted the baby DVD industry.

What led us to do the experiment? What were the theories and predictions at the time? And how did the finding lead me to a new hypothesis, the "social gating" hypothesis?

Two highly polarized theories shape the field of language acquisition, each elegantly argued by giants in the field. MIT professor Noam Chomsky favors a nativist position, positing a Language Acquisition Device (LAD) that triggers parameters of innate universal phonology and grammar through language input. Brown University professor Peter Eimas fleshed out this view, arguing that innate "phonetic feature detectors," encompassing the sounds of all languages, atrophied when the language infants heard did not include a particular phonetic feature.

Al Liberman of Haskins' Laboratories at Yale argued that "speech is special" – that brain systems were "modularized" such that other cognitive processes could not influence them.

The alternative view, expressed by Harvard professor B. F. Skinner, held that language required only operant conditioning and reinforcement to reward and eventually shape the behavior of children as they uttered words. Infants were, in effect, "blank slates," waiting for parental tutoring. The nativist and learning positions could not have been more disparate.

However, as data began to pour in from experimental studies on infants, a new view beyond the two alternatives appeared to be required.

A few of these findings were that: (a) infants were born with the capacity to discriminate all the phonetic contrasts of all languages, even if they had never heard these sounds – they were "citizens of the world," a feat not accomplished by their "language-bound" parents; (b) a "sensitive period" between approximately eight and ten months of age was identified, during which a dramatic change occurred in infants' perception of speech. During this period, infants' performance on native sounds increased significantly, while their ability to discriminate non-native contrasts declined. I had earlier shown that non-human animals show enhanced discrimination at the locations of phonetic "boundaries" between two categories, which suggested evolutionary continuity between complex auditory processing in animals and humans, and underscored the idea that infants' initial capacities did not necessitate the existence of phonetic feature detectors at birth.

The learning position took a significant step forward with the discovery that infants were capable of *implicit* learning – different from explicit learning, and distinct from operant conditioning à la Skinner. This gave infants computational strategies that helped them learn simply by listening to people talk. In effect, infants were shown to "take statistics" as they listened to us speak.

In laboratory tests, infants from an early age were shown to be sensitive to the distributional frequencies of phonetic units when exposed to a series of eight stimuli from a continuum. For example, in a series of stimuli ranging from the syllable /ra/ to the syllable /la/, infants exposed to a higher proportion of the endpoint stimuli became better at discriminating /ra/ from /la/. On the other hand, infants who heard a higher proportion of the intermediate stimuli became worse at discriminating /ra/ from /la/. This meant that infants in Japan, who hear intermediate sounds appropriate for Japanese, should get poorer during the sensitive period at discriminating /ra/ from /la/ – and, indeed, experiments show that they do. This kind of implicit "statistical" learning was occurring at an age well before parents were even aware that their children were learning, before parents were "rewarding" infants for learning. This kind of learning happened automatically.

This formed the backdrop for my design of the language exposure experiment. My initial goal was to test whether infants could learn the statistical properties of a new language if exposed to that language for the first time during the sensitive period. Infants hear their native language from birth, but the transition in phonetic perception does not occur until about eight months of age – why? Did it mean that infants needed eight months to build up statistical distributions of the sounds they heard in ambient language? If so, then twelve sessions of exposure to a new language, with its novel sounds and statistics, would not be sufficient to learn the sounds of Mandarin Chinese. But if twelve sessions – less than five hours – was sufficient, then something else was going on. Performance of infants in the control group ensured that simply coming to the laboratory for twelve sessions of listening to English did nothing to improve infants' Mandarin skills.

As the exposure experiment got underway, I began to notice how happy infants in the "live" group were as they sat in the waiting room prior to the experiment. They'd watch the door, smiling when one of the Mandarin tutors walked in. They were clearly happy campers. Control infants looked typical, but not exuberant. I began to wonder about the "social" component. What role was social interaction playing? The classic "statistical learning" experiments did not involve social interaction – infants hear audio tokens of speech, and they learn without the presence of a human being. But our experiment required learning from a complex, live, natural language interaction. Was there something about this natural social setting, with all its complexity, that actually enhanced language learning?

We tested this idea via the DVD and audio-only conditions. And voila! We had the answer – the human being was *essential* for learning. No learning occurred in the absence of a person.

This discovery gave rise to my "social gating" hypothesis: the idea that social interaction "gates" language learning. The finding caused many to suggest experiments and to offer explanations. The *contingencies* involved in natural interaction, something that's missing from a TV presentation, were often mentioned. The fact that infants could learn from following the gaze of the tutor, easier in the live as opposed to the DVD sessions, also came up often. Biologists offered the thought that pheromones, sensed only during "live" sessions, could be responsible. It was deeply satisfying to have been the catalyst for so much talk about infants' social brains!

The hypotheses I offered positioned the "social gating" hypothesis as an advantage infants accrued from two non-mutually exclusive sources: (1) enhanced *motivation* derived by face-to-face human interaction, and (2) enhanced *information* derived by tracking the tutor's eye movements and following their gaze. In further experiments (not yet published) we have demonstrated that both these factors play a significant role in infants' learning. We are using interactive screens, "social" robots, and even testing infant learning solo versus in pairs to test our hypotheses. We're having fun!

We are also exploring the brain basis of the effect in several experiments. One published result is intriguing: Using MEG brain imaging technology, we demonstrated that when seven- and eleven-month-old infants hear speech (but not non-speech), the brain's motor systems are activated – Broca's area and the cerebellum respond within milliseconds of the activation in auditory sensory cortex. This activation occurs for both native and non-native speech before the sensitive period. After the sensitive period, non-native speech shows even greater motor activation. Taking a cue from artificial intelligence, we argue that infants' brains, as they listen to us speak, are trying to "rehearse" the movements required to talk back. This is a social response, we believe, and we're following up on this idea with experiments that examine brain activation in response to DVD as opposed to "live" presentations while infants are in the MEG machine.

The discovery has affected educational systems as well as companies that develop videos aimed to teach languages to young infants. It has impacted developmental theories linking cognitive and social development and is leading to a new view of language acquisition.

I still do not fully understand how the social brain "gates" language learning, or indeed if this is the correct theoretical position. But stay tuned, and join me if you are so inclined. There are future discoveries to be made.

REFERENCES

Kuhl, P. K. (2004). Early language acquisition: Cracking the speech code. *Nature Reviews Neuroscience*, 5, 831–843.

Kuhl, P. K. (2010). Brain mechanisms in early language acquisition. *Neuron*, 67, 713–727.

Kuhl, P. K., & Rivera-Gaxiola, M. (2008). Neural substrates of language acquisition. *Annual Review of Neuroscience*, 31, 511–534.

45   The Importance of Developmental Plasticity

Newport, Elissa L.

The Importance of Developmental Plasticity

What do I consider my most important scientific contribution? There are actually two important contributions that are intertwined – one mostly not my own, and one that is to some degree mine. The first – a contribution of great importance that came primarily from the work of Ursula Bellugi, Edward Klima, and William Stokoe – concerns the discovery that signed languages of Deaf communities around the world are natural languages, equal in expressiveness and in grammatical complexity to spoken languages. When I was in graduate school and before, most psychologists and linguists believed that human language was uniquely connected to speech – that all languages around the globe were produced with the mouth and processed with the ear.

Thanks to the groundbreaking work of Bellugi and Klima and of Stokoe, we now know that, when speech is unavailable, humans readily use their hands and eyes for communication and that signed languages can become as complex and elegantly structured as spoken languages. I am proud to have done some of my research on the structure and acquisition of American Sign Language, in collaboration with Ted Supalla, a Deaf native signer whose native language is ASL (and who is also my husband). Our work on ASL has been in the context of another passionate interest that has been the main focus of my scientific career.

My own most important contribution, I think, concerns *developmental plasticity*. I've long been interested in mechanisms of learning: How do we learn, what are we especially good at learning, what are the principles and constraints on the way we learn? I've been particularly interested in why infants and young children are better than adults at learning certain types of skills, especially language. This issue was first raised by Eric Lenneberg, who suggested that there may be a "critical period" for language acquisition in humans. I read Lenneberg's famous 1969 *Science* article in a first-year proseminar in graduate school, and then his 1967 book *Biological Foundations of Language* (the *Science* article is a précis of his book). One idea in that work is that there may be a critical period for human language learning – a window of time during which we are especially good at learning languages but not as good thereafter, even with the same amount and type of exposure.

Lenneberg suggested this hypothesis in the context of arguing that language is a species-typical behavior in humans, like imprinting in ducklings or learning a mating song in songbirds, and follows many of the principles that are shown by these species-typical, partly instinctive and partly learned behaviors in animals. I was immediately fascinated by the then-novel idea that humans have these instinctive systems – a concept I had not heard during the behaviorist training in psychology that I had received in college.

Since that time, much of my work has focused on this question. I've tried to learn as much as I can about whether there really is a critical period for language learning, how it works, what makes it begin, and what makes it end. A better term for what I've learned is that there is, in language and many other systems, something called *developmentally regulated plasticity*. Plasticity – the ability of the brain and behavior to be modified by experience – can itself change over development. Many of the mechanisms that enable us to learn are altered by maturation: Learning is best when we are immature and neurons readily sprout new connections that can be strengthened by experience, and it is worse – much more difficult and qualitatively different – when we mature beyond this period and when more expansive cognitive abilities have appeared, along with the neural mechanisms that consolidate what we have already learned.

To investigate these questions in humans – where, of course, we cannot experimentally control exposure to language or keep groups of children in isolation to observe the outcome – I've studied groups of second-language learners of English whose ages of immigration (and therefore ages of immersion in the language) naturally vary; and, most important, I've studied Deaf children, who often learn their *first* languages (in the United States, usually American Sign Language) at different ages and from linguistic models that vary greatly in proficiency.

We've learned from them that languages are best acquired early in life, and that language input is not as important: Children can overcome remarkably inconsistent and impoverished input, as long as they receive this input to natural languages early in life. We've recently brought these questions into the lab, designing miniature languages whose properties we can manipulate and which we can present to adults and young children under controlled circumstances. Even in the lab, we can clearly see the better learning of young children and the ways in which adults – whose cognitive capacities are much greater in other ways – are not as good at learning languages or other types of complex sequential patterns.

My interest in developmental plasticity has been an enduring fascination with the idea that plasticity and learning can change over development and that infants and children can be better at many things than adults. But I have also been inspired by the important societal issues affected by understanding developmental plasticity. In the Deaf community, children have long been denied access to signed languages during their early years, in the hope that they might better acquire spoken languages – to which, unfortunately, they do not have adequate sensory access (no, cochlear implants do not solve this problem for most children). Now that we know that successful language depends on early exposure, and also that American Sign Language is an independent and remarkably beautiful language, more Deaf children are gaining access to fluent sign language input early in life.

My most recent work focuses on recovery from stroke and other brain injuries, where once again young children seem to be the shining examples. Young children recover remarkably well from strokes or other injuries to the language areas of the brain. They do this by acquiring language successfully in healthy brain areas that are not ordinarily used for language – a recovery and reorganization process that does not occur when strokes occur during adulthood. We are trying to understand the mechanisms by which this early language reorganization occurs, in the hope that we can help people who experience a stroke as adults to recover as well as children do.

Our future question concerns how to re-open early critical periods: How do we restore the remarkable learning abilities of infants to adults, especially when these capacities are needed in order to recover from injuries to the brain? This may sound like science fiction, but, in fact, in the animal lab, cutting-edge research involves learning how to re-open critical periods. My hope is that, in the future, we will understand these mechanisms so well that, for those who have brain injuries or develop neurological diseases, we can restore developmental plasticity exactly where and when we need it. This might mean that we could enable people to truly recover from neurological disease, just as they recover from breaking an arm or cutting their finger. I believe that this is not so far away in our understanding of an issue that has fascinated me for most of my career.

REFERENCES

Lenneberg, E. H. (1969). On explaining language: The development of language in children can best be understood in the context of developmental biology. *Science, 164,* 635–643.

Newport, E. L. (1990). Maturational constraints on language learning. *Cognitive Science, 14,* 11–28.

Newport, E. L. (2016). Statistical language learning: Computational, maturational and linguistic constraints. *Language and Cognition,* in press.

46   Levels of Analysis in Cognitive Aging

Salthouse, Timothy A.

Much of my professional life has been devoted to studying the relations between aging and cognition in order to understand why increased age is associated with lower levels of performance on different types of cognitive tests. This phenomenon of age-related cognitive decline is clearly evident in comparisons from standardized tests used to assess cognitive ability in adults, and significant negative age relations are typically found in tests as diverse as the assembly of blocks to match a design and the selection of items that best complete a sequence.

I began my career as a graduate student at the University of Michigan in the early 1970s, where my focus was on information-processing perspectives on cognition in normal (i.e., college student) adults. This approach to cognition emphasized the decomposition of cognitive tasks into sequences of processing operations, with the theoretical speculations often expressed in flow charts of the type used in computer programming. When I started studying relations between aging and cognition, I assumed that the information-processing perspective would be valuable in "localizing the loss" or "isolating the impairment" associated with aging to a few critical processing stages. Indeed, the dominant interpretations of adult age differences in cognition in the 1970s and 1980s emphasized task-specific explanations, such as ineffective strategy use or deficits in a critical component such as encoding or abstraction. However, as I read the relevant literature, I discovered that many different types of cognitive measures were negatively related to age, and not merely a few as one might expect if the age differences were caused by a discrete deficit in a specific cognitive process such as memory retrieval. In other words, adults in their sixties and seventies not only performed at lower levels than adults in their twenties and thirties on tests of memory, but also on tests of reasoning, spatial visualization, problem solving, etc. Although it was clearly possible that age differences in different cognitive variables had specific causes that were largely independent of one another, I began investigating an alternative interpretation that a small number of relatively broad and general factors might be contributing to the age differences across a wide variety of cognitive tasks.

214

My initial focus was on measures obtained from reaction-time and speeded paper-and-pencil tasks because they were postulated to represent how quickly simple cognitive operations could be performed. However, instead of assuming that adult age differences in the speed of performing a given task reflected a specific deficit, I examined how the performance of young and old adults varied across a range of different speeded tasks. The results of these analyses extended an earlier finding by Brinley of a systematic, and nearly linear, relation between the performance of older adults on a set of tasks and the performance of young adults on those same tasks. That is, young and old adults were very similar in terms of which particular tasks were easy and which were difficult, but the difference between the performance of older adults and that of young adults was typically greater as task difficulty increased.

I proposed that the relation represented the operation of general age-related influences common to different types of cognitive tasks, and that only if the measures from a given cognitive task deviated from the general function would a researcher be justified in postulating the existence of specific deficits. Because a great deal of research from many different laboratories revealed that results from a wide variety of speeded tasks could be accommodated within roughly similar linear young–old functions, the findings were interpreted by me and others as evidence for a substantial contribution of general, or task-independent, age-related influences on speeded measures of cognitive functioning.

The next phase in my research extended this multivariate perspective to different types of cognitive measures by using statistical procedures to hold constant the variation in one or more measures when examining age differences in other measures. For example, age differences in measures of reasoning were examined before and after effectively equating people on their performance in tests of speed. These methods required a different type of research than that prevalent at the time because multiple measures of different types of cognition were required from moderately large samples of adults, who ideally spanned a wide and continuous range of ages. That is, measures of several types of cognition were needed to investigate general influences, large sample sizes were needed to provide sufficient statistical power to detect differences in the magnitude of age differences, and a continuous range of ages was desirable to characterize the trajectories across all of adulthood. Of particular interest in the analyses was whether the age differences in the target cognitive measure were reduced after control of the variance in other measures: If so, one could infer that at least some of the age-related influences on the measures were shared, and were not independent of one another.

The results of these procedures revealed that the estimates of shared influences varied across different combinations of cognitive measures. However, in most cases the shared estimates were substantial, which was interpreted as evidence that general influences were contributing to the age–cognition relations in different types of cognition. To illustrate, the simple correlations of age with measures of block assembly and sequence completion were –0.48 and –0.53, respectively. However, after statistical control of an estimate of the variance common to these and other cognitive measures, the correlations were only –0.03 and –0.07, respectively. Results such as these imply that many of the age-related influences were shared, and that at least some of the age differences in the measures were likely attributable to general, rather than specific, factors.

Similar types of evidence have accumulated over recent decades, suggesting that adult age differences on measures of cognitive functioning reflect a mixture of domain-general and domain-specific influences. I suspect that any scientific visibility I might have is attributable to my role as one of the proponents of this position. There are still debates regarding the best methods of distinguishing general and specific influences, and about the relative contributions of each type of influence on individual cognitive measures. Nevertheless, I believe that there is compelling evidence that age-related differences on many (and possibly all) cognitive measures represent a mixture of general and specific influences.

Perhaps because I am personally involved in it, I also believe that this perspective has important theoretical and methodological implications. For example, a major theoretical implication of the perspective is that a shift will be required in what must be explained if both general and specific influences are contributing to the age differences in cognitive measures. That is, theoretical interpretations will not only have to account for the relations of age on a single measure, and the relations of age on a combination of variables assumed to represent the same ability construct, but also for influences that are shared across different types of cognitive measures and constructs.

One of the most important methodological implications of the general-and-specific perspective is that merely because a single variable is measured in a study does not mean that only influences specific to that variable are being observed. In other words, if general influences are operating, some of the age-related effects on the target variable are likely shared with age-related effects on other cognitive variables, and hence are not unique to that variable. This is an important consideration when investigating correlates of cognitive functioning because interpretations of the relations may be misleading if the observed variables reflect a mixture of general and specific determinants and their relative contributions are not distinguished.

I suspect that at least two directions will prove productive in extending these ideas. One potentially valuable line of research involves attempting to identify the mechanisms involved in both general and specific influences on age–cognition relations because specifying how the influences operate is essential for them to be fully understood. A second direction for future research is to extend the investigation of general and specific influences to other types of individual differences, such as child development and various patient populations. Not only would interpretation of other types of differences likely benefit from considering effects on particular measures of cognitive functioning in the context of broad effects on other cognitive measures, but research with other dimensions of individual differences may help clarify the nature of general influences.

In looking back at this overview of my research, it strikes me that one of the most important decisions in research concerns the level of analysis to be pursued when investigating the phenomena of interest. If the level is too narrow, broad principles may be missed, but if the level is too broad, critical details may be overlooked. This may seem a rather trivial observation, but it can have major implications for how research is conducted and interpreted. In my case, it has led me to the realization that the relations between aging and cognition may be both simpler (in the sense that many of the effects on individual cognitive measures appear to be shared) and more complex (in the sense that little is currently known about the mechanisms responsible for general influences) than was originally recognized.

REFERENCES

Salthouse, T. A. (1996). The processing speed theory of adult age differences in cognition. *Psychological Review, 103*, 403–428.

Salthouse, T. A. (2010). Selective review of cognitive aging. *Journal of International Neuropsychological Society, 16*, 754–760.

Salthouse, T. A., & Ferrer-Caja, E. (2003). What needs to be explained to account for age-related effects on multiple cognitive variables? *Psychology and Aging, 18*, 91–110.

47 The Longitudinal Study of Adult Cognitive Development

Schaie, K. Warner

My Most Important Scientific Contribution

I would consider the Seattle Longitudinal Study (SLS) to be my most important scientific contribution. This study has addressed the following questions:

1. Do cognitive abilities age at the same rate across people?
2. Do they decline at the same rate, starting when?
3. How can these topics best be studied?

This research began as a cross-sectional study, in which different groups of adults between twenty and seventy years of age were studied at the same time. The goal was to determine the impact of rigidity-flexibility on age differences in Thurstone's Primary Mental Abilities. This sample was then retested every seven years until 2012, with new samples added at each test occasions. We also converted the study of age comparisons to a long-term study of age changes in the same individuals. Data collections were added to study personality traits, family characteristics, health behaviors, and social-environmental variables, as well as records of health problems. The brains of some study participants were also studied by means of MRI scans over a ten-year period.

In addition, we have conducted family studies of the children, siblings, and grandchildren of our original study participants. Cognitive training studies were also conducted over a twenty-one-year period to determine whether it was possible to increase the cognitive performance of people over sixty years of age to the performance level of individuals who had been tested fourteen years earlier, as well as whether it was possible to increase performance of older persons by means of training interventions.

Why Is It My Most Important Scientific Contribution?

1. The study showed conclusively that cross-sectional data on age differences in cognitive performance cannot be used as an estimate of

218

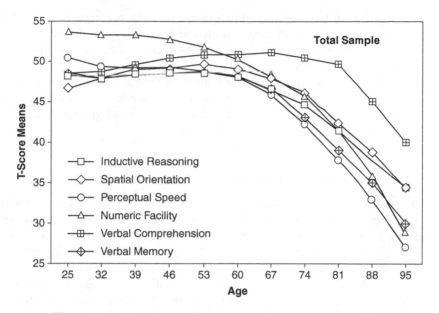

Figure 47.1. Age changes from estimated seven-year data of cognitive ability factors.From: Schaie, K. W. (2013). *Developmental influences on adult intellectual development: The Seattle Longitudinal Study* (2nd rev. edn., p. 162). New York: Oxford University Press.

longitudinal change within individuals over their life span. This is because cross-sectional data compare different people, while change over time and age always involves the same individuals.

2. We found vast individual differences in the rate of intellectual aging. People's thinking processes are differentially based on their educational attainment, occupational complexity, socioeconomic status, ability level of spouse, engagement in social and intellectual pursuits, and levels of cognitive flexibility.

3. Most individuals attain their highest level of cognitive function from the fourth to the sixth decade of life. Little decline is observed prior to the seventh decade for most abilities, and verbal ability remains at a high level until the eighth decade.

4. We found that people born more recently attain higher levels at later ages than people born at earlier times. Those born at the later times also show slower rates of cognitive decline in old age. Most adult children exceed the performance level of their parents, except for number skills, where the older generation excels.

5. Cognitive intervention studies suggest that the performance of older persons can be significantly improved by training, with the training effects being greater for those who had shown decline over the previous fourteen-year period.
6. Individuals carrying at least one allele 4 of the Apolipoprotein E gene are thought to be of increased risk to experience Alzheimer's disease in old age. In the SLS, such individuals also showed greater decline in early old age than those without that allele.

How Did I Get the Idea for the Contribution?

As an undergraduate in the department of psychology of the University of California at Berkeley I was introduced to the seminal work of L. L. Thurstone on what he called the "building blocks of intelligence" by the stimulating lectures of Professor Read Tuddenham, who eventually became my undergraduate advisor. Having discovered that Thurstone's Primary Mental Abilities had never been studied in adults, I conducted a directed study with Tuddenham, in which I administered the Primary Mental Abilities tests to some seventy adults, most of whom were recruited from the geriatric practice of my family physician, Robert M. Perlman. He encouraged me to submit an abstract for a presentation at the second International Congress of Gerontology in 1951 in St. Louis. Here, I first met many of the early players in American Gerontology, including James Birren, Jack Botwinick, Robert Butler, and Robert Kleemeyer. I was encouraged to submit my paper, which eventually became my first scientific publication. Having a paper "in press" may have been a major factor in my being accepted for graduate study in clinical psychology at the University of Washington.

The undergraduate project convinced me that while some older folks fitted the popular stereotype of being "doddering old fools," many others seemed to have maintained high cognitive levels and were now "wise old people." As I looked for a dissertation topic, I figured that these differential paths through the later two-thirds of life were worth studying further.

My graduate mentor at the University of Washington, Charles Strother, at this time was chairman of the board of one of the first large American health maintenance organizations, the Group Health Cooperative of Puget Sound. He worked out a deal wherein I was allowed to give the Thurstone tests to a random sample drawn from the HMO membership for my dissertation research in return for also collecting consumer satisfaction for the HMO. These data, of course, represent the beginning of what eventually became the Seattle Longitudinal Study, which continues to date.

How Does the Idea Matter for Psychological Science and Also for the World Beyond Academia?

1. The SLS conclusively demonstrated the vast differences in findings from cross-sectional and longitudinal study designs. It showed that cross-sectional data overestimated actual within-person age changes from young adulthood into old age.
2. The SLS has used a cohort-sequential design, which allows the psychological researcher to distinguish the impact of chronological age, birth cohort, and time of measurement effects in aging studies. This design is now widely used by researchers in geropsychology.
3. The SLS introduced the use of survival analysis (determining at which age a particular event or change occurs) into psychological science in order to predict the age at which a given individual is likely to first experience a significant decline for different cognitive abilities.
4. Data from the SLS have been used as significant evidence in several successful age discrimination lawsuits pursued by the federal Office of Equal Opportunity.
5. Data from the SLS constituted an important basis for the abandonment of rules for mandatory retirement by age for higher education faculty, police, and fire fighters.

What Would I Like to See as the Next Steps in Theory and/or Research?

Due to the availability of MRI technology for the study of age changes in brain structure and functioning, it will now be possible to engage in empirical studies of the hypothesis that well-functioning individuals develop cognitive reserves during early and middle adulthood, reserves that protect them against some adverse changes occurring with increasing age. The major question (to be answered by cross-lagged panel correlation designs) is whether behavior changes occur subsequent to brain changes, or whether brain changes follow significant behavioral changes.

REFERENCES

Schaie, K. W. (2013). *Developmental influences on adult intellectual development: The Seattle Longitudinal Study* (2nd rev. edn.). New York: Oxford University Press.

Schaie, K. W. (2016). The psychology of aging. In V. L. Bengtson & R. L. Settersten (eds.), *Handbook of theories of aging* (3rd edn.). New York: Springer Publishing Company.

Schaie, K. W. (2016). Theoretical perspectives for the psychology of aging in a lifespan context. In K. W. Schaie & S. L. Willis (eds.), *Handbook of the psychology of aging* (8th edn., pp. 3–15). San Diego: Elsevier.

48 How Does Change Occur?

Siegler, Robert S.

For as long as I can remember, I've been fascinated by change. How does an infant turn into a toddler, and then a preschooler, a child, an adolescent, an adult, and, eventually, a senior? What leads to changes in people's character, their intellect, their relationships with other people? What, if anything, unites evolutionary processes, regardless of whether they involve the evolution of species, the evolution of businesses, the evolution of national policies, or the evolution of a person's thinking about a specific topic?

This fascination with change led me to study the development of learning and problem-solving during childhood. Within the human lifetime, many of the greatest changes are seen from birth through adolescence; indeed, childhood can be defined as the period of life in which positive change is most dramatic.

Most of my research on learning and problem-solving during childhood has focused on the development of mathematical thinking. This interest began in childhood, when I became intrigued by the statistics on the backs of baseball cards: batting averages, hits, home runs, win-loss percentages, earned run averages, and so on. I spent innumerable hours engrossed in identifying from these statistics the best player at each position and which teams were most likely to win the World Series.

A variety of factors led to my pursuing this early interest in my research. When I began to do research, Piaget's theory, which was built in large part from observations of mathematical and scientific thinking, was the dominant approach to cognitive development. My early research was intended to show that Piaget had underestimated children's capacity for problem-solving and learning in these areas. Although the results of my early research supported this hypothesis, observing how tenaciously young children clung to their misconceptions about scientific and mathematical concepts led me to an enduring appreciation for Piaget's genius in designing revealing tasks, where answers and explanations on a single trial could lead to insights about children's thinking.

My appreciation for this aspect of Piaget's genius led to the discovery that I consider to be my most fundamental – fundamental in the sense that it provided the foundation for numerous subsequent discoveries. The discovery was that we can accurately assess individual children's problem-solving strategy on each problem by video-recording ongoing overt behavior during the problem and then immediately afterward obtaining the child's explanation of how he or she solved the problem. Combining the two types of data is more effective than using either alone; children sometimes do not generate any overt behavior, in which case the explanation can be used alone, and children sometimes cannot explain what they did, in which case the overt behavior can be used alone.

The first dividend of this discovery was to show that many models that seemed accurate when evaluated against data averaged across participants and problems were oversimplified or flat-out wrong. In some cases, the previously accepted model proved accurate on most problems but not on many others; in other cases, the previously accepted model proved accurate on a minority of trials; and in yet other cases, the model failed to accurately depict any individual children's thinking on any single trials, but, rather, was an artifact of averaging the data that arose from different approaches.

A second dividend of the trial-by-trial strategy assessments was richer and more accurate descriptions of children's problem-solving than was previously possible. Rather than all children of a given age using a single strategy to solve a given task, or some children using one strategy and other children using a different one, individual children have been found to use between 3 and 10 strategies on a wide variety of tasks. The tasks where such varied strategies are used include arithmetic, spelling, reading, scientific reasoning, attention, memory, tool use, estimation, inferences about other people's thinking, descending down ramps, and many others. For example, when adding small numbers, the same first grader might count from 1 on the first problem (e.g., "2+5 = 1, 2 – 1, 2, 3, 4, 5 – 1, 2, 3, 4, 5, 6, 7"), count from the larger number on the second (e.g., "2+7= 7, 8, 9"), draw an analogy to a related problem on the third (e.g., "2+9 = 2+10–1"), and retrieve the answer on the fourth (e.g., "2+3=5").

Appreciation of this strategic variability made possible a more nuanced portrayal of development than previously. Rather than development involving use of one way of thinking for a prolonged period, then a sudden hard-to-understand shift to a different way of thinking, and eventually another sudden shift to a third way of thinking, development was found to involve use of varied strategies at each age, with cognitive growth coming from increased use of more effective strategies, decreased use of less effective strategies, increasingly efficient execution of all of the strategies, and discovery of novel strategies. To continue with the example of simple addition, between kindergarten and second grade, counting from one becomes less common, retrieval from memory becomes more common, counting from the larger addend at first becomes more common and then becomes less common, and children discover that they can draw analogies to tie problems (e.g., "if 3+3 equals 6, 4+3 must equal 7"). Execution of all of these strategies becomes faster and more accurate during this period.

Discovering this strategic variability raised a new question: How do children (and adults) choose among the varied strategies that they know and use? There had been no reason to ask this question when people believed that children only used a single strategy at a single time. However, when the extent of strategic variability was documented, whether children chose wisely among problem-solving approaches became an important issue.

It turned out that children and adults usually do choose wisely. They often use a simple but effective rule of thumb for choosing among alternative strategies: Use the fastest strategy that you can execute accurately. Thus, if children can accurately retrieve answers to problems, they usually will solve the problems via retrieval, because retrieval is very rapid. On the other hand, if they cannot accurately retrieve the answer to a problem, they will more often use slower but more accurate strategies. In the addition example, even kindergartners usually retrieve the answer to 2+2, but on problems such as 2+5, they are more likely to count from one. These patterns are rarely all or none, though. Even college students use strategies other than retrieval to solve roughly 20 percent of single digit addition problems, and do so roughly half the time on problems such as 6+9.

Ability to assess strategy use on each trial also made possible microgenetic studies. These are experiments in which children are given greater amounts of relevant experience than is typical at their age, and their learning is followed on a trial-by-trial basis. This allows identification of a given child's discovery of new strategies, as well as the events that led up to the discovery and how it is generalized beyond its initial use.

Microgenetic studies have yielded a variety of consistent findings. One is that immediately before a discovery, performance usually becomes more variable. Children use a greater range of strategies, they generate short-lived transition strategies that often have elements of the more enduring discovery but are less effective, their solution times vary more, and they often have unusual difficulty explaining what they are doing. Another common finding is that even the most advantageous new strategies are often generalized slowly, with less effective previous approaches persisting for extended periods of time, even when children can explain why the new strategy is better. A third frequent observation is that newly discovered strategies that are very advantageous relative to alternatives tend to be generalized more rapidly than new strategies that are only somewhat better than previous ones.

My interest in numerical development, in the process of change, and in using psychological science to do some good in the world has led to my becoming increasingly interested in applying research to improving mathematics education. When children begin school, their numerical knowledge already varies greatly. Children from impoverished urban families typically start school already a year or more behind children from middle-income backgrounds in terms of numerical knowledge. These early differences seem to have long-term consequences: Four-year-olds' numerical knowledge predicts math achievement test scores in high school, above and beyond other relevant factors such as children's IQ and parents' income and education.

A very large amount of research indicates that people and many other animals organize numerical knowledge in a way that resembles a mental number line, with smaller numbers on the left and larger ones on the right. Preschoolers from low-income backgrounds, however, often have not yet organized numbers in this way. To help them do so, Geetha Ramani and I devised a numerical board game that had 10 squares in a row, with the numeral "1" at the left and "10" at the right. In playing the game, a child and an adult would alternate spinning a spinner and moving their token 1 or 2 spaces in accord with the spin; the first one to reach 10 would be the winner. Players were required to say the number in each square as they moved their token through it; thus, if the spin stopped on "2," a child whose token was on "3" would need to count "4, 5." The adult helped the child count when necessary. This game was expected to help children form a mental number line, because it would provide non-verbal cues to the sizes of the numbers. For example, it would take twice as many hand move-ments, twice as many counts, saying twice as many number words, and moving the token twice as far to reach 8 as to reach 4. Thus, playing the game provided visual, auditory, motor, and time-related cues to the sizes of the numbers.

This game proved effective not only in helping children learn the sizes of the numbers and organize them on a mental number line, but also in helping them learn to count, to identify printed numbers, and to learn the answers to simple addition problems. A version of the game involving a 10 × 10 matrix helped slightly older children learn about the numbers 1–100.

This merging of scientific research and educational application is a highly promising direction not only for improving mathematics instruction but also for improving instruction in reading, writing, science, and other areas. Insights from research are already being applied to these areas to some extent, but much greater benefits are within reach. The combination of investigators conducting research directly relevant to instruction and educators applying the lessons of the research in classrooms can make this promise a reality.

REFERENCES

Siegler, R. S. (1976). *Three aspects of cognitive development*. New York: Elsevier.

Siegler, R. S. (1991). *Children's thinking*. Englewood Cliffs: Prentice-Hall.

Siegler, R. S. (1996). *Emerging minds: The process of change in children's thinking*. New York: Oxford.

49   Cognitive Abilities of Infants

Spelke, Elizabeth

I entered psychology at an exciting time. An extraordinary scientist, Eleanor Gibson, had shown that a capacity for visual depth perception is innate: It is present and functional on first encounters with a visible environment.

Gibson, one of my two graduate advisors, thus settled a longstanding question concerning the development of perception, and she raised a broader possibility concerning the development of knowledge. Do infants not only perceive *where* surfaces are, but also *what* they are? Do they organize arrays of surfaces into meaningful objects and events?

My other graduate advisor, Ulric Neisser, was one of the founders of the modern field of cognitive psychology. At the time, he was studying the processes by which adults attend selectively and adaptively to events. He and others (especially Anne Treisman and Daniel Kahneman) discovered that attention tends to focus on discrete objects (whether people or things), rather than arrays of surfaces – so much so that if college students are watching a competitive ball game, they follow the players and the ball so well that they may miss a gorilla crossing the room. But are we built to perceive, attend to, and understand objects, or do these abilities develop as we explore objects and observe their behavior? I became fascinated by this question.

One of my first experiments asked whether infants who can't yet manipulate objects have separate or unitary experiences of objects' associated sights and sounds. To find out, I made simple, short movies of a person playing "peekaboo" and of a hand making a rhythmic pattern with a baton and tambourine. When both movies played side by side and each soundtrack was heard in alternation through a central speaker, four-month-old infants looked primarily at whichever movie currently accompanied the sound. Later studies in other labs showed that infants are exquisitely sensitive to the relations between sound and movement that accompany human speech, and that they detect some relations between sounds and visible objects even at birth. Thus, infants do not simply look and listen to people and things; they relate these separate sensory impressions to one

228

another. But do babies perceive objects as we do? As a new assistant professor, I began to address this question with students in my own lab.

Object perception is fascinating, because visual arrays of objects are complex. No opaque object is ever fully in view (its back is hidden), and most objects sit upon, beside, or behind other objects that partly hide them. Nevertheless, adults perceive arrangements of solid objects, not patchworks of visible surfaces. What do infants perceive? Philip Kellman and I took advantage of the fact that infants, like adults, get bored if they see the same thing repeatedly, and they perk up if it changes. We showed four-month-old infants a rod that moved back and forth behind a block that hid its center, until their looking declined. Then we took away the block and alternately presented one long connected rod and two short rods separated by a gap where the block had been. Infants looked longer at the latter display, suggesting that they found this display to be new and had perceived the visible ends of the original rod as one connected object. Like adults, infants appeared to perceive objects as solid bodies that continue behind other bodies. Many further experiments in my lab and others followed, confirming that suggestion and revealing that this aspect of object perception is present at birth.

My students and I then began to wonder whether infants' understanding of objects goes beyond perception. Experiments with Renee Baillargeon tested for "object permanence" in infants, inspired by the compelling demonstrations by the Swiss developmental scientist Jean Piaget that infants have limited abilities to act on hidden objects. If an interesting object moves behind a boring one, young infants fail to push the unwanted obstacle out of the way, but do they realize that the hidden object still exists? We used the same looking-time methods to address this question. First we familiarized infants with a screen rotating repeatedly on one of its edges, and then we placed a small block behind the screen – a block that disappeared completely when the screen rotated upward to vertical.

Although infants could no longer see the block, their looking patterns suggested that they remembered its existence and expected the screen to stop when it reached the block. Infants looked more when the screen underwent a superficially familiar but "magical" rotation that passed through the block, than when the screen stopped at the hidden block's location. These findings suggest that infants knew that a fully hidden object was still present in the scene, and that they understand on some level that objects don't wink out of existence or pass through other objects. Many experiments now support these suggestions, including one new finding: When infants are shown an event that violates the solidity of an object, as did the rotating screen, they tend to bang the object against other objects, actively attempting to reproduce the apparently magical event.

As adults, our understanding is organized around abstract concepts. Understanding of material objects and their interactions is organized around concepts of *mass* and *force*; understanding of other people is organized around concepts of *belief* and *desire*. And basic concepts of mathematics – of *number* and *geometry* – organize and enrich our understanding of diverse domains. When in development do abstract concepts emerge?

We and others have found seeds of these abstract concepts in human infants. One experiment with Veronique Izard, probing infants' number concepts, brings me back to my first method. We presented newborn infants with auditory sequences of matched duration containing either four or twelve syllables. As the sequences played, infants were shown alternating visual arrays of four and twelve objects. Just as in the peekaboo studies, infants looked longer at the visual array that corresponded to the syllable sequences, although here the correspondence occurred at the level of abstract number. Sensitivity to number is present at birth.

Thus far, it may sound as if babies share all our concepts and cognitive abilities, but that is far from the case. Each of the above lines of research has revealed striking gaps in infants' perception and understanding. For example, infants distinguish between numbers that differ by large ratios but fail to distinguish numbers that differ by smaller ratios: Children's sense of number remains imprecise until they learn number words and symbols. As a second example, young infants expect objects not to pass through walls or float in the air without support, but they do not expect that a ball, released on a slanted surface, will roll downward rather than upward. Infants share only a small but crucial part of our knowledge.

What, in general terms, do infants know? Research suggests that they conceive of objects as bodies that exist and move continuously through space and time and that interact on contact: the kernel of our mature, commonsense understanding of physics. Infants also conceive of animals, including people, as agents who act so as to change the world and themselves, and who direct their actions efficiently toward goals. Infants conceive of people not only as agents, but also as social beings who engage with them and with one another, sharing their attention and emotion. And infants have numerical and geometrical concepts that guide their emerging navigation and their sensitivity to the statistical structure of the environment. Evidence from my lab and others suggests that these conceptions are products of distinct, early emerging systems that humans share with other animals: what I have called systems of *core knowledge*. The core knowledge found in infancy serves as a foundation for later learning and remains central to our thinking throughout life. Thus, research on cognition in infancy sheds light on aspects of mature cognition and cognitive development.

Studies of cognition in infancy raise many questions for future work. We have learned quite a bit about what infants perceive and know, but we don't know how knowledge is represented and processed in infant brains, or how it is extended by learning. Infants are prodigious learners: They come to recognize the significant people and places in their environment, to interpret and produce actions such as eating from a spoon, to categorize diverse kinds of objects, and to distinguish and interpret the words and rules of their language. As part of the National Science Foundation's Center for Brains, Minds, and Machines, my lab has begun to participate in an interdisciplinary effort to create and test computational models of infant minds. I hope that these models will deepen our understanding of the foundations of human knowledge. Conversely, I hope that the effort to create artificially intelligent systems will benefit from research on infant learners, as the visionary and pioneering computer scientist Alan Turing suggested long ago. Studies of cognition in infancy also may serve to improve education, through curricula that build on young children's cognitive strengths and address gaps in their knowledge. I am especially hopeful that the insights from this research will inform programs to enhance the readiness of preschool children to learn science and mathematics. As in medical research, however, these efforts will require a new wave of controlled experiments, bridging from laboratories to classrooms.

Science is full of surprises: Although we can control the process of an experiment, we have no control over its outcome. This lack of control makes science exciting. Some of my best moments have come from utterly unexpected findings, showing that my thinking was wrong. Science also is a collective enterprise. Although this book focuses on specific people, discoveries always depend on legions of people with different ideas, working in different disciplines, living in far-flung places, and united by their unstoppable curiosity. When I was a young member of this diverse community, I was able to share the wisdom of an older generation; now I can share the energy of younger generations. I am perpetually amazed that work can be so much fun.

REFERENCES

Dehaene, S., Spelke, E., Pinel, P., Stanescu, R., & Tsivkin, S. (1999). Sources of mathematical thinking: Behavioral and brain-imaging evidence. *Science, 284* (*5416*), 970–974.

Feigenson, L., Dehaene, S., & Spelke, E. (2004). Core systems of number. *Trends in Cognitive Sciences, 8* (7), 307–314.

Spelke, E. S. (1994). Initial knowledge: Six suggestions. *Cognition, 50*(1–3), 431–445.

Section B

Social/Personality Development

50 The Power of Observational Learning Through Social Modeling

Bandura, Albert

When I began my career, behaviorism dominated the field of psychology. In this theoretical orientation, human behavior was shaped primarily by paired associations or rewarding and punishing consequences. Two major issues concerned me regarding this line of theorizing. The first was the exclusive focus on learning by direct experience. The second was the mismatch between time-honored psychological theories and the incredible transformative changes in the nature of the environment in the electronic era.

Learning by More than Just Direct Experience

For learning by direct experience, I found it difficult to imagine a culture whose language, values, complex competences, and the elaborate practices of its social, political, and cultural systems all were shaped in each new member by trial-and-error learning. Fortunately, in real life, social modeling (learning by example) of thinking and behaving can shortcut the laborious trial-and-error process. I launched a large-scale program of research to advance our understanding of this pervasive mode of learning and to apply this knowledge for individual and social change.

We showed that social modeling operates through four core processes. *Attentional* processes determine what people observe in the profusion of other people's behavior styles and the information they extract from what they observe. The second aspect of social modeling involves *representational processes*, whereby modeled events are converted into symbolic representations available for future recall. People cannot be much influenced by modeled events if they do not remember them. In the third aspect, *translational production processes*, symbolic representations are transformed into corresponding courses of action. *Motivational processes* determine whether people will act on what they have learned. People do not perform everything they learn through observation.

We found that virtually everything learned by direct experience could be learned much faster through social modeling. Further research clarified the four major ways social modeling exerts its influence. First, it instructs people in new ways of thinking and behaving. Second, it also affects motivation and self-regulation by conveying the functional value of modeled behavior. Seeing others gain desired outcomes by their actions creates outcome expectancies that serve as positive incentives. Conversely, seeing others punished for certain actions creates negative outcome expectancies that serve as disincentives. Third, people are easily aroused by the emotional experiences of others. This capacity for vicarious emotional arousal plays a key role in emotional learning. People acquire lasting attitudes and emotional reactions toward persons, places, and things through modeled emotional displays. Fourth, during the course of their daily lives, people have direct contact with only a small sector of the physical and social environment. Consequently, their conceptions of the vast social reality (with much of which they have little or no contact) are greatly influenced by media representations of society. The media portray ideological orientations, views of human nature, social and power relations, and the structure of social systems. Influence via the media is the most pervasive type of influence and shapes public consciousness.

Scientific advances in our understanding of social modeling's powerful system of motivation and learning required correcting some common misconceptions. Social modeling is not just response mimicry, as widely believed. Social modeling operates at a higher level of learning. Modeled judgments and actions may differ in specific content but embody the same principles. Once observers extract the underlying principles, they can construct new versions of that style of behavior, which go beyond the particular modeled examples.

Another misconception concerned the scope of modeling. Critics argued that modeling cannot build cognitive skills because thought processes are covert and not adequately reflected in modeled actions (which are the end-products). We saw this as a limitation of methodological ingenuity, rather than an inherent limitation of modeling. Cognitive skills can be made observable and are effectively cultivated by cognitive modeling. In this approach, the human models verbalize aloud their reasoning, strategies, and cognitive self-management, as they engage in problem-solving activities. Observers can socially learn cognitive skills.

Another misconception is that modeling is antithetical to creativity. Quite the contrary. Social modeling promotes innovativeness. Individuals who model unconventional styles of thinking and doing then foster innovativeness in others, whereas those who model conventional ways diminish creativity. Also, innovations are rarely entirely new. Innovators select useful elements from existing examples (models), improve on them, synthesize them into new forms, and tailor them to particular purposes. In these ways social modeling contributes to innovation.

Mismatch of Earlier Theories with New Media Environments

Our time-honored psychological theories were developed even before the advent of television, let alone the Internet. Because that was the lived environment at the time, the theories focused mainly on the influences operating within the immediate social and physical environment. However, revolutionary advances in communication technology radically changed how people live their lives, as well as the nature, scope, and sources of human influence. In this electronic era, extensive modeling in the cyberworld promotes ideas, values, belief systems, lifestyles, and sociopolitical movements worldwide. Ready access to the symbolic environment enables people to transcend the confines of their immediate lived environment. A major advantage of cyber and other symbolic modeling lies in its tremendous reach, speed, and instructive power. Unlike learning by doing, which requires shaping the actions of each individual through repeated consequences, in learning by observation a single model can transmit new ways of thinking and behaving simultaneously to vast populations in widely dispersed locales.

With the advent of television, diverse styles of thinking and behaving were transmitted to homes day in and day out. In much of their prime-time offerings, the television industry exploited gratuitous violence, in the erroneous belief that people crave it. Hence, gratuitous violence was used as the tactic to deliver viewers to advertisers. Families were watching the whole gamut of human brutality daily in the comfort of their homes – with growing concern about its possible effects.

As part of my research on social modeling, I included novel forms of physical and verbal aggression modeled in a televised format. (The ones that involved a model aggressing against an inflatable clown came to be known as the "Bobo Doll" studies.) Catharsis theory would predict that frustrated children could reduce their pent up anger by watching aggression, so they would be less aggressive in their behavior. Contrary to this prediction, children increased their aggression using the novel forms they saw modeled.

I was often invited to testify at congressional hearings on such media violence effects. The findings of these modeling studies did not sit well with the television industry. In this baptism in public policy, I was pilloried by the television industry and criticized in editorials in the 1969 *TV Guide* with titles such as "The Man in the Eye of the Hurricane." These critics, such as Efron, claimed that the "Bandura school ... won them center stage in Washington," and criticized the Surgeon General for acting "as if Rome were burning and Dr. Bandura were a fire extinguisher" (pp. 34–36).

The value of a theory is judged not only by its explanatory and pre-dicative power; in the final analysis, it is evaluated on its operative power to inform individual and social change. Modeling theory was widely applied in different fields of psychology and across disciplinary lines. The most ambitious applications of social modeling addressed urgent global problems. One inventive dramatist, Miguel Sabido at Televisa, drew on principles of social modeling from the Bobo Doll studies in creating long-running, serial dramas to alleviate societal problems and improve the quality of people's lives.

These dramatic productions are not just fanciful stories. The plotlines portray people's everyday lives and the impediments they face. They help people to see a better life and develop by modeling self-efficacy and coping skills to take the steps to realize their hopes. Hundreds of episodes over several years allow viewers to form emotional bonds to the models. Viewers are enabled by them to improve their lives. By including multiple inter-secting plotlines in subplots, one can address different aspects of people's lives rather than just a single issue. For example, the intersecting plotlines in a serial drama in Sudan included the benefits of family planning, educational opportunities for daughters, injustice of forced marriage, risks of early childbearing, prevention of HIV infection, engagement in drug activities, and genital mutilation. This flexible format contributes to its generalizability, versatility, and power.

Large-scale social change requires three complementary systems: a theoretical system that provides reliable principles of change, a transla-tional and implementable system that turns theory into effective practice, and a social diffusion system that adapts the successful practices for use in different cultural milieus. An international media center served as the diffusion vehicle. We psychologists often do not profit from our theore-tical successes because we lack creative translational systems and effective means to disseminate proven psychosocial approaches.

Modeling applications in Africa, Asia, and Latin America are raising literacy levels, enhancing the status of women in societies in which they are marginalized and denied their freedom and dignity, reducing unplanned childbearing to break the cycle of poverty and stem the soaring population growth, curtailing the spread of the AIDS epidemic, reigning in child trafficking for slave labor, reducing support for genital mutilation, and promoting conservation practices designed to preserve an environ-mentally sustainable future.

People often cite examples in the physical and biological sciences where basic research pursued for its own sake resulted in unforeseen beneficial applications. The Bobo Doll studies, which were designed to verify key processes governing social modeling, provided the principles for unforeseen global applications twenty-five years later.

REFERENCES

Bandura, A. (1997). *Self-efficacy: The exercise of control*. New York: Freeman.

Bandura, A. (2004). Social cognitive theory for personal and social change by enabling media. In A. Singhal, M. J. Cody, E. M. Rogers, & M. Sabido (eds.), *Entertainment-education and social change: History, research, and practice* (pp. 75–96). Mahwah: Lawrence Erlbaum.

Bandura, A. (2016) *Moral disengagement: How people do harm and live with themselves*. New York: Worth Publishers.

51   Human Development in Evolutionary-Biological Perspective

Belsky, Jay

It was the best idea I would ever have, I realized, as soon as I had it – a true eureka experience – while teaching a graduate seminar early in my career. I had been struggling with an intellectual issue as I had never done before, seeking insight that would enable me to test a provocative – even radical – new theoretical perspective on the ways in which the experiences children have while growing up shape who they become later in life. My best idea would not only revolutionize my thinking, but would stimulate a second important insight.

My training in and early research on human development was rather traditional, founded on the commonsense idea that there are good ways of caring for children that promote their well-being – or "optimal" development – and bad ways that foster problematic functioning. Thus, sensitive-responsive parenting, provided by economically secure and happily married parents, fosters children's emotional security, intellectual competence, and social skills, resulting, eventually, in an adult able to love and to work in productive and satisfying ways. In contrast, marital discord, economic insufficiency, and detached, intrusive, insensitive, or harsh parenting foster the opposite. These views were founded on classic developmental perspectives, including psychoanalytic, attachment, and social-learning theories.

But my thinking began to change after reading a fascinating anthropology paper that a colleague, Pat Draper, had written and left with me many months earlier. Pat's work introduced me to life-history theory, a branch of evolutionary biology which stipulates that ALL living things have the same fundamental goal – and it is not to be rich, happy, or healthy, but, rather, to pass their genes on to future generations. And that the best way to get this job of life done depends on the conditions in which the living organism finds itself, humans included. Notably, then, there is no optimal development. So what my training had taught me regarding what qualified as "good" parenting, "healthy" family life, and "optimal" child development turned out, when examined from the perspective of life-history theory and evolutionary biology, to be best only under particular circumstances, but not others.

From this perspective, a child growing up under conditions of poverty, child abuse, harsh parenting, or marital discord, for example, and who takes advantage of others, is sexually promiscuous, has children young, parents poorly, or experiences problems in marriage and life more generally, is developing in ways that Darwinian natural selection shaped humans to function when their early life experiences have led them – and their bodies – to understand that life is dangerous and precarious and others cannot be trusted. This shaping occurred because such an (often unconscious) approach to life increased the chances of such individuals successfully passing on their genes over the course of human evolutionary history.

However fascinating I found this evolutionary way of thinking, it reflected little more than "old wine in a new bottle." It just offered a new way of framing development, emphasizing reproductive fitness or the passing of genes down generational lines, rather than mental health. But what it didn't (yet?) do was offer any new predictions that would lead to new discoveries. Only such insights would make this intriguing perspective compelling. What was required, then, was a novel prediction, one that would lead to an empirical discovery that no other theory could explain, should it prove accurate. That was the issue I struggled with and which I resolved in a flash of insight.

If, according to life-history thinking, what was long regarded as "bad" from a mental-health perspective was actually "good" from a reproductive-fitness standpoint, then – and here's the prediction and the best idea I ever had – *adverse experiences growing up, such as harsh parenting, should lead to an earlier age of sexual maturation*. This was because such accelerated development would increase the chances that the person growing up in a risky environment could pass on his or her genes before it was too late, due to premature death or illness. Such a person whose life offered limited opportunity to develop skills to succeed in life, including attracting a good mate and raising healthy and productive children, also would benefit, biologically speaking, by bearing more children than those exposed to more advantaged conditions, even while providing lower quality care for them. Ultimately, it is better to have many offspring (even more than can be cared for well), beginning early, because this increases the chances, given the resources available, that at least some will survive to pass on their own – and their parents' – genes.

In other words, adversity-induced *accelerated sexual development* would pay off reproductively and reflect a quantity- rather than quality-oriented *reproductive strategy*. Essentially, the developing organism conceptualizes – not necessarily consciously – life in the following terms: "Since I cannot sufficiently control what happens to me and my offspring to make certain that I or they become healthy and capable adults, able to attract a talented mate and rear children well who will reproduce themselves, then I – and my offspring – should mature earlier, mate with many, bear multiple children and thereby increase the chances that at least some of them will grow up to pass on their own genes – and thus mine as well." So-called problematic development, then, involving taking advantage of others, being sexually promiscuous, having children at a young age and caring for them poorly becomes not so much a reflection of suboptimal development, but an excellent strategy for passing on genes under developmental conditions in which others can't be trusted and life itself is precarious. By the same token, developing in just the opposite manner is also a good approach – if one is raised in a well-functioning family, by happily married parents, with sufficient economic resources. Whereas early developers adopt a strategy of short-term gain by insuring reproduction despite long-term costs, the later developers pursue a strategy of long-term gain even if risking failure to pass on their genes by delaying reproduction (i.e., short-term cost).

Research designed to test my "puberty prediction" has generally confirmed it – in the case of females. The fact that growing up under adverse circumstances results in girls maturing earlier than would otherwise be the case is not something any traditional theory anticipated or can even explain, making clear that seeing the world through evolutionary lenses enhances understanding of human development. Indeed, the fact that this new framework can also explain long-established facts – that children who grow up under conditions of adversity are more likely to be aggressive, to have sex at younger ages, to become teen parents, and to care for their children poorly when they become parents – means that this new theory trumps the older ones. And this is because it explains what they also explain – and more! In consequence, we need to reconsider how we regard so-called problematic development, treating it as something that often makes biological sense rather than as some kind of error in development. We also need to understand how developmental experiences "get under the skin" or become biologically embedded so as to influence sexual maturation and reproductive strategy more generally.

Further evolutionary-developmental thinking made me realize that it would not make biological sense for everyone to have their future development and functioning shaped by their early experiences – as presumed by attachment theory, social-learning theory, and even my own evolutionary thinking about the development of human reproductive strategies: Because the *future is inherently uncertain* – and always has been – there would have been plenty of times in human history when later-life experiences turned out to be inconsistent with those of childhood, resulting in at least some individuals being poorly prepared by early life experiences for the world they would come to inhabit. To avoid everyone in such circumstances ending up mismatched to their later environment and thus misled by their early experiences, natural selection should have made some individuals more susceptible to the effects of early life experiences than others. This was my second – evolution-inspired – insight.

And guess what? Ever more research reveals that the very early life experiences presumed to shape development do influence some children much more than others. Indeed, evidence indicates that highly negatively emotional infants and toddlers, highly physiologically reactive children, and individuals carrying certain gene variants rather than others are more affected than others – for better and for worse – by a diverse array of environmental influences (e.g., parenting, peer relations, life events). Not only are they more likely to do poorly when exposed to conditions of adversity, but they are more likely to do well when they experience conditions of support and enrichment.

In sum, the two theoretical and empirical insights I have highlighted – that rearing experiences influence female pubertal development and that nurture matters more for some than for others – underscore my most important scientific contribution, while revealing the theoretical and empirical utility of looking at human development through an evolutionary-biological and not just a mental-health lens. To my way of thinking, then, psychologists must appreciate that the ultimate goal of *all* living things – to pass our genes on to future generations – plays an important and under-appreciated role in the when, why, and how of human development. In the same way that no architect designing a building can ignore the fundamental forces of gravity, no science of human development can ignore the fundamental forces of biological gravity.

REFERENCES

Belsky, J. (2012). The development of human reproductive strategies: Progress and prospects. *Current Directions in Psychological Science, 21,* 310–316.

Belsky, J., Bakermans-Kranenburg, M., & van Ijzendoorn, M. (2007). For better *and* for worse: Differential susceptibility to environmental influences. *Current Directions in Psychological Science, 16,* 305–309.

Belsky, J., & Pluess, M. (2013). Beyond risk, resilience and dysregulation: Phenotypic plasticity and human development. *Development and Psychopathology, 25,* 1243–1261.

52 Transitions, Timing, and Texture: A Developmental Psychologist Goes Transdisciplinary

Brooks-Gunn, Jeanne

For all of us who have contributed to this volume, and by definition have been conducting psychological research for many decades, it is difficult to pinpoint *the* most important scientific contribution. After all, we have been toiling our fields for three to four decades, and at the time that we were looking at a particular topic, it seemed to be critical, with scientific passion and thinking devoted to said topic. At the same time, some research has been viewed as seminal and has stood the test of time, which I suppose might be reasonable criteria with which to evaluate one's contribution to our field. Writing such an account seems quite immodest; perhaps others ought to be writing about any one scientist's legacy.

Much of my work has woven together the themes of transitions, timing, and texture, not surprising for a developmental psychologist. My contributions are not in defining these three themes, which presumably are present in all life-course developmental research – or at least ought to be. I am most proud of specific contributions to each of these three T's.

However, I was trained in conducting laboratory research, primarily descriptive of various social and cognitive phenomena (development of self-recognition, attention processing, learning of social cues, and maternal interactions with children, focusing on infants and toddlers). I was firmly situated in the traditional research paradigms of the time. Today, I am perceived as a developmental psychologist who does longitudinal long-term studies that are either nationally representative or at least representative of a large segment of the population (i.e., births in the late 1990s and early 2000s to women in cities with populations of 200,000 or larger) or a city (children in the city of Chicago in the mid-1980s). Today, I am seen not as someone who delves deep into developmental processes, but as a scholar who studies many individuals in more broad terms (since I have done both, I see the value of both approaches).

Two bodies of research seem most important. All involve colleagues from other disciplines. The two transitions are both reproductive in nature (although they involve biology, social, cognitive, and emotional processes): puberty and childbearing. The two textures involve income and related processes, as measured in the family and in the neighborhood. In addition, I am particularly proud of my role in translating research into policy, be it through specific analyses of longitudinal studies, directing large long-term studies, or evaluating interventions. As these are more general contributions, they will not be discussed.

Pubertal Changes in Girls

My study of puberty began because of an experience teaching undergraduates in the mid-1970s. Diane Ruble and I met in Princeton, where we both lived, and began discussing our similar experiences of teaching a Psychology of Women course (she at Princeton, I at the University of Pennsylvania). We were shocked by the paucity of research on reproductive transitions, especially on menarche and menstruation, and we were annoyed by what passed for knowledge – quotes from clinicians based on their patients' retrospective reports. We decided to remedy the deficit, designing and getting funded a series of studies, some cross-sectional and some longitudinal, interviewing girls about their expectancies and then their actual experiences of menarche. Along the way, we did studies on men's and women's expectancies, as well as boys' and girls'.

We had a terrible time getting schools to let us interview middle-school girls; principals would nervously usher us out of their offices. You would think that twelve-year-olds were not going through puberty in the United States. In retrospect, this squeamishness about reproductive changes during adolescence is illustrated in our relatively high teenage pregnancy rate compared with Western European countries (these higher rates continue today, even though rates of sexual intercourse are similar here and in Europe). We were saved by the Central New Jersey Girl Scouts, who allowed us to study their girls.

We learned that expectancies for symptoms are far more negative than actual experiences. We also learned from longitudinal work (following girls from before to after they had their first period) that, unlike the clinical literature, girls' emotional reactions to the first menstruation were not particularly negative (clinical reports characterized the experience as debilitating; girls, instead, were moderately excited and a bit nervous, mostly about the mechanics). Some of our work was used to revise the pamphlets on menarche that were given to virtually all girls in middle school by the personal-products industry.

I become interested in several related topics from this collaboration, including how girls respond to other pubertal events, how the timing of pubertal events (vis-à-vis peers) influences relationships with parents and friends, how contextual and hormonal changes influence eating problems, depression, and aggression, how early maturing girls navigate dating and attention from older boys, and how school characteristics influence girls' reactions to timing of maturation. Schools were just as wary of these lines of inquiry as they had been about menarche. Virtually all of our work in the 1980s and even the 1990s was done in private schools in New York City. Headmistresses and headmasters in the single-sex and coeducational private schools (unlike the heads of public schools) were very receptive, having realized that their students were experiencing pubertal changes and were talking about these changes and constantly comparing themselves to one another. While the work is well known, I am sorry to say that we had little success in altering school policy regarding discussing pubertal changes or the risks associated with early maturation for girls: depression and unwanted attention from older boys.

Much of this work was done in collaboration with an endocrinologist at Columbia University; Michelle Warren was also doing work on late puberty, using elite dancers in New York City as an exemplar of environmentally induced delays. With a dancer-turned-psychologist and two orthopedic surgeons who worked with dancers and baseball players, we wrote what became the definitive paper on links between hypo-estrogen (delayed puberty is associated, obviously, with relatively low levels of estrogen) and bone density (and fractures) – work that contributed to public health initiatives on bone fractures in post-menopausal women.

At the moment I am fortunate to be working with three young collaborators on issues such as whether the tempo of pubertal changes influences behavior, whether the timing of father absence and other environmental events influence timing of puberty, and whether links between early puberty and later behavior are moderated by markers of the serotonin and dopamine pathways.

Childbearing When Unmarried

I have also studied childbearing, first in teenage girls and later in adults. My interest has been in both the timing of childbearing (specifically during the adolescent years or in adulthood) and the context in which it occurs (specifically, in mothers who are married or unmarried at the time of the birth). This work has been done in collaboration with family sociologists. My first foray into this field was an outgrowth of the pubertal work, because early maturing girls were more likely to become teenage parents. And pregnancy and then early parenting are two other reproductive transitions.

I was introduced to a sociologist at the University of Pennsylvania by the head of a foundation who indicated that the two of us ought to follow-up Frank Furstenberg's sample of teenage mothers and their children. The children were then adolescents. We took up the challenge and saw the mothers about seventeen years after they first gave birth. With Phil Morgan, another sociologist, we examined the trajectories of the mothers and the children, as well as looking at how the mothers' life courses influenced their children's well-being. This study was one of the first to look explicitly at the timing of different experiences, as well as to differ-entiate among the teenage mothers, rather than focusing on their poorer outcomes as compared to older mothers. We found more variability in outcomes, with only a quarter exhibiting the failure-stereotype of the adolescent mother and another quarter having done very well. In addition, we found that certain situations increased their chances of success, including attendance at a special school for teenage mothers, living with their own mother during their child's preschool years, not getting married (only a few got married; those who did were very likely to get divorced), and delaying a second birth. Surprisingly, the children were not doing as well as the mothers, which later led to a series of studies with Lindsay Chase-Lansdale on how the young mothers and their own mothers interacted and raised the toddlers. Our work has been used for national policies on teenage mothers; for example, teenage mothers are now required to stay in school and to live with their parents in order to receive federal aid.

Conclusion

Perhaps my legacy will be in the fourth T of the title – transdisciplinary work. I have had the good fortune to have collaborated with scholars in endocrinology, pediatrics, economics, sociology, demography, genetics, and statistics as well as with social, educational, and neurodevelopmental psychologists. Lucky me. I began my career in the mid-1970s, at a time when cross-disciplinary work, while still rare, was seen as having value. Also, it was advantageous to have been involved in several longitudinal studies at a time when life-course work was emerging.

REFERENCES

Brooks-Gunn, J. (1990). Adolescents as daughters and as mothers: A developmental perspective. In I. E. Sigel & G. H. Brody (eds.), *Methods of family research: Biographies of research projects, Volume I: Normal families* (pp. 213–248). Hillsdale: Lawrence Erlbaum.

Brooks-Gunn, J. (2001). Autobiographical perspectives. In A. N. O'Connell (ed.), *Models of achievement: Reflections of eminent women in psychology* (vol. 3, pp. 275–292). Mahwah: Lawrence Erlbaum.

Brooks-Gunn, J. (2013). *Person, time, and place: The life course of a developmental psychologist.* In R. Lerner, A. C. Peterson, R. K. Silbereisen, & J. Brooks-Gunn (eds.), *The developmental science of adolescence: History through autobiography* (pp. 32–44). New York: Taylor & Francis.

53 Longitudinal Cohort Research: Sowing, Nurturing, Waiting, Harvesting

Caspi, Avshalom, and Moffitt, Terrie E.

Introduction

Our scientific contribution has been to study human development using the longitudinal birth-cohort method. This method starts with a list of all babies born in a defined place (typically a city or a country), within a defined period (typically a year). This list is referred to as a "cohort." The babies are enrolled in the study (sometimes before they are born) and then followed and assessed repeatedly throughout their lives, as they grow up and grow old. Researchers and participants collaborate on the project together for many decades, which makes this method quite different from the sorts of research projects that other psychologists typically do. The research participants generously give of themselves over and over all their lives, vouchsafing the scientists the details of their most intimate, delicate, and even dangerous behaviors and experiences, as well as their body tissues.

The scientists, in turn, accept the ethical obligations to ask important questions, publish findings rapidly, preserve the data carefully for use in future years, and guard the participants' confidentiality at all costs. We say "scientists" in the plural, because a longitudinal cohort study is far too ambitious an enterprise to be undertaken by one psychologist in his or her own lab. In fact, we are writing this chapter together because if we had worked alone, neither of us would appear in this book of high-achieving psychologists.

We think of a longitudinal cohort study as a scientific instrument, not unlike a large Hadron particle collider or a kilometers-wide radio-telescope antenna. Like one of these instruments, a cohort study is expensive, but pays for itself because it is a resource for many scientists who make multiple discoveries. Such scientific instruments are science-magnets; they attract collaboration among large numbers of scientists and staff from many different fields and nations. Like other large scientific instruments, a cohort study demands sustained dedication to fundraising. Instruments also require loving care and maintenance; in the case of a cohort study, this means dedication to keeping as many of the original cohort members as possible participating for decades. Our scientific careers have been devoted to two such studies. In both, well over 90 percent of the original cohort members still participate. The Dunedin Study follows about a thousand people born in 1972–1973 in New Zealand. The Environmental Risk Study follows over a thousand pairs of twins born in 1994–1995 in Great Britain.

We list eight contributions that we think are interesting, in reverse order, starting with what we are working on now. Papers can be found at www.moffittcaspi.com.

Hidden Aging Takes Place Inside the Bodies of Young People

As humans age, their risk increases for all diseases, including cancer, heart disease, diabetes, stroke, and Alzheimer's, to name a few. The ultimate scientific goal is to slow aging itself to prevent all of these disabling killers simultaneously. Anti-aging therapies will at some point be available and, for prevention purposes, therapies must target still-healthy young people. However, because gerontology studies senior citizens, virtually nothing is known about aging in young people. We tracked biomarkers of multiple organ systems (e.g., heart, lung, kidney, liver, metabolic, immune, and dental health) in people passing through their twenties and thirties, and we learned that aging shows in these organs just as it does eventually in seniors' gray hair and wrinkles, but far sooner. Young cohort members who were aging faster also scored worse on geriatric tests of balance, grip strength, walking up stairs, and solving unfamiliar mental problems. Of interest, the pace of youthful aging accelerates for people who have suffered early life adversity.

This work began with our discovery that adults in our cohort who were child-maltreatment victims years ago had elevated inflammation biomarkers. Our other papers pin down the timing; the inflammation emerges at the time of the maltreatment: in childhood. We also found erosion of telomeres (which cap the ends of chromosomes and deteriorate as a cell ages) from age five to age ten, in children who experienced maltreatment in the interim. Likewise, adults showed excess telomere erosion if they had stress-related mental disorders in the interim between blood tests. We recently published a paper inviting psychologists who design treatments for stress and trauma to add stress-sensitive biomarkers to randomized clinical trials testing their psychotherapies. Adding biomarkers before and after a randomized trial of psychotherapy can reveal whether the hidden body damage and premature aging caused by psychosocial stress is reversible.

Cannabis Users Have Both Healthy and Unhealthy Outcomes

Cannabis is the most widely used illicit drug in the world, and hence research is necessary to inform cannabis policy. We were among the first to report that young cannabis users had elevated risk for later psychosis (a risk that depends on genotype). We also showed that cannabis users who began using as teens and continued as adults showed declines on cognitive tests given in childhood and again in midlife, culminating in a loss of 8 IQ points. In our cohorts, long-term cannabis users ended up in lower-prestige occupations than their parents. Importantly, harm is clearest for long-term daily cannabis smokers; we did not detect harmful effects in recreational users. On the bright side, we reported that long-term cannabis users (unlike tobacco smokers) stay physically healthy and do not develop health problems, with the notable exception of gum disease. Because our cannabis work is unbiased objective science, it has featured prominently in public drug-policy debates.

The Importance of Self-Control for Success in Life

One of our projects that has attracted policy attention concerns the importance of self-control skills mastered in childhood for success in all aspects of adult life, including physical health, addiction, crime, suicidality, wealth accumulation, life satisfaction, and even parenting of the next generation. These findings lend support to the movement for early-childhood character education.

We investigated the self-control→health connection further, and reported that people who don't take care of their money also don't take care of their health. We used a unique data source: credit ratings. Our participants' credit ratings and their cardiovascular health were closely connected, and this connection was explained by the cohort members' childhood self-control. We further showed that a measure of the self-control ability called conscientiousness can identify which now-healthy young adults will develop health problems in the near future. A brief conscientiousness checklist completed in the doctor's waiting room could tell doctors which patients need motivational counseling to boost their self-control, promote health behaviors, and prevent later diseases.

Gene–Environment Interaction (GxE)

Humans' genetic endowment influences their risk of mental illness by shaping how we respond to environmental causes of mental illness. Of course, this idea has been around for decades, but it was just an abstract theoretical concept in psychology until our research provided evidence of GxE interactions: Genes predicted which abused children developed later antisocial violent behavior, and genes predicted which highly stressed young adults developed depression. These findings have been replicated by many teams, but not all, and the meaning of this track record is controversial. Meanwhile, our GxE work has transformed three groups. First, geneticists now study samples of people exposed to an environmental cause of mental disorder (stress, maltreatment, birth anoxia, airborne lead). Comparing those who become ill versus those who stay well can help find new genes for mental illness. Second, neuroscientists now show research participants environment-relevant stimuli during brain imaging. Doing so reveals connections from genes to brain to behavior. Third, our GxE research transformed the public's understanding of genetics. Our findings show that genetic effects on health and behavior often depend on factors under human control, vividly contradicting genetic determinism.

Schizophrenia's Childhood Roots

By interviewing the same people in childhood and adulthood, we discovered that a non-trivial percentage of children report having hallucinatory experiences and delusional beliefs, and that many such children later develop schizophrenia (or another serious disorder). Age ten–twelve is the right age to ask, because children are old enough to understand hallucinations and delusions, but too young to have learned by sad experience that they must keep them secret. Children should be assessed for psychotic symptoms by pediatric mental health professionals because these symptoms are often the first sign of mental illness yet to come. We have also studied the process of neurodegeneration in people who develop schizophrenia. We reported that the key deficit is in a mental ability called "processing speed." It lags in childhood for individuals who will later develop schizophrenia, and it deteriorates even further after the schizophrenia diagnosis. Recently, we discovered that poor quality of small blood vessels in retinal photographs relates both to poor childhood brain health and to adult schizophrenia. As part of the brain, the retina gives scientists a non-invasive window on the brain's vascular system.

Mental Disorders in the Population

Our research has yielded three novel findings about the epidemiology of mental illness. In 2003, we were first to report that over half of adult patients with psychiatric disorder have their first diagnosable disorder before age 15 (and 75 percent before age 18), suggesting that most of the burden of adult mental disorder could be prevented by effective screening and treatment for young people.

Second, we observed that if people are followed long enough, while being assessed frequently for mental disorders, almost everyone will experience diagnosable anxiety, depression, or substance dependence. Less than 20 percent of a birth cohort makes it to midlife without ever experiencing any mental disorder. This surprising finding has been replicated by several longitudinal studies.

Third, in 1998, we were first to report that adult mental disorders fit empirically into two large groups: internalizing (e.g., depression, anxiety, eating), and externalizing (e.g., substance, antisocial, ADHD). This finding has since become a central tenet of abnormal psychology. Continuing work on the structure of psychopathology, we showed that all psychiatric symptoms a person ever experiences can fit onto one single-dimensional scale of severity. Symptoms of thought disorder are at its extreme end. As a result of our contributions, researchers are asking why so many people experience mental disorder and what this means for the way we define mental health, design research, deliver psychiatric services, and count the economic burden of mental illness. At the least, our finding that most of us will experience disorder if we live long enough should reduce stigma against mental illness.

Life-Long Legacy of Temperament and Personality

We showed how temperament differences between young children shape their subsequent development. This research provided evidence that pre-school personality rivals social class and intelligence in shaping a child's life; preschool personality can predict most of the important outcomes in life, including educational attainment, mental illness, physical health, criminal behavior, love relationships, and financial success. It is often forgotten that when Avshalom began this work as a graduate student in the 1980s there was widespread skepticism about whether childhood personality existed, could be measured, or influenced people's lives. Today all this is accepted. Because of longitudinal studies of temperament and personality, early years intervention to build character has become national policy.

Life-Course Persistent Versus Adolescence-Limited Antisocial Behavior

Young people engaging in antisocial behaviors belong to two types: One type we called "life-course persistent." It is a neurodevelopmental disorder afflicting primarily males, with very low prevalence in the population, genetic predisposition, adverse family environment, early childhood onset, and persistence of violent offending into midlife. The other type we called "adolescence limited." It affects females as well as males, is common, limited mainly to the adolescent developmental stage, and emerges in the context of peer relationships. This developmental taxonomy, which Terrie began to develop soon after graduate school, has been cited more than 7,000 times and has influenced psychology, criminology, psychiatry, neuroscience, and the law. It has been codified in clinical diagnostic manuals and cited in Supreme Court decisions.

Conclusions

None of these findings would have been possible without the longitudinal cohort method. We have had false leads and bad ideas, but when our research has been successful we think it is for the following reasons.

First, longitudinal research is an inherently horizon-scanning enterprise; we constantly try to anticipate new trends and ask new questions, even when it means waiting years to learn the result. For example, the Dunedin Study was first to interview children about hallucinations and delusions more than thirty years ago, and this paid off by yielding insights into origins of schizophrenia.

Second, we have a track record as first adopters, incorporating new technologies into the cohort studies as soon as these became available. For example, we began collecting DNA in 1996; interviewed participants with life-history calendars based on advances in cognitive psychology; geocoded physical environments using Google Streetview; and worked with ophthalmologists to adopt retinal imaging as a tool to study brain health.

Third, we believe that crossing disciplines boosts creativity. In graduate school, Terrie sought training in clinical psychology, criminology, and the neuropsychology of aging. Avshalom sought training in child development, life-course sociology, and personality psychology. We collaborate with economists, geneticists, criminologists, neuroscientists, and medical scientists, even dentists. Our research is most innovative when we make surprising data combinations across previously unconnected disciplines (addiction research and dentistry; neuropsychology and criminology;

cardiovascular research and economics). As a result, many of our highest-impact studies were not part of any grant, because they fall into the gaps between traditional disease-oriented funding agencies.

Fourth, we get our ideas by paying close attention to the participants in our cohorts as they grow and change. For example, we cared deeply about puberty when the participants were adolescents, and now find ourselves caring more about cardiovascular health as they reach middle age. We constantly retool and retrain to keep up with our cohorts.

We are often asked: how is it, working together? Pretty good, for the most part. We model our longitudinal research after our grandparents who, as husband and wife, ran their farms together: sowing, nurturing, waiting, and harvesting.

REFERENCES

Arseneault, L., Cannon, M., Poulton, R., Murray, R., Caspi, A., & Moffitt, T. E. (2002). Cannabis use in adolescence and risk for adult psychosis: Longitudinal prospective study. *British Medical Journal*, *325*(7374), 1212–1213.

Caspi, A., McClay, J., Moffitt, T., Mill, J., Martin, J., Craig, I. W., ... & Poulton, R. (2002). Role of genotype in the cycle of violence in maltreated children. *Science*, *297*(5582), 851–854.

Caspi, A., Sugden, K., Moffitt, T. E., Taylor, A., Craig, I. W., Harrington, H., ... & Poulton, R. (2003). Influence of life stress on depression: Moderation by a polymorphism in the 5-HTT gene. *Science*, *301*(5631), 386–389.

Moffitt, T. E., & Caspi, A. (2001). Childhood predictors differentiate life-course persistent and adolescence-limited antisocial pathways among males and females. *Development and Psychopathology*, *13*(2), 355–375.

Eisenberg, Nancy

Much of my work has addressed two issues. One is the development of empathy-related responding in children and its relation to prosocial behavior (e.g., helping and sharing) and to moral judgment and behavior. The other is emotion-related self-regulation and its relation to individuals' positive social functioning and indices of maladjustment, including externalizing problems (e.g., aggression, defiance, and delinquency) and internalizing problems (e.g., depression, anxiety, and social withdrawal). Perhaps my most important findings are those that emerged from my work on empathy and led to my work on differences among people in the degree to which they regulate their emotions and associated behavior.

In my early work on prosocial behavior, I found that preschool children who spontaneously shared with other children at a cost to themselves (e.g., giving up toys they were using) were more likely than their peers to experience empathy or sympathy. Empathy is experiencing an emotion similar to that of another in response to comprehending what the other is feeling or is likely to experience (e.g., observers feeling sad when exposed to someone who is sad or likely to experience sadness). Sympathy is feelings of concern for another based on some understanding of their emotional state or situation (akin to compassion – e.g., feeling concern for a person who is sad rather than solely feeling sadness).

Those children who engaged in spontaneous prosocial behavior also were relatively likely to refer to others' needs or feelings when discussing hypothetical moral dilemmas in which children had to decide whether to assist others at a cost to the self. Moreover, they engaged in more neutral and positive social interactions with peers and were assertive when they needed to be; their peers also reacted positively to them when they did engage in prosocial actions.

In contrast, children who were high in prosocial behavior mainly in response to peers' requests (verbal or often non-verbal, e.g., reaching for an object) tended to be non-assertive and less social with peers than those who were spontaneously prosocial. Peers often would state or non-verbally indicate that they wanted help or reach for what children high in such requested or compliant prosocial behavior were playing with; thus, children high in requested prosocial behavior frequently seemed to be easy targets for peers wanting objects or assistance.

Pulling together findings across studies, it appeared that children who spontaneously shared with others at a cost to themselves were empathic/sympathetic and more socially skilled than other children who were lower in such behavior. When we followed up children in one study for twenty-seven years, we found that the preschoolers' spontaneous costly sharing with other children was related to greater empathy, sympathy, and prosocial behavior in later childhood, adolescence, and adulthood and higher levels of other-oriented values and caring for others in their twenties and early thirties.

In brief, individual differences among preschoolers in their tendencies to spontaneously assist others at a cost are related to childhood empathy/sympathy and social skills and predict differences in sympathy and related behaviors and values across nearly three decades.

Thus, we started to think about what it was about these socially competent, other-oriented children that accounted for such important differences in their subsequent functioning. One line of research pertained to the socialization of sympathetic responding in the home – which parenting behaviors and beliefs were related to greater sympathy or prosocial behavior in children. We did find that some aspects of parenting and parents' behavior related to children's sympathy: For example, children's sympathy was higher when their parents were sympathetic, when parents expressed their non-hostile negative emotions in the family (e.g., sadness), and when parents were restrictive in regard to children expressing hurtful emotions but non-restrictive when children expressed their own emotions that did not hurt others. Moreover, children were more sympathetic when mothers used various techniques to help children to relate to others' emotional experience, understand others' emotions, and deal with their own emotions. These findings provided some hints that the abilities to manage emotions might be important for children's tendencies to sympathize with others.

Consequently, we started to consider the role of emotion and its regulation in empathy/sympathy and, subsequently, children's broader social competence and adjustment. In research with both children and adults, there are relatively stable individual differences in both the tendencies to experience negative emotion and in the ability to regulate one's own emotions: These differences are discussed as part of the development of temperament and personality. It is also clear that these individual differences are partly due to heredity (i.e., differences among people in their genetics), although they also appear to be affected by the social environment. It seemed reasonable to assume that differences among children in these temperamental characteristics might play a role in explaining the array of individual differences observed in our research.

Thus, we began to examine the relations of individual differences in emotion, and especially self-regulation, in people's tendencies to respond with empathy or sympathy to others' distress or needs rather than personal distress. Personal distress (defined initially by Daniel Batson) is a self-focused aversion response to the emotions or condition of another. An example of personal distress is experiencing anxiety and wanting to avoid a person who is telling you about his or her problems. We argued that empathy often leads to sympathy, but when empathically induced negative emotion is strong and overwhelming, it leads to feeling of personal distress and self-concern rather than concern for the other person.

Based on this reasoning, we further suggested that people who are prone to negative emotions might be particularly likely to experience personal distress rather than sympathy, especially if they have difficulty regulating their emotions. Such people might tend to strongly experience others' negative emotions and become over-aroused and unable to lower their negative arousal; thus, they would be motivated to reduce their own aversive emotional state and be less concerned with the other person's emotion. Empathic over-arousal might also undermine children's social competence and adjustment by affecting their abilities to think clearly and their motivations. However, people who are skilled at modulating (regulating) their own negative emotions, compared with people who are less self-regulated, might be better able to feel others' negative emotions while avoiding becoming over-aroused and self-focused when empathizing. In addition, those who do not readily experience others' emotions might be expected to be low in empathy, sympathy, and personal distress.

We conducted a number of studies to test these ideas. In general, we found that people with a tendency to experience high levels of negative emotion are prone to personal distress. People who are prone to sympathy tend to experience some negative emotions, such as sadness, but they are not prone to hostile negative emotions such as anger and do not habitually experience high levels of intense negative emotion.

Moreover, children and adults who are relatively likely to experience sympathy, rather than personal distress, typically are well regulated. These people appear to be able to manage their attention, and attention can be used to modulate emotion. For example, the ability to shift attention away from a distressing event or thought is a technique for lowering emotional arousal; focusing on other thoughts or activities might serve to modulate negative emotion. Furthermore, people who can inhibit actions that they want to enact, but that are not appropriate or adaptive in a given context, are prone to sympathy, perhaps because they are skilled at controlling their own thoughts and behavior. We also found that being somewhat prone to relatively intense emotions (positive and negative) combined with high levels of self-regulation was associated with children being particularly high in sympathy. Finally, it appears that well-regulated people are not only more likely to experience sympathy, but also to assist other people.

In brief, the abilities to modulate attention and behavior seem to relate to the ability to maintain an optimal level of emotional arousal, which in turn predicts individual differences in sympathy. Well-regulated people are also more prosocial, probably partly because they are more sympathetic (sympathy has been shown to motivate children's and adults' prosocial behavior). These findings help us to understand why there are predictable differences in people over time in regard to prosocial tendencies (sympathy, helping) and how we might foster sympathy and prosocial behavior (e.g., by training children in self-regulation skills) – an important area for future research. In addition, our findings help to explain why we and other researchers have found that children who are high in self-regulation tend to be socially skilled, low in problem behaviors such as aggression, and relatively low in psychological problems such as depression and anxiety (emotions that require regulation). It appears that the development of children's abilities to manage their attention, behavior, and emotion is critical to many aspects of their social and emotional functioning. Thus, perhaps my greatest contributions have been to provide evidence of the role of self-regulation in moral functioning, such as sympathy and prosocial behavior, and to help stimulate the current body of research on the importance of self-regulation for children's social, emotional, psychological, and even academic competence.

REFERENCES

Eisenberg, N., Hofer, C., Sulik, M., & Spinrad, T. L. (2014). Effortful control and its socioemotional consequences. In J. J. Gross (ed.), *Handbook of emotion regulation* (2nd edn., 157–172). New York: Guilford Press.

Eisenberg, N., Spinrad, T. L., & Eggum, N. D. (2010). Emotion-related self-regulation and its relation to children's maladjustment. *Annual Review of Clinical Psychology*, 6, 495–525. doi:10.1146/annurev.clinpsy.121208.131208.

Eisenberg, N., Spinrad, T. L., & Knafo, A. (2015). Prosocial development. In M. Lamb (vol. ed.) and R. M. Lerner (series ed.), *Handbook of child psychology and developmental science. Socioemotional processes* (7th edn, vol. 3, pp. 610–656). New York: Wiley.

55 Follow the Evidence, Ignore the Words

Kagan, Jerome

Charles Darwin, not Albert Einstein, is the more appropriate role model for psychologists because he did not begin the Beagle voyage with a favorite idea he wished to prove. Rather, he was open to pursuing any puzzling observation without prejudice. Fortunately, nature furnished the evidence that his intelligence recognized as inconsistent with popular ideology. The rest is history.

I made the few modest discoveries that brought me a small measure of recognition because I adopted Darwin's strategy. I distrusted a priori hypotheses and remained vigilant for observations that were reliable and appeared to be related to a theoretically important issue. When chance presented such observations, I pursued them with the methods available at that time.

This approach generated several discoveries that, I hope, contributed to a deeper understanding of human development. The unexpected observation, in the 1970s, of an increase in attention to faces by infants of seven to nine months old implied an enhancement in working memory due to the maturation of a circuit connecting the temporal and frontal lobes. This discovery, which was later confirmed by others, was satisfying because it explained why seven to nine months is the interval when most infants cry when a stranger approaches them too quickly or their mother leaves them alone for a few minutes in an unfamiliar room. Infants cry because they compare the event with their acquired knowledge and cannot resolve the discrepancy. That comparison requires an improved working memory.

The research on temperament, conducted over the past thirty-five years, has brought more satisfaction, partly because most psychologists regard the discoveries as more significant. Hence, this short essay describes the events that led to the invention of the concepts of high- and low-reactive infants and inhibited and uninhibited children.

These ideas had their origin in the early 1960s, when Howard Moss and I were studying a large group of twenty- to thirty-year-olds on whom extensive observations from infancy to late adolescence were available.

A small number of adults whose personality was marked by caution, uncertainty, and a risk-averse posture to challenge typically also had retreated from unfamiliar people or events during their first three years. A second, equally small group showed the contrasting profile of an exuberant approach to, rather than avoidance of, unfamiliar people, objects, or places. These observations were puzzling in 1960 because most psychologists, including Moss and myself, resisted the notion that temperamental biases made an important contribution to adult personality. As a result, I failed to pursue this intriguing fact at that time, although I thought about it often.

Close to twenty years later, nature sent me a reminder when Richard Kearsely, Philip R. Zelazo, and I were studying the consequences of day-care attendance on European-American and Chinese-American infants and toddlers. The psychological differences between the two ethnic groups were more attributable to their temperaments than to the experiences that accompanied attendance at a day-care center from ages three to twenty-nine months. I did not need a third reminder.

The observations that led to the concepts of high- and low-reactive infants began with one trustworthy fact. I was convinced that one-year-old infants from affectionate families varied in the tendency to be cautious or bold when they encountered unfamiliar people, objects, or places. I called the former "inhibited" and the latter "uninhibited." My students and I wanted to know whether these biases were preserved as well as their biological origins. Because we believed that genes made an important contribution to these two behavioral styles, we treated inhibited and uninhibited children as members of discrete categories, defined by extremely cautious or bold behaviors, rather than as lying on a continuum. The data we gathered confirmed this premise. We did not use the words "fearful" or "fearless" to describe the two types of children, but rather chose a vocabulary that referred to observable behaviors. Hence, the title of this chapter.

The first study revealed that inhibited White two-year-olds, born to middle-class families, were likely to become shy seven-year-olds, whereas uninhibited two-year-olds were disposed to become sociable seven-year-olds. Equally important, the two groups displayed different patterns of heart rate, muscle tension, pupillary dilation, and cortisol levels that implied a different balance between the sympathetic and parasympathetic nervous systems. Research by other scientists, many studying animals, suggested that differences in the excitability of the amygdala, a small almond-shaped structure tucked inside the temporal lobe, could explain the evidence we had collected.

So the next project, which began in the 1980s, probed a trio of new questions. Is there a pattern of responses in young infants that predicts inhibited or uninhibited behaviors in later childhood? Are these infant profiles associated with biological measures that implicate the amygdala? Finally, do adolescents who display the different infant profiles vary in amygdala excitability? The answers to these questions turned out to be yes, yes, yes.

We filmed the behaviors of close to 500 four-month-old, healthy, White infants from middle-class homes while they encountered unfamiliar objects, sounds, and smells. I then viewed the films of the first 100 infants without any particular hypothesis. I wanted to see if there were distinctive profiles. This effort revealed that about 20 percent thrashed their arms and legs vigorously, arched their backs, and often cried to these innocent, but unfamiliar, events. I called these infants high-reactive. About 40 percent showed the complementary profile marked by minimal limb movement, little arching of the back, and the absence of crying. We called these infants low-reactive. The remaining 40 percent showed other patterns. The work of others led to the inference that the high- and low-reactive infants were born with different brain chemistries that rendered the amygdala either responsive or unresponsive to unexpected events.

These children were evaluated eight times up through age eighteen, with batteries that included observations of behaviors, interviews, and biological measures. This large corpus of evidence was consistent with the following conclusions. Although high-reactive infants were biased to become inhibited and low-reactive infants uninhibited during the second year, many high-reactives lost their extreme levels of shyness and timidity, and many low-reactives lost their extreme sociability as they matured. Their personas had moved away from the extremes. Nonetheless, very few high-reactives became extremely sociable and bold; very few low-reactives became unusually shy and timid. Each temperamental bias imposed a restraint on the acquisition of the traits of the other category.

The biological evidence implied greater preservation of the brain states we believed were the foundations of the behavioral profiles. This claim is supported by the fact that the four-month-old classification of high- or low-reactive was a better predictor of an adolescent's profile of biological measures than that child's later behaviors. This result is supported by the replies of adolescents to a woman who interviewed them in their home. Many high-reactives who were not obviously shy or timid said that they worried a great deal over visiting a new city, meeting new people, or taking on new challenges. Few low-reactives reported similar worries. Nathan Fox and his students at the University of Maryland have confirmed many of these results.

The contribution of my colleague Carl Schwartz provided critical support for the influence of variation in amygdalar excitability. The eighteen-year-olds who had been high-reactive as infants displayed larger surges of blood flow to the amygdala when they saw unfamiliar, unrealistic scenes – for example, an animal's body with a human face or a rose blossom with an animal for a stem – than the low-reactives.

A dissociation between behavior and biology was revealed in the answers to an interviewer who asked each eighteen-year-old about symptoms of social anxiety or depression. Although these symptoms were more prevalent among high-reactives, the small number of low-reactive females who reported either symptom did not display the biology that characterized the high-reactives. This observation supports the psychiatrists and psychologists who believe that the categories called social anxiety and depression, as well as others, have different origins. Clinicians treating patients suffering from social anxiety or depression should try to determine whether they possess signs of a high-reactive temperament or acquired their symptoms through life experience alone. These two groups might profit from different therapies.

This suggestion applies to all personality traits. Some adults who are introverts, psychopaths, workaholics, conscientious, compulsive, or impulsive possess a temperament that made it easier to acquire this trait. Others developed the same trait through a different cascade. Of course, life histories contribute to both types.

Two seminal questions remain unanswered. Would our results with middle-class, White children be replicated with children from other ethnicities and class groups? What patterns of genes and brain states make the critical contributions to the behaviors of high- and low-reactive infants from varied ethnic/class groups? I promise the students who pursue one or both questions a satisfying career.

REFERENCES

Kagan, J. (1994). *Galen's prophecy*. New York: Basic Books.

Kagan, J. (2010). *The temperamental thread*. New York: Dana Press.

Kagan, J., & Snidman, N. (2004). *The long shadow of temperament*. Cambridge, MA: Harvard University Press.

56 The Incredible Shrinking Conscious Mind

Nisbett, Richard E.

In the first experiment I ever conducted, I gave people a placebo and told some of the subjects it would cause heart palpitations, rapid breathing, and sweaty palms. These are the symptoms people experience when they're undergoing strong emotion. I then gave subjects a series of steadily increasing electric shocks, with instructions to tell me when the shocks became too painful to bear. I anticipated that subjects who were told the pill would cause arousal would mistakenly attribute their shock-produced arousal to the pill. They would consequently find the shock less aversive and would be willing to take more of it than control subjects who could only assume their arousal was being produced by the shock. And that was indeed the finding. After removing the electrodes I asked the subjects in the arousal-instruction condition who had taken a great deal of shock why they had taken so much. A typical answer would be, "Well, I used to build radios, and I got a lot of shocks so I guess I got used to it." I might then say, "Well, I can see why that might be. I wonder if it occurred to you that the pill was causing you to be physiologically aroused." "Nope, didn't think about the pills and didn't think about the arousal." I would then tell them what the hypothesis was. They would nod politely and say they were sure that would work for a lot of people. "But see, I used to make radios ... "

It was perfectly clear that subjects had no idea of what had gone on in their heads. At the time, believe it or not, this claim seemed to most people to be quite radical. There was a bedrock presumption that thought is basically linguistic. To show that this assumption was mistaken, and that quite elaborate cognitive processes can go on without people's awareness of them, I began to do experiments with Tim Wilson in which we would manipulate some aspect of the environment that would affect subjects' behavior in some way. For example, we might have people examine an array of nightgowns and tell us which they preferred. The order of the nightgowns had a big impact on preference: the later in the array, the more the subject liked them. Subjects had no idea this was true and when we asked them if the order of the nightgowns could have had an influence on their preference, they would look at us as if we were crazy. Or we would have subjects participate in a study in which they were to memorize word pairs: for example, parrot–bread. Later the subjects participated in "another study," this time on word association. They were to say the first word that came to mind when we asked them to provide an example of a category we suggested. Subjects who had studied the word pair ocean–moon were much more likely to respond with "Tide" when asked to name a detergent than subjects who had not studied that particular pair. When asked why they came up with Tide, subjects were likely to say, "that's what my mother uses," or "I like the Tide box."

To date, psychologists have done hundreds and hundreds of experiments where we find people engaging in unconscious cognitive processes. People tend to reject a persuasive communication when there is a "fishy" smell in the room where they read it. People choose more orange products in a consumer survey if they're answering with an orange pen. People are more likely to put the coffee money in the honesty box if there is a picture of a human face above it.

It became clear to me fairly early that we have no direct access to *any* kind of cognitive process that goes on. We understand that perceptual and memory processes are hidden in a black box, yet claim mistakenly that we can "see" the thoughts that produce judgmental and behavioral responses. But the unconscious nature of these thoughts shouldn't seem surprising when you consider the question "Why *should* we have access to our cognitive processes?" Being able to observe the complicated inference processes that go on would use up a lot of valuable real estate in the brain.

We nevertheless feel that we have access to our cognitive processes. Why is that? It's because I know I was seeing X and thinking about Y and then I did Z, and any fool would know that if you're seeing X and thinking Y you're going to do Z, because that's the sensible thing to do: "I saw the squirrel and I put on the brakes because I didn't want to hit it"; "I was nervous because I had to give a talk." And in such cases I'm usually right. It's just that I'm right because I know what was in my (conscious) mind, and I know what people do or feel in those circumstances. But a correct theory about process needn't come from inspection of process. (Plus, I hate to tell you, but we have a tremendous number of *in*correct theories about our cognitive processes. And in novel situations we're as likely to call on one of those as to apply a correct theory.)

If you believe what I'm saying here, it's scary. I'm constantly being influenced by things I hardly notice – many of which I would rather not be influenced by. Moreover, I can't know by direct inspection why I believe anything I believe or do anything I do.

But there it is, and we've got to make the best of it. We can start with the fact that if it's the case that we have very imperfect knowledge of why we do what we do, we're better off knowing it than not. In my book *Mindware: Tools for Smart Thinking*, I spell out some of the advantages of knowing how little we know about why we do what we do. It's valuable to know that I should be less confident about the accuracy of my opinions than I'm inclined to be. That makes me more likely to consider other people's possibly more valid views. And it makes it more likely that I would try to encounter people and objects in as many circumstances as possible. Abraham Lincoln once said, "I don't like that man. I must get to know him better" – to which I'd add, see him in as many different contexts as I can. We are particularly blind about the extent to which other people influence us. Realizing this makes it clear how important it is that you carefully select the folks you choose to hang around with.

A big advantage of believing that the unconscious mind is what's driving the bus is that you can make more effective use of it than you do. There's evidence that the conscious mind can make poor decisions – in part because it attends overly much to stimuli that can be described in words. Hard-to-verbalize stimuli may get less of a say than they should. So think over a decision consciously and then hand it over to the unconscious mind before signing off.

A second big advantage is that the unconscious mind can actually learn things that the conscious mind can't. Pawel Lewicki and his coworkers showed subjects a box divided into four quadrants and asked them to predict, for dozens of trials, where an X would appear. There were rules – extremely complicated ones – determining where an X would come up on each trial. Subjects learned those rules but had no inkling of what the rules were or even that there were any. They said they "just got a feel for where the X would come up." So expose yourself to situations where you know there's something to learn even though it's not obvious just what it is.

A third big advantage is that the unconscious mind is a great problem-solver – if you give it a chance. Brewster Ghiselin has collected essays by some of the greatest thinkers, artists, and scientists in history reporting on how they came up with their ideas. It turns out that the greatest discoveries are produced by the unconscious mind. Solutions typically appear out of nowhere when the thinker is occupied with some unrelated task or relaxing in a cafe.

What's true for geniuses is also true for the rest of us working on mundane problems. But you can't just tell your unconscious mind to go solve a problem. You have to do your homework and then pass the results along to the unconscious. Sit down and think about what the problem is and make a rough sketch of what a solution might look like. The noted writer James McPhee has said that he has to begin a draft of an article, no matter how crummy it is, before the real work on the article can begin.

Once you do knock off a hasty sketch, you may subsequently be doing very little conscious thinking about the article, but your unconscious mind is working for you for free 24/7. A good way to kick off the process of writing, McPhee says, is to write a letter to your mother telling her what you're going to write about!

REFERENCES

Ghiselin, B. (ed.) (1952/1980). *The creative process*. Berkeley and Los Angeles: University of California Press.

Nisbett, R. E. (2015). *Mindware: Tools for smart thinking*. New York: Farrar, Straus & Giroux.

Nisbett, R. E., & Wilson, T. D. (1977). Telling more than we can know: Verbal reports on mental processes. *Psychological Review, 84*, 231–259.

Wilson, Timothy D.

Many students take their first psychology class because they want to learn more about themselves and their loved ones. What better way to find out what makes people tick than to learn about psychology, probably diving into Freud and all sorts of interesting psychopathologies? But many of these same students are surprised to learn that modern psychology is not what they thought it was. An introductory-level course is about the scientific study of perception, cognition, social influence, development, and neuroscience, with nary a mention of how people come to know themselves better.

That's not to say that learning about such research is irrelevant to knowing what makes people tick. Discovering the principles of social psychology, for example, helps people understand their susceptibility to social influence, and learning the principles of cognitive psychology helps people understand the conditions under which they learn and retain new information. But there are unlikely to be units on how people come to know themselves, the value of such knowledge, and how accurate it is likely to be.

At least that's the way it used to be. If I were to point to my most important scientific contribution, it would be helping to bring the study of self-knowledge back into the mainstream of psychological research. Although there might not be specific units on self-knowledge in an introductory-level course, this topic has become a vibrant area of research in many areas of psychology.

How did this come about? The first step was showing that there is a lot that people *don't* know about themselves. When I was in graduate school in the 1970s, my graduate mentor, Richard Nisbett, and I published a paper arguing that a lot of what goes on in our minds happens outside of conscious awareness – not necessarily because we feel threatened by certain thoughts and feelings, as Freud argued, but because that's the way our minds are built. Human beings have a vast *adaptive unconscious* (as I came to call it) that allows them to process information about the world quickly and efficiently. And this is a very good thing, because it would impossible to rely solely on conscious thinking when going about our daily lives.

Imagine, for example, that you are walking down the street and run into an old friend from high school. The instant you recognize this person, a wealth of knowledge about her instantly comes to mind, as do your feelings toward her. You pick up your friendship where you left off, chatting about old times. Note how much of what just happened in your mind was unconscious: You recognized your friend instantly, your emotions and memories leaped into awareness, and you understood instantly what your friend was talking about when she referred to past events – all without any effort or conscious attention.

Imagine what the encounter would have been like if your unconscious mind had stopped working. You would have had to laboriously retrieve every fact from memory, like an old-fashioned clerk retrieving manila folders from a filing cabinet. Figuring out who the person is would be the first step: "Let's see, brown hair and brown eyes: let me look in that memory folder." After several minutes you determine that the person before you is your friend Sarah. Then you search all of the "Sarah" memory files to retrieve what you know about her, such as how you met, what your past encounters were like, and what happened the last time you saw her. Next you would have to deliberate about how these memories make you feel (e.g., "that time she kicked the winning goal on our soccer team still makes me happy, but I'm still mad about the time she stole my lunch money in fifth grade.") By now so much time has passed that Sarah is long gone (unless she was still consciously going through her memory files about you).

This is but one example of how the adaptive unconscious governs and facilitates our mental lives, from the initial perception of other people, retrieval of information about them, filling in the blanks of information we don't have, interpreting new incoming information, setting goals for ourselves, and triggering emotions. Without the ability to engage in such rapid, unconscious information processing, we would be helpless – still stuck on that street corner trying to figure out who Sarah was.

But the fact that so much of mental life occurs unconsciously comes with a cost, and that is that it is difficult to examine directly the workings of our own minds. In principle we could simply take a direct look, like a mechanic opening the hood of a car to see what's up with the fuel injection system. But the adaptive unconscious doesn't come with an engine hatch. Just as we can't directly observe the workings of our physiological processes, such as our digestive systems, so is it impossible to directly observe such things as our perceptual processes (e.g., how we transform retinal stimulations into 3-D images) or the workings of our own memories (e.g., how information about Sarah is stored and retrieved).

"But wait a minute," you might say, "there is a lot I can learn about myself by turning my attention inward. I know that I am anxious about my upcoming psychology test, infatuated with my boyfriend's roommate, and curious about what's going to happen on the next episode of *Game of Thrones*. No one else knows these things about me but me – they are private conscious experiences that are a key part of the richness of my own mental life."

Fair enough – obviously we all do have conscious mental experiences that are ours and ours alone. But the point is that these experiences are a very small part of what our minds are doing and accomplishing at any given moment, and we cannot just pull back the curtains and directly examine the workings of the adaptive unconscious.

But a crucial question is exactly *what* is out of view. Some would argue that it's just the "low level" stuff of daily living, such as the nuts and bolts of perception and memory. True, these folks would argue, we don't have direct access to how we perceive things in three dimensions or to the exact ways we store and retrieve things in memory, just as we don't have direct access to the way in which our skin, sweat glands, and blood vessels work together to regulate our body temperatures. As important as these processes are, they are not the higher-order psychological traits and emotions that define who we are as individual human beings. According to this view, I may not know how I perceive the world in three dimensions, but I know my hopes, dreams, peccadillos, beliefs, and attitudes that make me "me."

But here is where things get especially interesting, at least in my opinion. Yes, we know many of these things about ourselves, but how? Can we observe these personal characteristics directly, or did we learn about them in some other way? This is the second important step in the study of self-knowledge – studying how we come to know ourselves, and demonstrating that it is not the simple result of introspection. Instead, we take our conscious experiences and memories, as well as other sources of information (such as observations of what we actually do) and weave them into a narrative about who we are, why we do what we do, what our aspirations are, and so on. In short, self-knowledge is more of a construction, a process of story-telling, than direct observation.

For many of us, our self-stories are healthy accounts that direct our lives in fruitful directions. Sometimes, of course, people develop unhealthy narratives that lead to distress or unhappy outcomes. An important implication of the story metaphor is that people can change by editing their own stories. If a major overhaul is needed, psychotherapy is called for. But often our stories need little tweaks or tune ups, and social psychologists have developed a number of story-editing interventions to help people develop better narratives about themselves and who they can become. Exactly what those interventions are is the topic of another article – and exciting new research directions.

I'll end with one "story-editing" tip: An effective (but counterintuitive) way to change our self-views is to change our behavior first. We are excellent observers of ourselves and use our own behavior as "data" when inferring who we are. So, the first step to changing our self-view is often to act as we want to be. As Charlotte Brontë put it in *Jane Eyre*, "It seems to me, that if you tried hard, you would in time find it possible to become what you yourself would approve, and that if from this day you began with resolution to correct your thoughts and actions, you would in a few years have laid up a new and stainless store of recollections, to which you might revert with pleasure."

REFERENCES

Vazire, S., & Wilson, T. D. (eds.) (2012). *The handbook of self-knowledge*. New York: Guilford.

Wilson, T. D. (2002). *Strangers to ourselves: Discovering the adaptive unconscious*. Cambridge, MA: Harvard University Press.

Wilson, T. D. (2014). *Redirect: Changing the stories we live by*. New York: Little, Brown.

Part V

Motivation and Emotion: How We Feel and What We Do

Motivation

Amabile, Teresa M.

I started thinking about creativity at the age of five. I overheard my kindergarten teacher, Mrs. Bollier, say to my mother, "I think Teresa shows a lot of potential for artistic creativity, and I hope that's something she really develops over the years." Thrilled to hear it, I began imagining a life as a creative artist. Unfortunately, kindergarten was the peak of my artistic career. As I later revisited that flashbulb memory, I often wondered what happened to that promised creativity. Maybe Mrs. Bollier was wrong; I had no artistic talent. But maybe the cause had something to do with my art experiences in the ensuing elementary school years, when artistic activities, limited to one hour on Friday afternoons, consisted of trying to copy various great masterworks in painting. Limited to a few broken crayons and notebook paper, my classmates and I received no skill training; giving it my all, I nonetheless produced monstrosities that consistently earned poor grades. It was decades before I again felt like doing any sort of art.

The mystery of my missing artistic creativity receded into the background as I entered Canisius College, a small liberal arts school, as a chemistry major. I loved each science to which I'd been exposed, and chose chemistry because it looked excitingly challenging. I did well academically and, more importantly, had the opportunity to work in the labs of several research-active chemistry professors. (My first publication was in *The Journal of Chromatographic Science*.) In the summer after my second year, though, I had a life crisis. Impressed with the passion that my professors had for chemistry – I'd noticed the paper napkins covered with benzene rings and equations that they'd leave on the table after their intense lunch conversations – I realized I didn't enjoy thinking about chemistry on my own time. I didn't have that passion and doubted I ever would. But I wanted to find something that could captivate me that way.

I did find that something, the following year, when I took introductory psychology as an elective. The textbook, long since a classic, was by Ernest Hilgard and Richard Atkinson; the professors were Harvey Pines

275

and Dewey Bayer. I'd had no prior exposure to psychology, and I could hardly have been more excited: Here was a science, but it was not about the behavior of molecules; it was about the infinitely more fascinating (to me) behavior of humans.

When I entered the doctoral program in psychology at Stanford, I was fortunate enough to work with two young assistant professors of social psychology, Mark Lepper and Lee Ross. Mark had just begun publishing among the first experiments on the undermining of intrinsic motivation with extrinsic rewards, using concepts from attribution theory (on which Lee, among others, was doing pioneering work) and self-perception theory (which had recently been articulated by Daryl Bem, another of my Stanford mentors). The then-radical *over-justification effect* discovered in Mark's early work showed how extrinsic motivators, such as promised reward for doing an activity, can undermine someone's intrinsic motivation to do the activity for its own sake (i.e., because it's interesting, enjoyable, satisfying, positively challenging). I was fascinated by the notion that there could be different forms of motivation, and by this counterintuitive result.

As Mark and I developed our first co-authored paper (with William DeJong) on the effect of deadlines on intrinsic motivation, we began a debate. I speculated that motivational state – intrinsic versus extrinsic – must have an effect on performance. Mark was skeptical at first, noting the importance of having demonstrated the over-justification effect in the absence of performance decrements under reward. (He was right, of course.) But, I countered, certain kinds of performance on complex tasks – creativity, for example – could well suffer under extrinsic motivation. I found myself, at age twenty-five, making a link back to my childhood creativity puzzle, and I thought maybe I'd found a pathway to the answer. I've followed the intriguing twists and turns of that pathway ever since.

I initially pursued it with experiments, the first of which I did as a course project. In a field experiment conducted with children at my apartment complex, I examined the effect on artistic creativity of working for competitive rewards. Dissatisfied with the existing test-like paper-and-pencil measures of children's creativity, I decided to develop my own measurement technique based on judgments of actual products made by my study participants. Working with identical sets of materials, the children in both conditions (competitive reward vs. no reward) made collages that were later rated on creativity by independent experts who were blind to condition. I found that those experts agreed sufficiently in their judgments that I could combine their ratings into an overall creativity measure for each collage; I eventually published this methodology, expanded for use with both children and adults, as the *consensual assessment technique for creativity*.[1] More importantly, when I analyzed the creativity ratings in the two conditions, I found that the children in the no-reward condition made collages that were significantly more creative than those competing with each other for prizes.

That finding, tested further in a number of experiments over several years (many of them with my long-time collaborator Beth Hennessey, and many funded generously by the National Institute of Mental Health), yielded what I consider my most important scientific contribution: *the intrinsic motivation principle of creativity*: People are most creative when they are motivated primarily by the interest, enjoyment, satisfaction, and challenge of the work itself, and not by extrinsic motivators or pressures. In other words, creativity can vary significantly as a function of features of the immediate social environment.

Why do I see this as my most important contribution? There are several reasons. Most broadly, it enabled me to begin building the foundation for a social psychology of creativity (which my friend Dean Keith Simonton had simultaneously begun building with very different methods), a necessary expansion beyond the personality psychology of creativity that had long held sway. It formed the core of the comprehensive theory of creativity I developed, the *componential theory of creativity*, which highlighted the previously neglected roles of motivation and the social environment, and which I am still modifying and refining in light of new findings. Moreover, in order to conduct the experiments necessary to confidently articulate the intrinsic motivation principle of creativity, I had to develop the consensual assessment technique – which has now been used by dozens of creativity researchers. Plus, the publication of these experiments and my theory generated some controversy in the psychological literature (most notably in the form of papers by Robert Eisenberger and his colleagues), which I think is generally a good thing for our field. Finally, the intrinsic motivation principle bears significant implications for the use of extrinsic motivators and constraints in parenting, education, and organizations.

And this work has had a meaningful impact on my life. As I expanded my research program to examine creativity in other contexts, most notably organizations (initially in collaboration with Stanley Gryskiewicz of the Center for Creative Leadership), my work attracted the attention of Harvard Business School. Having spent nearly eighteen years in the

---

[1] Side-note of thanks to Bob Sternberg (then a fellow grad student), who helped me in the computer center when the punch card machine malfunctioned. Readers under fifty: look up "punch card"!

psychology department at Brandeis University, I was now recruited to join the HBS faculty. The trivial physical move of five miles from one institution to the other conceals the massive psychological and professional transition that this new appointment entailed. The broadened perspectives on organizational life that now surrounded me in the form of multidisciplinary colleagues, combined with the enhanced access to organizations as research sites and generous internal funding, allowed me to expand my research program immensely. For example, in a multi-year study involving the collection of nearly 12,000 daily diary entries with quantitative and qualitative data from more than 200 professionals working on innovation projects inside companies, my colleagues and I studied the micro-events that appear to establish optimal conditions for creative productivity. We found that, of all the positive work events that give rise to positive affect and intrinsic motivation, the single most prominent (by far) is making progress (even modest, incremental progress) in meaningful work. My co-author Steven Kramer and I call this *the progress principle*.

It's my fervent hope that someone reading this essay will be seized, as I was, by a strong intrinsic motivation to study the motivation for creativity rigorously and boldly. There are many next steps to take but, to me, the most essential ones will involve researching the interplay of intrinsic and extrinsic motivation as drivers of creative performance at different points in the creative process, particularly performance on significant projects in people's work at different points across the lifespan.

I'm still thinking about creativity, all these years later – wondering, perhaps not surprisingly, about creativity in later life. Thank you, Harvey and Dewey; Mark, Lee, Daryl, and Bill. Thank you, Beth, Stan, and Steve; NIMH, CCL, Brandeis, and HBS. Thank you, Mrs. Bollier.

REFERENCES

Amabile, T. M. (1996). *Creativity in context: Update to the social psychology of creativity*. Boulder: Westview Press.

Amabile, T. M., & Kramer, S. J. (2011). *The progress principle: Using small wins to ignite joy, engagement, and creativity at work*. Boston: Harvard Business Review Press.

Hennessey, B. A., & Amabile, T. M. (2010). Creativity. *Annual Review of Psychology*, *61*, 569–598.

59   Inner Processes Serve Interpersonal Functions

Baumeister, Roy R.

My mother was a schoolteacher, and many evenings she sat in our living room grading stacks of papers. I listened to her stray comments over the years enough to realize that grading papers is often boring, especially when they all say pretty much the same thing. I started to approach my own homework by first surmising what all the other students were likely to say and then finding something different to say. The hope was that by providing the teacher with a break in the monotony, I would persuade him or her to like my paper better. It probably helped my grades.

The habit of looking where no one else is looking has stuck with me for much of my career. One major theme of my thinking is that *inner processes serve interpersonal functions*. When I started graduate school in social psychology, I recognized quickly that almost all the ideas that dominated with the field focused on what happens inside one person. So I began to pay more attention to what happens between people.

To be sure, social psychologists were not completely indifferent to interpersonal processes, even though the 1970s were definitely a low point, coming after group research had mostly died out and before the 1980s boom in studying close relationships. But the dominant approach was to explain what happened between people as a consequence of what happens inside people. I tried to look at this in reverse: What happens inside people is often a consequence of what happens between them.

Many researchers were interested in issues of self and identity. Self-esteem was gaining ground as an important phenomenon, and it was common to interpret each laboratory finding about human behavior as reflecting people's concern with sustaining their self-esteem. I climbed on the self-esteem bandwagon too, but soon I began to think about inter-personal aspects. Self-esteem is what you think and feel about yourself. It seemed to me that what people think about themselves is only of secondary importance. It is much more useful and important to focus on how others regard you than on how you regard yourself. After all, your success or failure in life depends very much on whether other people accept you, like you, respect you, trust you, and so on. Loving (or hating) yourself doesn't put food on the table, put money in the bank, or establish a happy family. Those things depend on what other people think of you.

Hence, while everyone was talking about self-esteem, I began to study self-presentation – how people manage their reputations. To the consternation of my thesis advisor, I began to think that an important part of the self is the image of it that exists in other people's minds.

One way to tell whether behavior is driven by self-esteem or self-presentation is to compare public versus private situations – that is, to see whether the behavior changes when other people are present. Failing at a task or receiving computerized feedback on your personality, for example, should have the same effect on self-esteem regardless of whether other people know about it: It provides the same information for how you evaluate yourself. Hence, if research participants react differently depending on whether others know about it or not, that suggests they are concerned with self-presentation rather than self-esteem. My dissertation showed that people reacted much more strongly to personality feedback when others knew about it than when it was private and confidential. That meant they cared about the public self, more than the private self.

My first year as an assistant professor involved lots of time in the library. I had never taught a full social psychology course, so I was writing lectures, and for that I needed to read up on the latest findings. Each week's lectures brought me to a new topic, so I read different research literatures. I noticed that with each topic, somebody had published a study or two showing that behavior was different between public and private settings. These scattered findings emboldened me to think that the field's emphasis on inner processes such as self-esteem was missing out on lots of the real action – namely, in interpersonal phenomena. I discovered that some research journals would publish papers that simply summarized the literature, rather than reporting original data from one's own experiments. (This had never come up in graduate school.) So I managed to write up and publish a paper surveying all these findings about differences between public and private reactions. It made a big theoretical splash and helped me get tenure.

Much of my career since then has pursued the idea that inner processes serve interpersonal functions. I attended a series of conferences that were also frequented by several thinkers who were pursuing the idea that fear of death is the fundamental human motivation and the basis for anxiety. Really? I rarely heard anyone talk or worry about death, but they worried plenty about being socially rejected – divorced by spouse, abandoned by friends, rejected by graduate or medical schools, fired from jobs. Another literature review article concluded that most anxiety is in fact rooted in interpersonal relations, not private fear of eventual death. In other words, the anxiety that troubles and motivates people in their daily lives is not fear of death but, rather, fear of social rejection.

A colleague, Mark Leary, said he thought my anxiety paper was correct but didn't go far enough. He and I surveyed massive amounts of other literature to look for interpersonal roots behind all sorts of phenomena. The article summarizing our conclusions, titled "The Need to Belong," elucidated the motive to connect with others as the basis for emotion, thinking patterns, behavior, mental and physical health, and much else. Judged by impact, it is my most successful paper, having been listed in the bibliographies of more than nine thousand scientific papers. (Even one hundred times is enough to count as a "classic"; most papers get zero or one such listing.)

After that paper was published, my PhD students and I began to do experiments on what happens when the need to belong is thwarted, such as when a person is socially rejected by others. These turned out to yield large, strong effects, even in lab studies where you are being rejected by a stranger. Other researchers have picked up this work, making it into a thriving area of study.

Ultimately, my contrarian emphasis on interpersonal processes led to a new set of ideas that has become the foundation of my thinking. What is the essence of human nature? I think humans evolved to create a new kind of social life, namely culture. In evolutionary terms, culture is human-kind's biological strategy: It is how our species solves the universal problems of survival and reproduction. We create complex social systems that include sharing information, working in groups with different but interlocking roles, developing economic marketplaces, and the like. In modern life, we rely on culture (e.g., hospitals, supermarkets, restaurants, governments, sewers and utilities, universities) for both survival and reproduction. Even our drinking water comes to us from public services rather than directly from nature.

I came to this insight in a roundabout way. I was frustrated by how frequently experts in other fields (e.g., literary criticism, anthropology) turned to Freud when they wanted to use psychology in their work. Freud was a genius, but his ideas have become obsolete over the years, as new research accumulated. So I undertook to construct a new, comprehensive, integrative theory of human nature based on modern research findings. I wrote chapters on the main questions theorists ask psychology about: what do people want, how do they think, what drives emotions, how do people interact, and so forth. When done, I tried to step back and see what sort of creature this is. And, contrary to many prevailing views, I concluded that people are really well designed and well equipped to join complex social systems. When this insight came to me I was sitting outside by a rooftop pool at a friend's apartment building, and I had already sent the book to the publisher. I contacted the publisher to retract the manuscript and then re-wrote the entire book with this new theme and emphasis.

The idea that humans are social animals has been much repeated, dating back to Aristotle. To me, the key is that people are also cultural animals. That became the title of my book.

I have always felt myself to be something of an outsider in social psychology. Yet, ironically, I consider myself to be one of the most social of psychologists. My colleagues study single persons. Increasingly, most social psychologists conduct research by having college students sit at computers and make ratings. They study inner processes. These are important. But we should also attend to what happens between people. Inner processes are there to enable people to relate to each other.

REFERENCES

Baumeister, R. F. (2005). *The cultural animal: Human nature, meaning, and social life*. New York: Oxford University Press.

Baumeister, R. F., & Leary, M. R. (1995). The need to belong: Desire for interpersonal attachments as a fundamental human motivation. *Psychological Bulletin, 117*(3), 497–529.

Carver, Charles S.

I have been privileged to contribute to several distinct topic areas in personality, social, health, and abnormal psychology. Many of these contributions have had the label "self-regulation" attached to them at one time or another. To a personality psychologist (which is what I am), self-regulation refers to the use of mental reference points to guide one's behavior so as to create end states that correspond to those mental reference points.

My most important scientific contribution has probably been to help make this concept (and term) commonplace across psychology. At least two parts of that statement require more words. First, although I did play a role in popularizing self-regulation as a concept, I certainly didn't do it alone. Early in our careers, my collaborator Mike Scheier and I essentially caught a wave that was forming at the time. Our own contribution to the use of the term occurred in the context of that broader wave. (We did, however, spend an entire afternoon deliberating about using it in the title of our first book together.)

The second point that requires more words concerns the origins of the concept. Although I would be happy to avow my utter brilliance in synthesizing it, I did not do any such thing. Rather, having run across the concept in various guises early in my career, I decided that it mattered a great deal and that others should also realize it. So I tried over the years to make people aware of it and its relevance to the broader issues they were interested in.

There is a subtext here that students of psychology (and probably anything else) should realize. Almost everyone in any field, including psychology, would like to be widely known as the person who created some particular new idea (and, just as importantly, thought of a clever label for it). But ideas invariably have roots in other ideas. There are fewer new concepts than you probably think there are, but there are a lot of new twists on older concepts. I don't think I am entirely without creativity, but a startlingly high proportion of what I have done in my career turns out to have involved taking concepts others had created and applying them in slightly different ways to slightly different contexts.

How I Found It

In the spirit of our marching orders from the editors, however, let me describe as best I can how I got the idea for my most important contribution. When I was in graduate school I was not a very good student. Not lazy or argumentative, but not much interested in anything I was being exposed to in courses or seminars. I may have been well on my way to drifting gradually farther afield and perhaps out of psychology altogether. In my third year, however, two things happened, roughly simultaneously, that changed my life.

The first was that a couple of my more gregarious friends had been talking with fellow students in the social psychology program, and had become interested in a theory of "objective self-awareness" that had been proposed by a young faculty member (Robert Wicklund) and his graduate student (Shelley Duval). This theory held that when attention is directed to the self as an object, it causes the person to compare the self's current state to whatever is the currently salient standard for behavior (e.g., a salient standard while driving in the US is to keep to the right of the center line and reasonably distant from the car in front; a salient standard when being introduced to other people is to be polite; a salient standard for a dieter is to choose low-calorie food). One potential consequence of that comparison is an adjustment of one's behavior to conform more closely to the standard.

The second thing happened in the context of a seminar on cognitive development. The seminar was supposed to be about Piaget, but the professor who taught it (Mark Bickhard) inserted many bits of whatever else he was interested in at the time. One of the things he was interested in (more or less as a side-line really) was ideas about feedback processes and the structure of behavior (how people use information about their current conditions to adjust their behavior as needed to reach desired goals – more or less the definition of self-regulation in the arena of behavior). It took me about three minutes to look at those ideas, put them beside self-awareness theory (see previous paragraph), and say (to myself, I presume, rather than out loud), "well *that's* obviously pretty much the same thing as *that*." (I didn't realize for another year or so how annoying that conclusion – which seemed pretty obvious to me – would be to the people whose self-awareness theory I was about to intrude on, but that's another story.)

Juxtaposing these ideas sparked the first real interest I had had in graduate school. I fairly quickly thought of two simple experiments extending self-awareness theory slightly (one of which became my doctoral dissertation project). And those experiments led to other studies.

Once the dam cracked, the river flowed fairly freely, and I did a lot of work in the context of self-awareness theory. But I always thought of the processes I was studying in terms of feedback control (self-regulation).

Later I was pointed to other sources of ideas in the same general vein. William Powers had written an important book on feedback control as a model of human functioning. In it, he proposed a hierarchy of multiple layers of control systems, ranging from very concrete (control of muscle tensions) to very abstract (e.g., control of one's manifestations of honesty or of social responsibility). The notion of hierarchical organization allows the self-regulation principle to be applied to essentially anything people do, while simultaneously addressing how it might actually happen physically. That is, "doing something" generally requires making things happen at several levels of abstraction – ultimately, making muscles move – and this is true whether the overall goal is to pick up a coffee cup or to become successful in business.

Why the Idea Matters

As I said earlier, to a personality psychologist self-regulation implies the use of mental reference points to guide behavior so as to create end states that correspond to those mental reference points. For example, self-regulation occurs when we use intentions to guide actions. This is a way of thinking about behavior as inherently goal directed, conveying the sense that we have a vague image of where we are trying to go, and that we use information about where we presently are as a guide to adjust actions as needed to keep ourselves on course.

Of course, it's not just physical states that we regulate. Developmental psychologists such as Nancy Eisenberg and clinical psychologists such as James Gross emphasize the regulation of emotions, keeping them under control as situationally appropriate. In all these cases, though, the assumption is that behavior (in the broadest sense) has some internal guidance, with aims that are in some manner (though often quite vaguely) internally represented.

In more recent years, the concept of self-regulation has taken on stronger overtones of self-control, promoted partly by the writings of Roy Baumeister and his collaborators. Self-control occurs when a person overrides the impulse to do one thing in order to maintain conformity to some other goal value. This is a bit more complicated than simply staying on track toward one's intended goal. Both involve a desired goal and efforts to move toward it. In self-control, though, there is also a competing goal. Eating a salad requires self-regulation, in order to move the salad to your mouth successfully. Eating a salad instead of a piece of pie, on the other hand, may require self-control, in order to override the impulse to eat the pie instead.

I have always thought of self-control as an important subset of self-regulation, though only a subset. In some ways, though, it may turn out to be the most interesting subset. These days the idea that people have incompatible desires that have to be sorted out in one way or another occupies a lot of my thought. The processes by which people are able to overcome impulses – particularly emotionally based impulses – are a focal point for my current work. For example, when some people feel the desire for something, they reach out and grab it. When other people feel the same desire, they take it to the cash register and pay for it. Why they differ in their behavioral responses is an important question.

To me the self-regulation concept matters for several reasons (which some people might even see as being internally contradictory). One point of interest is that the self-regulation view assumes that people are trying to do something (i.e., they have a goal) pretty much all the time. They may not realize what it is they are trying to do, but there generally is something. It can be useful to look closely at one's thoughts, feelings, and actions to see what the goal is. For example, you may find yourself taking courses that don't interest you, maybe even majoring in something that bores you. But perhaps those behaviors are helping attain the goal of making your parents happy. Realizing that that's what you are doing may lead you to think about whether there is a way to make your parents happy that doesn't involve torturing yourself (or even whether making your parents happy should be your major goal right now).

Another point of interest is that self-regulatory processes can occur in very disparate sorts of systems, so that the concepts involved form a link between the understanding of human behavior and the understanding other kinds of systems, even self-organizing non-living systems. The existence of this link can seem very weird when you think about it hard (e.g., some of the behavior of people in groups and the behavior of weather systems appear to reflect similar principles). But I find the link aesthetically pleasing.

There is also a practical side, though I must admit that practicality has never been my main interest. The practical side relates to self-control as a facet of self-regulation. Self-control is incredibly important in many aspects of life. Many of the pressing problems of the world at large – and of the smaller slice of the world that represents your own life space – are partly issues of self-control and its failures. In the long run, humans will be well served by developing a better understanding of how self-control works and how it can be better fostered and nurtured. Many people are at work on this question, and I for one will be very interested in seeing whether we can learn to do this before the world is beyond saving.

REFERENCES

Carver, C. S., & Scheier, M. F. (1998). *On the self-regulation of behavior.* New York: Cambridge University Press.

61 Intrinsic Motivation: The Inherent Tendency to Be Active

Deci, Edward L.

Traditionally, when psychologists and laypeople alike have talked about motivation, they have usually referred to the amount of motivation someone has (or doesn't have). "How can I get my child *more* motivated to do schoolwork?" or "How can I get my employees *more* motivated to do their jobs?" someone might ask. The implication, of course, is that more motivation would make the child do more schoolwork and make the employees work harder at their jobs.

It makes sense that if these individuals have more motivation, the child would do more schoolwork and the employees would do more work. However, having more motivation would not necessarily lead them to do high-*quality* work. When I think about motivated behavior, I am generally interested in seeing high-quality behavior rather than just a large quantity of behavior.

Take learning, for example: One person who is highly motivated to learn might spend time memorizing facts, whereas another who is highly motivated might spend time learning concepts and themes that tie facts together. In general, I find the second type of learning preferable, but if all you know is the amount of motivation a person has for learning, you would not be able to predict whether the learning would be the lower-quality learning (viz., memorization) or the higher-quality learning (viz., conceptual understanding).

When I was a graduate student, it occurred to me that predicting the quality of learning (or playing basketball, or managing a company, or solving problems) would require differentiating the concept of motivation into *types* of motivation rather than just focusing on the *amount* of motivation. In other words, I thought that some types of motivation might lead to higher-quality behavior than other types. I also thought that perhaps the high-quality behavior would be accompanied by greater well-being.

At about that time I became captivated by the concepts of *intrinsic motivation* and *extrinsic motivation*, which very few people were writing about back then. I knew immediately that that was what I wanted to

288

research. The concept of intrinsic motivation, which means doing an activity because it is interesting and enjoyable, resonated deeply within me, and when I looked at young children playing, I knew I was watching a beautiful example of intrinsic motivation. And the children seemed to be learning while they played. However, when I observed upper-level elementary school classrooms, I wondered why some students seemed to have little intrinsic motivation for their schoolwork while others had a great deal.

Extrinsic motivation, in contrast to intrinsic, means doing a behavior to attain some separate consequence – a reward, a praising statement, or avoidance of a punishment. This is the so-called carrot-and-stick approach to motivation, which many people believe is the gold standard for motivating others. But thinking about these types of motivation led me to predict that intrinsic motivation was a type of motivation that would lead to higher-quality behavior, whereas extrinsic would lead to lower-quality.

The Undermining Effect and Enhancement

Because motivational psychologists were focusing on the amount of motivation, a few psychologists suggested that the best way to motivate people was to use both intrinsic and extrinsic motivation so the two would add together to yield a total amount of motivation. I was skeptical and wondered what would happen if I combined the two types of motivation. If a person were intrinsically motivated for an activity – playing golf, solving puzzles, or reading novels – and the person was paid to do it, would the payments affect the person's intrinsic motivation for that activity? Would they increase it, decrease it, or leave it unchanged?

So, I did an experiment. I had college students come into the lab individually and asked them to solve four really interesting "building-block" puzzles. I knew the puzzles were intrinsically motivating because I had pre-tested them and students had rated them as highly interesting and enjoyable. I offered half the students in the experiment monetary payments for each puzzle they solved, but I didn't mention money to the others.

After participants finished the puzzle-solving I left them alone in the lab with more puzzles and with some interesting magazines. I found that those people who had been paid to do the puzzles were less likely to do puzzles during this free-choice period than were those who had not been paid. Something had happened that decreased paid participants' intrinsic motivation for the puzzle-solving. This indicated that the two types of motivation were not additive because, when you put them together, the extrinsic diminished the intrinsic. Subsequently, Lepper and colleagues found the same undermining with preschool children. Years later, colleagues and I did a meta-analysis of 128 experimental effects and confirmed the original findings. And since then an experiment by Murayama and colleagues using brain scanning replicated the undermining effect of rewards and highlighted brain processes involved with the phenomenon.

Threats of punishment had a similar undermining effect. So, it seemed that the carrot-and-stick approach actually undermines people's natural intrinsic motivation. And studies by various researchers have shown that evaluations, deadlines, and imposed goals also decreased intrinsic motivation.

Other strands of research showed that intrinsic motivation did lead to deeper, more conceptual learning, to greater creativity, and to better psychological health. The carrot-and-stick approach, in contrast, led to routine behaviors, memorization, and lower levels of well-being. So, it has become clear from many studies that this natural, intrinsic motivation has profound advantages over the external types of pressured motivation that are so often used to motivate people and that not only lead to lower-quality behavior, but also undermine a type of motivation that leads to higher-quality behavior.

I also examined the effects of positive feedback on intrinsic motivation using a paradigm similar to the rewards paradigm, and I found that positive feedback led to enhanced intrinsic motivation relative to the no-feedback group.

Basic Psychological Needs

I became curious about why positive feedback enhanced intrinsic motivation whereas tangible rewards undermined it. I turned to the concept of psychological needs – specifically, the needs for competence and self-determination – which had been linked to intrinsic motivation in the 1950s and 1960s by Robert White and Richard de Charms. It made sense to me that people need to feel competent or effective, as well as autonomous or self-determined, and that competence and autonomy were intertwined with intrinsic motivation. So I proposed that positive feedback satisfied the participants' need for competence, leading them to be more intrinsically motivated.

As for rewards, although people like to get rewards, rewards are often used as a way to control them, so rewards can easily take on a controlling meaning for people and therefore thwart their need for autonomy. So too could evaluations, deadlines, and impositions, which are also used to control people, and they too undermined intrinsic motivation. In contrast, offering people choice, which satisfied their need for autonomy, increased their intrinsic motivation.

Cognitive Evaluation Theory

In 1980, Richard Ryan and I teamed up to review all of this research and integrate it by making a formal statement of cognitive evaluation theory, which had the idea of needs for competence and autonomy (i.e., self-determination) at its core. As we did that, it became clear that the concept of intrinsic motivation represented an entry point for the empirical exploration of autonomy – that is, of psychological freedom – which interested me deeply. Serendipitously, I had found a way to study human autonomy by starting with an exploration of intrinsic motivation.

After doing several laboratory experiments about the effects of rewards, feedback, and other external factors, Rich Ryan and I took to the field to see if we could find, in a variety of real life situations, the phenomena we had been able to produce in the lab. For example, we went into a Fortune 500 company and trained managers to be more supportive of their employees' competence and autonomy. We found that the trained managers were more supportive of their employees' needs, and their employees were more satisfied with their work and had more trust in the corporate management.

In elementary schools, when teachers were more supportive of the students' competence and autonomy, the students were more intrinsically motivated, showed deeper learning, and felt better about themselves. But teachers also have needs for competence and autonomy, which must be satisfied for them to have the vitality and enthusiasm to provide the students with the supports they need.

In time, Rich Ryan and I moved forward to develop self-determination theory, initially by examining whether extrinsic motivation, although often controlling and detrimental, could sometimes be autonomous and have more positive consequences. Rich took the lead on that work, which he describes in his chapter for this volume (Chapter 66). In short, we found that extrinsic motivation can become autonomous through the process of internalization, and when it does, it shares various qualities with intrinsic motivation. We use the term autonomous motivation to refer to the combination of intrinsic motivation and well-internalized extrinsic motivation. When studying internalization, we realized that it was necessary to posit a third psychological need – the need for *relatedness to others*. People internalize values, regulations, motivations, and beliefs because they want to be related to others who hold those values and motivations.

292   *Deci, Edward L.*

This work has led us to focus on the degree to which people's behaviors are autonomous versus controlled and on the degree to which the interpersonal environments – in such places as schools, athletic teams, medical clinics, workplaces, families, virtual worlds, and close personal relationships – support versus thwart the three basic psychological needs for competence, autonomy, and relatedness. To the extent that environments are supportive, people are more autonomously motivated, engage in higher-quality behavior, have better close relationships, and display greater psychological well-being.

REFERENCES

Deci, E. L., & Ryan, R. M. (1980). The empirical exploration of intrinsic motivational processes. In L. Berkowitz (ed.), *Advances in experimental social psychology* (vol. 13, pp. 39–80). New York: Academic Press.
Deci, E. L., & Ryan, R. M. (2000). The "what" and "why" of goal pursuits: Human needs and the self-determination of behavior. *Psychological Inquiry*, *11*, 227–268. doi:10.1207/S15327965PLI1104_01.
Ryan, R. M., & Deci, E. L. (2016). *Self-determination theory*. New York: Guilford, in press.

62 Mindsets: From the Classroom to the Middle East

Dweck, Carol S.

When I was in college, I fell in love – with the scientific method. Could I imagine a better career than using the scientific method to uncover the workings of the human psyche? No, and I still can't. It's been a long and fruitful relationship, and I'd like to share with you some of the fruits.

My most important scientific contribution so far has been my research on mindsets. (From now on I will say "our" and "we," because all of the research is collaborative, which makes the enterprise all the more stimulating and enjoyable. We are not lone scientists toiling in isolation.) It all started with the following question: What makes some people seek challenges and thrive in the face of obstacles, while others, no less able, avoid difficulty and crumble when they encounter setbacks? I came to realize that I was interested in this question for personal reasons. Many of us psychologists do not just do *re*search, but what we call "*me*-search" – research on a topic that is really about us, such as our bad memory or our inability to exert willpower or our concern with others' opinions. As for me, I had always done well at everything I tried, but I didn't try everything. I was reluctant to step out of my comfort zone and was alarmed by the prospect of ever failing at anything I valued. As I began my me-search, I encountered something that would change me for good.

While working with ten-year-old students, at some point in the experiment I gave them problems that were too hard to solve. As I expected, some students were a bit distraught. But, counter to my expectation, some were pleased. They didn't just cope with what I thought of as the "failure" problems, they welcomed them as an exciting opportunity to learn. It was as though the whole experience was now worth their while. After I got over my shock, I vowed to understand these children's secret, not just for myself, but so I could share it with others.

Some years later, we came to understand that these students were in a "growth mindset." They believed that their intelligence and abilities could be developed, and they believed that the way to do that was by taking on challenges and sticking to them. The students who crumbled were instead in a "fixed mindset." They believed that their basic abilities were fixed – that they had a certain amount and that's that – and they believed that the hard problems reflected badly on their fixed ability. They worried that the hard problems meant they were somehow deficient and always would be.

Over the years we have learned that being in a growth mindset has real benefits for students' motivation to learn and their achievement. In many studies, students in a growth mindset significantly outperformed their peers who were in a fixed mindset, especially when they were making difficult school transitions or confronting challenging courses. We and other researchers have also showed that teaching a growth mindset and how to apply it has benefits for students' motivation and achievement. In our intervention studies, students learn that they can grow their brains: that every time they take on hard tasks and stick to them, the neurons in their brain form new or stronger connections, and over time they can increase their abilities. They learn that effort and difficulty should not make them feel less competent, but, rather, should make them feel like they are increasing their competence, for they are creating the very circumstances for growing their brain. These studies have shown that students who learn these lessons subsequently learn more, learn more deeply, and enjoy their learning more, leading them to do better in school.

We have also learned that praise can influence the mindsets. Work with Claudia Mueller, Melissa Kamins, Andrei Cimpian, and others shows that praise for intelligence or ability can foster a fixed mindset, with all of its vulnerabilities, whereas praise for "process" (such as the hard work or strategies that led to learning or success) can foster more of a growth mindset. Ironically, telling kids they're smart can sap their intellectual vigor.

It has been extremely rewarding that our mindset research has had an impact on public policy. Many schools and school systems have been influenced by this work. Some new schools have been founded on growth mindset principles. The Secretaries of Education of the United States and of the United Kingdom, and the President and the First Lady of the United States, have described this work and its implications in their speeches. The Khan Academy built a whole public service campaign, called "You Can Learn Anything," around the growth mindset (https://www.khanacademy.org/youcanlearnanything).

Can whole fields, whole academic disciplines, have mindsets? New work by Andrei Cimpian, Sarah Jane Leslie, and their colleagues shows that they can. What's more, they found that the more the scholars in an academic discipline said their field had a fixed mindset (i.e., believed that it took innate brilliance to succeed in that field), the fewer women and

African Americans earned PhDs in that field. These more fixed mindset fields included math, physics, economics, and philosophy. They believed that some people had this brilliance and others did not, perhaps creating an atmosphere in which women and minorities did not feel that they would be welcomed, as the haves versus have nots. Armed with this knowledge, we can begin to figure out how these disciplines can send out a more growth-mindset-oriented message, one that welcomes women and minorities to take their courses and grow their abilities.

Following our initial discovery of the mindsets, our research exploded into many new directions. For example, work with Sheri Levy, Steve Stroessner, Jason Plaks, and Priyanka Carr shows that the belief in fixed traits can foster stereotypes about and prejudice toward others. Work with Catherine Good and Aneeta Rattan shows that holding a growth mindset can make women less susceptible to the negative academic stereotypes about their math ability; despite encountering negative stereotypes in their calculus course, those who believed their abilities could be developed maintained their interest in math, their sense that they belonged in their math course, and their intention to take math in the future.

Work with David Yeager is showing that mindsets about personal qualities (as fixed or capable of being developed) are at the heart of adolescent aggression and depression, and that teaching more of a growth mindset about personal qualities can decrease both. When adolescents learn that they and others are capable of change, they no longer feel that instances of exclusion or rejection define them as permanent victims or losers, or define the perpetrators as permanently mean people deserving of aggressive retaliation.

In recent years, Veronika Job, Greg Walton, and I have shown that mindsets about willpower can be powerful determinants of the willpower we actually display. One current view of willpower portrays it as a very limited resource that is easily depleted. We find that this is only true if you believe it. People who instead believe that willpower is abundant and even self-generating (the harder you work, the more you want to work; the more you resist temptations, the stronger you feel) are able to maintain their willpower for a long time and in the face of demanding tasks. We find, for example, that during final exams these people focus better and do better.

Finally, in recent years, we have found that teaching a growth mindset about *groups* – the idea that groups don't have a fixed evil or aggressive nature but are capable of growth and change – can affect people on both sides of the Middle East conflict. Both Palestinians and Jewish Israelis, after learning a growth mindset about groups, liked each other a bit more and became more open to entertaining serious compromises for the sake of peace. We have recently shown that Israelis, after attending a growth mindset workshop, maintained this more positive attitude about the possibility of peace over a six-month period, even though it was a period of intense conflict and domestic political upheaval.

I am often asked, "How do I develop more of a growth mindset?" The first step is to realize that we're all a mixture of mindsets, and then begin to observe what triggers your fixed mindset self. Does it appear when you're out of your comfort zone and make you anxious or insecure? Does it emerge when you're struggling with something and make you think, "If I were really smart, this wouldn't be so hard"? Does it leap out when you've made mistakes or failed at something and make you feel ashamed or defensive? Does it make you feel jealous or inferior when you meet someone who seems smarter than you? Watch carefully for those triggers and notice what happens to you, how you feel, and how it affects your behavior. Then, give that fixed mindset persona a name (Gary, Harriet, Uncle Duane, Aunt Maisie) and, when it appears, talk to it from a growth mindset perspective. Tell it how important it is to take on challenges, teach it that mistakes and setbacks are a natural part of learning, show it how you can learn from people who are currently more skillful, focus it on your longer-term growth rather than your short-term performance.

I hope you've seen how research can take you on an exciting journey to unforeseen places. A journey begun to understand obstacles to achievement in American classrooms took us to a better understanding of prejudice, aggression, and willpower, and ended up shedding light on a conflict on the other side of the world.

REFERENCES

Dweck, C. S. (2006). *Mindset*. New York: Random House.

Dweck, C. S. (2008). Can personality be changed? The role of beliefs in personality and change. *Current Directions in Psychological Science*, *17*, 391–394.

Moser, J. S., Schroder, H. S., Heeter, C., Moran, T. P., & Lee, Y-H. (2011). Mind your errors: Evidence for a neural mechanism linking growth mind-set to adaptive post error adjustments. *Psychological Science*, *22*(14), 1484–1489.

63 Whether You Think You Can, or You Think You Can't – You're Right

Furnham, Adrian

1. A Modest Contribution to Science

I have never been a good judge of reactions to my work. Some of what I think are my most innovative ideas and experiments seem to attract little attention. I have to rely on others and such things as citation counts to get some idea of the contribution. I consider my research on the *psychology of culture shock, the psychology of alternative medicine,* and *the psychology of money* to be my best work, but I am going to discuss another issue: self-estimated intelligence. I believe this is important for science as much as for application.

I got the idea from reading a very short paper by a fellow academic at Edinburgh University. Hanna Beloff, an early feminist and social psychologist, wrote a short, semi-academic paper in the British Psychological Society journal *The Psychologist.* She reported in 1992 that she asked students to estimate their own and their parents' IQ scores and found striking sex differences, which she attributed to the modesty training given to girls.

I thought it might be really interesting to replicate this finding, which I did. It seemed surprising to me that the difference was so large, particularly among bright students who had benefited from the women's liberation movement and from much gender equality legislation.

This, in turn, led me to do around forty studies looking first at cross-cultural differences, then at differences in estimates of multiple intelligences as well as at the relationship between psychometrically measured ("actual") intelligence and self-assessments.

I started simply by showing students the well-known bell curve of intelligence and asked them to "honestly and accurately" estimate their score. With colleagues, I collected data in countries from Argentina to Zambia, always showing a sex difference.

Then I started asking about different types of intelligence, using first Gardner's model but then others, including Sternberg's and Cattell's work on different types/facets of intelligence. I then got the subjects to estimate how they would do on the various tests that make up the best IQ tests, such as the Stanford-Binet or the Wechsler Adult Intelligence Test. This provided a finer-grain analysis, and it appeared that the sex differences in estimations were mainly about mathematical and spatial types of intelligence.

In the first study Beloff had asked students to estimate their parents' scores. In a number of studies we asked people to estimate scores not only of their parents but also of their grandparents, as well as of their children and peers. We did one study on people estimating the intelligence of famous people. I remember being very surprised to find in many studies done in many countries, including China and Japan, that parents, on average, thought their sons brighter than their daughters. This could of course lead to self-fulfilling prophecies, with parents investing more in their sons than in their daughters.

Journal editors soon pointed out that it was important to look at the relationship between "actual" test-derived intelligence and self-estimates. Were males, they asked, overestimating their test scores and females under estimating theirs, or were both true at the same time? The answer seemed to be "both," but there was more evidence of male hubristic over-estimates than of female humble under-estimates.

We did notice that the over- or under-estimation effects were reduced if the subjects made the estimations soon after taking an intelligence test. Currently we are looking at giving people accurate or distorted feedback on their scores and seeing what effect that has. However, we have concluded that you cannot use estimates as a good proxy for actual scores: That is, that people's self-estimates are not accurate enough to be used as a substitute for getting an accurate test score.

The work has generated some interest, with a few meta-analyses. Others have picked up the baton.

2.   The Psychology of Self-Estimated Intelligence

To summarize, my findings from over forty studies in this area are:

First, males of all ages and backgrounds tend to estimate their (overall) general intelligence about 5 to 15 IQ points higher than do females. Those estimates are always above average, and usually around one standard deviation above the norm. This difference is much larger than the actual differences one finds in test manuals. Males tend most to "suffer from" hubristic over-estimation.

Second, when judging "multiple intelligences," based on Gardner's model, males estimate their spatial and mathematical (numerical) intelligence higher but their emotional intelligence lower than do females. On some multiple intelligences (verbal, musical, bodily-kinesthetic), there is little or no sex difference. When they consider the traditionally defined intelligences, which are usually verbal, mathematical, and spatial intelligence, people of all ages and cultures believe males are more intelligent.

Third, people believe these sex difference occur across the generations: People believe their grandfather was/is more intelligent than their grand-mother; their father more than their mother; their brothers more than their sisters; and their sons more than their daughters. That is, through-out the generations in one's family, males are judged as more intelligent than females. This trend is, however, more noticeable in males compared to females. People estimate their own scores lower (3–5 points) than those of their children, but 3–5 points higher than those of their parents and 8–15 points higher than those of their grandparents. The sex difference in estimation remains consistent across the generations. In this sense, unless they believe their IQ scores change, people believe there are generational effects and people (their relatives) are getting brighter every generation.

Fourth, estimated sex differences are cross-culturally consistent. While Africans tend to give higher estimates, and Asians lower estimates, there remains an estimated sex difference across all cultures. Differences seem to lie in cultural definitions of intelligence as well as norms asso-ciated with humility and hubris.

Fifth, the correlation between self-estimated and test-generated IQ is positive and low, in the range of $r=0.2$ to $r=0.5$, suggesting that you cannot use self-assessments as proxies for actual IQ test scores. Some people are accurate, but there are too many outliers who seriously over- or under-estimate their tests scores and ability.

Sixth, with regard to outliers, those who score high on IQ but give low self-estimates tend nearly always to be female, while those with the opposite pattern (high estimates, low scores) tend to be male.

Seventh, most people say, in the abstract, that they do not think there are sex differences in intelligence, despite the fact that we always find females give lower self-estimates, on average, than do males. We also found that those who said they have taken IQ tests and received feedback seem to give higher self-estimates. This may be because brighter people choose to do tests or are at institutions that do IQ testing.

4.   Where Next?

I am not sure there is anything one could grandly see as a theory in this area. However, I would very much welcome the following research:

I would like to further explore beliefs about intelligence, such as Dweck's Mindset theory and self-estimated intelligence. Dweck has distinguished between Entity theorists, who essentially believe that intelligence cannot be increased, as opposed to Incremental theorists, who believe that with sustained effort everyone can become more intelligent.

Most of all, I would like longitudinal research on a large sample, tracing the relationship between "actual" psychometrically assessed intelligence and self-estimated intelligence, over time, to explore causal relations. I could then ask the question of whether self-estimates have an impact on test achievement, or the other way around – or, indeed, both.

I would like to explore the relationship between self-rated intelligence, general measures of self-confidence, and life-success variables such as health, income, and relationship stability. I would also like to explore ways of giving people feedback on their intellectual capabilities to help them to ultimately explore and exploit their potentials.

REFERENCES

Freund, P. H., & Kasten, N. (2012). How smart do you think you are? A meta-analysis on the validity of self-estimates of cognitive ability. *Psychological Bulletin, 138*, 296–321.

Furnham, A. (2001). Self-estimates of intelligence: culture and gender difference in self and other estimates of both general (*g*) and multiple intelligences. *Personality and Individual Differences, 31*, 1381–1405.

Szymanowicz, A., & Furnham, A. (2011). Gender differences in self-estimates of general, mathematical, spatial, and verbal intelligence: Four meta-analyses. *Learning and Individual Differences, 21*, 493–504.

Higgins, E. Tory

For centuries, the dominant principle of motivation has been the hedonic principle that people are motivated to maximize pleasure and minimize pain. This principle continues to be central not only in psychology but in other disciplines as well, such as economics. Within psychology, the idea that people want to approach pleasure and avoid pain has been basic to theories of emotion, conditioning, achievement, and decision-making. When Freud discussed motivation "beyond the pleasure principle," it was to emphasize that avoiding pain is almost as important as approaching pleasure.

Two decades ago, I proposed that scientists need to go beyond pleasure and pain to understand how motivation works. Why? Because there are two separate and distinct systems for approaching pleasure and avoiding pain, and the difference between them is critical for understanding what people feel, how they make judgments and decisions, and what they strive for. The scientific discoveries that were made by distinguishing between *promotion* motivation and *prevention* motivation have been my most important scientific contribution.

How do promotion and prevention motivation differ? At the highest level of analysis, promotion and prevention have different survival concerns. When individuals have a promotion focus, they are concerned with growth and mastery. When they have a prevention focus, they are concerned with safety and security. Individuals with a promotion versus prevention focus also differ in how they represent their goal pursuits, with promotion-focused individuals representing their goals as hopes and aspirations (ideals) and prevention-focused individuals representing their goals as duties and obligations (oughts).

This latter difference produces emotional differences as well because ideal versus ought goals are also used in self-evaluations of success or failure in goal pursuits ("How am I doing?"). Success versus failure produces happy-versus-sad emotions in the promotion system and calm-versus-anxious emotions in the prevention system. This means that what pleasure and pain actually *feel like* is different for promotion versus

301

prevention. This is one way that the promotion–prevention distinction goes beyond the hedonic principle per se.

Finally, and importantly, there is a basic difference between promotion and prevention in what conditions produce pleasure and pain. A person's current state-of-affairs is the *status quo* for that person. It can be thought of as "0." Importantly, this "0" is *not* neutral. And not only is it not neutral, its valence is different for promotion versus prevention. What matters to individuals with a prevention focus is to maintain safety and security, to meet duties and obligations. What they want is to maintain a satisfactory status quo "0" and not lose it by moving to a worse state of "–1". Pleasure is maintaining "0" (a non-loss) and pain is moving to "–1" (a loss).

In contrast, maintaining "0" is not enough for promotion. What matters to individuals with a promotion focus is to grow and advance, to move toward hopes and aspirations. What they want is to attain a better "+1" state than the current status quo "0." Pleasure is attaining "+1" (a gain), and pain is staying at "0" (a non-gain). Importantly, this difference between promotion and prevention means that what *is* pleasure and what *is* pain is different. This is another way that the promotion–prevention distinction goes beyond the hedonic principle per se.

These three differences between promotion and prevention produce many significant differences in people's lives. The difference in people's emotional lives has already been mentioned. Other important differences have also been discovered. One difference is in the goal-pursuit strategies that are preferred and sustain motivation in promotion versus prevention. Pursuing goals in an *eager* manner sustains promotion, whereas pursuing goals in a *vigilant* manner sustains prevention. Receiving success feedback supports being eager, whereas receiving failure feedback supports being vigilant. Consistent with this, promotion-focused individuals perform better after receiving success than failure feedback, but the opposite is true for prevention-focused individuals. Moreover, promotion-focused individuals tend to be optimists (anticipating success in the future), whereas prevention-focused individuals tend to be defensive pessimists (focusing on the possibility of failure if they don't prepare enough). There is even evidence that promotion-focused individuals' self-esteem rises after success (sustaining eagerness for the next task), but prevention-focused individuals' self-esteem falls (maintaining vigilance for the next task).

Another important difference between promotion- and prevention-focused individuals is when they are and are not motivated to make risky (vs. conservative) choices. When individuals are currently at a satisfactory status quo "0," those with a promotion focus are generally more willing to take risks and are more open to change. But there is more to this story. When promotion-focused individuals have clearly made progress already, have clearly moved to a better "+1" state, they become relatively risk averse. Even more interesting is the fact that prevention-focused individuals become risk seeking when they find themselves at "−1." Being at "−1" is unacceptable because it is an unsafe, insecure place to be. They need to return to safety and security, and they will make a risky choice if it is the only way to achieve this. Notably, making risky choices is more determined by a prevention focus in the domain of "−1" losses and a promotion focus in the domain of "+1" gains.

The promotion–prevention difference also contributes to differences in moral concerns and moral behaviors. Prevention-focused individuals want to meet their duties and obligations, behave as they ought to behave, and avoid breaking the rules. Promotion-focused individuals aspire to being better persons, want to make progress toward ideals, and don't want to miss opportunities for advancement. This difference translates into prevention-focused individuals being more concerned about sins of commission than sins of omission, while the opposite is true for promotion-focused individuals. In addition, prevention-focused individuals are more concerned with maintaining proscriptive moral rules (e.g., "Thou shalt not ... "), whereas promotion-focused individuals are more concerned with moving toward (perhaps unreachable) ethical standards of excellence, such as being inspired by noble or saint-like figures.

Note that the promotion–prevention difference is not just a personality difference. People, and other animals as well, do vary chronically in whether they are more promotion- or prevention-focused. But momentary situations can make individuals either promotion- or prevention-focused because we all have some growth concerns and some security concerns. Different situations can also vary in terms of whether gains or non-losses are emphasized ("playing to win"; "playing to not lose"). Moreover, teams or groups can be more promotion-focused or more prevention-focused, and this affects how they perform and what decisions they make. There are also cross-cultural differences in whether the cultural members are more promotion-focused (e.g., Italy, United States) or more prevention-focused (e.g., South Korea, Japan). Thus, the motivation distinction between promotion and prevention is wide-ranging. Indeed, it is a pervasive part of all of our lives.

I have been asked how I got the idea for this distinction between promotion and prevention. I have also been asked how this distinction matters in everyday life. My answer to the first question also provides one answer to the second question. The idea began with my wanting to understand why a highly stressful life event, such as getting divorced or losing your job, can lead to depression for some people but generalized anxiety disorder (GAD) for others. The answer, from my self-discrepancy theory, was that people are more likely to suffer from depression when they experience a negative event as a failure to attain their hopes (ideals), whereas they are more likely to suffer from GAD if they experience a negative event as a failure to meet their obligations (oughts).

Over several years studying this distinction, I began to realize that something more general was going on. First, a momentary situation can activate ideals or activate oughts; activating discrepancies (failures) in these momentary situations can also produce, respectively, depression-like and GAD-like syndromes. Second, there are ideal and ought successes and not just failures, and they also produce different kinds of (positive) emotions. This suggested that two different motivational systems underlay these differences – the beginning of the idea of distinct promotion and prevention systems.

The insights from the promotion–prevention difference have been used to develop new, and effective, therapeutic interventions for depression and GAD. There have also been applications to improving performance, such as framing success in a vigilant way for prevention-focused individuals and in an eager way for promotion-focused individuals. For example, when German professional soccer players were told in a shoot-out of 5 shots to try either to gain 3 or more scores (eager pursuit) or not to lose more than 2 scores (vigilant), performance was enhanced for promotion-focused players in the former case and for prevention-focused players in the latter case. There is also evidence that consumers will offer more to buy the same product if it was chosen using eager (vs. vigilant) means by promotion-focused individuals but vigilant (vs. eager) means by prevention-focused individuals. As a final example that promotion–prevention differences matter, couples in long-term relationships are more satisfied with their relationship when one partner has a promotion focus and the other has a prevention focus – a complementarity that allows for division of labor.

What would I like to see in future research? Most important is to understand more fully when promotion and prevention work together effectively – both within individuals and within teams. The marital example above illustrates how they can work together effectively by partners dividing an activity (e.g., cooking) into eager subtasks that fit promotion and vigilant subtasks that fit prevention. More generally, there are often parts of tasks where eagerness works best and other parts where vigilance works best. This would be true for scientists working alone and working in teams. Because promotion and prevention each have motivational benefits and motivational costs, we need to find a way that they can *work together* effectively by sometimes supporting and sometimes constraining each other in order to reap their benefits and decrease their costs. This is the next great challenge.

REFERENCES

Halvorson, H. G., & Higgins, E. T. (2013). *Focus: Use different ways of seeing the world for success and influence*. New York: Hudson Street Press (Penguin).

Higgins, E. T. (1997). Beyond pleasure and pain. *American Psychologist, 52,* 1280–1300.

Higgins, E. T. (2012). *Beyond pleasure and pain: How motivation works*. New York: Oxford University Press.

65 The Letter to a Friend That Helped Launch a Career

Ross, Lee

Over the course of my fifty-year career, I have written three books and a number of well-cited papers and chapters. Each of these books, and several of the papers and chapters, had their genesis in a written exchange with a friend while I was still in graduate school. We both had done work on the misattribution of one's own emotional state, but the provocative paper he sent in draft form broke new ground. In my otherwise positive two-page response, I raised two issues. The friend was Richard Nisbett, who had been my senior classmate at Columbia and who by then was an assistant professor at Yale. The 1971 paper co-authored by Ned Jones soon became a classic in the attribution theory literature. It was titled "Actors and Observers: Divergent Perceptions of the Causes of Behavior."

Jones and Nisbett offered a compelling mix of empirical observations, anecdotal examples, laboratory findings, and plausible mechanisms in support of the claim that actors are inclined to attribute their own actions, preferences, and choices to features of the relevant situation, but attribute the responses of other actors to the "dispositions" of those actors. My comments included two questions.

Two Questions Posed to My Colleague

Is there a more fundamental main effect than the actor–observer difference? One issue I raised was the possibility that the phenomenon Jones and Nisbett had identified reflected a difference in the degree to which actors and observers, albeit to different degrees, were succumbing to a more "fundamental" bias. This issue was pursued in my 1977 chapter in the *Advances in Social Psychology* series titled "The Intuitive Psychologist and His Shortcomings" and explored at length in each of the three books I subsequently co-authored. My own contribution consisted mainly in naming this "fundamental attribution error" and in pointing out the role it played in the seeming non-obviousness of so many classic research findings, whereby particular situational pressures and constraints led research participants to act in ways that challenge our notions about how "ordinary" people behave. But that is not the story I shall tell in the remainder of this chapter. (If that story interests you, *Human Inference* and later *The Person and the Situation*, both co-authored with Richard Nisbett, are the places to find it.)

Might actor–observers differences in attribution reflect differences in own vs other actions? The second issue I raised was prompted by the attribution "cube" proposed in 1967 by Harold Kelley and by the 1965 discussion of "correspondent inference" by Jones and Davis. Both of these seminal papers suggested that in making inferences about the causes and implications of particular actions and choices, people give weight to the commonness and normativeness of the relevant choices. In my letter to Dick I asserted (without evidence) that people are bound to overestimate the extent to which others share their choices and preferences, and as such to see actions and choices that differ from their own as more reflective of distinguishing personal dispositions than their own actions and choice. So, I set out to see whether actor–observer differences in attribution would remain after "correcting for" the relevant differences in presumed "commonness."

The false consensus effect. The answer to that question proved to be *yes* (although this "correction" reduced the actor–observer discrepancy). But before submitting a report on this finding (in a 1977 paper co-authored by David Greene and Pam House), it dawned on me that what we had "corrected for" was itself worth pursuing. We described this *false consensus effect* as the tendency for people who make a given choice to assume that choice to be more common – and less revealing about personal dispositions – than do people who make the opposite choice in the same situation.

One source of this bias in consensus estimates, we suggested, is that the people we observe and associate with are apt to share our preferences, priorities, and life situations. The second source of this bias is less obvious but richer in its psychological implications. Different actors respond in a given situation in part because they "construe" that situation differently. What people fail to recognize and make sufficient allowance for is the fact that others are apt to have different construals and to act accordingly. For example, we asked research participants to walk around campus wearing a sandwich-board sign bearing the message EAT AT JOE'S, with the assurance that if they opted not to do so they could opt for some other later study. When they were asked what percentage of their peers would agree to wear the sign, they showed the expected false consensus effect. This result, we suggested, reflected the fact that participants who imagined that classmates they encountered would respond with interest and good humor were likely to say *yes*, and to assume that most others would similarly agree to the request. In contrast, participants who imagined a far more negative response – perhaps shaking of heads, snickering, and turning away without giving them any chance to explain – were likely to say no and assume that most peers would do likewise.

In 1990, Tom Gilovich provided direct evidence for this interpretation of the false consensus effect. He showed that the magnitude of the effect depended on the degree to which there was ambiguity, and hence latitude for differences in construal, in the response options participants were considering. He further showed that when that latitude was greatly reduced, so was the magnitude of the false consensus effect.

In the decade that followed, some of my empirical work focused on the impact of situational labels. But my larger interest was in the extent to which differences or changes in construal held the key to a number of important phenomena, including heightened enmity and distrust in the context of interpersonal and intergroup conflict. I also came to see that there was a truly fundamental source of bias that made its influence felt in all social perception, and all self-reflection as well.

Naïve Realism

People necessarily have the conviction that what they perceive, or reason to be the case, or even feel, when they respond is attuned to reality – that is, they believe they see things the way those things "really" are. There is an obvious corollary to this conviction. If one believes one's "take" on the world reflects reality, then those holding and acting on different perceptions, assessments, and responses must be doing so because of something about *them*. Depending on the context, that something may involve their personality traits, the misinformation and indoctrination they have received, their tendency to see and believe what serves their self-interest, the cultural lenses through which they are seeing things, or some other distorting perceptual, informational, cognitive, or motivational bias.

My colleagues and I have explored some of the implications of such "naïve realism." In particular, we documented people's failure to recognize that they are just as subject to various sources of distortion in judgment as are others – including those on the "other side" of issues. In one study, students examined the political attitudes of an unknown peer and then were asked to assess both the similarity of those views to their own and the extent to which those views were the product of normative inferential processes versus various biases. Our findings confirmed the observation that the wise statesman Benjamin Franklin made more than two centuries ago:

Most men, indeed as well as most sections in religion, think themselves in possession of all truth, and that [to the extent that] others differ from them, it is so far error.

The naïve realism framework has also helped to explicate various other phenomena we had worked on earlier (notably, partisan perceptions of media bias and overconfident prediction about future events). It has also prompted research on other phenomena – for example, the failure of dyad members to give adequate weight to the input of a partner in various estimation tasks, and the price they pay for this failure in terms of accuracy. Finally, an appreciation of naïve realism has helped my colleagues and me at the Stanford Center on International Conflict and Negotiation to appreciate a source of mutual enmity and mistrust in the context of protracted intergroup conflicts, and to devise strategies to overcome this barrier to negotiated agreements.

As my attention increasingly turns from empirical research to observation of everyday events, I keep noticing everyday manifestations of naïve realism. These include "thermostat wars" (complaints that one is being forced to suffer a "too hot" or "too cold" home in order to accommodate a spouse), generational differences of opinion about whether rap is "real music," comments about "odd cultural practices" of new arrivals to our shores, and, of course, the mutual misunderstandings and recriminations we observe between "red-staters" and "blue-staters." I could go on in this vein, as Gilovich and I do in our new book, *The Wisest One in the Room*, but instead I will close with quotations from two wise non-psychologist observers of human folly.

The great satirist George Carlin asked: "Ever notice that anyone going slower than you is an idiot and anyone going faster is a maniac?" The insight underlying Carlin's quip could be broadened from freeways to include perceptions of who wants to go too fast or too slow when it comes to political reforms and changes in social practices, and, indeed, what problems in our society are being ignored versus overemphasized by various political constituencies. George Bernard Shaw (in *Man and Superman*) wrote "Never do unto others as you would have them do unto you. Their tastes may be different" – a wry warning about the mischief caused when we assume that our own view of the good or balanced life is the enlightened view to which others should be brought through persuasion and education. I envy the next generation of social psychologists who might pursue the implications of these quotations, or, better still, undertake long and satisfying research journeys on the own.

REFERENCES

Gilovich, T., & Ross, L. (2015). *The wisest one in the room*. New York: Free Press.

Nisbett, R. E., & Ross, L. (1980). *Human inference: Strategies and shortcomings of social judgment*. Englewood Cliffs: Prentice-Hall.

Ross, L., & Nisbett, R. E. (1991). *The person and the situation*. New York: McGraw Hill.

66 The Empirical Study of Human Autonomy Using Self-Determination Theory

Ryan, Richard M.

Among the most important concerns of people across the globe are issues of freedom and control. Indeed, despite some horrific exceptions, the modern world is trending toward greater human rights, tolerance for diversity, and allowance for individual choices in vocations and lifestyles. Everywhere people fight against oppression and dictatorial controls, and groups that have been stigmatized struggle for equal rights and respect. At a more individual level, people move during their development toward greater self-regulation. They suffer under excessively controlling care-givers, teachers, clinicians, coaches, and bosses. In general, people are more likely to thrive and be positively engaged and motivated in settings where they are empowered and feel a sense of autonomy.

Although most laypeople grasp the import of these issues in everyday life, when I was a young clinical psychologist studying motivation, these topics – human freedom, people's capacities and needs for choice, and development toward increased self-direction and autonomy – were mostly treated as pseudo-phenomena, and were at best topics peripheral to mainstream empirical psychology. Some humanistic and psychodynamic psychologists had made such issues their central themes, but they were often not applying strong scientific methods to support their ideas.

Could it be right that people's concern with freedom and choice – and, oppositely, their feelings of alienation and frustration when overly controlled – are merely illusory issues? Could it be, as a famous cover of the *American Psychologist* once claimed, that human behavior is actually "involuntary"?

Despite the strong pull of clinical work, I was decidedly preoccupied with such questions during graduate school and was convinced, in part because of philosophical training, that psychologists had largely misconceptualized the issues in this area. I was also, in my everyday work in hospital and outpatient settings, confronted with the costs of compromised human autonomy, and I felt that understanding how autonomy and volition could be better supported could have implications in every

311

applied field, from workplaces and schools to sport fields and psychotherapy clinics.

Thus, despite my initial plan to pursue full-time clinical practice,
I began to research this topic, in part occasioned by my friendship and
collaborations with Edward Deci, who also has a chapter in this volume
(see Chapter 61). Deci had been doing experimental work on *intrinsic
motivation*: those behaviors that are driven by spontaneous interest and
enjoyment of activities. Intrinsic motivation reflects our evolved tendencies to actively engage our environments, exercise capacities, and assim-
ilate novel ideas; it plays a big role in development and learning,
representing nature's "push" from the inside. Yet, however natural this
propensity, Deci found that under circumstances that were controlling –
where others were attempting to compel behaviors through rewards and
punishments –people lost their intrinsic motivation. To me this seemed
like an inroad to the study of the broader issue of human autonomy, which
was my intellectual passion. Thus began our collaborative development
of a broader *self-determination theory* (SDT), which has engaged us in
research for more than three decades.

In our early joint studies we looked at teachers' approaches to motivating children in the classroom. We found that teachers who employed
more controlling strategies (e.g., those who relied on rewards and punishments to motivate) had students who were less motivated and felt less
confident and competent than did teachers who supported children's
autonomy. Subsequent longitudinal studies verified these as causal
effects, with teachers increasing and decreasing children's motivation
and well-being as a function of autonomy-supportive or controlling styles.
Seeing such robust effects, we knew this was about more than just
intrinsic motivation. We were tapping into a much bigger topic.

From Intrinsic Motivation to the Autonomy Continuum

Intrinsic motivation is characterized by *autonomy* – or, in cognitive attribution terms, an *internal perceived locus of causality*. People experience
these behaviors as self-initiated and willingly done. When intrinsically
motivated, people experience enjoyment and often "fun."

Yet human life is not all fun and games. As group animals, we engage in
many behaviors that are not intrinsically motivated, including many
chores, work tasks, and social obligations. We often engage in activities
because socializing agents expect, promote, and sometimes even compel
us to do them. These non-intrinsically motivated behaviors can vary a lot
in terms of their perceived locus of causality or *relative autonomy*. In some
contexts, people feel pressured to fulfill social obligations; in others, they

quite volitionally and willingly undertake them. Thus, as many philosophers have argued, one can fully endorse an activity that a society advocates or even demands of its members. Yet, just as surely, people often perform such activities with a resigned sense of compulsion or alienation.

Types of Internalization and Regulation

Together with developmental psychologist James Connell, I began working on a new taxonomy of motivation that represented various types of behavioral regulation that could energize behaviors that were not intrinsically motivated and that varied in relative autonomy. In initial studies we identified four distinct regulatory styles. At the low-autonomy end of this continuum is *external regulation*, when people act because others are controlling them with rewards and punishments. Although external regulation can be powerful (as operant-learning theorists have compellingly shown), it can also lead to poor-quality behavior, as people take the shortest route to reach the reward or escape from the punishment. It is also associated with low interest, and often with more negative affect.

Somewhat more autonomous is *introjection*, in which, instead of being externally controlled, people are self-controlling – pushing themselves around with feelings of guilt or contingent self-esteem. In introjection the individual has internalized others' standards, but not really accepted them as his or her own. Again, although introjection can strongly motivate, it is associated with negative experiences and unstable motivation.

Still higher on this continuum of relative autonomy is *identification*, when people engage in a non-intrinsically motivated activity because they personally value it and find it worthwhile. Behaviors motivated by identification are more persistent, and performance is of higher quality, than behavior motivated by external or introjected regulations.

Finally, as previously described, *intrinsic motivation* is a highly autonomous form of motivation, representing behavior propelled by interest and excitement about the activity rather than its instrumental value.

In the 1980s we began developing both experimental and self-report methods to tap each of these types of motives and their functional consequences. Studies confirmed that these varied motivations differ systematically in their perceived locus of causality, with some experienced as autonomous and others as controlled. Research also showed how these motives are causally connected with social contexts, with more controlling contexts engendering external and introjected regulations, and more autonomy-supportive contexts fostering greater internalization and relative autonomy. Publications on these efforts provided others with assessment tools and hypotheses that were then applied across developmental and behavioral settings, and methods were extended to include self-reports, experimental inductions, implicit measures, and, more recently, neurological assessments.

Today, literally hundreds of studies apply this SDT taxonomy of regulations in both basic and applied research. Findings routinely show not only unique qualities to each of these motives, but also the fact that the more autonomously people are motivated overall, the higher quality their behavior and the more positive their experience. For instance, students' well-being and learning outcomes are strongly enhanced by greater autonomy, a finding well sustained across development and cultures. Interventions with teachers also show that autonomy-support can be enhanced, in turn improving student outcomes. In clinical settings, we have developed interventions to facilitate greater autonomy, and randomized clinical trials show significant improvements in areas such as weight loss, diabetes management, and smoking cessation, among others. In workplaces, relative autonomy predicts lower turnover and higher employee vitality and wellness, and, as in other domains, is strongly affected by controlling versus autonomy-supportive leadership styles. A voluminous research literature has emerged in other areas as well, including parenting and socialization, physical activity and sport, media use, and psychotherapy. The model has utility for almost every behavioral domain in which motivation matters – and that is pretty much all of them.

There is still a lot to be done. On the mechanistic end, understanding better the neuropsychological bases of SDT's varied regulatory states is one agenda, and it represents a very active area of current research. On the macro end of the spectrum, studies of how cultural and political climates impact autonomy and its effects on well-being and motivation are equally important. In between these micro and macro foci, research on how both developmental and situational factors affect autonomy and motivation continues to be refined. Finally, intervention work is important not only for its practical human value, but for the feedback it provides to the basic sciences of SDT.

Of course, intrinsic motivation and the internalization continuum are just some aspects of SDT, which has grown to be a comprehensive macro-theory addressing issues such as people's basic psychological needs, the role of awareness and mindfulness in behavior regulation, the relevance of eudaimonia and intrinsic versus extrinsic life goals to well-being, the dynamics of vitality and depletion, and many other topics. Yet, in the development of our work in SDT, moving from intrinsic motivation to a broader conceptualization and operationalization of human autonomy was an especially pivotal change. It afforded us not only a richer basis for theory and experimentation, but also the capacity to develop more effective interventions in workplaces, clinics, schools, sport-fields, and families. And of course for me, as a clinician-researcher, this was the point of doing psychology in the first place.

REFERENCES

Ryan, R. M., & Connell, J. P. (1989). Perceived locus of causality and internalization: Examining reasons for acting in two domains. *Journal of Personality and Social Psychology, 57,* 749–761.

Ryan, R. M., & Deci, E. L. (2000) Self-determination theory and the facilitation of intrinsic motivation, social development and well-being. *American Psychologist, 55,* 68–78.

Ryan, R. M., & Deci, E. L. (in press). *Self-determination theory.* New York: Guilford.

67 Behavioral Self-Regulation: A Little Optimism Goes a Long Way

Scheier, Michael F.

Thinking back over my academic career, there are several things that stand out to me. The first derived from my good fortune to collaborate with Chuck Carver (who also has a chapter in this book; see Chapter 60). We were both graduate students at the University of Texas, and we were doing work on self-awareness, trying to understand more fully how thinking about oneself impacts how one behaves. At the same time, Chuck audited a course that offered on overview of control theory. Control theory provides a framework for thinking about self-regulating or self-guiding systems. Most importantly, it helps to identify the component processes that are needed in order for a system to be self-correcting.

When people think about self-guided or self-correcting systems they often think of things like thermostats in heating systems, which function to keep the temperature at a set level, or, perhaps more recently, how self-driven cars keep themselves in the proper lane as they go down the highway, self-correcting as they negotiate turns and curves, and get buffeted back and forth by wind. At some point, Chuck had the epiphany that these same principles might apply when people try to make progress toward the goals they are striving to reach.

It was Chuck's insight that caused us to begin to recast the work we had been doing on self-awareness in terms of behavioral self-regulation. That is, the research findings on self-awareness were showing that the behaviors people engaged in were more closely aligned with their intentions and goals when they were more self-aware or more self-reflective. This sounded a lot like something a self-regulating system would do. The system would operate in a way that kept the person's behavior aligned with the endpoints the person was trying to achieve (e.g., the person's intentions, values, attitudes, and beliefs).

At some point, our thinking began to shift from what happens when goal pursuit is going smoothly to what happens when it's not going so smoothly. We began to think harder about what happens when people are engaged in goal-directed action and they are having a hard time making progress attaining what they want to attain. After all, challenges arise repeatedly in life, whether those challenges have to do with getting a certain grade in a course, finishing a race in a certain period of time, or trying to get a date with someone you'd really like to know better. Expectancies played an important part in our ideas about what happens under these circumstances.

The idea was (and still is) that when people encounter difficulties doing what it is that they intend to do, some sort of mental calculation takes place that results in the generation of an outcome expectancy – the person's subjective assessment of the likelihood that he or she will succeed. We thought these expectancies played a role in the nature of the affect that was experienced as well as the person's subsequent behavior. That is, to the extent that expectancies are positive, positive affect is experienced and the person is motivated to continue striving to attain the goals toward which they are working. As expectancies become more negative, the person's affect turns more negative and there is a tendency to give up and stop trying to attain what the person is after.

Initially, we considered outcome expectancies in a very limited way. We focused on specific situations that were manipulated in controlled experimental contexts to validate our ideas. For example, we studied snake phobics who all had moderate fear of non-poisonous snakes, but varied in their confidence that they could approach and hold a snake if asked to do so. In this case, we weren't interested in snakes or phobias per se, but in how the person's expectations drove her or his behaviors. In turned out that confident phobics (those with positive expectations and greater confidence) were able to approach the snake more closely than those whose expectations were more negative (and, interestingly, this effect was magnified among people who were induced to think more about themselves by the presence of a mirror that was hanging on the wall behind the snake tank).

After several years conducting laboratory studies on expectancies, things changed. A number of our colleagues in health psychology – Karen Matthews, Sheldon Cohen, and David Krantz, among others – urged (or maybe even challenged) us to consider applying some of our ideas to real-world settings, particularly those that might be relevant to well-being. It also was the case that our formal area of study in graduate school was personality. I started to hear the voice of my advisor, Arnie Buss, in my head, urging us to return to what it was that we had been trained to do.

This confluence of events started us thinking about expectancies in a broader way, in a way that might be more reflective of stable, generalized expectancies for positive or negative outcomes. And voila! We found ourselves interested in dispositional optimism, which we define as the general expectation that good (versus bad) things will happen across important life domains. My guess is that if you asked people in the psychology research community what I'm known for, they'd say the work that I've done on optimism and pessimism. Indeed, I've spent the better part of my professional life studying optimism and its effect on psychological and physical well-being. So, if I'm known for something, it might as well be that.

A lot of research has been done since Chuck and I published our first paper on dispositional optimism; the vast majority of this research has examined the relationship between optimism and well-being. I think it's now safe to say that optimism is clearly associated with better psychological health, as indicated by lower levels of depressed mood, anxiety, and general distress, when facing difficult life circumstances, including situations involving recovery from illness and disease. A smaller, but still substantial, amount of research has studied associations with physical well-being. And I think most researchers at this point would agree that optimism is connected to positive physical health outcomes, including decreases in the likelihood of re-hospitalization following surgery, the risk of developing heart disease, and mortality, to name but a few. For example, Hilary Tindle spearheaded a project that observed over 95,000 women over an eight-year period. The women were all free of heart disease when they entered the study. Compared to those more pessimistic in outlook, the more optimistic participants were 9 percent less likely to have developed coronary heart disease (CHD), 14 percent less likely to have died from all causes, and 30 percent less likely to have died specifically from CHD-related causes over the course of the study.

We also know why optimists do better than pessimists. The answer lies in the differences between them in the coping strategies they use. Optimists are not simply being Pollyanna-ish. They're problem solvers who try to improve the situation. And if it can't be altered, they're also more likely than pessimists to accept that reality and move on. Physically, they're more likely to engage in behaviors that help protect against disease and promote recovery from illness. They're less likely to smoke, drink, and have poor diets, and more likely to exercise, sleep well, and adhere to rehab programs. The positive expectations held by optimists seem to spur them on to do what they can to make those good things happen. Pessimists, on the other hand, tend to deny, avoid, and distort the problems they confront, and dwell on their negative feelings. It's easy to see now why pessimists don't do so well compared to optimists.

What still needs to be figured out? Two things. First, how do optimism and pessimism develop? We know from studies comparing the similarity between identical and fraternal twins that dispositional optimism is heritable, although the specific genes that underlie the differences in personality have yet to be identified. It's also likely that parenting styles and early childhood environment play a role. For example, research has shown that children who grow up in impoverished families have a tendency toward pessimism in adulthood. Still, the specifics have not been well delineated.

The other missing link has to do with how to construe optimism and pessimism. I've been describing them as though they are opposite ends of a continuum, and this may not be the case. Optimism and pessimism may represent related, but somewhat distinct dimensions. This is so because not expecting bad things to happen doesn't necessarily imply that the person expects good things to happen. The fact that they're somewhat separable leads to the question of what is important for the beneficial health outcomes we see: the absence of pessimism, or the presence of optimism?

Ultimately, it is very gratifying that other psychologists have found aspects of the work valuable enough to incorporate some of the ideas into their own research. Collectively, we have accomplished a lot in the last forty or so years.

REFERENCES

Scheier, M. F., Carver, C. S., & Armstrong, G. H. (2012). Behavioral self-regulation, health, and illness. In A. S. Baum, T. A. Revenson, & J. E. Singer (eds.), *Handbook of Health Psychology* (2nd edn., pp. 79–98). New York: Psychology Press.

Watson, David

I have conducted research on many different topics, including personality, psychopathology, life satisfaction and subjective well-being, mate preferences and marital satisfaction, sleep, organizational behavior, attitudes, and values. To make progress in each of these areas, researchers have had to answer two basic questions. First, what basic concepts (known formally as *constructs*) do we need to study? Second, how do we measure these constructs? My most important scientific contribution is that I played a key role in supplying plausible answers to both of these questions in the domain of affect, which is the area of science that examines moods, feelings, and emotions.

Development of the Model

How I Became an Affect Researcher

My work in this area arose from an improbable series of events. Early in my fourth year of graduate school at the University of Minnesota, I started dating Lee Anna Clark, who was a student in the Clinical Psychology program (I was in the much smaller Personality Research program). When it was clear that our relationship was becoming serious, she informed me that she recently had received a Fulbright International Fellowship to conduct her dissertation research in Japan the following academic year (1979–1980). We eventually decided that we would get married and I then would take a year off from graduate school and accompany her to Japan for her Fulbright year.

I scheduled a meeting with my graduate advisor, Auke Tellegen, to break the news to him. I had some trepidation about this, because I expected him to react negatively to the news. However, he actually was pleased, as he saw this as an opportunity to test the cross-cultural replicability of a model he had developed. Most mood/emotion researchers at that time emphasized the importance of specific, "discrete" affective states, such as fear, sadness, anger, joy, and attentiveness. In contrast, Auke had collected data indicating that emotional experience was dominated by two broad and non-specific dimensions, which he labeled *Negative Affect* (i.e., the non-specific tendency to experience aversive emotional states such as anxiety, depression, and hostility) and *Positive Affect* (i.e., the tendency to experience pleasurable and rewarding states such as happiness, enthusiasm, and alertness). He suggested that I spend my year in Japan collecting mood data to test the generalizability of this model in a non-Western culture. I agreed to do so; this eventually became my doctoral dissertation research and formed the basis for my first major empirical article (published in the *Journal of Personality and Social Psychology* in 1984).

The Two-Factor Model of Affect

There was one small problem, which was that I knew almost nothing about the scientific evidence related to the subjective experience of emotion. Fortunately, psychologists had shown little interest in mood over the previous several decades, so the sparse literature in this area was quite easy to master. I focused particularly on structural studies that sought to identify the basic underlying constructs within the domain. These studies used a variety of techniques, but most commonly employed exploratory factor analysis (EFA) to clarify the underlying structure of mood. EFA is a technique that infers the existence of latent constructs – or factors – from clusters of moderately to strongly correlated variables; these latent factors, in turn, are assumed to be the underlying cause of these observed associations. For example, people who report feeling cheerful also tend to describe themselves as happy and joyful. The observed correlations between these variables can be used to model a factor, which in this case would be given a label such as *Joy*.

As noted earlier, mood researchers at this time mostly were interested in specific types of affect. This also meant that they were interested in identifying narrow and specific latent variables in EFA, typically using five to eleven factors to model the observed correlations between mood terms. I had received good training in EFA at Minnesota (mostly from Auke), and I had learned one important fact about how it works: As one models an increasing number of factors in a dataset, large general dimensions (such as Negative Affect and Positive Affect) tend to break apart and decompose into smaller, specific factors (such as Fear, Anger, Joy, and Interest). As I examined the results of these factor-analytic studies carefully, I observed strong hints that the general Negative Affect and Positive Affect factors actually were present in these data. In fact, I became convinced that if we could restrict these analyses to only two factors, the results would fully support Auke's general factor model.

I discussed these ideas with Auke at our next meeting. I had assumed we were stymied and could not pursue them further, but Auke knew how to reanalyze the results from most of these studies to extract only two factors. I performed these reanalyses and they provided amazing support for his two-factor model. These reanalyses were included in my dissertation, and subsequently formed the basis for a highly influential synthesis of affective structure that was published in *Psychological Bulletin* in 1985 (it currently is my second most highly cited work; as of this writing, it has been cited more than 4,000 times, according to Google Scholar). In this 1985 article, we were able to show that these Positive Affect and Negative Affect factors consistently can be identified in analyses of self-reported mood across a broad range of methodological conditions. Furthermore, we demonstrated how these factors could be integrated with the groundbreaking work of James Russell, who had developed a two-dimensional circumplex model based on analyses of facial and vocal emotional expressions. Thus, we were able to establish that the same two-dimensional model fit all major types of mood/emotion data. Consequently, we presented it as the basic structure of affect at the general factor level.

Development of the Measure

Creation of the PANAS

This article quickly generated a lot of excitement and stimulated increased interest in the study of affect. After all, we had provided a simple and parsimonious answer to the first fundamental question by clarifying the constructs that needed to be assessed. Still, the problem of how best to assess them remained. For the first few years, we used factor scores, which involves applying regression weights to standardized item responses. This approach was cumbersome and was difficult to explain to other researchers, particularly those with limited quantitative expertise.

One day, Lee Anna (who had begun collaborating on this work during our time in Japan) suggested that we drop these factor scores and instead create simple, unit-weighted scales. I thought this was a great idea, so I started collecting the necessary data. This took some time because we wanted to create a highly flexible instrument that could be used with several different time instructions (e.g., how you do feel right now; how have you felt today; how have you felt during the past few weeks; how do you feel in general) and so needed to collect responses from multiple samples. We eventually amassed enough data to create two ten-item scales that we could show were reliable and valid measures of Negative Affect and Positive Affect. These were simple, unit-weighted scales that were extremely easy to administer and score (one sums the responses to the ten items in each scale). We called the resulting instrument the Positive and Negative Affect Schedule, or PANAS. Lee Anna, Auke, and I described the development and preliminary validation of the PANAS in a 1988 article in the *Journal of Personality and Social Psychology*; this quickly became my most highly cited paper (currently more than 19,000 citations, according to Google Scholar).

Response to the PANAS

The response to this paper was overwhelming. Over the next several years, Lee Anna and I each received dozens of testimonials (initially, these were letters; later, they were emails) from excited researchers who reported obtaining great results using the PANAS. The development of the PANAS made it simple and easy to assess self-rated mood in research (we subsequently adapted it so that one can use the PANAS to obtain informant ratings as well). Thus, we had provided a simple and parsimonious answer to the second basic question regarding the assessment of key constructs, which further stimulated the scientific study of affect.

Subsequent Work and Future Directions

Since then, I have continued to refine both the underlying model and our approach to assessing affect. In the 1990s, for example, Lee Anna and I created the Expanded Form of the PANAS, or PANAS-X. In addition to measuring the non-specific dimensions of Negative Affect and Positive Affect, the PANAS-X allows researchers to model specific emotional states such as Fear (i.e., feeling nervous and scared), Sadness (i.e., feeling blue and lonely), Hostility (i.e., feeling angry and disgusted), Joviality (i.e., feeling happy, excited, and energetic), and Self-Assurance (i.e., feeling bold and confident). In a 2015 article in *Assessment*, several colleagues and I reported on the development and validation of the Temperament and Affectivity Inventory (TAI), which provides an alternative approach to assessing stable individual differences in the experience of various specific affective states.

We have made tremendous progress over the past thirty years, but we still have a way to go. In particular, we still must clarify the nature of the constructs that need to be included in any comprehensive assessment of affect at the specific factor level. Instruments such as the PANAS-X and the TAI represent a good start, but they are based on imprecise models that require further explication. In my lab, we currently are particularly interested in distinguishing between healthy and adaptive versus dysfunctional and maladaptive forms of positive affect (the latter are implicated in important clinical disorders, such as narcissism and mania). So, future generations of researchers will need to supply us with better, more complete answers to the two fundamental questions.

REFERENCES

Watson, D., Clark, L. A., & Tellegen, A. (1988). Development and validation of brief measures of positive and negative affect: The PANAS scales. *Journal of Personality and Social Psychology, 54,* 1063–1070.

Watson, D., Stasik, M. R., Chmielewski, M., & Naragon-Gainey, K. (2015). Development and validation of the Temperament and Affectivity Inventory (TAI). *Assessment, 22,* 540–560.

Watson, D., & Tellegen, A. (1985). Toward a consensual structure of mood. *Psychological Bulletin, 98,* 219–235.

Section B

Emotion

69   Human Aggression and Violence

Anderson, Craig A.

Even as a child I was interested in aggression. There likely are many reasons, including having an older brother who was much larger, stronger, and smarter; being the smallest boy in my grade level; and hating to lose. I was both frustrated and angry a lot. My favorite TV shows all involved violence, including classic Westerns (e.g., *Maverick*, *Sugarfoot*) and World War II shows (e.g., *Combat*, *Rat Patrol*). By the time I was fourteen, though, I knew that being angry and breaking things was neither enjoyable nor productive. In high school I paid close attention to the ongoing Vietnam war and the growing student protest movement. The killings at Kent State University had a major impact on my thinking and my bewilderment about violence. Army Basic Training yielded another major insight; it is trivially easy to learn how to kill another person with an M16 rifle.

At a theoretical level, my most important scientific contribution has been the development of a broad-based interdisciplinary model of human aggression: the General Aggression Model (GAM). Its roots lie in contributions by many scholars going back many years, from scholars whose primary work was in the aggression and violence domain, and from scholars whose primary work was in basic social, cognitive, developmental, personality, and biological psychology. Briefly, GAM illustrates how factors from the current situation (e.g., provocation) interact with personality factors (e.g., attitudes toward and expectations about aggression) and life history (e.g., growing up in a family that hunts animals for recreation) to increase or decrease one's likelihood of behaving aggressively when faced with potential conflict. It views the development of personality as a learning process that is rooted in biological processes but also is strongly influenced by events that a person experiences and observes.

My path from graduate student to aggression scholar was convoluted, and not at all "planful." My early focus was on human inference and decision-making, a focus that required understanding how people think, what heuristics they use, and what kinds of situational variables influence the inference process. A parallel interest was in attribution processes – that is, how people come to explain events that they experience or observe. I was dissatisfied with current models, but was learning the scientific tools that could test and create better models. I was also interested in personality theory – more specifically, in individual differences in how people explained events to themselves, and how these differences influenced emotional and behavioral variables, such as depression, loneliness, and shyness.

My graduate school and early faculty years yielded a number of contributions in domains that I perceived as highly interrelated, though many others did not see the connection. For example, my interest in basic explanation processes led me to view now-classic human inference and decision-making phenomena such as belief and theory perseverance, attribution and attributional processing, and judgmental heuristics as all being part of the same broader social–cognitive–emotion decision-making system. Thus, with input from numerous colleagues (e.g., Bernard Weiner), we created a model of the explanation process that encompassed attribution theory and current models of judgment and decision-making. It was relevant to understanding phenomena ranging from priming effects on persistence after failure (e.g., hearing some describe a task as being one that requires finding a good strategy leads to more effort and more thoughtful attempts), to interventions for depression, loneliness, and shyness, to the effects of different types of persuasive communications on attitude and behavior change.

This dual-process model describes how quick, automatic types of decisions are made with little or no conscious effort, as well as how slow, thoughtful decisions are made by means of, and are in fact based on, automatic cognitive processes. Indeed, our focus on the importance of the accessibility of causal explanations to belief perseverance and change (and to consequent behaviors) led to experiments by Morgan Slusher that showed that the then-current CDC public service announcements about how HIV is spread failed to persuade people precisely because they didn't evoke the kind of causal explanations that people could understand and incorporate into their world view. Our simple causal-scenario-based persuasive communication significantly changed beliefs about HIV transmission and behaviors toward persons with AIDS, such as willingness to work with people with AIDS.

None of my early work on how people think and make decisions (both automatic and controlled aspects) was specifically done in the context of aggression. Partly this reflected the interests of my graduate school faculty advisors, and partly it reflected aspects of my first faculty position at Rice University (e.g., very small subject pool, no PhD program in Social

Psychology). Nonetheless, my personal interest in aggression persisted, and showed up in my work on temperature effects on violent behavior. Indeed, my first professional publication was on the relation between ambient temperature and civil riots in the United States. This work led to a host of field studies and to some experimental lab studies on temperature effects. As this work progressed, it became clear that a broad theoretical framework was needed to effectively explain numerous (and occasionally paradoxical) findings. That theoretical framework was heavily guided by my prior general model of explanation processes and consequences.

My move to the University of Missouri in 1988 afforded me resources that enabled a greater focus on aggression and violence research. My students and I began conducting experimental studies on the effects of pain, frustration, and temperature (among others). We incorporated individual difference variables in many of these studies. We attempted to delineate the underlying psychological processes by which situational (e.g., pain) and individual difference (trait hostility) variables increased or decreased aggressive behavior. One particularly satisfying line of studies (the last of which was carried out at Iowa State University) involved the "weapons effect." The mere visual presence of a weapon, even a photo of a weapon, increases the likelihood of aggressive behavior, found in both lab and field experiments. Our initial studies tested the hypothesis that this phenomenon was based on priming – i.e., that seeing a weapon increases the accessibility of aggressive thoughts. In later studies, we added an important individual difference variable – hunter status – to further test what was soon to become GAM. If the weapons effect was based on gun images priming aggressive thoughts, there should be different effects for hunters (versus nonhunters) because these two types of people likely have different thoughts and memories associated with guns. Moreover, this effect should differ based on whether the gun image is a hunting or an assault gun. Our experiments confirmed these predictions, supporting not only GAM but also supporting any general social–cognitive-developmental model in which life experiences influence the development of knowledge structures, which in turn influence one's reactions to stimuli.

I was already quite familiar with Albert Bandura's and with Walter Mischel's social learning and social–cognitive theoretical and empirical work, having taken classes from both of them in graduate school and from continuing to follow their work. As I read more in the aggression domain, it dawned on me that many people (e.g., Leonard Berkowitz, Nicki Crick, Kenneth Dodge, Russell Geen, Rowell Huesmann) were fundamentally saying the same things that Bandura and Mischel and other generalists were saying about the development of thought, emotion, and behavior patterns. Thus, GAM was essentially born in the 1990s, as I tried to create a simple model that summarized the many contributions of many leading theorists, and did so in a common language that would enable aggression scholars from different backgrounds to communicate clearly with each other.

While working on the early versions of GAM, it became clear that any aggression model claiming to be "general" had to successfully incorporate the large media violence research literature. Brad Bushman's early work fit well with this social–cognitive framework. So, my students and I did a few media studies of our own, mainly to see how well GAM fit the media violence literature. Because of my long-time interest in video games as a player (going all the way back to text-based Star Trek games on the Stanford mainframe) and as a parent, my students and I began a series of studies on violent video game effects, a series that continues to the present.

About this time (1999), I moved to Iowa State University. This move was fortuitous in several ways: I had a leading media violence expert as a faculty colleague (Bushman); the subject pool was large enough to allow the large sample sizes needed for media violence research; and there was considerable meta-analytic expertise available. Although unintended, this move led to a longstanding focus on violent video game effects. Indeed, one could argue that my most important empirical contribution has been in developing and promoting high-quality research methods in the video game domain.

Our first major article on video-game violence appeared in 2000. Our first comprehensive meta-analysis of violent video-game effects appeared in 2001 (the most recent in 2010). We found that both short-term exposure in the immediate situation and repeated exposure to violent video games led to increases in aggressive behavior, aggressive thoughts, and aggressive affect; and to decreases in empathy and helpful behavior.

Our first major theoretical GAM article appeared in 2002. The coincidental timing of this paper and our first video game meta-analysis led some scholars to confuse these events to the extent that they claimed that GAM was merely a model of media violence effects. Of course, this wasn't – and still isn't – true. Recently, GAM has guided research by many scholars in a broad range of aggression/violence domains, including intimate partner violence, cyberbullying, outgroup stereotypes and aggression, juvenile delinquency, major personality disorders, and the impact of rapid climate change on aggression and violence.

In the future, I would like to see GAM used to create and test interventions designed to improve the people's lives. For example, GAM's emphasis on the importance of learning experiences in the development of personality, combined with its delineation of both automatic and controlled decision-making processes, suggests ways in which child-rearing practices might be modified to increase prosocial thinking and feelings. For example, decreasing children's exposure to violent events (both real and in entertainment media), increasing exposure to prosocial events and ways of thinking, and reframing their understanding of aggression all lead to more prosocial, less aggressive children and young adults. Similarly, GAM suggests ways in which already-aggressive people can learn to be less aggressive and more prosocial. Some such interventions might focus on at-risk populations, others on treating violent populations, and still others on broad-based changes in how children are raised and socialized. It also could be used to inform debates about the importance of dealing with rapid global warming, based on its predictions that this will likely increase war and other forms of violence.

REFERENCES

Anderson, C. A., & Bushman, B. J. (2002). Human aggression. *Annual Review of Psychology, 53,* 27–51.

Anderson, C. A., Shibuya, A., Ihori, N., Swing, E. L., Bushman, B. J., Sakamoto, A., Rothstein, H. R., & Saleem, M. (2010). Violent video game effects on aggression, empathy, and prosocial behavior in Eastern and Western countries. *Psychological Bulletin, 136,* 151–173.

Bartholow, B. D., Anderson, C. A., Carnagey, N. L., & Benjamin, A. J. (2005). Interactive effects of life experience and situational cues on aggression: The weapons priming effect in hunters and nonhunters. *Journal of Experimental Social Psychology, 41,* 48–60.

70   Research on Automatically Elicited Aggression

Berkowitz, Leonard

Many discussions of aggression emphasize only controlled actions in which the aggressors deliberately attempt to achieve some goal. Without minimizing the importance of these analyses, I will here present a sampling of my own research highlighting the determinants of impulsive, relatively uncontrolled, aggressive conduct. This research program was narrowly focused at the start, and was especially concerned with the effects of frustrations. But then, as time went by, my studies became much more general in nature and considered the effects of a variety of other aversive occurrences. The implicit theorizing governing these investigations was at first also fairly narrow, and was guided by a simplified version of the S-R associative learning concepts prevalent at the time. My analyses also broadened as the studies continued, making more use of cognitive notions. Then, as I came closer to retirement, I made increasing use of associative-network ideas.

Although my initial research publication appeared in 1953, I began my systematic attention to aggression in 1958, with an examination of the frustration–aggression hypothesis, principally as published in 1939 by Dollard, Doob, Miller, Mowrer, and Sears. These authors defined "frustration" as an "interference with the occurrence of an instigated goal response" (with this interference supposedly produced either externally or within the person). This blocking, according to Miller's later modification, produces an instigation to aggression along with other inclinations. If the perceived frustrating agent is injured, the Yale group held, the aggressive drive theoretically will be lessened, but will increase if the frustrater is not hurt for one reason or another.

In my early 1962 book on aggression, and in other discussions of this topic, I frequently spoke of the resulting aggressive drive as anger. I later went on to propose that the arousal of anger will not produce open aggression in the absence of aggressive cues – "stimuli associated with the present or previous anger instigators" in the external environment or in the mind. These cues presumably "pull" (evoke) aggressive responses from the angry person. However, this insistence on the necessity of aggression-associated stimuli is probably too strong a statement, and I now prefer to say that these cues only automatically intensify the ongoing aggressive drive.

A series of experiments from my laboratory illustrate the operation of such aggression-heightening stimulation. Basically, in these investigations a supposedly fellow student angered the participants, who then watched a brief, filmed fight scene. The anger-instigator, whose name linked him/her to the witnessed aggressive event, subsequently was punished most severely. The angering person's name-mediated connection with the observed aggression apparently increased her/his aggression-cue value, serving to strengthen the attacks on the disturber.

The aggressive cue value of the anger instigators can be modified by certain kinds of further cognitive processing. For example, in several experiments by former students of mine, angry people seeing film violence they strongly believed to be unrealistic were subsequently less punitive to the anger source than were there their counterparts who thought the fighting was real. The "fictitious" label evidently caused the viewers to "distance" themselves somewhat from the violent movie. Yet another former colleague went on to show that viewers were also less hostile after the film if they had believed at the time that their task was to judge the aesthetic quality of the scene.

These studies were followed by yet another theoretical change, this one having to do with people's feelings when they are thwarted. A number of tests of the Dollard et al. thesis did not find the predicted increased aggression, leading the writers to criticize the original sweeping formulation. However, as my 1989 review of animal and human research indicated, it could be that the basic principle holds only when the frustrations are sufficiently unpleasant. A broad variety of negative occurrences in laboratory experiments, such as pain arousal, irritable cigarette smoke, foul odors, disgusting scenes, and high room temperatures, have all been shown to heighten the hostility exhibited or punishment given to another person, even when the aggression cannot lessen the unpleasant events. All in all, then, it's the evoked negative affect that presumably leads to the aggressive inclinations.

Here again, thinking can modify the degree to which the negative affect leads to intensified hostility. As an example, in one of our experiments many of the participants had to keep their hands in decidedly cold water as they evaluated a supposedly fellow student's task performance by giving him reward and punishments. Half of them believed they had to keep their hands in the cold water for a relatively long time, while the others in this unpleasant condition had been reassured beforehand that they could take their hands from the water any time they wanted. Even though none of these suffering people actually took advantage of the escape possibility, those who thought they could *not* escape from the unpleasant situation became angrier and more punitive than those who believed they could get away. All in all, the mere thought that their negative affect could not be alleviated if they desired had led to a relatively persistent high-felt discomfort and relatively greater punitiveness.

My cognitive-neoassociation model of aversively stimulated events (similar to the more complicated embodiment theorizing) proposes that the negative affect gives rise to a variety of expressive motor reactions, feelings, thoughts, and memories which promote inclinations to both fear and anger (i.e., to escape/avoid and to fight). If the latter, rudimentary anger-related reactions are stronger than the former, fear-related ones, visible angry feelings and hostile/aggressive reactions could occur.

Going further, both the cognitive-neoassociation model and embodiment theorizing say that anger-related muscular movements might intensify already existing angry feelings. One of the experiments in a doctoral dissertation carried out in my laboratory attests to such an effect (but without dealing with aggression). The female participants were first asked to think of, and talk about, an event in their lives that was either affectively neutral in nature or that had made them either angry or sad. At the same time they were to squeeze a hand dynamometer with little force or with great force. The strong squeeze muscularly resembled a tight fist, whereas the other hand movement was very much less fist-like. After 3.5 minutes the participants stopped talking about the specified incident and rated their present feelings. The data analysis showed that the women's feelings were now very much as had been expected. Although the fist clench hadn't affected the angry feelings of the people who had recalled either a sad or neutral occurrence, those who had thought and talked about the angry incident now reported feeling angrier than the women in any other condition, including their counterparts in the angry recollection/no fist group. Just as we had predicted, the fist clench had intensified the felt anger elicited by the recollection of the angry event.

I have generally assumed that, with the exception of the people in the early studies of the frustration–aggression hypothesis, the participants in the experiments summarized here were largely unaware of just why their aggressive actions occurred. But, as many psychologists have proposed, consciousness can come into play as people attend to their feelings. With this attentiveness, they then may take steps to regulate their emotions, perhaps by considering what reaction is best under the circumstances.

Some years ago one of the students in my laboratory carried out a fairly complicated study to show how people's attention to their negative feelings can affect their judgment of others. Greatly simplifying what was done, the female participants listened to a brief, tape-recorded autobiographical statement said to have been made by a fellow student applying for a dormitory position. Half of the women experienced a good degree of muscular discomfort as they listened because they extended their non-dominant arms out unsupported for six minutes, whereas their counterparts just rested their arms on the table and felt little discomfort. When the recording ended, the participants rated their judgments of the target. Just before they expressed these evaluations, half of the people in each discomfort-level condition were led to be self-attentive because they briefly had to describe their present feelings.

I will here describe the outcome only for those women who had been informed earlier that the target had been accepted by the house-fellow selection committee (so that a favorable judgment of the target was implicitly deemed to be right). The participants feeling high discomfort but who were induced to be self-attentive gave the target the best ratings. Their unpleasant feelings presumably prompted them to evaluate the job applicant unfavorably, but, as a consequence of their self-attention, they apparently decided to rate her in accord with the house committee's positive assessment.

Human aggression is clearly far more complicated than is widely supposed. Angry persons do at times deliberately attack a person in keeping with their conscious intentions. But they also can assault a target impulsively, automatically, and non-consciously, driven by their emotions, motor reactions, ideas, and learned behaviors. We would do well to understand these automatic, impulsive actions, and also learn how they can be controlled.

71 The Nature of Emotion and the Impact of Affect

Clore, Gerald L.

1. What Do You Consider to Be Your Most Important Scientific Contributions?

Consider Miranda, a first-year college student, whose parents informed her that they were separating. There had been tension at home, but the news was a shock. She was upset and found it hard to think about much else. Beyond being upset, what emotions might she feel, and what impact might they have? A theory of emotion I developed with colleagues addresses the emotion question, and research on emotion with other colleagues and students addresses the impact question.

Emotions depend on one's focus of attention. Ortony, Clore, and Collins' emotion theory says that one can focus on *outcomes*, *actions*, or *objects*, which are evaluated on the basis of *goals*, *standards*, and *tastes*. Outcome emotions concern goals. For example, Miranda's loss of family security might make her *fearful*, but the reduced family conflict would be a *relief*. She could also focus on actions, which are evaluated on the basis of standards. Miranda might feel *admiration* at a family member's praiseworthy action or *pride* in her own. She might feel *anger* at another's blameworthy action or *shame* at her own. Finally, she could focus on the appealing versus distasteful attributes of objects, including individuals. Object-focused emotions include *like*, *dislike*, *love*, *hate*, or *disgust*. Additionally, as her attention shifts back and forth, she might experience several different emotions almost at once. What any of us feels depends on what we attend to and evaluate. We can control our attention, but evaluations are automatic and generally unconscious, so our emotions can surprise us.

Let's turn to the question of how Miranda's emotions might influence her. *Affect-as-information* theory (developed with Norbert Schwarz and elaborated with Jeffery Hunsinger and Linda Isbell) says that it depends on her current mindset. Most people have a moderately broad, global scope of attention. If positive affect says "yes" to that inclination, it would

336

promote a big-picture focus, creativity, and confidence in her thoughts. But Miranda's sad feelings should say "no" to those impulses, narrowing her focus, making her less creative, but maybe better at spotting problems. The "take home message" is that such influences are not fixed but changeable. Affect confers value on whatever is in mind at the time, regulating the mind to fit the moment.

2. Why Do You Consider Them to Be Your Most Important Contributions?

Imagine an ant taking a complex path along a beach around rocks and other obstacles. How should one explain its behavior? Are ants complex? Do they have complicated strategies for foraging? This ant was a teaching example from Herbert Simon, originator of the field of artificial intelligence. The lesson was that the ant's complex behavior reflects complexity not in the ant, but in its environment.

Our work carries a similar lesson about the apparent complexity of emotions. Whereas people think of emotions as complicated, much depends on the contexts in which they occur. Consider, as an analogy, how to explain the accuracy of cat owners' understanding of their cat's meows as "I want to go outside" or "I'm hungry." Research finds that it depends on the environment – whether the cat is near the door or near the food bowl. Similarly, when we study mood effects, we find that positive affect experienced as "liking" when focused on an external object of judgment is experienced as "confidence" when focused on internal thoughts about the object.

The same applies to specific emotions. What distinguishes among fear, sadness, and anger? All are negative, but fear signals the *possibility* of bad outcomes; sadness signals *actual* bad outcomes; and anger signals bad outcomes from *blameworthy* actions. They differ simply because they reflect different psychological situations. But such simple differences can have complex consequences. Psychologists, however, have generally tried to explain such consequences by putting motivations, "action readiness," and so on, inside emotions. The problem is that the occurrence of emotional expressions, psychophysiological changes, or other behaviors depends on the context. Thus, facial expressions may occur if others are present, and psychophysiological reactions occur if action is required. In contrast, fearful situations always involve anticipations of possible bad outcomes.

Our research on affect-as-information further illustrates the wisdom of Simon's ant example. Recall that feeling happy triggers big-picture thinking and creativity, not because of something about happiness itself, but because positive affect says "yes" to the default tendency to adopt a global, broad focus. In contrast, negative affect says "no." Therefore, the complexity of emotional consequences turns out to be due not to something in the emotions, but to something in their interactions with the environments in which they occur.

3.   How Did You Get the Ideas for These Contributions?

The emotion theory began during a sabbatical at Stanford, when University of Illinois colleague Andrew Ortony invited me to Berkeley to discuss emotion with a few cognitive scientists. Two days of furious note-taking on coffee shop napkins began our account of emotions as embodiments of psychological situations. Back at Illinois, two mornings a week we alternately dictated, typed, and scribbled on a whiteboard. We were still at it by my next sabbatical at Oxford University seven years later. I recall many night-time bicycle trips to the computer center to find a terminal to send drafts back and forth.

Work on the impact of emotion began earlier in graduate school, studying interpersonal attraction with Donn Byrne at the University of Texas. At one point, I recorded two-person conversations to see what made people likable. I found that liking for one's partner reflected not what partners said, but how participants felt about themselves during the conversations. That encouraged further study of affect and judgment. Later, when Norbert Schwarz came to Illinois as a postdoc, we proposed the *affect-as-information* hypothesis. In one experiment, we took advantage of weather extremes in the Midwestern United States to induce mood. On the first warm, sunny days of spring, people were in better moods than on subsequent cold, rainy days. We found that mood affected people's judgments of their life satisfaction. But, in addition, when we asked first about the weather, the effect disappeared, showing that affective influences are not automatic, but depend on the apparent information about the object of judgment.

4.   How Do the Ideas Matter for Psychological Science and Also for the World Beyond Academia?

Our account of emotion was designed to be computer implementable. It has been influential in the field of "affective computing" to create "believable agents" for games, tutoring programs, and other applications (Googling "OCC," "emotion," "computing," etc., leads to numerous examples).

Principles of the affect-as-information approach are evident in advertising, politics, law, and elsewhere. In advertising, examples abound. In politics, the Republican initiation of negative ads in the 1988 US elections may have been successful because, as we propose, negative affect says "no" to habitual responding, and Americans at the time habitually voted Democratic. Finally, legal philosophers worry about the influence of emotion on juries, leading highly evocative material to be barred from courtrooms. Research shows, however, that a failure to use emotion can lead to poor decisions.

5.   What Would You Like to See as the Next Steps in Theory and/or Research?

One scholar reduced the history of drama to sixty-four plot situations and sixty-four emotions. The number is debatable, but, in our account also, emotions are viewed as embodiments of situations that characterize the human condition. It would be useful to study common elements in people's concepts or schemas of anger, fear, love, sadness, jealousy, and other emotions. Widely shared schemas of emotion do a great deal of cognitive work, shaping how people understand and communicate about their experience. When a friend describes her distress, for example, we feel we understand once we interpret it as embarrassment, hurt feelings, or some other emotion. Watershed moments in psychotherapy also often involve interpreting inchoate feelings as anger, disappointment, or guilt. We all have cartoon-like schemas of common emotions with mental slots for causes, characteristics, and consequences, which shape our experience and memory. Perhaps much of what we have learned in psychology about the influences of emotions, therefore, is really about the influences of emotion schemas.

One planned project asks when affect-as-information is about the world versus about one's own thoughts. We found, surprisingly, that feeling happy can lead to especially negative judgments. Why? Because if people already dislike something, feeling happy increases confidence in their negative opinions. This is interesting because previously we treated affect as information about the world, whereas these results show that it can also be information about one's own thoughts.

I am also interested in potential clinical applications of affect-as-information. Mindfulness, which can help reduce stress, seems to operate like our affect misattribution manipulations. Both involve focusing directly on feelings rather than on reasons for the feelings. Once affect becomes an object of perception it loses its power to modify our views of other objects. Our general finding of malleable rather than fixed influences of affect may therefore have practical as well as theoretical implications.

REFERENCES

Clore, G. L. (2016). How do emotion and cognition interact? A new view. In R. Davidson, A. Shackman, A. Fox, & R. Lapate (eds.), *The nature of emotion: a volume of short essays addressing fundamental questions in emotion.* Oxford: Oxford University Press.

Clore, G. L. (2016). What is an emotion? In R. Davidson, A. Shackman, A. Fox, & R. Lapate (eds.), *The nature of emotion: a volume of short essays addressing fundamental questions in emotion.* Oxford: Oxford University Press.

Ortony, A., Clore, G. L., & Collins, A. (1988). *The cognitive structure of emotions.* New York: Cambridge University Press.

72 The Rediscovery of Enjoyment

Csikszentmihalyi, Mihaly

Personally, I think that my most important conceptual contribution to science might turn out to be the work I have done trying to adapt evolutionary theory to human development, and particularly to creativity; and in terms of methodology, the work with the Experience Sampling Method, or ESM, which has resulted in the beginnings of a systematic phenomenology that I expect will be widely used in psychology. I must repeat, however, that this is only my personal opinion. In terms of how others evaluate my work, I am quite sure that those who have heard about it at all would single out the concept of *flow* as being my main contribution – however small. As defined here, flow is complete absorption in what one is doing.

So let's talk about flow. I think flow is important mainly for two reasons: because it is (a) an essential aspect of life that almost everyone recognizes as being something they have experienced, yet they had no name for it or way to understand it; and (b) the recognition of the phenomenon I ended up calling "flow" helped to add a new perspective to understanding human behavior, a perspective that eventually helped establish the subfield of *Positive Psychology*.

My original interest in this phenomenon probably started when, as a child, I was caught up in the tragic events of World War II. The stupid cruelty around me was hard to tolerate and impossible to understand. My two older brothers disappeared – the oldest snatched away from his family to spend years in Soviet prison camps, the younger one drafted out of college and killed in the defense of Budapest. Nobody knew what was going to happen. Powerful, wealthy, well-educated men acted like frightened children. Daily air raids chased us into basement shelters, and buildings crumbled in flames up and down the streets. I was ten years old while all this was going on, and could not figure out how grown-up people I had assumed to be rational and in control of their lives could suddenly become so clueless.

One small remaining island of rationality was that I had just learned how to play chess. The game was like an oasis in which rules provided predictable outcomes to one's actions. I remember that once I made the opening moves in a game, the "real" world seemed to disappear, and you could plan the future without having to fear irrational violence. In retrospect, I realize that losing myself in the game constituted a denial of the larger reality of my surroundings; yet the experience of order within chaos that playing chess provided left a lasting – albeit almost entirely unconscious – impression: It suggested an alternative possibility to the senseless reality that humankind had chosen when opting for war.

It took several decades for this seed of intuition to bear any fruits. After the war, when we became refugees fleeing the approaching Soviet armies, the problems of daily survival were too pressing for giving much thought to the human condition in general. Just having enough food so as not to go to bed on an empty stomach was a success. Still, whenever I could, I also read extensively from the work of philosophers, spiritual leaders, historians, and political scientists, hoping to find an explanation as to why a race that could build nuclear bombs and devise trigonometry was unable to find a peaceful and fair way to live. But I did not have much time to devote to such questions. By the time I was fifteen years old, I had to drop out of school and start working at various jobs. My father, who had become the head of the Hungarian Embassy in Italy, resigned his job in 1948 when the Soviets imposed a Communist government in Hungary. So I had to serve tables at a restaurant in Rome, pick peaches for canning near Naples, manage a hotel in Milan, and lead trains full of pilgrims to Lourdes and Fatima. In the meantime, however, I stumbled on some books by C. G. Jung, and discovered psychology. Reading Jung's work suggested the possibility that psychology might be a key to understanding why human beings behave so strangely.

I decided to study psychology, but there were a few obstacles to overcome. First, at this time psychology in Italy was taught only as part of doctoral programs in medicine or philosophy. Second, even if there had been courses in psychology I could take at university, I would not have been able to take them, given that I had quit school when I was fifteen. To get around these obstacles I decided to apply for a visa to the United States, start a college career while I worked at night, and then become a psychologist. It took a few years to get a visa, but in 1956, just as I turned twenty-two years of age, I finally was able to set foot in America – specifically Chicago, Illinois, where I arrived with $1.25 in my pocket, but full of good intentions.

Working eight hours each night was not very pleasant, but then going to school each day (I did pass the high school equivalency exams, so I was admitted to the University of Illinois at Chicago) made it an exhausting drill that left no time for anything else. What was worse, however, was that the psychology taught in the 1950s was nothing like the books by Jung

I had read: much about rats, nothing about the human spirit. It looked like coming to the USA had been a mistake; the miserable life in Chicago was much more miserable than the miserable life in Rome had been, and the psychology I had come to study turned out to be a dud.

After two years of college, I decided to transfer to the University of Chicago. I knew by then the reputation of that school, and read some of the work of teachers at that school that promised to be quite rat-free.

It turned out to be a good decision. At Chicago I became a student of Jacob W. Getzels, who wrote about values and creativity, and soon we started to write articles together. In 1963 I was writing my dissertation in psychology on a group of young artists, trying to understand how they moved from a blank canvas to a finished painting. During this study, I was struck by the fact that these young artists were deeply involved with the process of painting, to the point of not eating or sleeping for long periods of time, but as soon as the painting was finished, they seemed to imme-diately lose interest in it, and stack it against a wall with all the other canvasses they had painted before. What made this behavior so interest-ing was the fact that it seemed to contradict the generally accepted paradigm of psychology. According to behaviorist theories, people, like other organisms, were motivated to behave by the expectation of a desirable external state, such as food or the cessation of electric shocks. The young artists, however, knew that their work was very unlikely to be noticed or bought – yet as soon as they finished one painting, they were eager to start a new one. Clearly they were not motivated by *having* the painting, or by *selling* it for money; instead, it looked very much like what motivated them was *making* the painting.

From that point on, I became more and more focused on understand-ing this apparent anomaly in human behavior. What did the artists get from the process of painting that made them so eager to engage in the activity for its own sake? There were similarities between the artists' work and children's play, and for several years I studied various play-forms to see if there was an underlying pattern between different forms of play, and also the creative process of artists. The result of all these studies – which were facilitated by many students, friends, and colleagues – has been the recognition that some of the best moments in human life are the results of acting in ways that express who we are, what we are good at doing – as athletes, artists, thinkers, mothers, healers – or, simply, as just good human beings. This way of acting is what I ended up calling *flow*; the history of how the idea evolved has been chronicled elsewhere, and need not be repeated here.

The recognition that human beings are motivated by the intrinsic rewards of the flow experience, and not just by external rewards, has had a reasonably strong impact on psychology, and on society as a whole. The book I wrote twenty-five years ago for a general audience, *Flow*, has been translated into twenty-three different languages, plus two different translations in Portuguese and in Chinese. An extensive flow research network has been organized in Europe. IPPA, the International Positive Psychology Association, which was built on conversations I had with Professor Martin Seligman of the University of Pennsylvania and now has tens of thousands of members among psychologists all over the globe, was strongly influenced by flow research.

Outside of academic psychology, flow has also found an unusual number of applications. In the field of *education*, it has influenced US magnet schools, Montessori, and public education; studies of flow and learning in schools have been conducted in Denmark, Japan, Korea, Hungary, Finland, and France. Clearly, young people all over the world learn more when they can experience flow in the process. In *business*, organizations that have adopted flow as a management tool have reported very encouraging results in the United States, Sweden, and South Korea. Makers of *computer games* have modeled many of their products on flow theory, and an interactive management simulation game based on flow won the Gold Medal at the US Serious Play Association meetings in 2013. And this is just a start. The possible uses of the flow perspective to improve quality of life are truly innumerable. It is poetic justice, perhaps, that an idea and concern born amidst the ruins of an inhuman conflict should blossom into a set of practices that help make the world a better place.

REFERENCES

Csikszentmihalyi, M. (1990). *Flow: The psychology of optimal experience*. New York: Harper & Row.
Csikszentmihalyi, M. (1993). *The evolving self: A psychology for the third millennium*. New York: HarperCollins.
Csikszentmihalyi, M. (2003). *Good business: Flow, leadership and the making of meaning*. New York: Viking.

73   Happiness Is a Virtue – Good for You and Good for the World!

Diener, Ed

Subjective well-being refers to people's evaluations of their lives in both thoughts and feelings, and includes states such as life satisfaction, positive feelings, and happiness. Deciding which of my laboratory's findings on subjective well-being are the most important is a tough decision. In 1984, I authored an influential review of the field. At that time there were a few important studies of subjective well-being, but not many of them, and very much was unknown. In 1981, the year I entered the field, there were fewer than 100 studies per year on happiness; in 2014, there were 14,000! I have conducted research on most areas in this field. Thus, nominating one important finding is difficult with such an array of choices.

The findings I've chosen as my most important are those showing the many benefits to later behavior of high subjective well-being. My research and reviews of the literature indicate that those who are high in subjective well-being on average exhibit superior health and longevity, social relationships, work performance, and citizenship. It is not that these factors simply cause high subjective well-being, but that subjective well-being is likely to increase them! There seems to be a virtuous circle between positive feelings and desirable behavior, in which each reinforces the other. Think of the implications of these findings: Happy people not only enjoy life more, they also tend to be healthier and have more friends, and they are better citizens who are successful at work as well.

Thinkers have expressed very different opinions about the value of happiness. On the one hand, philosophers such as the Utilitarians have held happiness to be the true goal of life, the one outcome that makes all life worth living. In contrast, other thinkers describe happy people as shallow and narcissistic, not able to see problems and improve the world. A third view sees happiness as desirable as long as it results from virtue and fulfilling needs, such as for meaning and purpose in life. My view, now supported by substantial research, is that happiness is itself a virtue. This new approach argues that although happiness is pleasurable, it is much more than hedonism because it so often helps people function more effectively and less selfishly.

Evidence for the Beneficial Outcomes

I noticed that scholars were worried about what causes happiness, and how people might increase it, but few seemed very interested in the questions of whether happiness is a good thing, or whether we should be happier. Happiness was assumed to be desirable because it is pleasant. I began to believe that happiness is more than just a pleasant feeling – that in fact it helps people function better. I was surprised at the strength of findings supporting this claim.

Health and Longevity

People who score high in positive feelings tend to be healthier and live longer. There is substantial research on why happy people might be healthier – stronger immune functioning and cardiovascular fitness, for example. There are also studies indicating that happier individuals are more likely to have healthy habits, such as exercising and wearing seat belts. In both the counties of the USA and the nations of the world there are relationships between happiness and health, with happier places experiencing greater longevity. Educated readers know the factors leading to better health – for example, not smoking and getting exercise. They now should add being happy to this list.

Social Relationships

Those who are frequently in a positive mood are likely to have more friends and to be more sociable. They have happier marriages that are less likely to end in divorce. Happier individuals have more supportive relationships, and they in turn are more likely to give support to others. People who are lonely might ask whether their moods and emotions might be partly to blame.

Work Performance

Happier workers tend, on average, to be better workers. They are less likely to quit their job and less likely to take unnecessary sick days, for example. They are more likely to be rated high in customer service, and they are more creative. In contrast, people who are depressed or angry are more likely to quit their jobs or be fired, and are more likely to suffer from maladies such as alcoholism and drug abuse. Wise employers seek out happy workers, and also try to create the conditions for happiness in their work environments.

Citizenship

Research in social psychology reveals that, in most instances, when people are put into a good mood they often become more altruistic. Similarly, scientists also find that happier individuals are more likely to donate money to charity, and to volunteer time for worthy causes. In the workplace, people who are high in job satisfaction are more likely to be good "organizational citizens" – that is, to help others and do things that benefit the organization. The stereotype that happy individuals are hedonistic and self-centered widely misses the mark.

The Unknowns

Despite all that is known, there are important questions remaining for future research. For instance, we do not know how much happiness is needed for desirable outcomes, and whether more is always better. It could be that a mix of feelings, with occasional negative emotions, is desirable. Another open question is under what circumstances is high subjective well-being most helpful? Is a happy disposition equally beneficial in an impoverished environment as in a resource-rich one, for instance? Finally, we need to know what other personal characteristics, such as conscientious and achievement motivation, might be needed in addition to high subjective well-being to lead to specific desirable outcomes. The unanswered questions are exciting because they point to important research that the next generation of scientists will conduct.

Exciting Finding

The finding that subjective well-being is beneficial moves it from the category of pleasure and hedonism to also being a virtue. Thus, perhaps the most important finding from my decades of studying subjective well-being is that happiness is the best of both worlds – both enjoyable and virtuous. This suggests that we should be actively teaching children and adults how to live happy lives, and create the societal conditions for this as well. An important question for each reader is how he or she might become a happier person.

The finding that happiness helps effective functioning and success in life is a real game-changer. It means that societies need to enact policies that raise happiness. This will have the wonderful effect of making life more enjoyable as well as more successful. For me this is a once-in-a-lifetime discovery, because I think it might just change the world!

REFERENCES

DeNeve, J.-E., Diener, E., Tay, L., & Xuereb, C. (2013). The objective benefits of subjective well-being. In J. F. Helliwell, R. Layard, & J. Sachs (eds.), *World happiness report 2013* (vol. 2, pp. 54–79). New York: UN Sustainable Development Solutions Network.

Aronson, Elliot

Throughout my life as a social psychologist, I have had two major goals: to design and conduct controlled experiments that shed light on how the human mind works, and to make discoveries that might be useful to people and perhaps even improve society. When I was about to enter graduate school, I had stars in my eyes so, understandably, the second goal was far more prominent than the first. However, by the time I earned my PhD, I had discovered that, as a scientist, there is no way to do good in the world without first being able to do good research.

My great good fortune was that I entered Stanford as a student the same year that Leon Festinger joined the faculty as a professor. At that time, Festinger was developing his theory of cognitive dissonance, which proposed that when a person simultaneously holds two contradictory cognitions, he or she experiences an unpleasant feeling of discomfort (dissonance). The person is motivated to reduce that dissonance by altering one or both cognitions, bringing them into consonance. This simple theory led us to make predictions about human behavior that were bold, exciting, and innovative.

For example, in the first experiment I ever designed, Jud Mills and I demonstrated that people who went through a severe initiation to join a group later liked the group better than those who went through a mild initiation. We didn't try to convince people that their group was terrific; rather, we set up a situation where they convinced *themselves* that the group was terrific. The cognition "I went through hell and high water to get into this group" was dissonant with the fact that the group was actually pretty boring. Therefore, following a severe initiation, they were inclined to convince themselves that those boring group members were quite charming. The people who didn't have to go through a severe initiation saw the group for what it was.

In another experiment, my students and I showed that children who were threatened with severe punishment if they played with a forbidden but attractive toy were eager to play with it anyway as soon as they had the chance. But children who had been threatened with mild punishment resisted the temptation and avoided the toy. Why? Because those under threat of mild punishment lacked justification for ignoring the toy (in the form of severe punishment), they convinced themselves that the toy was not worth playing with ("it is a lousy toy anyway").

These experiments not only formed the foundation of dissonance theory, they also taught me one of the enduring lessons that guided my research for the next fifty years: Although it's true that changing people's attitudes (through communication) sometimes changes their behavior, to produce a more enduring change it is imperative to induce a change in behavior first; attitude change will follow.

After conducting several experiments testing this theory, I proposed a change in the definition of cognitive dissonance. I argued that the essence of the theory is not inconsistency between any two cognitions; rather, the theory makes its most powerful predictions when the individual's behavior is dissonant with his or her self-concept (e.g., "I am a moral person" but "I have just committed an immoral act," or "I'm incompetent at this" but "I have done really well on this assignment"). Thus, in one experiment, we showed that people who didn't expect to do well on a task actually felt dissonance when they succeeded. In another experiment, we showed that when we bolstered people's general level of self-esteem, they subsequently resisted the temptation to behave dishonestly – because "I'm a terrific person" would be dissonant with "I just cheated."

The experiments inspired by dissonance theory changed the way psychologists thought about how the mind works, challenging the prevailing behaviorist view that people are primarily reinforcement machines, motivated almost exclusively by rewards and punishments. These experiments also underscored the importance of the self-concept in cognitive and social psychology.

Whatever became of my initial starry-eyed desire to do good? The opportunity emerged in 1971, while I was teaching at the University of Texas. The Austin public schools were abruptly desegregated; contrary to liberal hopes that increased contact between ethnic groups would reduce prejudice, all hell broke loose. Within a few weeks, the schools erupted in hostility, with interracial taunting and fistfights in the schoolyards. It became vividly clear that desegregation wasn't working in Austin – or anywhere else, for that matter.

The school superintendent asked for my help – and, because the system was in crisis, he agreed to implement any suggestions I might make. After spending a few days observing classrooms, my students and I determined that the hostility had two interrelated causes: unequal preparation and relentless competition. The schools in the minority areas of Austin were inferior to those in the more affluent white neighborhoods; as a result, a typical sixth-grade minority student was reading at a fifth-grade level. With desegregation, minority kids were thrust into a highly competitive situation where they were guaranteed to lose. This exacerbated the existing stereotypes. If someone had intentionally designed a system guaranteed to make school desegregation fail, they couldn't have done a better job.

What was needed was a complete restructuring of the classroom atmosphere to reduce competition and increase cooperation. We invented the jigsaw classroom, so named because it works like the assembling of a jigsaw puzzle. We organized the students into ethnically diverse six-person groups. Each student was given a unique piece of the lesson (e.g., one paragraph of a six-paragraph biography), and required to teach it to the others so that, at the end of thirty minutes, all students could gain mastery of the entire biography. To accomplish this, the students needed to pay close attention to their teammates, helping and encouraging those having trouble presenting their segment.

We conducted a controlled experiment, comparing students in jigsaw classrooms with students being taught the same material by some of the best teachers in the system using traditional techniques. The results were striking: After only six weeks, students in the jigsaw classroom had higher self-esteem, higher scores on objective exams, lower absenteeism, less prejudice, and greater empathic ability than students in traditional classrooms. Close friendships developed within and across racial boundaries. In short, jigsaw made school desegregation work. We replicated the original experiment several times.

Elated by jigsaw's stunning success, I spent the next decade doggedly trying to give it away – mostly in vain. I learned that educational bureaucracies are reluctant to adopt radical structural changes. Happily, I also learned that patience is necessary. Novel ideas often need time to marinate. Over the next four decades, jigsaw gradually caught on and is now being used in thousands of classrooms throughout the United States, Europe, and Asia.

Having had my appetite whetted by the success of doing good research to do good in the world, in the 1980s I turned my attention to the AIDS epidemic. Because AIDS is caused primarily by sexual contact, and because condoms are effective at preventing sexually transmitted diseases, AIDS prevention therefore seemed merely a matter of convincing sexually active people to use condoms. Merely? Across the nation, public-service information campaigns were producing a negligible effect on condom use. For example, on my campus, after a vigorous information campaign, the percentage of sexually active students regularly using condoms increased from 16 percent to 19 percent. Although almost all college students believed condoms could prevent AIDS, most considered their use to be an unromantic nuisance.

My graduate students and I turned to cognitive dissonance theory. We reasoned that because self-esteem is an important aspect of cognitive dissonance, and because nobody wants to believe that he or she is a hypocrite, we set out to put people in a position where they were not practicing what they were preaching – i.e., where they were in danger of behaving hypocritically. We predicted that once sexually active people were confronted with the fact that they were advocating behavior that they themselves were not practicing, they would be motivated to modify their behavior to preserve their integrity.

In our experiment, we instructed college students to compose a speech describing the dangers of AIDS and advocating the use of condoms. In the hypocrisy condition, students (1) recited their speech to a video camera and were informed that the video would be shown to high school students, and (2) were made mindful of their own prior failure to use condoms by reciting the circumstances in which they failed to use them in the past. In the control conditions, students either videotaped their speech without having been made mindful or were made mindful without videotaping their speech. Several months later, as part of an "unrelated" telephone survey, participants were asked about their sexual behavior. Almost 60 percent of the people in the hypocrisy condition reported using condoms regularly – about three times the number in the control conditions. Subsequently, my students applied the hypocrisy paradigm, with great success, to induce people to conserve water during a drought, exercise regularly for their health, and apply sunscreen to prevent skin cancer.

My contributions to dissonance theory and to improving classroom structure are interwoven themes in my life's work. Both reflect my deep belief in the importance of doing controlled, theory-based experimental research, whether in the laboratory or the real world. Both reflect the excitement of making meaningful discoveries that have staying power over the decades. And they both show how good science helps us understand the wonders and complexities of the human mind, and is the first step to doing good in the world.

REFERENCES

Aronson, E. (2002). Drifting my own way: Following my nose and my heart. In R. Sternberg (ed.), *Psychologists defying the crowd: Stories of those who battled the establishment and won*. Washington, D.C.: APA Books.

Aronson, E., & Patnoe, S. (2011). *Cooperation in the classroom: The jigsaw method* (3rd edn.). London: Pinter & Martin. (See also https://www.jigsaw.org/)

Gonzales, M. H., Tavris, C., & Aronson, J. (eds.), (2010). *The scientist and the humanist: A festschrift in honor of Elliot Aronson*. New York: Psychology Press.

75   The Incredible Little Shrinking Man
in the Head

Bargh, John A.

My career as a psychologist began in the 1970s. It was a time of ideological ferment in the field, a period of consolidation after the cognitive revolution of the 1960s. In high school, there was Skinner on the cover of *TIME* magazine in 1971, his face painted blue (apparently to show what a cold unfeeling human being he was), his new book *Beyond Freedom and Dignity* scathingly attacked and ridiculed. The antagonism that his book provoked stirred the contrarian within me: I wanted to understand Skinner's position and why it met with such resistance.

The main battleground was the role of intentional conscious thought in producing the higher mental processes, especially social behavior. The radical behaviorists held the position that consciousness was an epiphenomenon, playing no causal role in our thoughts and lives, and that instead we were all controlled by responses automatically triggered by external environmental stimuli. The cognitive psychologists held the opposite extreme position: that hardly any higher mental processes are under the direct control of external environmental stimuli. Instead, internal, goal-directed, and conscious (intentional, aware) executive processes ran the show. In a span of just ten years – from the publication of Skinner's *Verbal Behavior* in 1957 to Neisser's *Cognitive Psychology* in 1967 – the dominant assumption had swung like a pendulum from one extreme to the other.

Back then, the assumption that the higher mental processes were all under conscious control was just that: an assumption. Neisser in his 1967 book was acutely aware that a causal vacuum existed after the removal of the behaviorist's external environment – and that replacing it with a homuncular conscious "executive" calling the shots was not a satisfactory *scientific* solution by any means. Thus, he explicitly called for research into the cognitive mechanisms of the higher mental processes, and for researchers to strive to shrink the homunculus until it eventually disappeared, just as *The Incredible Shrinking Man* did in the 1950s science fiction movie.

It was an exciting time also because cognitive psychology was starting to provide new tools that allowed us to ask these important existential questions of *human beings* for the first time. The behaviorists, after all, had generated their grand theories of the higher mental processes in humans based almost entirely on their extensive research on pigeons and rats. It was this leap of generalization that doomed Skinner's heroic attempt in *Verbal Behavior* from the start – his attempt to account for language and complex human interactions in purely S-R terms. The radical behaviorists had eschewed any causal role of internal mental processes in part because there were no reliable scientific methods to measure those processes. But now there were.

Using these new methods, I started to test – taking baby steps at first – whether there could be *any* external environmental causation of internal, cognitive, higher mental processes. My dissertation at Michigan used both dichotic listening (developed by pioneering attention researchers in the 1950s, it involves presenting different information simultaneously to the two ears via stereo headphones, with participants attending and responding to only one ear and thus not conscious of what is presented to the other ear) and, with fellow graduate student Paula Pietromonaco, subliminal verbal priming using a then very high-tech PDP DEC-10 computer that was as big as a bookshelf.

The basic idea tested in these two studies was that if *any* form of external information could be processed without need of conscious involvement, it would be very highly frequently processed – i.e., much thought about – information. Shiffrin and Schneider's landmark work on automatic processes had just showed that high frequency of processing was necessary for these non-conscious, "automatic" processes to develop. In social psychology, there was no more frequently processed type of information than that which was related to oneself – so, I reasoned in Study 1 that self-relevant information would be the most likely candidate to be capable of processing outside of conscious awareness in the unattended channel of a dichotic listening task. The second study used the PDP computer to subliminally present common personality-trait words such as "kind" or "hostile," to see if they too could be processed outside of awareness and influence impression formation. Together, the results of these two studies, one in the auditory and one in the visual domain, suggested that at least some forms of social information, the most frequently processed, were capable as external stimuli to influence internal cognitive, higher mental processes.

Following those first baby steps, my colleagues and I kept testing ever more complex and realistic psychological phenomena as to whether they required conscious intention and awareness to occur. First, we tested the processing of social behavioral information under time pressure in impression formation, showing that people who thought a lot about a certain kind of social behavior (because it was important to whether they liked a person or not), such as *intelligent* or *generous*, were then able to process that kind of information even when it was rapidly presented to them with just enough time to read it once, with no time to stop and consider it. Other people, for whom those particular kinds of behavior were not as important, under the same rapid presentation conditions couldn't tell the difference between someone who was mainly honest and someone who was mainly dishonest.

In social psychology, other researchers such as Russell Fazio were showing that one's attitudes became active and influential in the presence of the object of that attitude, without the need for conscious reflection or retrieval of it. Shelly Chaiken and I confirmed in a series of studies that, if anything, conscious intentional processes *interfered* with the natural activation of many attitudes, far from being necessary to activate them. Eventually we and others arrived at social behavior itself, showing that the participant's own behavioral tendencies could be put into motion, unintentionally and without their awareness, by a variety of external means, including personality-trait words, stereotype-related content (including subliminal faces of members of the stereotyped group), and the physical behavior of an interaction partner (in imitation and mimicry effects).

But I would consider our most important contribution to have been the application of this same logic to motivations and goal pursuits, because this came back full circle to Neisser's "executive processes" and the homunculus problem. What if these top-down, show-running executive processes, the person's goals and purposes, could *themselves* be activated by external environmental information – a hybrid combination of the behaviorists' external (distal) and the cognitivists' internal (proximal) control? Peter Gollwitzer and I reasoned that motivations should correspond to internal cognitive representations and so should be just as capable of activation by relevant external stimuli as attitudes and stereotypes had already shown to be. Accordingly, we used subtle and indirect means of activating the participants' goals – e.g., with words in a purported language test directly relevant to that goal (e.g., *strive, achieve, success* for achievement motivation), and by situations and contexts with which those goals are associated (e.g., triggering the participant's goals associated with having *power* by having them incidentally seated behind a professor's desk, compared to the "student's chair" in front of the desk, when filling out some forms).

Since our initial studies, others have used realistic goal activation methods in naturalistic settings: Gary Latham activated high-performance goals in actual workplace settings through photographs of a successful athlete; Esther Papies and her colleagues used recipe handout flyers to activate goals of dieting in actual grocery stores (significantly reducing the shoppers' purchase of snack items); and developmental researchers have shown that even eighteen-month-old toddlers become more helpful to the experimenter after seeing two dolls facing each other in a friendly manner compared to facing away from each other. And importantly, few if any participants in these studies show any awareness of how their goals had been activated and their behavior had been affected.

Today, although some still seem to be fighting the cognitive revolution, insisting that higher mental processes are exclusively consciously chosen and guided, many others are recognizing the value of the middle ground. Goal pursuits and social behaviors can be influenced and instigated either by external stimuli or by conscious thought and choice. The best way to make further scientific advances is to rid ourselves of axiomatic assumptions, cherished and humanistically motivated as they may be, that by default any given psychological effect or phenomenon requires conscious intention and awareness to occur, until proven otherwise. After all, the cognitive revolution and its aftermath have shown us that while conscious thought is not epiphenomenal, neither is it always necessary.

REFERENCES

Bargh, J. A. (2016). The devil made me do it. In A. Miller (ed.), *The social psychology of good and evil* (2nd edn.). New York: Guilford.

Bargh, J. A., & Ferguson, M. L. (2000). Beyond behaviorism: On the automaticity of higher mental processes. *Psychological Bulletin*, *126*, 925–945.

Bargh, J. A., & Gollwitzer, P. M. (1994). Environmental control over goal-directed action. *Nebraska Symposium on Motivation*, *41*, 71–124.

76 Ethnocentrism and the Optimal Distinctiveness Theory of Social Identity

Brewer, Marilynn

Most behavioral scientists today accept the basic premise that human beings are adapted for group living. Even a cursory review of the physical endowments of our species – weak, relatively slow-footed, extended infancy – makes it clear that we are not suited for survival as lone individuals, or even as small family units. We require groups to survive, and our psychology has been shaped by the necessity of accommodating to, cooperating with, and coordinating with others as members of social groups.

My own work as a social psychologist has focused on this group-living aspect of human nature. I have sought to understand more about our need to belong to groups and how our social group memberships influence the way we think about and act toward others. The framework for my research is the concept of *social identity* – the idea that individuals' sense of self includes more than their personal, individualized identity, but also incorporates the collective identity of the groups to which they belong. Social identity involves a shift from "I" to "we," so that the sense of self (and well-being) becomes inextricably tied to the fortunes and destiny of the group as a whole.

One consequence of our strong need to belong and our social identification with groups is *ethnocentrism*. The term "ethnocentrism" was coined in 1906 by William Graham Sumner in his book *Folkways*. Sumner made the observation that human societies are universally characterized by differentiation into "ingroups" and "outgroups" – the distinctions that demarcate boundaries of loyalty and cooperation among individuals. Attitudes and values are shaped by this ingroup–outgroup distinction in that individuals view all others from the perspective of the ingroup (hence the term, ethno*centrism*).

Sumner's conceptualization of ethnocentrism contained two important assertions. First, that all human societies divide the world into "us" (ingroup) and "them" (outgroups); and second, that people favor their ingroups, evaluating them more positively than outgroups and reserving loyalty and trust for fellow ingroup members. Since the conceptualization, results from years of social psychological on intergroup relations have strongly substantiated Sumner's claims about ethnocentric attitudes. Hundreds of studies in the laboratory and the field have documented ingroup favoritism in myriad forms. Preferential treatment and evaluation of ingroups relative to outgroups appears in evaluations of group products, judgments about others' behavior, allocation of resources, application of rules of fairness, and the decisions we make about whom to trust and cooperate with. Even arbitrary groupings that create us–them distinctions are sufficient to engender preferential attitudes toward one's own group.

Studying the nature and consequences of ingroup favoritism has been an extremely fruitful and important area of social psychological research. But I became interested in the other aspect of Sumner's ethnocentrism concept – why do we humans have such a strong propensity to divide the world into ingroups and outgroups in the first place? The answer, it seemed to me, lies in the necessity for group living and how this has shaped human psychology and social motivations.

The Origins of Optimal Distinctiveness Theory

My theorizing began with thinking about the nature of groups and what structural features are necessary for a cooperative group to work effectively. In particular, I focused on the issue of group size. On the one hand, there are advantages to be gained by extending a group to a wide circle in order to gain more resources, protective strength, and potential helpers in times of need. But expansion comes at the cost of increased demands on obligatory sharing and need for regulation and control. Physical resources can only be stretched so far before the carrying capacity of the environment is exceeded. In addition, the limits on ability for distribution of resources, aid, and information inevitably constrain the potential size of cooperating social networks. Thus, effective social groups must be restricted to some optimal size – sufficiently large and inclusive enough to realize the advantages of extended cooperation, but sufficiently exclusive to avoid the disadvantages of spreading social interdependence too thinly.

Based on this analysis of one structural requirement for group survival, I hypothesized that the conflicting benefits and costs associated with expanding group size would have shaped social motivational systems at the individual level. A singular drive for belonging and inclusion would not have been adaptive without a counteracting drive for differentiation and exclusion. Based on this reasoning, I proposed that humans are characterized by two opposing needs that govern membership in social groups. The first is a *need for inclusion*, a desire for belonging that motivates immersion in social groups. The second is a *need for differentiation* from others that operates in opposition to the need for immersion.

Opposing motives hold each other in check, with the result that human beings are not comfortable either in isolation or in huge collectives. As group membership becomes more and more inclusive, the need for inclusion is satisfied, but the need for differentiation is activated; conversely, as inclusiveness decreases, the differentiation need is reduced, but the need for assimilation is activated. Both needs can be satisfied simultaneously by belonging to groups that are *optimally distinct* – groups that are inclusive enough to satisfy inclusion needs but different enough from other groups to satisfy differentiation needs. The opposing social motives at the individual level create a propensity for adhering to social groups that are both bounded and distinctive.

A salient example of optimal distinctiveness at work is provided by adolescent peer groups. Each generation of adolescents develops its own distinctive clothing, hairstyles, music preferences, and other group norms. Individual teens strive to conform to their peer group style, to be as similar as possible to others of their age. But the norms they are adhering to are fashioned to be as distinctly different as possible from those of other (older) generations – thereby allowing group members to be the same and different at the same time. Somewhat less dramatically, all groups maintain distinctive symbols and practices that members conform to but that distinguish them from members of other groups. Preserving group distinctiveness is essential to meeting the underlying social motives that create strong social identity, member loyalty, and cooperation.

Social Implications: The Upside and the Downside of Optimal Distinctiveness

On the positive side, social identity with distinctive ingroups motivates much prosocial behavior. Mere knowledge that another individual shares our group identity is sufficient to engage trust, empathy, and cooperative orientation. The dilemma, however, is that the social motives postulated by optimal distinctiveness theory create a propensity for adhering to social groups that are both bounded and distinctive. Secure inclusion implies *exclusion*. A consequence is that individuals modify their social behavior depending on whether they are interacting with ingroup or outgroup members. Ingroup positivity and trust are not extended to those outside the ingroup boundary.

At the same time that groups promote trust and cooperation within, they caution wariness and constraint in intergroup interactions. Psychologically, expectations of cooperation and security promote positive attraction toward other ingroup members and motivate adherence to ingroup norms of appearance and behavior that assure that one will be recognized as a good or legitimate ingroup member. Assimilation within and differentiation between groups is thus mutually reinforcing, along with ethnocentric preference for ingroup interactions and institutions. Thus, even in the absence of overt conflict between groups, the differentiation between ingroup and outgroup behavior creates a kind of self-fulfilling prophecy. People expect that outgroup members will not treat them as well as ingroup members do, so they behave less trustingly and more defensively with outgroups than they do with ingroups, and hence intergroup distrust is reinforced.

As a consequence of our evolutionary history, our sense of personal security and certainty are maximized in the context of shared ingroup membership and clear ingroup–outgroup distinctions. The dilemma that optimal distinctiveness theory poses for the modern world is this: How do we accommodate the need for distinctive ingroup identities that is rooted in our evolutionary past under conditions where interdependence transcends group boundaries at a global level?

The complexity of the modern world does provide us with multiple ways to meet identity needs, with multiple group identities that are optimal within different contexts. In a large and complex society, persons are differentiated or subdivided along many meaningful social dimensions, including gender and sexual orientation, life stage (e.g., student, worker, retiree), economic sector (e.g., technology, service, academics, professional), religion, ethnicity, political ideology, and recreational preferences. Each of these divisions provides a basis for shared identity and group membership that may become an important source of optimally distinct social identification. Further, most of these differentiations are cross-cutting in the sense that individuals may share a common ingroup membership on one dimension but belong to different categories on another dimension. Hence, having multiple group memberships has the potential to reduce the likelihood that one's social world can be reduced to a single ingroup–outgroup distinction. To the extent that we recognize the multiplicity and complexity of our own group identities, we may enhance the capacity for acceptance of intergroup differences and life in a pluralistic social system.

REFERENCES

Brewer, M. B. (1991). The social self: On being the same and different at the same time. *Personality and Social Psychology Bulletin, 17*, 475–482.

Brewer, M. B. (1999). The psychology of prejudice: Ingroup love or outgroup hate? *Journal of Social Issues, 55*(3), 429–444.

Tajfel, H. (1970). Experiments in intergroup discrimination. *Scientific American, 223*(2), 96–102.

77   Psychology of Gender: Nature and Nurture Working Together

Eagly, Alice S.

In the first half of my career I happily concentrated on the study of attitudes, a core area of social psychology. This work investigated how attitudes are structured in people's minds and how they influence all stages of their information processing, from exposure and perception to interpretation and memory. Although strong attitudes are often enduring, they can be changed by information and life experience. Attitude theory and research deal with the nuances of these processes.

As a culmination of my work on attitudes, I wrote a book, *The Psychology of Attitudes*, with Shelly Chaiken, that summarized everything that I knew about attitudes as of the early 1990s. Writing this book was an intellectual adventure, a high point in my work in psychology. I then carried my understanding of attitudes into work on other topics.

Even as I concentrated on the study of attitudes, I began to work on the psychology of gender, another area presenting fundamental questions about human psychology. My grounding in social psychology, especially in attitudinal processes, gave me intellectual capital that is critical to understanding how gender is created and played out in everyday behavior. Also useful was my educational background, which incorporated sociology and anthropology along with psychology.

I began my research on gender during the women's movement of the 1970s, when these questions took on special urgency. Many people were asking questions about gender that deserved answers based on scientific research. The overarching question was – and still is – the extent to which women and men are psychologically different, and, if they are different, why that is so. Are differences rooted in nature or nurture? Most psychologists, as well as most people who have taken a psychology course, would say that nature and nurture act together to produce some differences and many similarities in women and men. That view is scientifically valid as far as it goes, but of course it is the details that matter.

In studying a broad area such as gender, it is helpful to have a theoretical stance. I have done that with social role theory, which posits that sex differences and similarities arise primarily from the positioning of men and women in social roles within their society. In all known societies, social roles are to some degree segregated by sex. This segregation is present even in contemporary, highly industrialized societies, where in many occupations the work is carried out mainly by one sex, and in families women usually take on more responsibility than men do for domestic work. As I will explain, these role distributions are consequential for the psychology of gender.

Social role theory raises the question of why such a division of labor exists at all. What are its evolutionary origins? As I argued in my collaborations with Wendy Wood, the roles of women and men in part reflect evolved bodily differences. These critical differences are women's childbearing and nursing of infants and men's greater size, speed, and upperbody strength. Women's reproductive activities can make it challenging for them to participate as much as men do in tasks that require uninterrupted activity, extended training, speed of locomotion, or longdistance travel. In addition, men's greater size and strength equip them to engage in especially strength-intensive manual labor. Less understood by psychologists is the extent to which the division of labor reflects inherited temperamental sex differences – specifically, the greater surgency (i.e., approach tendencies), including greater motor activity, that is more typical of young boys, and the greater effortful control, or selfregulatory skill, that is typical of young girls. These temperamental differences emerge in adult personality and therefore can influence the roles that people occupy.

The implications of these inherited bodily and temperamental differences between the sexes depend on the social, economic, technological, and ecological forces present in a society. For example, women's childbearing and lactation constrain their activities more if birth rates are high and infants are dependent on long-term breastfeeding. Men's physical prowess takes on greater importance to the extent that highly strengthintensive activities are crucial to a society's survival – for example, in some societies, activities such as warfare, hunting large animals, or mining are essential. Through the mediation of social psychological processes, a society's division of labor yields the psychologies of women and men, which differ across societies because of variability in the ways that the division of labor is constituted.

The division of labor produces gender roles, which are shared beliefs about the attributes of women and men. These beliefs derive from divided roles because people infer the traits of men and women from observations of their everyday behaviors and generally do so spontaneously. For example, if women are greatly overrepresented in the care of young children, people infer that women are warmer and more nurturing than men, and, in fact, the childcare role constrains women to develop such qualities.

Also important is the concentration of men and women in different types of occupations. In industrialized societies, women dominate service and caring roles (administrative assistant, teacher of children), and men dominate roles involving making and interacting with things (carpenter, engineer). Men are also more common than women in leadership roles, especially at higher levels. Observations of all of these aspects of the female–male division of labor contribute to people's beliefs about differing male and female traits. When psychologists study these traits directly as gender stereotypes, the most consistent pattern that emerges is that warm and interpersonally sensitive qualities, named *communal* by psychologists, are ascribed more to women than to men, and assertive and competitive qualities, named *agentic* by psychologists, are ascribed more to men than to women.

As these gender roles are shared within cultures, they shape the socialization of girls and boys in gender-stereotypical directions that enable them to fit into the prevailing division of labor. As children mature, and in adult life, gender roles influence behavior by working through a trio of biosocial mechanisms to influence behavior in role-appropriate directions. As I detail below, the mechanisms implicate (a) conformity to others' stereotypic expectations, (b) influence by one's own gender identity, and (c) supportive hormonal processes. These three types of influences interact to yield both differences and similarities in male and female behavior.

The first set of processes thus takes the form of people tending to behaviorally confirm gender roles in response to others' expectations that they do so. People thus learn that behavior inconsistent with gender roles often elicits negative sanctions, including dislike and social exclusion. These sanctions make it easier to follow gender roles than to disregard them.

A second set of processes takes the form of adopting gender roles as personal standards for judging one's own behavior. Although people may adopt more or less traditional versions of these gender norms, they regulate their behavior according to what version they have incorporated into their self-concepts. Both men and women evaluate themselves favorably to the extent that they conform to these standards and unfavorably to the extent that they deviate from them.

The third set of processes pertains to hormonal changes, especially in testosterone, oxytocin, and arginine vasopressin, which generally act to facilitate culturally masculine and feminine behaviors in relevant social contexts. These biological processes, which stem from ancient selection pressures, implicate hormones and related neural structures as central to human sex differences. In summary, all three sets of processes – normative, self-regulatory, and hormonal – work together to yield both differences and similarities in male and female behavior.

Over the years, this social role theory of gender has expanded into an encompassing theoretical structure. From its central construct – the division of labor – the theory looks upward in a nomological (i.e., conceptual) net to address the evolutionary origins of this social structural pattern. The theory also looks downward from roles to behaviors by illuminating the social psychological and biological processes by which gender roles are translated into the behaviors of women and men.

The theory that I have outlined provides an organizing structure for much gender research in psychology. One of my missions is to help organize the many thousands of psychological studies that pertain to these gender issues. The very abundance of these studies presents challenges for understanding their meaning and importance. To facilitate this task, many psychologists have engaged in meta-analyzing, or quantitatively organizing, studies in various content areas. For example, I meta-analyzed studies that compared the behavior of men and women in the domain of helping or altruistic behavior. Another project pertained to aggressive behavior. Several of my other meta-analyses addressed aspects of leadership by answering questions, for example, about the leadership styles of women and men. These meta-analytic projects, as well as individual studies, have provided empirical support for the various causal links proposed by social role theory.

All in all, has my research and writing made a difference? The work on gender has drawn attention to sociocultural factors that influence gender, thus strengthening the view that gender equality may be possible in human social organization. This perspective about gender has filtered out to journalists and popular writers. In terms of writing that has directly reached the public, the best example is my analysis of gender and leadership roles. The book that I wrote with Linda Carli, *Through the Labyrinth: The Truth About How Women Become Leaders*, has reached a broad audience and produced understanding of the challenges that women face in attaining equal participation in leadership as well as possibilities for overcoming these challenges.

REFERENCES

Eagly, A. H., & Carli, L. L. (2007). *Through the labyrinth: The truth about how women become leaders*. Boston: Harvard Business School Press.

Eagly, A. H., & Chaiken, S. (1993). *The psychology of attitudes*. Fort Worth: Harcourt Brace Jovanovich.

Eagly, A. H., & Wood, W. (2012). Social role theory. In P. van Lange, A. Kruglanski, & E. T. Higgins (eds.), *Handbook of theories in social psychology* (vol. 2, pp. 458–476). Thousand Oaks: Sage Publications.

78 How Warmth and Competence Inform Your Social Life

Fiske, Susan T.

Successful scientific contributions are equal parts serendipity, synthesis, integrity, and passion. My most-cited papers all have reflected ideas that happened to be in the right place at the right time – they pulled together competing perspectives, strived for scientific integrity, and were fueled by moral outrage. Of my most-cited work, our model for the two fundamental dimensions of social cognition – warmth and competence – best illustrates these principles.

When we are making sense of other people, we need to know immediately what the other individual or group intends toward us. Are they friend or foe? If they are on our side, then they seem trustworthy, sincere, friendly – in short, warm. If they are against us, they seem none of these. After inferring their intent, we need to know how capable they are of acting on it. If they have high status, we infer they are capable, skilled, effective – in short, competent.

This simple two-dimensional space has synthesis and predictive validity going for it. The combinations of warmth × competence describe common stereotypic responses to all kinds of people, whether at work or in societal groups around the world. For example, in most countries, their own citizens and their middle class generally are viewed as both warm and competent; people are proud of them. Homeless people and undocumented immigrants are stereotypically viewed as neither, and people report being disgusted by them. The mixed combinations are unique to this model: Older or disabled people are stereotyped as warm but incompetent, and people pity them. Rich or business people stereotypically come across as competent but cold; people envy them. Each combination elicits not only its distinctive emotional prejudices, but also a distinct behavioral response by the rest of society. So the model describes distinct stereotypes that predict both emotional prejudices and discriminatory tendencies.

The stereotype content model has proved useful in dozens of countries around the world, allowing us to compare across cultures. For example, any group without an address – migrants, refugees, Roma (gypsies), Bedouins (desert nomads), hobos – is viewed with distrust and contempt across the globe. Likewise, rich people are envied, yet resented as competent but cold everywhere, regardless of whether being rich is simply associated with social class or with an outsider entrepreneurial group (e.g., Jewish or Chinese people in various times and places). The model also describes people's relationships with animals (e.g., predators are competent but cold; prey are stupid) and with corporations (e.g., everybody loves Hersheys; everyone is disgusted by BP). And individual people fit this warmth-by-competence space, according to our work and related work by others. All this evidence has synthesis (conceptual integration) and scientific integrity (rigorous evidence), as evidenced by peer-reviewed publications from our lab and others.

Serendipity and passion come into play as well. As immigration and globalization increase, all countries (especially developed democracies) are coping with greater diversity than ever before. Although American and European psychological scientists have studied stereotyping and prejudice for decades, the US research focused on Black–White relations (and, to a lesser extent, anti-Jewish bias), and the EU research focused on national identities. In the twenty-first century, we need to understand biases based on all kinds of ethnic, religious, gender, sexual, age, class, and ability distinctions. (We won't be out of work any time soon.) At this time of societal flux, our model went beyond existing blunt ingroup–outgroup analyses to describe some apparently universal, applicable principles. Although related ideas had been kicking around the field, our model jelled at an opportune moment.

My own passion for this topic comes from a sense of moral outrage about people mistreating (even killing) other people because of arbitrary group categories. Stereotypes and prejudices are historical accidents of who allies or competes with whom, and what their relative status is. People underestimate these demonstrably circumstantial predictors of stereotype content that our model and research have shown. What are accidents of immigration at a particular place and time often get generalized to an entire ethnicity. Similarly, gender roles get essentialized as biological destiny. And so forth. These fundamentally unfair societal processes can yield to scientific analysis, careful theory, and rigorous evidence. Moral outrage is not enough, of course. Science prevails.

The idea for this stereotype content model came from several sources. On an implicit level, I had been acquainted with the warmth and competence dimension since graduate school. My dissertation manipulated a target person's apparent sociability and civic competence. My readings had built on Solomon Asch's 1946 research, which manipulated warm–cold traits among a list of competence traits, and on Seymour Rosenberg's 1968 identification of two dimensions – social good–bad and task good–bad – in trait impressions. Shortly after graduate school, I published a paper with Robert Abelson and Donald Kinder on impressions of presidential candidates, which used integrity and trustworthiness as the two trait predictors of voting intention. In the 1990s, Peter Glick and I published the ambivalent sexism inventory, which identified two major types of sexist prejudice: hostility toward women seen as competitive and threatening (i.e., competent but cold) and subjective benevolence toward women seen as cooperative and subordinate (i.e., warm but incompetent). If you squint, these all are precedents for the warmth and competence dimensions, but I did not see that until afterwards.

My more explicit development of these ideas came when I was organizing the stereotyping, prejudice, and discrimination literature for a 1998 handbook chapter. The extant research, it seemed to me, focused on social cognitive processes presumed to be the same for all groups: in the United States, as noted, mainly Black–White relations, but extended without qualification to, for example, Latinos, women, and gay men. Our own analyses of gender relationships had already suggested that they differ from, for example, race relations, because men and women have greater independence, among other societal factors. So I started thinking about whether there are different kinds of outgroups and whether one could make a systematic and psychologically meaningful typology that would predict other variables.

Upon going public in talks describing our preliminary data, I discovered other people were thinking about parallel issues: Marilynn Brewer and Michelle Alexander, Andrea Abele and Bogdan Wojciszke, Steven Neuberg and Cathy Cottrell, among others. Over my career, I have learned that no one owns an idea, only the published work – especially empirical – on it. Also, in a way, it is intellectually reassuring when others are discovering related phenomena: it suggests that there's a "there" there.

Presumably real, the apparently universal dimensions of warmth and competence matter for our field and for the world beyond academia. For our field, they suggest researchers not glossing over the differences among various outgroups, clusters of which have particular relationships to each other and distinct resulting perceptions. Not all outgroups are equivalent. For applied work, this means that diversity programs and human resource management must acknowledge the systematic variety of outgroups subject to distinct patterns of bias. On a broader scale, the apparently universal dimensions of social cognition mean that any seemingly intent-having entity will be seen in these ways: human individuals, human groups, corporations, nations, animals, robots, nature, gods. Accordingly, if these dimensions are universal, how early do children apply them? Some work suggests that infants distinguish good actors from bad ones, as well as higher-status, more-competent actors from lower-ranked ones. Some researchers are investigating whether even dogs and primates make these same distinctions.

More work remains, besides exploring extensions. We and others have explored the psychometrics of these dimensions. Andrea Abele has proposed that competence comprises both agency and capability, while warmth consists of both trustworthiness and sociability. Also, we and others are exploring patterns in how the dimensions are used across cultures. For example, East Asian cultures seem not to place societal reference groups in the high–high quadrant, as Westerners do, perhaps because of norms about modesty. In other work, income inequality predicts a greater number of groups in the two mixed quadrants, consistent with the idea that inequality requires more complex explanations. Other cultural variants are likely to emerge. For example, societies in conflict (e.g., conducting a war, or a civil war) may be more polarized than societies at peace.

Other future directions could pursue the neural signatures of these phenomena. We did find distinct responses to allegedly disgusting targets, with less medial prefrontal cortex activation and less conscious reflection directed at considering their minds. And envied targets evoked physiological responses and self-reports consistent with Schadenfreude (malicious glee) at their misfortunes. If the dimensions and their combinations are indeed universal – and perhaps evolutionarily old – then the other quadrants and the warmth/competence dimensions themselves might have characteristic neural manifestations. Stay tuned.

REFERENCES

Fiske, S. T. (2015). Intergroup biases: A focus on stereotype content. *Current Opinion in Behavioral Sciences*, 3, 45–50.

Fiske, S. T., Cuddy, A. J., Glick, P., & Xu, J. (2002). A model of (often mixed) stereotype content: Competence and warmth respectively follow from perceived status and competition. *Journal of Personality and Social Psychology*, 82, 878–902.

79   Two Routes to Persuasion

Petty, Richard E.

In the course of our daily lives, we make tons of decisions ranging from the relatively trivial to the more consequential. What should I wear to work? What soap should I buy? For whom should I vote in the Presidential election? The work that my colleagues and I have done over the past several decades has tried to address how people go about evaluating their options and deciding what to do. Our goal has been to build a general model of attitude formation and change that can be applied to virtually any situation in which a person must make a decision or decide on a course of action. As social psychologists, our focus has largely been on how people's own views are influenced by the information provided to them by other people, but we have also studied self-influence.

Although I was very interested in persuasion as a teen – mostly because of the practical benefits of the rare win in arguments with my father – I first became interested in social influence as an academic topic as an undergraduate Political Science major at the University of Virginia. I was intrigued by Richard Neustadt's dictum that the power of the president was merely the power to persuade. Yet, little evidence was available to indicate *how* voters made their decisions and what factors determined whether citizens were drawn to one side over another. As luck would have it, a social psychologist was offering a small advanced seminar on political psychology that I was allowed to join despite not being a psych major. The course proved so fascinating and relevant to my interests that I vowed to forgo my original law school plans and become a social psychologist instead.

When I arrived in Columbus to enter the social psychology PhD program at Ohio State University, I wasn't entirely sure what to expect. However, as luck would have it once again, I began a friendship and ultimately long-term scientific collaboration with another student entering the program at the same time, John Cacioppo. Ohio State was the perfect place for us to do our individual and collaborative work because of the stellar resources and atmosphere. My initial academic advisor was Robert Cialdini, visiting OSU at the time, and his influence was monumental, as was that of Tim Brock, Tony Greenwald, Tom Ostrom, and

Bibb Latané. John and I read the existing literature on persuasion, but also engaged in various field trips to see persuasion in action, from negotiating with used car dealers to making a strange visit to the Church of Scientology.

Reading the literature in social psychology on persuasion at the time (mid-1970s) was quite depressing. The prevailing textbooks stated that although the study of attitudes once reigned supreme, the topic was no longer at the forefront. The primary reason was that so much research had yielded contradictory findings that it seemed impossible to make sense of it all. Even for the seemingly simplest persuasion variables, such as the credibility of the source, some studies obtained the obvious effect – that high credibility led to more persuasion than low – but other studies revealed the opposite, and some failed to find any effect. This replication crisis was so severe that some scholars suggested that research on this topic be abandoned until more clarity could be obtained. Adding to this depressing state of affairs were additional findings indicating that sometimes the changed attitudes endured over time and predicted behavior, but, at other times, attitude changes were short-lived and seemingly inconsequential.

Against this backdrop, and following many long night conversations and debates, John and I concluded that a new approach was needed if the study of attitudes was to be restored to prominence and provide any useful guidance in important domains of application. Our key insight was that despite the long-standing tradition of assuming that learning messages and careful deliberation were the keys to persuasion, attitudes could also be changed if thinking was low, but the processes and consequences would be different. In what became our *Elaboration Likelihood Model* (ELM) of persuasion, we proposed that in some contexts people were motivated and able to engage in careful thought about a message, and, in such situations, persuasion would be determined primarily by the cogency of the information available. In other contexts, however, people would be relatively unmotivated or unable to engage in message scrutiny. In such situations, people could be influenced by simple cues in the situation (e.g., source credibility, their mood, mere number of arguments) that could help them form a reasonable opinion with relatively little cognitive effort. Furthermore, we proposed that low-thought attitude change would not be as enduring and predictive of behavior as that produced by high thought.

How did this framework help to bring coherence to the field? Most importantly, it explained why contradictory results for any given persuasion variable would be expected. Prior results were not really contradictory at all, if the underlying processes involved were understood, because different processes could lead to different outcomes. The ELM held that thoughtful (central) and non-thoughtful (peripheral) routes to persuasion anchored the ends of an elaboration continuum. Some variables pushed people toward the high-thinking end (e.g., high personal relevance, accountability), and other variables pushed them toward the low end (e.g., distraction, low knowledge). We also identified a way to assess individual differences in the likelihood of thinking in our *need for cognition scale*. The ELM was also a theory about theories, in that it specified that some prior persuasion theories postulated high-thought mechanisms (e.g., cognitive dissonance) that were more likely to operate at the high-thinking end of the continuum, whereas other theories proposed low-thought mechanisms (e.g., classical conditioning) that were more likely to operate at the low-thinking end of the continuum. Thus, it was not that some prior theories were right and some wrong, or that there was only one direction of effect for any given variable, but, rather, that different outcomes and processes operated at different points along the elaboration continuum.

For example, consider the question of whether providing three or six arguments is better for persuasion. According to the ELM, the answer depends on how much thinking the person is doing and whether the arguments are strong or weak. If people are not doing much thinking (e.g., low relevance topic), presenting six arguments is better than three regardless of quality because people will just reason that if there are more, it must be better. However, if thinking is high, then six arguments will be better than three only if the arguments are strong. If they are weak, six will be *worse* than three because with more weak arguments, people will become increasingly convinced that there is little merit to the proposal. This example shows how the effect of a given variable can reverse its impact by invoking a different process depending on the extent of thinking. Many other variables behave similarly.

The ELM has now been around for over three decades, and it has prospered because it has brought some coherence to what had been a confusing state of affairs, by proposing that judgments can be formed in different ways with different consequences. The ELM was an early example of what became an explosion of subsequent dual-process and system theories of judgment. It also became influential because the basic principles of the theory could be used to understand and influence all sorts of judgments, from the election of politicians to jury outcomes to one's personal health and consumer choices. Now that the ELM has gained acceptance and several meta-analyses have confirmed the predictions of the theory, the time is ripe to use the theory in additional applied settings and to flesh out when the variables identified by the ELM will have their largest effects.

That is, although the ELM is good at identifying the direction of expected effects for different variables in different situations, an important step in using the ELM in applied contexts is to understand how to implement the variables of the theory. For example, what serves as a credible source in one context may not do so in another, so pretesting of variables is advised. In using the ELM, the magnitude of effects that should be expected will depend on how variables are operationalized. For example, take the prediction that as the personal relevance of a message increases, the quality of the arguments will have a larger impact on attitudes, such that enhancing personal relevance will increase persuasion if the arguments are strong, but decrease persuasion if the arguments are weak. How large an effect should this be? The answer is that the size of the effect will be influenced by how argument quality and personal relevance are instantiated in any given setting as well as the presence of all other variables in the situation that could also affect the extent of thinking. In general, to observe a larger effect for personal relevance on thinking, it is better if other variables that influence thinking are set at a moderate level so relevance has the most room to operate. For example, if studying the impact of personal relevance on a group of individuals who are highly accountable for a decision (versus low in accountability), thinking will already be high, so increasing personal relevance will not be able to increase it much further.

Of course, the variables that are most under the influencer's control and the possibilities for their implementation will vary from situation to situation. Nonetheless, the ELM provides useful guidance as to which variables are potentially important and makes clear predictions about the direction of effects these variables should have, in what contexts they are most likely to operate, and whether the resulting changes will tend to be consequential or not.

REFERENCES

Petty, R. E., & Cacioppo, J. T. (1984). The effects of involvement on response to argument quantity and quality: Central and peripheral routes to persuasion. *Journal of Personality and Social Psychology, 46*, 69–81.

Petty, R. E., & Briñol, P. (2012). The elaboration likelihood model: Three decades of research. In P. A. M. Van Lange, A. Kruglanski, & E. T. Higgins (eds.), *Handbook of theories of social psychology* (vol. 1, pp. 224–245). London: Sage.

Personal Relationships

80   The "Next One"

Berscheid, Ellen

If at any time during my professional career I had been asked, "What do you consider your most important scientific contribution?" I would have said, "The next one!" Like the Biblical Lot, I believe that looking back can be an unrewarding distraction from current endeavors. As I now glance in my rear view mirror, I see only a long stream of "nexts" in the general areas of interpersonal attraction and close relationships. No one piece of work stands out as "most" important, or even as particularly important in itself. I must hope that if the whole is not greater than the sum of the parts, it at least is not significantly less.

Identifying *your* most important contribution would be difficult in any case because scientific contributions are rarely made by one person alone. Any contribution attributed to me has been the result of collaboration (formal or informal) with others, and might have never been made without their knowledge and effort. A useful piece of advice to a young aspiring researcher might be: "Always try to work with those who have more relevant knowledge than you do and, preferably, people smarter than you are."

My answer to another question, "How did you get the idea?" for each piece of work also remains the same as always: curiosity! Not the idle kind of curiosity, but an involuntary personal compulsion to seek the answer to a question. It is the kind of curiosity that dominates conscious thought and usually is the spawning ground for an active and organized quest to find the answer. Being captured by curiosity is not always welcome. For one thing, the search for the answer may crowd out personal relationships and previous activities, some essential to health and home. For another, failure is always a real possibility.

Success of a new pursuit is always in doubt because the answers to large questions – and most things that matter and that we are curious about are very large questions – are usually yielded by Mother Nature in a series of droplets, each one granted only in response to a small question associated with the larger question. Despite obtaining many drops of knowledge after expending much effort and time – perhaps one's entire professional life – the large question that prompted the search may be only partially answered. Even the combined efforts of many researchers over decades – centuries, even – may not succeed in providing a wholly satisfactory answer to the larger question. Moreover, whether the work "matters" is the province of others, not the researcher; one's own curiosity may be satisfied, but others may regard the question as unimportant or be unsatisfied with the answer offered.

Although I suspect that all researchers vaguely hope to make an important scientific contribution to their discipline and to the world, I doubt that hope trumps curiosity as the primary motivation for undertaking the work in the first place. Moreover, a desire to make an important scientific contribution is neither necessary nor sufficient for making one. Seasoned writers tell their aspiring students, "Write what you know!" Aspiring researchers might be advised, "Research what you are curious about!" The corollary is: if you're not curious about anything, you should find another occupation because research *always* begins with a question, and if you are not personally compelled to seek the answer to that question, you will never have the will or the energy to sustain the effort it inevitably takes to find the answer.

My early work, with Elaine Hatfield, in the area of interpersonal attraction may illustrate what I mean. People have always been curious about why we like some people but not others, as shown by the stupendous success of Dale Carnegie's 1936 *How to Win Friends and Influence People*, which made history by staying on the best-seller list for a decade and has remained popular for well over half a century. At the time it was published, psychologists were not particularly interested in the large question of the dynamics of interpersonal attraction. By the mid-1960s, however, and with the growth of social psychology, enough had been learned that Hatfield and I thought it should be compiled into a book, *Interpersonal Attraction*, in 1969. It was a thin book.

We not only were curious about why some people were liked and others weren't but, like most young people, we also were curious about romantic love. At that time, romantic love was simply viewed as a strong form of liking – that is, liking and romantic love were viewed as two points on the same continuum. Thus, it was assumed that if you identified the causal antecedents of liking, you also would have identified those of romantic love, their magnitude simply being stronger in the case of love. It followed, then, that if you kept on liking another person more and more, you'd eventually find yourself at the love end of the continuum. We'd had some personal experiences in that arena, however, and had our doubts. It seemed to us that liking someone more and more just led to a whole lot of liking – not to love, and especially not to romantic love.

At lunch one day, alternately discussing our book project and commiserating about our current relationship problems, I recall saying that if there were a pill I could take that would banish romantic love from my life forever, I would take it. At the same time, of course, some of our friends were lamenting that they weren't in love and feared they might never be. There was no pill then – nor is there now – for getting out of love or for getting in love, and illuminating knowledge was unavailable. Nevertheless, we decided to add a last chapter to our book, titled "Romantic Love"; never mind that we had next to nothing "scientific" to put in it. Only nineteen pages long, it consisted mostly of our musings, including our suspicion that strong liking (which we called "companionate love") and romantic love were not on the same continuum – they were different phenomena.

There were many obstacles to the study of interpersonal attraction at that time. For example, many in the "world beyond" thought research would be a waste of time and money because the mysteries of attraction and love were impenetrable. Still others, including one influential US senator, feared that, if successful, research would destroy the mystery and the experience of love. In addition, many elite departments of psychology had issued encyclicals excluding "applied" phenomena from the purview of their faculty and students. This excluded phenomena associated with people's experiences in their close relationships. Being women at a time when many psychology departments would not admit women for graduate study and most would not hire a woman into their faculty, Hatfield and I found ourselves in marginal university positions, isolated from the psychology department and its faculty. As a result, we were little influenced by their declaration of unacceptable research topics and relatively immune to the prejudices and fads of colleagues we did not have. We felt free to research what *we* were curious about.

Early on, it became clear that physical attractiveness played an outsize role in heterosexual romantic attraction among college students, trumping all of a person's other attributes. Hatfield, Karen Dion, and I wondered why, and found a powerful physical attractiveness stereotype – the "what is beautiful is good" stereotype – underlying the effect; that is, an attractive exterior was assumed to cover an attractive interior of personality traits and other positive and less visible qualities. We suspected (and perhaps hoped) that the stereotype was limited to callow adolescents, but subsequently found them to be no different from anyone else. Even later, we found that physical attractiveness was potent not just in the romantic realm but in most others as well, including the classroom and the workplace. But it was our finding that physical attractiveness played a significant role in a child's popularity with his or her nursery school playmates, as well as in the personality traits the other children attributed to him or her, that stunned me. It is difficult now to appreciate how deeply embedded the cultural belief that "all children are beautiful" was at that time and, thus, that they could not be differentiated in their physical attractiveness. I shared that belief; I thought the study would be a waste of time and resources, but the intense curiosity (and pestering) of my graduate student, Karen Dion, won me over. Though I suspected (perhaps hoped) our finding wouldn't replicate, it subsequently was confirmed by hundreds of studies showing that physically attractive children (as young as infants) receive preferential treatment (even from their mothers), in contrast to the less attractive (who, for example, receive harsher punishments for the same transgression).

Today there are many theories and studies of romantic love, as well as of other varieties of love, that are as important to people as the romantic variety (see, for example, Berscheid, 2010). Many books survey the now voluminous physical attractiveness literature. Both bodies of research subsequently became central to the development of "relationship science," a fast growing sub-discipline of psychology, as Harry Reis has documented.

I end this essay by confessing that, if I have made a contribution to psychological science, it is dwarfed by the contribution it has made to me. It cured me of the debilitating disease of boredom that afflicted me throughout adolescence (during which I was viewed as a serious "disciplinary problem" by teachers and others) until late in college when I was forced to take a course in psychology to graduate. There I discovered that human behavior is an Aladdin's cave of curiosities, and that by exploring its riches with my own "special magic lamp" – my mind – I could banish boredom forever.

REFERENCES

Berscheid, E. (2010). Love in the fourth dimension. *Annual Review of Psychology*. *61*, 1–26.

Berscheid, E., & Regan, P. (2005). *The psychology of interpersonal relationships*. Englewood Cliffs: Prentice-Hall. (Reprinted by Taylor and Francis, 2015)

Hatfield, E., & Berscheid, E. (2016). In research as in love, one is the loneliest number. In R. Zweigenhaft & E. Borgida (eds), *Collaboration in psychological science: Behind the scenes*. New York: Norton.

81   Human Mating Strategies

Buss, David M.

My research obsession with mating started in the early 1980s. I sought to test several evolution-based hypotheses that derived from Darwin's 1871 theory of sexual selection. Darwin observed that many qualities of animals seem to have no survival advantage whatsoever. Think about the brilliant plumage of peacocks, the bulky antlers of male deer, or the loud mating croaks of frogs. Darwin's theory of sexual selection identified two critical causal processes by which these weird survival-impairing characteristics could evolve: preferential mate choice, and same-sex competition. Potential mates possessing qualities desired by one sex have a mating advantage; they get chosen, while those lacking desired qualities do not. Qualities linked with winning same-sex competitions also evolve, or get passed on in greater numbers, because victors gain increased sexual access to members of the opposite sex. I became fascinated with these causal processes of sexual selection. It struck me as awe-inspiring that so much evolutionary action revolved around mating, even though many erroneously see evolutionary theory as all about survival.

There were two problems. First, back in the 1980s I was not aware of any psychologists who actually used evolutionary theory to guide their empirical research. Second, although biologists were using sexual selection theory to make discoveries about insects and birds, next to nothing was known about these processes in humans. So I set out to test a few hypotheses about gender differences in the content of mate preferences – that men would prefer fertility in a mate, such as cues to youth and health; that physical appearance provides this bounty of cues; and that women would prefer potential mates who have resource-acquisition potential, in part to offset their large obligatory investment of a nine-month pregnancy (none of this is conscious, of course).

The results supported these predictions, but there was another problem. If the hypotheses anchored in sexual selection were correct, they should be universal, not just found among a couple of undergraduate samples. Over the next five years, I launched the International Mate Selection Project, and ended up assembling a team of fifty collaborators in thirty-seven countries occupying six continents and five islands. I knew

383

that whatever I found would be controversial. In retrospect, I was naïve about how controversial. Emotions run high when talking about evolution, higher when talking about evolved gender differences, and higher still when adding sex and mating to this volatile mix. But the thirty-seven-culture study provided an important start. It identified universal gender differences in mate preferences (e.g., desire for youth, attractiveness, and financial prospects), some universal desires shared by women and men (e.g., desire for kindness, intelligence, dependability), and some important cultural differences (e.g., the desire for virginity).

But the study also left many questions unanswered. I had studied preferences in long-term mates such as marriage partners, but what about casual sex partners? How do desires change across environments or social circumstances? How do men and women translate their desires into mating strategies in trying to attract the mates they want? How do women and men compete for mates, that second key causal process of sexual selection? Are people higher in mate value better able to translate their desires into actual mating outcomes? How do people deal with challenges after mateships are formed, such as the presence of mate poachers, the potential for sexual infidelity, or partners who want to break up?

Some Key Discoveries About Human Mating Strategies

These and other questions led to a raft of research projects that my lab, students, and colleagues conducted over the ensuing years. Here are a few highlights of what we discovered:

- *Temporal context matters.* Although men value physical attractiveness more than women in long-term mating, women dramatically increase their valuation of appearance in short-term mating.
- *Desire for sexual variety differs between the genders.* Men, compared to women, desire a larger number of sex partners, have a stronger desire for casual no-strings sex, let less time elapse before seeking sex, fantasize about a larger number of sex partners, and are more likely to consent to sex with strangers.
- *Men and women have different inferential cognitive biases.* Men show a sexual over-perception bias, over-inferring sexual interest when women display minimal cues such as a smile or a glancing arm touch. We hypothesize that this bias exists to minimize the cost of missed sexual opportunities. Women show a commitment skepticism bias, under-inferring cues to a man's commitment, a bias hypothesized to avoid costly forms of male deception.

- *Mate value matters.* Those high in mate value demand and actually obtain mates who are higher on a host of qualities, including resources, attractiveness, good parent qualities, good partner qualities, and "good genes" qualities.
- *Ecological environment matters.* In cultures with a high prevalence of parasites, both genders ramp up the importance they attach to physical appearance, likely due to the fact that parasites degrade physical appearance.
- *Sex ratio matters.* In cultures with a surplus of women, men are better able to implement their evolved desire for sexual variety, causing both sexes to shift to a short-term mating strategy. When there is a surplus of men, marriages become more stable and casual sex rates decline.
- *Mate competition tactics embody mate preferences.* The most effective tactics of mate attraction are those that embody the mate preferences of the opposite sex. In online dating, for example, men higher in higher-status occupations and higher income brackets receive more responses. Younger and more physically attractive women receive more responses.
- *People derogate their mating rivals in predictable ways.* Although men and women verbally slander their competitors with equal frequency, we found that they do so in different content domains. Women more than men derogate their rival's physical appearance (e.g., "Did you notice that her thighs are heavy?") and sexual promiscuity (e.g., "She's had so many sex partners she's lost count"). Men more than women derogate their rival's future prospects (e.g., "He's a loser and not going anywhere") and their physical prowess (e.g., "He's a wimp"). These tactics, a key part of human mate competition, are predictable from the mate preferences of the opposite sex, linking the two key components of sexual selection.
- *Deception on the mating market is common, especially in short-term mating.* Women and men both deceive each other, but about different things. Men are more likely to deceive about their status, income, height, and commitment. Women are more likely to deceive about cues to potential sexual access, their appearance, their age if older, and their weight. Deception tends to be more common in short-term mating, as when men feign greater emotional involvement or long-term interest for purely sexual goals.
- *Jealousy tracks gender-linked adaptive problems.* Because of internal female fertilization, men face the problem of paternity uncertainty. Mothers are always 100 percent sure that their children are their own. Men can never be sure. Women face the problem of the diversion of

a man's resources to another woman. Sexual jealousy tracks these adaptive problems, with men more than women displaying more jealousy at cues to sexual infidelity, women more than men at cues to emotional infidelity. In studies of forgiveness or breakup following a violation, men have greater difficulty forgiving a partner's sexual infidelity, women a partner's emotional infidelity.

- *Mate retention tactics track adaptive problems.* Mates gained must be retained, at least for a time when pursuing a long-term mating strategy. Our lab discovered nineteen tactics people use to guard and retain their mates. These range from vigilance to violence. They include benefit-bestowing tactics, as when someone showers their partner with more love and affection. And they sometimes get cost-inflicting, causing stalking and battering. People calibrate the intensity of mate retention efforts to the mate value of their partner. Younger and more attractive women and higher-status and higher-income men are guarded and retained more vigorously.

- *Sexual regret tracks gender differentiated adaptive challenges.* Looking back at your life when you are fifty, what will you regret in the mating domain? Our studies found that women tended to have regrets about having sex with the wrong partner in the wrong time and the wrong place. Men tended to regret missed sexual opportunities.

The mating mind turns out to be extremely complex, and new discoveries continue to be made, with no sign of slacking.

Objections and Misunderstandings

The volatile mix of mating, gender differences, and evolution produces a fair volume of objections and misunderstandings. Objections come from both ends of the ideological spectrum. Those on the religious right tend to object to evolutionary theory in general, and especially to its application to understanding the human mind. Those on the political left tend to see the work as somehow antithetical to social justice goals such as gender equality. If there are evolved gender differences, some believe, then they will be used to justify discrimination against women and otherwise doom interventions designed to change the status quo. One recent article attempted to refute one of my former student's work on mate preference that found shifts as a function of women's ovulation cycle. The purported refutation was entitled "Women Can Keep the Vote," strangely implying that if women's psychology changes at all with their cycle, then somehow that would justify depriving them of full citizenship! The inappropriate infusion of ideology into science, of course, is not new. When it comes to evolutionary theory, it dates back to Darwin's time when Lady Ashley, upon hearing about his theory, remarked "Let's hope that it's not true; but if it is true, let's hope that it doesn't become widely known." The list of misunderstandings about evolutionary psychology is long and deep. There is even evidence that humans have evolved cognitive biases that actually interfere with the ability to understand the logic of evolutionary theory itself, making the evolutionary science of the mind an uphill battle.

Other objections have been made about specific evolutionary hypotheses and specific empirical findings. Gender differences in the desire for sexual variety and sexual jealousy have been especially favored targets of challenges. When cogent alternative hypotheses have been advanced, our lab and others have attempted to pit the competing hypotheses against each other in critical empirical tests. Although some claim to have falsified certain specific mating hypotheses, in my judgment, the competing hypotheses have not fared well empirically. Ultimately, science uses the weight of the empirical evidence to adjudicate among competing hypotheses.

From my perspective, although it is extremely unlikely, it would be fine if future competing hypotheses did falsify those previously proposed. Indeed, there exist competing evolutionary hypotheses about the same set of findings, and they cannot all be scientifically correct. Even if all evolutionary hypotheses about human mating psychology turned out to be wrong, they would still have served science well in guiding researchers to make important empirical discoveries, such as those mentioned above, that were entirely unknown prior to bringing an evolutionary lens to human mating.

Mate selection is the most important decision a person can make. At a personal level, that decision affects the day-to-day environment you will inhabit from the breathing body next to you in the morning through to your last glance before sleep. It can bestow daily happiness or condemn you to conflict. At a social level, it influences the parties you go to, your network of friends, and alliances of your newly extended family. It affects the reach of your social influence and, reciprocally, the social influences to which you will be exposed. Your choice can raise or lower your social status. If you have children, mate selection influences the genetic make-up of your offspring and the parental and family environment to which your children will be exposed. Mate competition and preferential mate selection affect the evolution of our species, as Darwin's theory of sexual selection brought to light. Human mating strategies have turned out to be far more important to science than we psychologists ever envisioned.

REFERENCES

Buss, D. M. (2013). Sexual jealousy. *Psychological Topics, 22,* 155–182.
Buss, D. M. (2013). The science of human mating strategies: An historical perspective. *Psychological Inquiry, 24,* 171–177.
Buss, D. M. (2015). *Evolutionary psychology: The new science of the mind* (5th edn.). Boston: Allyn & Bacon.

Hatfield, Elaine

In 1963 I graduated with a PhD from Stanford University. My advisor, Leon Festinger, casually opined that he could get me a job anywhere I liked. "Choose," he said. I chose Harvard, Yale, or Bell Labs. (This was the post-Sputnik era, when jobs were so plentiful that it was a seller's market). Leon was supremely egalitarian, but the academic world was not. After a fistful of rejections – almost all saying that a woman wouldn't fit in at their premiere university – Leon began to fret. Then (as my aspirations declined) came similar rejections from junior colleges, and finally from all-boys' prep schools. Leon just about gave up on finding me an academic job. Finally, in desperation, he called his long-time friend, Dean E. G. Williamson, at the University of Minnesota, who offered me a job at the Student Activities Bureau. It would be my task to arrange activities for incoming freshmen. Happily, and with some luck, I soon found my way to the Laboratory for Research in Social Relations, which in its short history had housed such luminaries as Leon, Stanley Schachter, Harold Kelley, Gardner Lindsey, Elliot Aronson, Ellen Berscheid (who was then a graduate student), and the like. I was accepted as a sort of an honorary sidekick.

I have always been intrigued by passion (what graduate student is not?) but in the early 1960s, passionate love and sexual desire were considered topics too silly, too trivial, too evanescent, and too mysterious to warrant investigation. But, as an organizer of University of Minnesota's Orientation activities, I was free to investigate anything I wanted. And what I wanted to do was to discover the underpinnings of romantic love and sexual desire – specifically the influence (if any) of market conditions on what young people yearn for, what they expect, and what they eventually settle for in a mate. Thus, in 1963, my friends and I designed the Computer Dance study – one of the first studies to investigate love, sexual desire, and mate selection, and certainly one of the first to match couples up with computers.

The Matching Hypothesis

In fairy tales, Prince Charming often falls in love with the scullery maid. In real life, however, after some experience, people – whether they are young or old, gay, lesbian, or heterosexual – generally end up settling for "suitable" partners. In the end, market conditions would prevail. Or so we thought.

To test this notion, we invited incoming freshmen to a get-acquainted dance. Couples were promised that a (then) new innovation, a state-of-the-art (dismal) IBM computer would match them with an appropriate blind date. (In truth, the students were randomly matched with one another.) When the freshmen arrived to purchase tickets, a trio of ticket sellers surreptitiously rated their physical attractiveness. From student records we also assembled information on their self-esteem, scholastic aptitude, intelligence, grades, and personality (we possessed their scores on the prestigious *Minnesota Multiphasic Personality Test* and the *California Personality Inventory*).

At the dance, the 400 matched couples chatted, danced, and got to know one another. Then, during the 10:30 p.m. intermission, we swept through the dance hall, rounding up couples from the dance floor, lavatories, and fire escapes – even adjoining buildings. We asked the students to tell us frankly (and in confidence) what they thought of their dates. How much did they like them? How much did they think their dates liked *them*? Did they plan to ask them out again? If *they* were asked out, would they accept? Six months later we contacted the participants again to find out if they had, in fact, dated.

We found that all young men and women yearned for the stars. Everyone – regardless of how low their self-esteem, what *they* looked like, how dismal their intelligence or personality – preferred (in fact, insisted on) being matched in the future with the most self-confident, best-looking, most charming, brightest, and most socially skilled partners available. During the dance, those whom blind chance had matched with handsome or beautiful dates were eager to pursue the relationships (whether those dates liked or despised them!)

When couples were contacted six months after the dance, participants (whether they were good looking or homely, well-treated or not) had in fact attempted to wangle a date with the best-looking. The more handsome the man and the more beautiful the woman, the more eagerly he or she was pursued. *Interestingly, men and women cared equally about their dates' appearance.* Every effort to find anything else that mattered failed. Men and women with high self-esteem and exceptional IQs and social skills, for example, were not liked any better than those who were less well endowed.

This study demonstrated that (as predicted) young people yearn for perfection – especially in appearance. Alas, there is indeed a difference between what people desire (perfection) and what they can get (imperfection). Subsequent research made it clear that, all too soon, young optimists find they must be more realistic. Aim too high and you discover (after undergoing the humiliation of rejection) that someone is "out of your league." Settle for too little, and friends counsel that "you can do better." Eventually, like Goldilocks, you settle for someone who is "not too hot, not too cold, but just right."

Of course, in the dating and mating marketplace, physical appearance is not the only thing of value. Couples can be well- or ill-matched in a variety of ways. For example, a collection of young beauties all chose Seth Rogen, who, although he is hardly handsome, is charming, intelligent, famous, and very funny. A variety of assets all contribute to one's "mate value" – a general indicator of how desirable a person is in the dating market.

In conclusion: Research, much of it now emanating from Equity theory, seems to indicate that in the *early stages* of dating relationships, considerations of the marketplace prevail. Men and women strive to attract socially attractive partners and are profoundly concerned with how rewarding, fair, and equitable their budding relationships appear to be. Were we to review recent Equity theory research, we would find that in longer-term relationships, as love and shared interests grow stronger and family ties increase, market considerations generally grow less important . . . but that is a topic for another day.

What changes have occurred in the fifty-plus years since the original Computer Matching study was run! Instead of research on love and sexual desire being taboo, it is now ubiquitous. Today, a vast army of scholars from a daunting variety of theoretical disciplines – social psychologists, neuroscientists, cultural psychologists, anthropologists, evolutionary psychologists, sociologists, and historians – are all addressing (and answering) the same theoretical questions with which we once struggled. They are also employing an impressive array of new techniques as well. Primatologists are studying animals in the wild. Neuroscientists are pouring over fMRIs. Chemists are examining the chemical bases of love. Historians are now studying demographic data (birth and death records; records of marriage and divorce), architecture, medical manuals, church edicts, legal records, song lyrics, and the occasional private journal that floats to the surface. Love research is now a gargantuan and still-growing industry.

In the last half-century, society is finding new ways for people to meet potential romantic partners. From the innocent beginnings of the 1960s Computer Matching study and its peers, new and improved web sites offer more innovative opportunities. Whereas some sites – such as Match.com, e-Harmony, Zoosk, Badoo, and Tinder – are for the general population, other sites target special niches of the population. There are those designed to appeal to various age groups (HookUp .com, SilverSingles.com), political groups (ConservativeMatch.com, LiberalHearts.com), religious groups (CatholicSingles.com, Jdate .com, ChristianCafe.com, HappyBuddhist.com), and sexual orientation (GayWired.com, superEva.com). Social media (such as Muslima .com, Muslims4marriage.com, Meet IsraeliSingles.com) are flourishing even where forbidden – in the Middle East, for example. Dating sites also exist for people who possess mental and physical disabilities, unusual sexual preferences, and so forth. Even people who wish to find dates for themselves and their favorite pets can sign on to a site (DateMyPet .com). Currently, there are more than 8,000 dating websites servicing the world. What impact this Brave New World will have on the dating and mating habits of its citizens is a fascinating, unsettled, and unsettling question.

REFERENCES

Hatfield, E., Aronson, V., Abrahams, D., & Rottmann, L. (1966). The importance of physical attractiveness in dating behavior. *Journal of Personality and Social Psychology*, 4, 508–516.

Hatfield, E., Rapson, R. L., & Aumer-Ryan, K. (2008). Social justice in love relationships: Recent developments. *Social Justice Research*, 21, 413–431.

Sprecher, S., Schwartz, P., Harvey, J., & Hatfield, E. (2008). TheBusinessofLove .com: Relationship initiation at internet matchmaking services. In S. Sprecher, A. Wenzel, and J. Harvey (eds.), *Handbook of relationship initiation* (pp. 249–265). New York: Taylor & Francis.

Group and Cultural Processes

Deutsch, Morton

I have been much honored for my theoretical and research work in the following areas: cooperation and competition, conflict resolution, social justice, interdependence, psychological orientation, peace psychology, and prejudice. Much of this work was stimulated by my experiences in World War II, where I served in combat with the US Air Force. When I started my PhD graduate study at Kurt Lewin's Research Center for Group Dynamics (RCGD) at MIT in September 1945, I wanted to do work that would contribute to the development of a peaceful world.

Cooperation and Competition

At the time, I wondered whether the recently developed UN Security Council would be a cooperative or competitive group, and what the consequences would be of the two different types of functioning. Under the influence of the atmosphere at the RCGD and Lewin's dictum "There is nothing so practical as a good theory," I turned these questions into my dissertation research. This was a theoretical and research study on the different effects of cooperation and competition on the functioning of small groups. This study laid the foundation for much of my subsequent work in conflict resolution, social justice, and peace psychology.

My theory, in brief, distinguished two basic types of interdependence between people (groups, nations): *cooperative* (where people win or lose together) and *competitive* (where if one gains, the other loses). It also described three basic processes that would be affected differently by the two types of interdependencies: *substitutability* (where one party's actions can satisfy the intentions of another), *inducibility* (where one party can influence another), and *cathexis* (in which positive or negative attitudes are developed toward another). I hypothesized that cooperative interdependence would lead to positive substitutability, inducibility, and cathexis; while competitive interdependence would have negative effects on these variables. A second independent variable in our theory was type of action: *effective* or *ineffective*. The effective action facilitates the actor's goal attainment; ineffective action hinders it. The preceding statements about the effects of cooperative and competitive interdependence assume effective actions. With ineffective actions, cooperative interdependence becomes more like competitive interdependence and competitive interdependence becomes more like cooperative interdependence.

The research was conducted in small groups of five, who were students from a large introductory psychology course I was teaching at MIT. The cooperative groups were graded cooperatively (how well they did as a group); the competitive groups were graded in competition with one another. The members of the cooperative groups learned more than did the members of the competitive groups. This result led one of my students, David W. Johnson, to do much to further the development of cooperative education.

The results of the study supported my theoretical predictions. In the cooperative as compared to the competitive groups, communication among members was more informative and honest, there was a good sense of trust and warm personal relations, more readiness to help others and to enhance their power, more division of labor, and greater group productivity. The results also indicated that when conflicts occurred between members, they were resolved more constructively in the cooperative as compared to the competitive groups. This led to our study of conflict and negotiations and to the theory relating to conflict resolution.

The Resolution of Conflict

In many studies, my students and I investigated the question of what determines whether a conflict will take a constructive or destructive course. We used a variety of negotiating and bargaining solutions, as well as the Prisoner's Dilemma, with many different experimental variables. Our results essentially indicated that introducing a cooperative process into a conflict or negotiation situation typically led to a constructive ("win–win") resolution. The typical effects of a competitive process led to a destructive conflict resolution process. Since the typical effects of cooperative and competitive processes were known from our preceding research on cooperative and competitive processes, we had a theory of conflict resolution. This result was generalized into *Deutsch's Crude Law of Social Relations: The typical effects of a given social relation tend to induce that relation.*

Our work on conflict resolution has stimulated much further development of theory, research, and practice in this area. And, something I'm most proud of, in Poland the key negotiators for the Communist Party (Professor Reykowski) and for the Solidarity Movement (Professor Grzelek), who helped to negotiate the peaceful transfer of power from the Communist Government to the Solidarity Movement, have indicated that our work helped them to engage in a constructive process of conflict resolution.

Social Justice

Our work revealed that conflict often was related to social justice issues. And, as we pondered this area, it became clear that our earlier research on cooperation and competition was about two different principles of distributive justice. Stimulated by these thoughts, I began doing more systematic, theoretical, and research work on distributive justice. I began with a critique of the limitations of Equity theory, which was then the predominant theory of justice in social psychology. This was followed by a series of studies by my students and myself on the effects of different types of distributive systems ("winner takes all," "equity," "equality," and "need") as well as of factors affecting the choice among the different systems. Among the interesting findings were: (1) the use of an "equality" distribution was as task productive as the use of an "equity" or "merit" system of rewarding group members; and (2) the choice of a distributive system followed Deutsch's Crude Law of Social Relations. Thus, as in our studies of conflict resolution, the typical effects of a distributive system tend to induce that distributive system. I also wrote about the processes of awakening the sense of injustice and overcoming oppression.

Interdependence and Psychological Orientation

In one effort, I tried to describe the key dimensions of social relations and the psychological orientations associated with them. This was a means of going beyond the one-dimensional nature of my work on cooperation–competition. Five basic dimensions of social relations were included: cooperation–competition; power distribution; orientation to task or social relations; formal versus informal; and importance of the relationship. I indicated that different combinations of these five dimensions would require different psychological orientations. I suggested that a psychological orientation was composed of three kinds of orientation: cognitive, motivational, and moral. Thus, for example, the relationship between "lovers" compared with that of "prisoner and guard" differ systematically from each other, and the psychological orientation of the participants in the relationship must fit the type of relationship; otherwise, one or the other will change. I believe the ideas in this paper present an important, original framework for social psychology and require much additional work.

Peace Psychology

As indicated earlier, I always wanted my work in psychology to be useful in promoting peace. I believed my work on cooperation–competition, conflict resolution, and social justice was useful. This work led me to be active in writing various articles analyzing psychological factors promoting war and to co-edit a book on *Preventing World War III*. I also was very active in presenting my views to officials in government, to professional groups, and to the public.

Prejudice

The first study that I was involved in after obtaining my PhD was a comparative study of the effects of segregated and integrated public housing. This study helped lead to the desegregation of public housing and played a role in the US Supreme Court decision on Brown versus the Board of Education that made public segregation illegal. I was very active in the 1950s in discussing the results with public officials at professional meetings, and at public events.

Other Activities of Note

More recently, impelled by the potentially catastrophic consequences of climate change for the people who inhabit planet Earth, I have turned my attention to the social psychological factors involved in developing a global community and working with colleagues on a theoretical paper and a research study of attitudes toward actively participating in a global community.

Conclusion

Under the influence of my mentor, Kurt Lewin, I have mainly done theoretical and research work in areas that are central to all the social sciences: cooperation–competition, conflict resolution, and social justice. My work is very much indebted to the many outstanding doctoral students who were in my "work groups" as students. They were active participants in developing these areas.

Although my work was mainly in the laboratory, the work has had some important positive social impacts, due mainly to the contributions of former students and colleagues. Throughout my career I have also always tried to point out the important social implications of this work.

REFERENCES

Full references for works cited can be found here: http://icccr.tc.columbia.edu/wp
  -content/uploads/2012/05/Deutsch_Chapter_Making-a-Difference.pdf.
For suggested readings, see chapters 3, 4, and 5 in P.T. Coleman and M. Deutsch
  (2015). *Morton Deutsch: A Pioneer in Developing Peace Psychology.* New York:
  Springer.

84 The Collective Construction of the Self: Culture, Brain, and Genes

Kitayama, Shinobu

Early in the fall of 1982, I arrived in Ann Arbor from Japan as a new social psychology graduate student, and met Hazel Markus. She was on the University of Michigan faculty back then. Over the next five years, we frequently discussed cultural differences between her country (the United States) and mine (Japan). This conversation eventually culminated in a *Psychological Review* paper. We argued that many aspects of the East–West cultural variations in thinking and feeling, as well as in behavior, could be linked to cultural construals of the self as either independent (dominant in the United States) or interdependent (dominant in Japan). We reviewed a wide range of available evidence. Fortunately for us, the notion of independent and interdependent self-construal gained traction, not only on our home turf of social and cultural psychology, but also in a wide range of other fields, including cognitive psychology, marketing, organizational behavior, education, and, more recently, neuroscience and genetics.

In this essay, I would like to reflect on this development. In particular, I would like to highlight two lines of work I have done. The goal is to shed new light on future directions of the study of the human mind as biologically prepared and, yet, culturally completed.

What Was New?

At the highest level of abstraction, our proposal was analogous to some existing ideas in sociology, anthropology, and cross-cultural psychology. All these ideas, ours included, pertained to the ways in which social structures or cultural meaning systems are organized. Like all others, we also spent a lot of pages to delineate how collectively shared ideas and institutions could be patterned by the cultural models of independence and interdependence.

However, we went a step further by proposing that the cultural patterns and social structures are related to basic psychological processes. This means that the sociocultural is inherently intertwined with the psychological, including the nature of agency. The proposal to delineate this

400

interdependence, or mutual constitution, between culture and the self, in some empirically tractable fashion was new back then. It still is current today.

How Can the Self Be Collectively Constructed?

This idea of mutual constitution between culture and the self became a central obsession of mine during the 1990s. The idea seemed both intriguing and puzzling. There was some ring of truth. It seemed obvious that some aspects of our mind are influenced by culture and, conversely, that culture is a product of many such minds. But at the same time it seemed to me like a Zen dialogue – profound, but vague; deep, but convoluted; and seemingly true, but not clear why it matters. It was not at all obvious how all this could really work. How could the seamless whole of the mind-in-culture be dissected and deconstructed? Intrigued by these questions, we started out by translating the idea of mutual constitution of culture and the self into something more tangible and concrete.

It was already clear by then that self-esteem as assessed by a standard psychological scale was much higher for Americans than for Japanese. It thus seemed possible that Americans have a stronger tendency toward self-enhancement as compared with Japanese. That is, Americans might work harder than Japanese to focus on positive self-relevant information and to elaborate on it, instead of focusing on negative, self-threatening information. But why do Americans have such a strong tendency toward self-enhancement? The principle of mutual constitution would posit that this must be due to their culture. That is, American culture may foster and encourage the tendency of self-enhancement, whereas Japanese culture may not do so. But how can we know that this is the case?

To address this question, we tried something straightforward. We randomly sampled social situations common in both the United States and Japan and tested how people from these two cultural groups would respond to the situations that had been sampled in one or the other culture. We asked both Japanese and American undergraduates to write down as many situations as possible in which their self-esteem went up (i.e., success) or went down (i.e., failure). We then randomly selected 400 situations in total, with half of them from Japan and the remaining half from the United States. Moreover, half of the situations from each culture pertained to success experiences, and the remaining half pertained to failure experiences. We anticipated that the American-made situations and the Japanese-made situations would be quite different in the potential they offer to boost the self-esteem of someone who experiences the respective situations. We then had a new group of both Americans and Japanese read each situation and estimate the degree to which their self-esteem would increase or decrease.

The findings from this study fascinated us. Americans were highly self-enhancing, consistent with what was already known. That is, American respondents reported that their self-esteem would go up more in the success situations than it would go down in the failure situations. In contrast, Japanese were self-critical. They reported that their self-esteem would go down more in the failure situations than it would go up in the success situations. This latter finding is consistent with subsequent evidence that Japanese people are quite sensitive to negative information in part because they try to improve on short-comings. Most importantly, however, the cultural difference in the self-evaluative bias (self-enhancement versus self-criticism) was most pronounced when the respondents responded to the social situations that had been sampled from their own culture. Thus, it appears that the culture-typical response tendencies (i.e., self-enhancement and self-criticism for Americans and Japanese, respectively) are fostered or afforded by the ways social situations are defined in the respective cultural contexts.

In a very concrete, and tangible, fashion, the study illuminated how culture and the self could be mutually constitutive. I liked that. Americans (or Japanese) are self-enhancing (or self-critical) because social situations that are common in their culture foster this psychological tendency. Moreover, these situations are common in the United States (or Japan) precisely because Americans (or Japanese) are self-enhancing (or self-critical).

Cultural Neuroscience: Neuroplasticity, Social Learning, and Genes

The Kitayama et al. study showed one tangible way in which culture and the self could be mutually constitutive. Ultimately, however, it was not satisfactory. The study was limited because it dealt only with what individuals reported about them themselves. What about behaviors that could happen spontaneously or even unconsciously? More importantly, what about neural mechanisms underlying such behaviors? If culture is truly constitutive of the self or the mind, it should penetrate into the core of the mind. Whatever that core might be, it would include the brain. So, it occurred to us that it would be very useful to explore cultural differences with methods of neuroscience. Following some pioneers in this area, we employed an electroencephalogram (EEG) and tested cultural differences in several different domains. This work has helped create a new field known as cultural neuroscience.

What makes cultural neuroscience truly intriguing comes from a simple realization that the brain is a biological entity. The possibility that the brain could plastically change as a function of cultural experiences would suggest that the brain might have evolved so as to adapt to the environment humans themselves had created – namely, culture. The brain must now be capable of accommodating to this environment so that it can be functional in it, and, perhaps, only in it. There must have been certain genetic changes that facilitated the cultural accommodation and cultural learning. Given the fact that culture, as we know it today, has become an integral part of human existence rather recently (i.e., only during the last 10,000–50,000 years), it would stand to reason that these genetic changes must also have occurred in this same time period. If the field of cultural psychology looked at the question of mutual constitution between culture and the psyche, cultural neuroscience expanded the scope of the question exponentially because it aspired to address mutual influences between human culture and genes (and, most likely, gene expression).

Concluding Thought

Since my initial meeting with Hazel, my intellectual journey has taken some unexpected turns. An initial observation of cultural differences gave rise to the hypothesis of independent versus interdependent self-construal, which was used by many to motivate much of the work that is now collectively known as cultural psychology. In the meantime, we began asking how culture and the mind might be mutually and dynamically linked. One landmark in my mind was the situation-sampling study we discussed earlier. Our current effort in cultural neuroscience can be placed squarely in this context. It's hard to tell what unexpected turns this effort might bring to us. However, I remain optimistic that it will eventually bring about a better and more comprehensive understanding of what it is that makes us all truly human.

REFERENCES

Kitayama, S., King, A., Hsu, M., Liberzon, I., & Yoon, C. (2016). Dopamine-system genes and cultural acquisition: The norm sensitivity hypothesis. *Current Opinion in Psychology*, 8, 167–174. http://escholarship.org/uc/item/9p24k3n0#page-1.

Kitayama, S., Markus, H. R., Matsumoto, H., & Norasakkunkit, V. (1997). Individual and collective processes in the construction of the self: Self-enhancement in the United States and self-criticism in Japan. *Journal of Personality and Social Psychology, 72*(6), 1245–1267. http://doi.org/10.1037/0 022-3514.72.6.1245

Markus, H. R., & Kitayama, S. (1991). Culture and the self: Implications for cognition, emotion, and motivation. *Psychological Review, 98*(2), 224–253. http://doi:10.1037/0033-295X.98.2.224.

85 The Personal Is Political ... and Historical and Social and Cultural

Markus, Hazel Rose

The personal is political. As a college student deciding between a major in psychology or journalism, the statement stuck with me. I couldn't shake it. As a feminist, I knew it meant that questions of who should do the housework and childcare were not just women's personal problems but also societal problems of power and patriarchy. But as a young social psychologist, I sensed there was even more to this provocative statement. I came to see that the more you peer inside the personal, the more you discover not only the political and its twin, the economic, but also the historical and all forms of the social and cultural. And this, for me, was a central psychological insight.

What feels so personal – *my* identity, *my* subjectivity, *my* agency, *my* self, *my* I, or *my* me – is not just mine, not fully my own creation, and not just my private property. To be sure, my self requires genes, neurons, and hormones, but also my self belongs to others and rests in the eyes, minds, and actions of others, current, past, and future. Being is thus inherently social. Who we are, what we want, what we care about, what we are supposed to do, what moves us to action, what is possible for us is shaped by the cultural. For me, the cultural is an umbrella term that also covers the political, the economic, the historical, and the social. Specifically, culture is not just the symphony or the ballet or what we eat or how we worship; it includes all the institutions, interactions, and ideas that guide the thoughts, feelings, and actions of individuals. Individuals are born biological beings, but they become people only as they inhabit the many intersecting cultures that give form and meaning to their lives. Understanding selves and cultures and, as Rick Shweder says, the ways in they "make each other up" has been an ongoing theme of my research.

The self or the *me* at the center of experience is the sense of being a more or less enduring agent who acts and reacts to the world around and to the world within. It is the part of you that perceives, attends, thinks, feels, learns, imagines, remembers, decides, and acts. It is a story you are writing, whether you know it or not. If you lose the plot, you are in trouble. The self connects your present to your past and your future, and lets you know that the person who went to bed last night is the same one who woke up this morning. The self is also the all-important meaning maker.

In laboratory studies, I examined the self as a system of self-schemas or interpretive structures that help you make sense of your experiences and figure out what to do next. As these studies reveal, all that is self-relevant takes on a special glow. We quickly attend to, learn, and remember what is relevant to our needs, goals, and interests and ignore what is not. This means, as Anais Nin wrote, we don't see the world the way *it is*, but as the way *we are*. For psychologists who hope to know the mind and behavior of others, selves matter.

Understanding our selves in turn depends on understanding the many forms of culture crisscrossing our lives – those associated with nation, region, origin, gender, race, ethnicity, social class, sexual orientation, profession, sports team, birth cohort, and so on. These cultures help create different ways of being a self, and these selves, in turn, help create different cultures. Cultures are like water to the fish; they are often hard to experience unless someone takes them away. Understanding the ways in which the personal is deeply political, such that my *I* and my *me* was a European-American cultural product and process, began with trips to Japan and questions I traded with my long-time collaborator, social psychologist Shinobu Kitayama.

Why was it, I wondered, that after lecturing in Japan to students with a good command of English, no one said anything – nothing: no questions, no comments. What was wrong with these Japanese students? Where were the arguments, the debates, and the signs of critical thinking? And, moreover, if you asked somebody a completely straightforward question such as "Where is the best noodle shop?" why was the answer invariably, "It depends." Didn't Japanese students have their own preferences, ideas, opinions, and attitudes? What is inside a head if it isn't these kinds of things? How could you know someone if she did not tell you what she was thinking?

Shinobu listened and replied with his own questions. He was curious about why students shouldn't just listen to a lecture and asked why American students felt the need to be constantly active, to talk all the time, often interrupting each other and talking over each other and the professor? And why did the comments and questions of his American students and colleagues reveal such strong emotions and have such a competitive edge? What was the point of this arguing? Why did intelligence seem to be associated with getting the best of another person, even within a group where people knew each other well?

These questions about the peculiarities of everyday life in different cultural contexts led me first to see that my way of being a self was not *the* way to be a self, but *a* way to be a self, and that there were other viable ways to be a self, and finally to a theory of how different cultures reflect and foster different ways of being a self. I learned something about Japanese selves, but, most of all, I saw my own self and national culture in high relief. US cultural ideas, institutions, and interactions reflect and promote an *independent* model of self: a "good" self is a separate, stable, autonomous, free entity possessing a set of defining attributes – preferences, attitudes, goals – that guide behavior. I understood that standing out and expressing one's opinions and preferences was normative and appropriate – necessary, even – in the United States. In contrast, Japanese cultural ideas, institutions, and interactions reflect and promote an *interdependent* model of the self: a good self is a connected and flexible being, defined by relations to others and not fully separate from the social context. Listening, fitting in, being similar to others, adjusting to situations and the needs of others was normative and appropriate. At heart, independence is the sense of the self as a free agent, while interdependence is a sense of the self as an agent committed to significant relationships.

Both ways of being a self are necessary, often coexisting within the same person, but, depending on which self mediates a person's responses, behavior can differ. Researchers now have a good grasp of why the squeaky wheel gets the grease in the United States and why, in contrast, the duck that squawks the loudest gets shot in East Asia. We know, for example, that North Americans speak up more in schools and workplaces than their Asian American counterparts, that high parental expectations can have opposite motivational effects in Asian American and European-American families, that helping others is a moral obligation whether or not one likes a person in India but not in the United States, and that the brain's medial prefrontal cortex activates to judgments about the self in the United States, but to judgments about both self and one's mother in China.

Beyond the East–West divide, researchers also know that people in West African settings claim more enemies and fewer friends that those in North America, that Western Europeans are less likely than North Americans to associate happiness with personal achievement, that Latino dyads talk, smile, and laugh more than Black or White dyads, that Protestants are more likely than Jews to believe that people have control over their thoughts, that people from the US South respond with more anger to insults than do Northerners, and that working-class Americans are less concerned than middle-class Americans with having their choices denied. At the root of most of these differences is the question of whether cultures foster a relatively independent self or a relatively interdependent self.

Some independent American selves resist the idea the cultures shape selves. But this resistance is itself a product of a culture that makes and mirrors an independent self. The very idea of independence suggests that people should be free from the influence of others. Yet the notion of the independent self is not an empirically derived fact, but, instead, a philosophical and historical construction rooted in the idea of the authority of the individual – a product of Western enlightenment thinking, Christianity and the Protestant Ethic, the Declaration of Independence, the frontier, the American Dream, and all the institutions and interactions that continue to animate these ideas. Some believe that interdependence is a secondary, weaker, or compromised way of being. Yet outside the middle-class West, interdependence is the more familiar, practiced way of being a self. Until we understand how our culturally different ideas about how to be a self mediate our thoughts, feelings, actions, and interactions, we do not have a comprehensive psychology, but a partial and culture-specific psychology, grounded in the middle-class West.

So, the personal is political. Here I have sketched how the political can shape the personal. But because individuals are part of and actively construct their cultures, they are not slaves to them. They can trigger change at all levels of their cultures. As an example, acting independently is currently the most pervasive, promoted, valued, and psychologically beneficial style of behavior in the United States. Yet virtually of all society's pressing social challenges (e.g., environmental degradation and economic inequality) require that people recognize their shared fate and work together – to think and act interdependently. There is reason for optimism: those who desire change can claim their role in culture-making and promote more interdependence in the ideas, institutions, and interactions of their cultures. In this case, the personal can shape the political.

REFERENCES

Markus, H. (1977). Self-schemata and processing information about the self. *Journal of Personality and Social Psychology*, 35, 63–78.

Markus, H. R., & Conner, A. C. (2013). *Clash! Eight Cultural Conflicts that Make Us Who We Are*. New York: Penguin (Hudson Street Press). [Paperback (2014): Clash! How to Thrive in the Multicultural World (Plume)].

Markus, H., & Kitayama, S. (1991). Culture and the self: Implications for cognition, emotion, and motivation. *Psychological Review*, 98, 224–253.

Pinker, Steven

One of the delightful features of our field is that a man who wrote an undergraduate thesis on auditory perception, a doctoral thesis on visual imagery, two technical books on children's acquisition of syntax, and a series of monographs on the psychology of irregular verbs could name as his most important scientific contribution an analysis of the causes of war and peace, crime and safety, barbarism and humanity. This analysis appeared in my 2011 book *The Better Angels of Our Nature: Why Violence Has Declined.* The subtitle is about history, but the main title is defiantly psychological: it's about the components of human nature that inhibit us from causing physical harm.

It was easy to designate this book (and the papers I have written in its wake), as my most important contribution, because that's what the world has told me. It's been discussed by columnists, politicians, diplomats, generals, even a president and prime minister or two. Given the book's topic and message, this should not have been surprising. I wrote in its preface:

This book is about what may be the most important thing that has ever happened in human history. Believe it or not – and I know that most people do not – violence has declined over long stretches of time, and today we may be living in the most peaceable era in our species's existence . . .

No aspect of life is untouched by the retreat from violence. Daily existence is very different if you always have to worry about being abducted, raped, or killed, and it's hard to develop sophisticated arts, learning, or commerce if the institutions that support them are looted and burned as quickly as they are built.

The historical trajectory of violence affects not only how life is lived but how it is understood. What could be more fundamental to our sense of meaning and purpose than a conception of whether the strivings of the human race over long stretches of time have left us better or worse off? How, in particular, are we to make sense of *modernity* – of the erosion of family, tribe, tradition, and religion by the forces of individualism, cosmopolitanism, reason, and science? So much depends on how we understand the legacy of this transition: whether we see our world as a nightmare of crime, terrorism, genocide, and war, or as a period that, by the standards of history, is blessed by unprecedented levels of peaceful coexistence.

409

What led an experimental cognitive psychologist to write about the history and psychology of violence? The circuitous career path began with a drive to explain how children acquire language. That problem was put on the agenda of scientific psychology in the late 1950s by the linguist Noam Chomsky, who noted that it was a remarkable accomplishment of our species, and that any explanation must identify the innate mechanisms that make it possible. After having been familiarized with the data on children's language development by one of my graduate advisors, Roger Brown (who had pioneered the empirical study of children's language development in the 1960s), I attempted to meet Chomsky's challenge in my 1984 book *Language Learnability and Language Development*. And that, in turn, set off an unlikely cascade of questions that culminated, preposterously, in my interest in genocide, rape, torture, and world war.

The existence of innate circuitry dedicated to acquiring language raised the question of why our brains might have it, and the answer, I suggested, lay in Darwin's theory of natural selection as it applied to our brainy, social species. In *The Language Instinct* I argued that language was a biological adaptation for communication: for sharing information and coordinating behavior. The possibility that humans evolved with an adaptation for language then raised the question of what other adaptations we evolved with, and I tried to answer that question in *How the Mind Works*, a synthesis of cognitive science with evolutionary psychology which argued that the human mind is a system of organs of computation that evolved to help our ancestors outsmart objects, animals, plants, and each other.

The responses to *How the Mind Works* showed me that questions about human nature are not just scientific but moral, political, and emotional. Critics feared that if the mind is a rich system of adaptations, rather than a blank slate that is inscribed by parents, culture, and society, then hopes for social reform are futile (since flawed humans will screw their lives up no matter what), that inequality is written into our genes, that free will and moral responsibility will be shown to be mirages, and that life will be drained of meaning and purpose. I took on these reactions in yet another book, *The Blank Slate: The Modern Denial of Human Nature* (2002), which argued that the equation between a belief in human nature and fatalism about the human condition was spurious. Human nature is a complex system with many components. It comprises mental faculties that lead us to violence, but also faculties that pull us away from violence, such as empathy, self-control, and a sense of fairness. It also comes equipped with open-ended combinatorial faculties for language and reasoning, which allow us to reflect on our condition and figure out better ways to live our lives.

Not only does a robust conception of human nature make social improvement possible in principle, I argued, but social improvement is an undeniable fact, so any debate on whether it's possible is empirically moot. In both *How the Mind Works* and *The Blank Slate*, I presented several kinds of evidence that violence had declined over time. Then, in 2007, through a quirky chain of events, I was contacted by scholars in a number of fields who informed me there was far more evidence for a decline in violence than I had realized. Their data convinced me that the decline of violence deserved a book of its own. Not only were most people unaware that violence had declined (most of us, misled by mass media and the Availability Heuristic, believe the opposite), but *explaining* this massive and surprising decline posed a delicious challenge for a psychologist. Many of the historical declines are far too quick and recent to be explained by the generation-by-generation process of Darwinian natural selection. But it seemed to me that the synthesis of cognitive science, affective and cognitive neuroscience, social and evolutionary psychology, and other sciences of human nature that I explored in my previous books held the key. If the mind is a complex system of cognitive and emotional faculties which owe their basic design to the processes of evolution, then some of these faculties could very well incline us toward various kinds of violence, while others – "the better angels of our nature," in Abraham Lincoln's words – could incline us toward cooperation and peace. The way to explain the decline of violence is to identify the changes in our cultural and material milieu that have given our peaceable motives the upper hand.

Granted, writing a work of history (a field in which I had no formal training) seemed daunting to an experimental psychologist. But *Better Angels* concentrates on *quantitative* history: studies based on datasets that allow one to plot a graph over time. This involves the everyday statistical and methodological tools of social science, which I've used since I was an undergraduate – concepts such as sampling, distributions, time series, multiple regression, and distinguishing correlation from causation.

What's next? Though *Better Angels* was an account of the past and the recent present, not an extrapolation into the future (I certainly don't believe that violence will ever disappear), it's important to check whether I happened to catch the world in a coincidence of random fluctuations in violence that happened to hit bottom around 2010, or whether I was explaining a more systematic development. So, every year I update my datasets with the latest year's statistics. The most recent update (2015) suggests that the trends are indeed systematic. Of the many categories of violence I had plotted in the book, one of them – civil war – showed a bit of a reversal. The Syrian Civil War and other conflicts with Jihadist forces on one side had wiped out about twelve to fifteen years of progress in the seventy-year process by which wars all kind have been in decline. Even that reversal has left the world more peaceful than it was in the 1950s–1990s, to say nothing of the eras with world wars. And all the other major categories of violence continued their declines: interstate war, autocracy, homicide, rape, domestic violence, violence against children, capital punishment, hunting, even violence in sports.

The other question for the future is whether the decline of violence is a part of a more general process of human improvement, driven by advances in institutions that foster our better angels such as science, democracy, education, public health, and international organizations. The answer seems to be "yes." To my pleasant surprise, the historical decline of violence is just one part of a quantifiable improvement in the human condition. At the same time that our lives are becoming more peaceful, they are also becoming longer, healthier, richer, and smarter. In an age of dire predictions and gruesome headlines, it is the greatest story seldom told.

REFERENCES

Pinker, S. (2012). *The better angels of our nature: Why violence has declined.* New York: Penguin.

87   Focusing on Culture in Psychology

Triandis, Harry C.

When I started graduate school in 1954, culture was a peripheral topic in psychology. Most cross-cultural work consisted of verifying that the American findings of psychological science replicated in other cultures. When my career ended in 1997, culture had become an important factor in psychology. Thousands of publications now include data from many cultures. Of course, I was not the only one that contributed to this change. Many others made significant contributions. Some of these scholars told me that my work inspired theirs, and that was a most gratifying aspect of my career.

In my first year in graduate school I wrote to Charles Osgood and suggested that it would be desirable to replicate his work on the structure of affective meaning (evaluation, potency and activity) in a different culture. Since I came from Greece to study in North America (McGill University for my bachelor's, The University of Toronto for my master's, and Cornell University for my PhD degrees), it would be easy for me to collect the data in Greece. Osgood was enthusiastic, and we obtained a $5,000 grant for me to spend the summer of 1955 in Europe. Since I was in Greece anyway, I also collected the data to replicate the three dimensional structure of emotions that was found in the USA by Harold Schlosberg. Both the Osgood and Schlosberg findings were replicated in Greece and two articles reported the results in the *Journal of Abnormal and Social Psychology*, the best journal in social psychology at that time.

When I completed my degree in 1958 Osgood went to Lyle Lanier, the Head of the Psychology Department at the University of Illinois, and told him that I would be a good person to hire. Lanier hired me without meeting me.

Illinois was a marvelous place for a new psychologist to learn more about psychology. My colleagues were distinguished psychologists such as Ray Cattell, Lee Cronbach, Fred Fiedler, Lloyd Humphreys, Joe McVicker Hunt, William McGuire, Hobart Mowrer, Charles Osgood,

I thank Michael Bond, Susan Fiske, Michele Gelfand, Jim Georgas, Robert Sternberg, and Pola Triandis for valuable comments on earlier drafts.

and many others. I learned as much about psychology from them as I had in graduate school.

Fred Fiedler was asked by the Office of Naval Research if he was interested in researching the following problem: How can sailors become good-will ambassadors for the USA? Fred assembled a team: Osgood to study communication, Stolurow to study how information about culture can be put into computers so the sailors could learn about other cultures, and I was given the job of analyzing culture.

I went around the world in 1965 presenting lectures on the way psychological methods might be used to study culture. I also discussed how culture-comparable measures could be developed to analyze culture. The former was a controversial issue at that time. I was on a panel with Margaret Mead at the New York Academy of Sciences and Mead objected to the use of psychological methods instead of the usual fieldwork. I argued that both approaches are valuable and should cross-validate each other.

I identified collaborators in Japan (Yasumasa Tanaka), India (A. V. Shanmugam), and Greece (Vasso Vassiliou). Over the next three years we collected data from these cultures as well as from the United States, resulting in a book titled *The Analysis of Subjective Culture.*

One of the themes that emerged in that work was the contrast between individualistic cultures, such as those found in the West, and collectivist cultures, such as those found in East Asia and elsewhere. Over the following years I was involved in much empirical work to determine the meaning of these constructs, the best way to measure them, and how they emerge when the data are correlated across cultures as opposed to across individuals. Individualism and collectivism emerge when the mean responses of individuals to many items, across many cultures, are correlated. When the data on those items are correlated within a culture and across individuals, one obtains personality differences, with *allocentrics* behaving the way people in collectivist cultures behave, and *idiocentrics* behaving the way people in individualist cultures behave. A good fit between culture and personality (e.g., allocentrics in collectivist cultures) results in good mental health, while a poor fit (e.g., allocentrics in an individualist culture), results in poor mental health. Michele Gelfand and I summarized this topic in the 2012 *Handbook of Social Psychological Theories,* edited by P. A. M. Van Lange, A. W. Kruglanski, and E. T. Higgins. We also discussed numerous situational and demographic factors that increase the probability that a sample of individuals will be individualist or collectivist. For example, social class is relevant: The upper classes in most societies are more individualist than the lower classes, so that a sample from a collectivist culture may be idiocentric.

Over the years we examined many other dimensions of cultural variation, such as tight versus loose cultures (cultures where norms are imposed tightly, and where deviations from these norms are punished severely; Michele Gelfand has published extensively on that dimension), and horizontal versus vertical cultures (cultures that emphasize equality vs. hierarchy).

There are also combinations of these dimensions. For instance, horizontal collectivist cultures, such as the Israeli kibbutz, are different from vertical collectivist cultures such as one finds in India, where caste leads to much hierarchy. Horizontal individualist cultures, such as Sweden and Australia, are different from vertical individualist cultures, such as one finds in the USA and in academia. In Sweden one must avoid "sticking out." In academia one must shine.

In 1976 I was asked to edit the *Handbook of Cross-Cultural Psychology*. After it appeared (1980–1981, in six volumes), Lee Cronbach said that I had started a new subfield of psychology.

After retiring in 1997, I spent my time reviewing journal articles. But 9/11/2001 had a profound effect on me, because I read in the *New York Times* that Mohammed Atta, the chief terrorist, had a *Manual for the Raid* in his luggage that described his action as "God's work." I wanted to know how killing 3,000 innocent people might be construed as God's work. For the next six years I studied the world's religions, and concluded that we humans have a tendency to see the world the way we want it to be rather than the way it is. So I wrote *Fooling Ourselves: Self-Deception in Politics, Religion, and Terrorism*. This book received the William James Award of Division 1 of the American Psychological Association. There I argue that "good" cultures are those that promote four criteria:

1. Good health (both physical and mental),
2. Well-being (satisfaction with life and happiness),
3. Longevity, and
4. The protection of the environment.

No culture does a good job on all those criteria, and cultures whose members are high in self-deception are especially poor in meeting them. In that book I discuss the factors that lead to the maximization of the four criteria, and one of the most important ones is that we should help as many others as possible to reach those criteria. That is an immense task, and it is unlikely that we can succeed, but it is good for us to have a lofty goal that will "stretch" us, and give benefit to others and to society.

The motivation for studying culture came from my experience: I came from one culture and lived in another, and I could see that the way culture works has its own logic. Ecology (climate, geography, economic system, political system) generates culture, and since ecologies differ, cultures differ. I got the idea of studying self-deception when I realized how much self-deception there is in politics (e.g., President G. W. Bush: "Iraq has weapons of mass destruction"), religion (e.g., Osama bin Laden: "the whole world will become Islamic and I will be the Caliph"), and terrorism (the "martyr" thinks he is going to paradise, but that is a self-deception).

Looking back, what do I consider my most important contribution? Was it the work on culture or the work on self-deception? My biased opinion is that it was the latter. However, all objective indices, such as citation counts, textbook pages covered, and number of awards, indicate that it was the former. Posterity must decide . . .

Does the work on culture matter for psychology? Yes, because culture is an important factor in the way we perceive the world, and it determines our cognitions, emotions, and behaviors. The world is better by having a more accurate psychology that takes culture into account. Does the work on self-deception matter? I think that if we are to succeed in fighting the jihadists we need to know how their self-deceptions influence their actions.

What work do I want to see in the future? I think the most exciting work now is in brain science, and there are already discoveries that link culture with that work. For example, collectivists differ from individualists in the distribution of some genes and the way their brains operate. Much more will be discovered in these areas. The work on self-deception will examine how culture influences its members' self-deceptions. Some cultures are extremely susceptible to self-deception and other cultures are not. Discovering the factors that result in this difference would be most interesting.

In sum, culture is essential to psychology and our planet's future; exciting work remains to be done!

Part VII

Clinical and Health Psychology: Making
Lives Better

Section A

Stress and Coping

88 Psychological Stress, Immunity, and Physical Disease

Cohen, Sheldon

I received my doctorate in social psychology in 1973 and began my career studying the effects of environmental stressors, such as aircraft and traffic noise, on children's cognition and behavior. In the 1980s, I became interested in the role of stress in physical health, particularly through its effects on the immune system. To pursue my new interest, I needed to expand my knowledge base. I convinced the National Institutes of Health to provide me with support to train in immunology, endocrinology, and virology. Questions I planned to address included: Does stress influence the immune system's ability to fight off infectious disease? What types of stressful events put people at risk for getting sick? How does stress influence the immune system to increase vulnerability to disease?

During the next few years, my laboratory and others found that experiencing stressful events (e.g., death of a loved one, taking an important exam); feeling stressed, anxious, or depressed; and performing stressful tasks in the laboratory all were associated with poorer functioning of the immune system. Immune measures used in these studies were primarily tests of the ability of immune cells drawn from participants' blood samples to respond to foreign (non-self) substances. It was unclear whether these stress-associated immune changes observed *in laboratory petri dishes* represented the type or magnitude of change necessary to influence the body's ability to fight infection.

Does Stress Influence the Immune System's Ability to Resist Infectious Disease?

In 1985, I traveled to Great Britain to meet with Dr. David Tyrrell, a physician and virologist who headed the British Common Cold Unit (CCU) in Salisbury. The CCU was founded just after World War II with the mission of learning the causes of, and developing a cure for, the common cold.

I convinced David to collaborate on a study investigating whether stress plays a role in people's ability to resist infection and illness. Between 1986 and 1989, we collected data from more than 400 healthy

419

volunteers, using questionnaires to measure the number of recent major stressful life events (e.g., death of spouse, job loss), perceived stress (perception that demands on them exceed their ability to cope), and negative emotions (e.g., anxiety, depression). Subsequently, through nasal drops, we exposed each volunteer to one of five viruses that cause a common cold, and then we followed them in quarantine at the CCU for six days to see if they developed colds. A cold was defined as both being infected (study virus replicates in the body and is found in nasal secretions) and showing symptoms of illness. Overall, about one-third of exposed participants developed a cold. We found that the more stress participants reported (on any of the stress measures), the greater the likelihood that they developed a cold when later exposed to a cold virus.

In this and subsequent studies, we measured stress *in healthy participants before they were exposed to a virus.* Consequently, we could rule out the possibility that either existing illness or developing a cold in our study caused participants to report more stress. Moreover, we were able to measure and eliminate (through statistical adjustment) other explanations for our findings, such as heightened stress and disease susceptibility both being caused by participant age, education, sex, weight, height, or pre-existing immunity (antibody level) to the experimental virus.

Budgetary constraints resulted in the CCU closing in 1990. Nevertheless, we were able to continue our work because one of the five remaining laboratories in the world that conducted viral exposure studies with human participants was located in Pittsburgh, where I lived and worked.

What Types of Stressful Events Put People at Risk for Getting Sick?

In the first Pittsburgh study, instead of stress questionnaires, we used a life-event *interview* that identified each individual's most stressful life event, the *type of event* (e.g., interpersonal, educational, financial), and *how long it lasted.* After the interview, we exposed each of 276 participants to one of two viruses that cause a cold, and then monitored them in quarantine. We found that the *longer* participants' most stressful event lasted, the greater their probability of getting sick following viral exposure. Moreover, the types of events that were most predictive of colds were *enduring interpersonal problems* and being *under- or unemployed.*

How Does Stress Influence the Immune System to Increase Vulnerability to Disease?

In the Pittsburgh study, we also tested whether stress predicted increased risk of disease because of its possible associations with elevated levels of "stress" hormones (epinephrine, norepinephrine, cortisol), poorer immune function (measured by *in vitro* assays), or poor health practices such as smoking, excessive alcohol consumption, poor diets, low levels of physical activity, and poor sleep. Contrary to expectations, none of these (alone or together) explained why stress was associated with greater risk of developing a cold.

New insights about the function of the immune system provided another possibility to explore. Chemicals called pro-inflammatory cytokines are released by the immune system in response to infections. These chemicals elicit an inflammatory response, drawing immune cells to the infected area to help orchestrate the immune defense against the infectious agent. However, if the immune system produces *too much* of these inflammatory chemicals, the results can be toxic. In the case of infection with a common cold virus, producing too much pro-inflammatory cytokine triggers cold symptoms, such as nasal congestion and runny nose.

In 1999, we published a study that established the role of inflammation in the link between stress and colds. We measured perceived stress by questionnaire and then exposed participants to a cold virus. Following viral exposure, we measured how much pro-inflammatory cytokine was produced in participants' nasal secretions. We found that participants reporting high levels of stress both produced high levels of these inflammatory chemicals and, in turn, experienced more symptoms.

These results raised a dilemma for us. Acute stress exposures in the laboratory and natural settings had been found to *increase* circulating levels of cortisol, a glucocorticoid hormone which *normally reduces inflammation* by turning-down the release of pro-inflammatory cytokines. Yet even though acute stress was associated with increased cortisol (and hence would presumably decrease cytokine release), we found that people who suffered from chronic stress produced more, not less, pro-inflammatory cytokine. In response to this apparent contradiction, we hypothesized that when people are exposed to major stressful events over a prolonged period, their bodies adapt to the initial increase in cortisol by reducing immune cell responsiveness to cortisol (a process called glucocorticoid resistance). As cells become less responsive, the body loses the ability to turn down the inflammatory response.

We began testing this hypothesis by examining whether chronic stress in humans was associated with reduced responsiveness to cortisol.

In a paper published in 2002, we identified a population that was experiencing an intense and chronic stressful event – parents of children with cancer – and compared them to similar non-stressed parents of healthy children. As expected, when we added a synthetic cortisol-like glucocorticoid, dexamethasone, to blood samples from parents of healthy children, it reduced their immune cells' ability to produce inflammatory chemicals. However, adding dexamethasone to blood samples from parents of cancer patients was relatively ineffective in reducing the production of these chemicals. That is, immune cells in chronically stressed parents were insensitive to the regulatory effects of this cortisol-like glucocorticoid.

Finally, in two studies published in 2012, we tested the implications of stress-elicited insensitivity to cortisol for susceptibility to disease. We found that interpersonal stressful events lasting a month or longer were associated with a decrease in immune cells' sensitivity to cortisol. In turn, less sensitivity to cortisol was associated with both greater production of pro-inflammatory cytokines in response to being infected by a cold virus, and with a greater risk for developing a cold.

In sum, in over 30 years of research, we found that psychological stress increases the risk of developing a common cold for those exposed to a cold virus; that long-lasting stressors, interpersonal stressors, and unemployment are particularly potent; that the association between stress and disease occurs because chronic stress interferes with the body's ability to turn off the immune system's production of inflammatory chemicals; and that this failure in regulation (maintaining a proper level) of immune response occurs because chronic stress results in immune cells becoming insensitive to cortisol.

What Are the Implications of This Research?

This work provides a broad psychobiological model of how stress influences health. It supports work by our lab and others on the importance of interpersonal and socioeconomic stressors, and the potent and unique effects of chronic stressful events. It also highlights that effects of enduring stress on health may not be driven by stress suppressing immune function, as we believed in the 1980s, but instead by stress interfering with the ability to *turn off* immune response when it is no longer needed.

Our demonstration of a relationship between stress and susceptibility to infectious disease has played an influential role in the medical community's increasing acceptance of the importance of psychological stress in health. Moreover, the hypothesis that chronic stress effects occur because immune cells become resistant to cortisol regulation is central to current understanding of how chronic stress influences risk for and progression of a broad range of diseases (e.g., heart disease, autoimmune diseases, diabetes) where inflammation plays an important role.

REFERENCES

Cohen, S., & Herbert, T. B. (1996). Health Psychology: Psychological factors and physical disease from the perspective of human psychoneuroimmunology. *Annual Review of Psychology, 47,* 113–142.

Cohen, S., Janicki-Deverts, D., & Miller, G. E. (2007). Psychological stress and disease. *Journal of the American Medical Association, 298,* 1685–1687.

89   A Goldilocks Idea: Not Too Big, Not Too Small, Just Right

Folkman, Susan

When we think about emotions that characterize psychological stress, we are likely to name negative emotions such as sadness, anxiety, and fear. During most of the twentieth century, positive emotions were essentially dismissed as unimportant or irrelevant, especially in relation to psychological stress.[1]

Despite their low status, I have had a long-standing curiosity about positive emotions and whether they have any role in the stress process. I can't say exactly when I first thought about this question, but it was on my mind by the time I began my doctoral work with Richard Lazarus in 1975.

Professor Lazarus – or Dick, as he preferred to be called – was the author of a theoretical framework for the study of psychological stress that remains the foundation for much of the research in the field today. I joined Dick as co-author of an updated and expanded version of the theory in *Stress, Appraisal, and Coping*, published in 1984.

One of the central tenets of the theory is that stress is a dynamic process influenced by cognitive appraisals through which the individual determines whether ongoing interactions with the environment are relevant to valued goals, whether there are options for controlling interactions that have been or are potentially harmful to those goals, and, if so, whether the resources for controlling their outcomes are available.

Emotions are a part of the stress process from start to finish. Emotions express the nature of the appraisal at the outset of a stressful encounter – whether the situation signals harm or threat, or perhaps an opportunity for mastery and gain. Emotions also reflect changes in the stressful circumstances as the situation unfolds. And emotions are regulated by coping processes, especially when emotion intensity interferes with problem solving.

Although stress and coping research has typically focused on negative emotions, we did develop a few ideas about positive emotions while I was still a graduate student. We proposed, for instance, that such emotions

[1] Emotion, mood, and affect are used interchangeably throughout this chapter.

424

could help restore psychological and physical resources by providing a break from distress. The chapter disappeared into relative obscurity for about fifteen years and then was rediscovered as the new field of positive psychology began to take hold in the late 1990s.

In 1988 I moved from the University of California, Berkeley, to the University of California, San Francisco (UCSF). There I talked with Dr. Tom Coates, a psychologist who, with a colleague, had just established a center for AIDS behavioral research at UCSF. The HIV/AIDS epidemic was raging and no viable treatments were in sight. Tom suggested that I might want to pursue my coping research by studying people with HIV/AIDS. The idea was compelling, but I modified Tom's suggestion slightly. I asked, "What about studying the partner/caregivers of the men with AIDS instead?" People with HIV/AIDS were already being enrolled in many studies, and the clinical course of their disease would probably overwhelm any secondary effects. By contrast, little attention was being directed to their caregiving partners. Tom agreed. That single conversation shaped the course of my research for the next twelve years.

Many factors contributed to the stress experienced by the caregivers of men with HIV/AIDS. First, caregivers were in their thirties and forties, ages when people are typically building relationships and careers, not providing care to a partner who is terribly sick and likely to die. Second, many gay men had already experienced stigma because of their sexual orientation. Now they also had to deal with AIDS-related stigma. Third, the clinical course of HIV was horrific, moving from one opportunistic infection to another, each occurrence presenting both the infected partner and his caregiver with new and often more complex demands for skilled nursing care, psychological support, and physical stamina. Finally, many of these caregivers were themselves infected with HIV, although not yet diagnosed with AIDS. In effect, these caregivers were witnessing what lay ahead for them. With support from the National Institute of Mental Health, in 1989 we began a longitudinal study with 314 gay men that included HIV-positive caregivers, HIV-negative caregivers, and HIV-positive partners of healthy (HIV-negative) men.

Nearly half the caregivers experienced the death of their partners during their first two years in the study. We expected and found high levels of distress, depressive symptoms, and anxiety in these caregivers, with some tapering in years three through five. The pattern was very similar to patterns of distress observed in conjugal bereavement.

We also included two measures of positive affect – one that measured mood, and another that measured psychological states of well-being. I wasn't sure what to expect, and I was right to be unsure: Although caregivers reported lower frequencies of positive mood in the months before and after the death of their partners than did non-caregivers, the frequency of their positive mood was actually comparable to the frequency of their negative mood. The only significant bifurcation was at the time of the partner's death, when distress peaked. Even then, participants reported experiencing some positive mood during the previous week. And with respect to the measure of positive states of mind, scores were similar to those in the general population except during the weeks immediately surrounding the partner's death, at which time they dropped a bit, but only for a short time.

These findings were also true of the group I had thought would be at greatest psychological risk – caregivers who were also HIV-positive. They could see what lay ahead for them, and they knew it was likely to be nightmarish. Yet their psychological states were no worse than those of their HIV-negative counterparts.

When I first presented these findings at conferences, several people commented that these data were from the San Francisco gay community, and as one audience member commented sarcastically, "We all know they are on drugs." So I asked a colleague in Nova Scotia if she would add our measures to a study she was conducting with parents of children with serious illness. Not surprisingly, though her participants were clearly heterosexual and lived across the continent on the east coast, the same pattern was revealed. We also discovered that other researchers had observed positive affect in people dealing with profound stress, such as the death of a child or a spouse, but the findings had not been pursued.

The positive and negative emotions reported in our study did not appear to be two sides of the same coin. Except during the weeks immediately before and after the partner's death, positive and negative mood were only weakly or moderately correlated, suggesting that the causes of positive and negative mood tended to differ.

Years of research on coping with stressful situations had given us a good understanding of coping strategies, such as distraction or distancing, that regulate distress. But, with a few exceptions, the coping strategies that regulated distress here were weakly correlated with positive emotions.

We collected narratives about participants' recent stressful events in every interview. Unlike most caregiver studies, in which participants tend to be elderly and often reticent or limited in their ability to speak, the participants in this research were mostly in young middle age, well educated, and comfortable talking about their experiences. In their narratives we found that positive emotions were often expressed when their stories touched on underlying values and goals that brought meaning to the moment. For example, an acknowledgment by the ill partner that he really appreciated the care his partner was providing was interpreted as an affirmation of their shared love. Completing a challenging medical procedure such as wound cleansing was interpreted by the caregiver as evidence of his increasing clinical skill. These experiences were imbued with personal meaning that created positive affect – if only momentarily – in the caregiving partner.

Today the neuroscience of emotion has captured the attention of many investigators in both stress and emotion research. While this new field is providing exciting insights into emotions and the brain, it will not provide all the answers regarding the origins of positive emotions during stressful encounters, the extent to which they are protective of mental and physical health, and their social and psychological sequelae during and following stressful periods. These themes need to be pursued.

Three reasons motivated my decision to write about findings on positive emotion for this essay:

- First, the story illustrates the importance of being open to findings that challenge the status quo, such as finding positive emotion in the midst of intense stress. Sometimes the unexpected findings contain gold.
- Second, the ideas lead directly to practical application. Physicians and other health care professionals often comment: "Interesting findings, but how will they help me do my job? How will they help my patients?" Happily, our findings can shift our efforts from the often frustrating task of trying to minimize distress that is a response to loss, harm, or threat, to leveraging normally occurring positive emotions that emerge during prolonged stressful periods. We can learn to be aware of those moments and how to get the most benefit from them whenever distress is on the rise.
- Third, while the work my colleagues and I have done over the past several decades addressed important theoretical and methodological issues, I chose to discuss the findings on positive emotion in this essay simply because they are a lot more fun to talk about, and because ... they are not too big nor too small, but just right for a chapter of this length.

REFERENCES

Folkman, S. & Moskowitz, J. T. (2000). Positive affect and the other side of coping. *American Psychologist, 55,* 647–654.

Lazarus, R. S., Kanner, A., & Folkman, S. (1980). Emotions: A cognitive-phenomenological analysis. In R. P. H. Kellerman (ed.), *Theories of emotion* (pp. 189–216). New York: Academic Press.

Section B

Understanding Mental Disorders

90   Why Study Autism?

Frith, Uta

I first met autistic children as a trainee clinical psychologist, and I was captivated for life. I thought them hauntingly mysterious. How could they do jigsaw puzzles straight off, and yet never respond to my simple requests to play with them? What was going on? How could they be tested? Here was a challenge that cried out for basic research.

My mentors, Beate Hermelin and Neil O'Connor, knew how to do elegant experiments with children who hardly had any language and were more than a little wild. I was elated when they offered to supervise me, and I got my dream job in their lab after I finished my PhD. I was hooked on the experimental study of cognitive abilities and disabilities in young children with autism and I wanted to know how they differed from other children. One of the innovations that O'Connor and Hermelin had introduced me to was the mental-age match. They argued that comparing bright and intellectually impaired children would get us nowhere. The brighter would do better, and this told us nothing that we didn't know already. Instead, they compared, say, eight-year-old children who on psychometric tests had a mental age of four, with four-year-old, typically developing children with a mental age of four.

I was proud of one memory experiment I did during my apprenticeship as a PhD student. We observed that autistic children often had a remarkable facility in remembering words by rote. This allowed us to compare autistic and non-autistic children who had the same short-term memory span. What we found gave me a key insight: Typically developing children could remember many more words when these words were presented in the form of sentences than if the same words were presented in a jumbled up fashion, but autistic children failed to show this advantage. I followed up this finding in experiments with binary sequences with clear structure, such as abababab, versus those without, such as aababaaa. The results suggested that structure or "meaning" allowed stimuli to be packaged into bigger units and thereby extended memory span. Did autistic children not see meaning in the way other children did, I wondered? Did meaning not exert the same dynamic force in their information processing?

431

This question occupied me for a long time. Some years later, it became a theory that I termed "weak central coherence." Briefly, the information we process is usually pulled together by a strong drive to cohere. We like things to make sense, we like a narrative, we like the big picture. In autism, I proposed, this drive is less strong. The downside is that individuals with autism do not see the forest for the trees. But there is also an upside: Not being hampered by a strong drive for central coherence could actually give you far better attention to detail. You are not lured away by an overall Gestalt to forget about its constituents, and you won't fall prey to certain perceptual illusions. For the first time, here was a way to think about autism not just in terms of disabilities, but also in terms of special talents.

As I was developing this idea, I was worried that in all our experiments we were missing the social features of autism. My search for a glitch in processing social information would have been a hopeless quest, had it not been for Alan Leslie and Simon Baron-Cohen. Alan had asked the exciting question how young infants were able to understand pretend play while they were still learning about the real world. How on earth could they distinguish which was what? This reminded me of a finding nobody had paid much attention to: Autistic children show little, if any, pretend play. Alan proposed a cognitive mechanism that could underpin the ability to decouple representations of an event so that they could become second-order representations. They could then be freely embedded into an agent's mental states: the agent can wish, pretend, or believe the original event. Could it be that the decoupling mechanism was missing in autistic individuals? In that case, they should not be able to understand that another person can have a false belief.

Why should this matter? Beliefs and other mental states, such as pretense, wishes, and knowledge, are what enable us to predict what others are going to do. We don't predict this on the basis of the physical state of affairs. So, John will open his umbrella because he believes it is raining, regardless of whether it is actually raining. Tracking mental states is grist to the mill of our everyday folk psychology, also known as Theory of Mind. To be able to talk about this ability, we coined a new word: *mentalizing*.

Simon, Alan, and I were excited to find out more about this ability. One of the tasks we developed was the Sally Ann task. It is played out with two dolls, Sally and Ann. Sally has a marble and puts it in her basket. She then leaves the scene. While she is out, Ann takes the marble from the basket and puts it into her box. Sally comes back and wants to play with her marble. The critical question is: "Where will she look for the marble?" The right answer is, of course, "in the basket," because that is where she believes it is.

The results amazed us, as they were so clear cut: Typical four-year-olds and older learning disabled children passed this task, while autistic children didn't. They had failed to understand that Sally had a false belief and therefore made the wrong prediction of where she was going to look. This and other experiments threw new light on the social communication problems in autism: If you don't understand mental states, then you wouldn't understand deception, nor would you get the point of most jokes. You wouldn't get the point of keeping secrets, nor would you understand any narratives that depended on "she doesn't know that he knows" scenarios. It would limit ordinary social interactions in just the way that interactions with autistic people are limited.

With the advent of the new neuroimaging methods, we could now try to visualize this cognitive mechanism in the brain. One of the pioneers in neuroimaging was my husband, Chris Frith, and he and his colleagues were sufficiently interested to set up a then still daring series of studies. We designed stories, cartoons, and animated triangles, which could be presented in carefully matched conditions, which either did or did not require mentalizing. This difference allowed us to see a difference in brain activity in several critical brain regions, forming a mentalizing network. Other labs were able to replicate this.

One disappointment was that we could not immediately see what was different in the brains of autistic people during mentalizing. But to unravel this required many studies by many people in many different labs. This led us to a better understanding of mentalizing, and has already resulted in differentiating two forms: an apparently innate and unconscious form, and an acquired conscious form that is influenced by culture. This second form can be acquired by autistic people through compensatory learning.

Is there a lesson from my studies beyond the world of autism? I believe that the studies have demonstrated the usefulness of the cognitive level of explanation. The purely behavioral level is not sufficiently transparent for us to deduce the underlying causes; there are just too many. But, we can predict what behaviors might arise if a particular cognitive process were faulty. This was the point of the Sally Ann test: Nobody before had observed that autistic children failed to understand false beliefs. The beauty of this result was that it suddenly made sense of a range of hitherto unconnected behavioral observations, such as the poverty of pretend play, the inability to tell lies, and the incomprehension of irony.

Our concept of autism has changed enormously since the 1960s. There are likely to be many different phenotypes hidden in the autism spectrum. It is now time to split up subgroups and relate specific cognitive processes to specific causes, in the brain and in characteristic patterns of behavior.

Mentalizing is not all there is to being social. There are other cognitive processes that underpin our social behavior that might be faulty and give rise to different problems and possibly different forms of autism. We simply need the right theoretical glasses to see differences in the spectrum, which are now blurred. Whether these subgroups conveniently map onto specific biological causes is another question. It is likely that there are hundreds of genetic and other biological causes, too many to make meaningful subgroups. At the behavioral level, each individual is in a class of his or her own. In contrast, at the cognitive level, there is a nexus, which might hold a manageable handful of phenotypes. My money is on cognition.

REFERENCES

Frith, U. (1989, 2003 [2nd edn.]) *Autism: Explaining the enigma.* Oxford: Wiley Blackwell.

Frith, U. (2012) Why we need cognitive explanations of autism. *Quarterly Journal of Experimental Psychology, 65*(11), 2073–2092.

Frith, U., Morton, J., & Leslie, A. (1991) The cognitive basis of a developmental disorder. *Trends in Cognitive Sciences, 14*(10), 433–438.

Gotlib, Ian H.

Have you ever been depressed? Not just sad or despondent for a few days – I mean *really* depressed, where you can't get out of bed, don't want to see people, feel like you'll never recover from feeling as badly as you do. Like everyone else, I've had times when I've been down, but for me such times have passed quickly. But I've known many strong, effective people who have been tortured for weeks or months by a sadness and hopelessness that seemed difficult to fathom. I wanted to understand why some people snap out of these feelings while others succumb to the debilitating condition we call clinical depression. In this chapter, therefore, I briefly describe my involvement in what I believe are two significant scientific contributions: adapting experimental cognitive paradigms to assess cognitive functioning in depression, and integrating psychological and biological assessments to elucidate mechanisms underlying the intergenerational transmission of risk for depression.

Information-Processing Approaches to Understanding Cognitive Functioning in Depression

At the time I became interested in trying to understand the causes and consequences of depression, in the mid-1970s and early 1980s, most psychologists were using self-report measures to characterize the functioning of depressed adults. Aaron Beck had just formulated his cognitive theory of depression, positing that depressed individuals have a negative view of themselves, their world, and the future. And indeed, when filling out self-report questionnaires assessing cognitions, depressed participants indicated that they had negative thoughts, apparently confirming Beck's theory. But it seemed to me that that this conclusion might be based on something known as "common method variance"; that is, people who were reporting negative behaviors and affect in an interview that got them diagnosed as depressed were also reporting negative cognitions on a questionnaire ("I feel bad and I'll tell you that on every measure you give me").

Starting with a collaboration with Doug McCann (now a professor at York University), and continuing more recently with Jutta Joormann (now a professor at Yale University), I began to adapt tasks and paradigms developed by experimental cognitive psychologists to circumvent the problems inherent in the use of self-report questionnaires to assess cognitive content and processes. We began by modifying the Stroop task (trying to quickly name the ink color in which different color names are presented, such as the word "RED" presented in blue ink) to include emotional words presented in different colors. We reasoned that if Beck was correct, depressed individuals would be "primed" to attend to negative stimuli, and the content of the negative words on this Emotional Stroop Task would interfere with the competing task of naming the colors of these words. That is precisely what we found: Depressed people were slower to name the colors of negative words. This was the first application of experimental paradigms to understand the cognitive-emotional functioning of depressed persons.

Since that study was published in the mid-1980s, we have extended our use of experimental tasks to obtain a more precise understanding of the cognitive functioning of depressed individuals. We developed and adapted tasks to assess attentional capture of negative stimuli for depressed persons, as well as their (in)ability to remove negative material from working memory. In fact, this particular impairment in depressed individuals' ability to expel negative information from working memory is a nice "cognitive psychology" example of the clinical phenomenon of rumination – the difficulty experienced by depressed people of stopping unwanted thoughts from recurring. Our studies in this area have led us to posit that the attention of depressed individuals is captured "automatically" by negative material or stimuli; once captured, this negative information stays in their memory because depressed people cannot remove it. It then continues to further guide their attention to additional congruent negative material, increases the intensity of their negative affect, and hinders depressed individuals' ability to use positive stimuli to repair or reduce this negative affect, thereby prolonging their depressive episode.

At the same time that we were conducting these studies, neuroscientists were beginning to make breakthroughs in assessing patterns of brain activation as people engaged in various tasks in the scanner, a method known as functional magnetic resonance imaging (fMRI). We saw this as an opportunity to gain an even more comprehensive understanding of the functioning of depressed persons, examining neural activations in depressed individuals as they viewed and processed negative stimuli in the scanner. Working with John Gabrieli (now a professor at MIT), we were among the first to demonstrate that depressed people activate limbic structures, such as the amygdala and subgenual anterior cingulate cortex, to a greater extent than non-depressed people do when they view negative stimuli; moreover, excitatory patterns of activation between these limbic structures and the medial prefrontal cortex, an area of the brain involved in self-referential processing, help to explain the strength and pervasiveness of rumination in depression.

Psychobiological Mechanisms Underlying the Intergenerational Transmission of Risk for Depression

A second area of research in which I believe my collaborators and I have made a significant contribution to the field involves our understanding of risk factors for the development of depression. Many more scientists were studying how to *treat* depression, when I believed we should be working to understand how to *prevent* this disorder. And that means trying to identify risk factors for the development of depression, such as having a family history of the disorder. Since the 1980s, and until recently, much of the research on familial risk for psychopathology focused on children of schizophrenic parents, due in large part to findings that schizophrenia has a significant hereditary loading. But children of depressed parents are at even greater risk for developing psychopathology than are offspring of schizophrenic parents. Early studies examining children of depressed parents focused primarily on demonstrating that the children had a higher likelihood of developing depression than did children of non-disordered parents. We took this as a given, and were more interested in understanding *why* these children developed depression – what are the mechanisms by which risk for depression is increased in offspring of depressed parents?

We initiated a study in which we recruited ten- to fourteen-year-old daughters of two groups of mothers: mothers who had recurrent episodes of depression during their daughters' lifetime, and mothers who had no history of any emotional disorder – none of the daughters in either group had (yet) experienced any diagnosable disorder. Based on our research with depressed adults, we assessed cognitive, biological, endocrinological, and neural factors, and specific genetic polymorphisms, that we thought might contribute to the increased risk of the daughters of depressed mothers to develop depression themselves. Thus, we examined cognitive biases in attention and memory in these daughters in the same way that we did in depressed adults; we also examined telomere length and cortisol secretion as measures of stress exposure and reactivity, and we assessed abnormalities in brain structure and patterns of neural activation in the daughters. Because this was a longitudinal study, we were also able to use these measures of psychobiological functioning, obtained before any of the girls had experienced a depressive episode, to predict the onset of depression over the following five to ten years.

The results of this project have been both striking and alarming. Despite not having yet experienced an episode of depression or exhibiting depressive symptoms themselves, daughters of mothers with recurrent depression look remarkably like depressed adults with respect to both cognitive and biological functioning: their attention is captured by negative material, they secrete high levels of cortisol both in response to stress and throughout the day, they have smaller hippocampi than do daughters of never-disordered mothers (brain structures that are involved in memory), likely because the high levels of cortisol are interfering with normal hippocampus development, and they have stronger limbic activation to negative stimuli. Moreover, at the time of writing, about 60 percent of the daughters of depressed mothers have now developed an episode of clinically significant depression. Importantly, these same anomalies at baseline are predicting which of the daughters will become depressed: greater attention to negative stimuli, higher levels of cortisol, smaller hippocampus volume, etc. Because it is becoming increasingly clear that difficulties in stress reactivity and recovery from stressors are involved in the onset and maintenance of depression, we are using neurofeedback with a new but similar sample of young girls at familial risk for depression. With this procedure, we are training these high-risk girls in an fMRI scanner to learn to reduce the magnitude of their limbic activation to negative stimuli, and are examining the effects of this training on levels of stress reactivity. So far, it appears that this training is successfully reducing the girls' physiological responses to laboratory stressors; we are following these participants to assess longer-term effects of this training on the development of depression.

Beyond the Laboratory

I have focused in this chapter on our laboratory studies of depressed adults and young children at risk for developing depression. Although these investigations were conducted in the laboratory, I believe that they have "real-world" implications for the prevention and treatment of depression. For example, the greater precision in our understanding of the cognitive functioning of depressed individuals that comes from our research using information-processing paradigms permits more targeted and, hopefully, more effective interventions for depression that focus on altering specific forms of maladaptive cognitive functioning. Indeed, the class of interventions now known as Cognitive Bias Modification is based almost fully on research like the studies I described earlier. Similarly, our identification of stress reactivity and its psychobiological consequences as important factors that may lead to the development of depression has allowed us to develop approaches that we think will help prevent the occurrence of the first episode of depression, which may lead to life-long improvements in mental health.

Depression remains the leading cause of disability worldwide. Certainly, there is much more for us to do in this area of research. By staying open to learning new areas of research and by always thinking about how we can apply new methodologies and technologies to increase our understanding of psychopathology, we can work to reduce the prevalence of debilitating emotional disorders.

REFERENCES

Gotlib, I. H., Joormann, J., & Foland-Ross, L. C. (2014). Understanding familial risk for depression: A 25-year perspective. *Perspectives on Psychological Science, 9*, 94–108. doi:10.1177/1745691613513469.

Kircanski, K., Joormann, J., & Gotlib, I. H. (2012). Cognitive aspects of depression. *Wiley Interdisciplinary Reviews: Cognitive Science, 3*, 301–313. doi:10.1002/wcs.1177.

Singh, M. K., & Gotlib, I. H. (2014) The neuroscience of depression: Implications for assessment and intervention. *Behaviour Research and Therapy, 62*, 60–73.

Kessler, Ronald C.

Unlike the vast majority of contributors to this volume, I originally trained in sociology rather than psychology. The path from my early academic studies on social altruism to my current interdisciplinary work in psychiatric epidemiology was circuitous, and was guided over thirty-five years by an interdisciplinary set of mentors and colleagues. I entered graduate school at New York University in the early '70s with an interest in survey methodology and mass communications. My first substantive research involved designing blood drives at the New York Blood Center and evaluating recruitment success using general market research techniques.

Afterwards, I was hired in the market research department at the NBC television network, primarily to study effects of television violence on children. The study's numerous design and analysis challenges, however, also stimulated in me a lasting interest in modeling quantitative change over time in ways that might help inform the design and evaluation of real-world applications. About the same time, I was also involved in a study of teenage drug use at the New York State Psychiatric Institute. This twin focus on imitative violence and addiction got me wondering more seriously about the broader field of psychiatric epidemiology. Knowing that I needed more training, I embarked on a two-year post-doctoral fellowship in psychiatric epidemiology at the University of Wisconsin before joining the Department of Sociology at the University of Michigan as an assistant professor in 1979.

I was hired at Michigan to teach Medical Sociology in an emerging subspecialty known as "the sociology of mental illness" – what public health professionals would today refer to as social psychiatric epidemiology. By then, although I had five years' post-doctoral experience, all of it was obtained outside sociology departments, in settings where I focused largely on refining my skills in survey methods and applied statistics. This expertise grew exponentially over the next decade due to interactions with the methodology group at the Survey Research Center at Michigan's

Institute for Social Research. I also became involved during those years in a series of community epidemiologic surveys on a wide range of topics, including the effects of the auto industry economic downturn on the mental health of unemployed auto workers (led by James House), the effects of the recently discovered HIV epidemic on the mental health of gay men (led by Jill Joseph), and the effects of spousal death on the mental health of surviving spouses (led by Camille Wortman). I also carried out secondary analyses of the *Americans View Their Mental Health* national study (led by Joseph Veroff and Elizabeth Douvan) during those years.

There was only one major psychiatric epidemiologic study in the United States during those early years of my career at Michigan: the NIMH *Epidemiologic Catchment Area (ECA) Study*, a large (over 20,000 respondents) community epidemiologic survey of the prevalence and correlates of common mental disorders in the catchment areas surrounding five of the major centers of psychiatric research in the country (Duke, Johns Hopkins, UCLA, Washington University, and Yale). The ECA was a landmark study for psychiatric epidemiology, but was limited in that it was based on samples that were atypical even of their local areas, so they were consequently incapable of providing information about the national patterns of interest to policy-makers regarding prevalence, correlates, and unmet need for treatment of common mental disorders.

Recognizing this limitation, NIMH released a Request for Proposals in 1988, asking for bids on a national survey that would build on the ECA. I was fortunate to be awarded that grant and to carry out the first national epidemiologic survey of mental disorders in the United States, which became known as the *National Comorbidity Survey* (NCS). The term *comorbidity* means having two or more disorders. Mental disorders are characterized by the presence of high comorbidity, with up to half the people meeting criteria for one disorder also meeting criteria for one or more other disorders. Some of the most common co-morbidities, like panic with agoraphobia, have been codified in the existing diagnostic system as disorders in their own right, but there are many other common co-morbidities and multi-morbidities (i.e., the presence of three or more disorders) that are still treated as clusters of distinct disorders. It is quite clear that the existence of high comorbidity among mental disorders reflects imprecisions in our current diagnostic system rather than the true co-occurrence of distinct disorders. The new NIMH Research Domain Criteria (RDoC) initiative is an attempt to tackle this problem in a serious way. The NCS was a first step in that direction based entirely on the analysis of symptom data. A decade later, I conducted a trend survey (the *National Comorbidity Survey Replication*), as well as a follow-up survey of the original NCS respondents and a parallel national survey of the mental health of adolescents. The bulk of my work over the fifteen years beginning with the award of the initial grant to carry out the NCS was devoted to the design, implementation, and analysis of the data collected in those surveys (www.hcp.med.harvard.edu/ncs).

During the middle of this time period, as the NCS was becoming increasingly visible, the World Health Organization (WHO) asked me to direct a consortium that would replicate the NCS in interested countries around the world so as to provide information for health policy planners on the magnitude of the problem of unmet need for treatment of mental disorders in their countries. This *WHO World Mental Health (WMH) Survey Consortium* (www.hcp.med.harvard.edu/wmh) subsequently helped investigators in twenty-eight different countries carry out nationally or regionally representative psychiatric epidemiologic surveys that interviewed more than 200,000 respondents. The WMH investigators have now collaborated in publishing more than 700 papers and a growing series of books. I consider the establishment and nurturing of WMH – including the dissemination of the technology for psychiatric epidemiologic research and mentoring of a new generation of researchers in all the WMH countries – my most important scientific contribution. Some of the important findings of WMH were that mental disorders are highly prevalent in all countries in the world; that these disorders are typically chronic-recurrent and usually have early ages of onset (with the median age of onset of a first mental disorder occurring in early adolescence in most countries); and that early age of onset and comorbidity are both associated with persistence and severity of these disorders,

WMH was not the first international consortium of psychiatric epidemiologists. A number of large community epidemiological surveys based on the ECA Study were carried out before the NCS, and an international consortium was created to pool the results across these ECA replications more than a decade before the establishment of WMH. But that earlier effort did not have nearly as much impact as the NCS or WMH. Why? I think the answer can be found in the fact that my position as a relative outsider to the field of psychiatric epidemiology when I designed the NCS allowed me to ask novel questions, and that my background in market research led me to make sure these questions had a practical focus that appealed to clinicians. In addition, my broad methodological training made it possible for me to design the NCS and subsequently the WMH interview schedules in ways that allowed these research questions to be addressed with subtle assessments and innovative statistical analysis methods. The end result was captured by a clinical researcher who, a number of years ago, introduced me as a grand rounds speaker in a medical school by saying that he always knew psychiatric epidemiology existed but never thought of it as relevant to him until he started reading papers from the NCS and WMH surveys.

One way I tried to bridge the gap between epidemiologic and clinical research as the NCS and WMH initiatives progressed was by creating measurement cross-walks between the two areas of research. In the early days of the NCS, when we published our first papers reporting that more than 50 percent of the US population was projected to meet DSM-III-R criteria for a mental disorder at some time in their life (a finding subsequently confirmed in prospective studies), there was understandably a good deal of skepticism. I initially tried to address this skepticism by embedding blinded clinical reappraisal sub-studies in each of my surveys.

Subsequently, I went beyond this to include in the core survey instruments short-forms of the fully structured versions of standard clinical severity scales that were at that time just beginning to appear in the clinical literature (e.g., the short self-report version of John Rush's Inventory of Depressive Symptomatology, a scale that has been shown to have very high correlations with scores on the clinician-administered Hamilton Rating Scale for Depression [HAMD]). This allowed me to report such things as the depression severity classification distribution in the US general population based on imputed HAMD scores to clinical researchers who were otherwise skeptical of the high major depression prevalence estimates in our surveys. I could also show that the subsamples of survey respondents who reported having been in treatment had distributions on these classification schemes similar to those found in clinical studies. We also found that the vast majority of people with persistent mental disorders eventually obtain treatment, but that delays in first seeking treatment are common. Interestingly, early age of onset is one of the most powerful predictors of delays in seeking treatment, but also a predictor of persistence and severity. This means that many of the people with the most persistent-severe disorders delay seeking help the longest. By virtue of the fact that we had information about patients both before they ever sought treatment and after they sought treatment, we were able to study patterns and predictors of the course of illness in more depth than in clinical studies. We also were able to see that treatment dropout is much less of a problem than it seems to be in clinical studies that consider a patient a "dropout" if they do not return for treatment, as we saw that many of those patients sought help elsewhere and hence were really treatment "switchers" rather than dropouts. And we found that this kind of switching is often a good thing, as many patients told us that they had to try three or four different kinds of treatment providers before they found someone who helped them. One important weakness of the mental health treatment system is that it provides patients with no guidance on this kind of matching of patients to optimal treatments. Our efforts to bridge this gap between epidemiological and clinical research have been useful in increasing the influence of NCS-WMH findings.

This effort to bridge the gap between community epidemiologic and clinical research is far from complete. I have devoted an increasing proportion of my time in recent years to clinical epidemiology: that is, to the implementation of epidemiological studies in clinical populations. Clinical epidemiology is a central component of epidemiologic research in other areas of medicine, yet it remains under-developed in psychiatry. But this is changing. For example, a number of psychiatric epidemiologists are now doing screening in primary care waiting rooms for common mental disorders to understand the magnitude and distribution of undetected cases. My colleagues and I are developing an extension of this design to inform screening and outreach efforts aimed at reducing the problem of unmet need for treatment of common mental disorders. My group is also carrying out prospective epidemiologic surveys with patients beginning (and followed through until the end of) treatment of anxiety and mood disorders. Our hope is to develop predictive analytic models of differential treatment response. We plan to do this to draw provisional causal inferences about the ways in which optimal treatments differ for different patients. If successful, the models we develop could be used to provide clinical decision support for precision medicine treatment selection decisions. I feel strongly that efforts such as these to blend epidemiologic and clinical research, in many cases taking advantage of new technologies (e.g., smart phones, wearable sensors) and including diverse biomarkers with more conventional epidemiologic data collections, are the future of psychiatric epidemiology.

REFERENCES

Kessler, R. C., Chiu, W. T., Demler, O., Merikangas, K. R., & Walters, E. E. (2005). Prevalence, severity, and comorbidity of 12-month DSM-IV disorders in the National Comorbidity Survey Replication. *Archives of General Psychiatry, 62,* 617–627.

Kessler, R. C., McGonagle, K. A., Zhao, S., Nelson, C. B., Hughes, M., Eshleman, S. et al. (1994). Lifetime and 12-month prevalence of DSM-III-R psychiatric disorders in the United States. Results from the National Comorbidity Survey. *Archives of General Psychiatry, 51,* 8–19.

Nock, M. K., Green, J. G., Hwang, I., McLaughlin, K. A., Sampson, N. A., Zaslavsky, A. M. et al. (2013). Prevalence, correlates, and treatment of lifetime suicidal behavior among adolescents: results from the National Comorbidity Survey Replication Adolescent Supplement. *JAMA Psychiatry, 70,* 300–310.

93   Closing the Divide: Psychological Science, Basic and Applied

Lang, Peter J.

When I began graduate study of psychology in the early 1950s, I entered a theoretically divided house. Most experimental psychologists could be described as neo-behaviorists, studying classical and operant conditioning, paired associate learning, psychophysics, and the like. The data collected were measures of physical events in animals and humans. Theories described connections between objective measures, as in other physical sciences; inferences about mediating mental phenomena (hypothetical constructs) were highly controversial and prompted vigorous debate.

Clinical psychology was, however, a very different matter.

Based on the great need for mental health workers, occasioned by the flood of psychiatric casualties among war-veterans in the aftermath of World War II, an increasing proportion of university psychologists were treating patients and training students in clinical practice. The then general view of mental disorder was, as for psychiatry, dominated by the theories of Sigmund Freud, his colleagues, and disciples.

In the 1950s, clinical evaluation did not involve the measurement of behavior or physiology, but depended on analysis of patients' symptom reports and personal memories, gathered in a prolonged series of interviews – a "talking cure." The therapist's interpretations were intended to uncover patients' hidden (unconscious) foci of distress. Treatment was achieved when the patients gained emotional "insight": a conscious realization of the dark motives determining their dysfunctional behavior.

In graduate school, I took the sequence of clinical courses and associated practicum, along with the required program in experimental psychology. I vividly recall a curious sense of "split-personality" that developed during these studies. In experimental psychology, careful objective measurement, statistical analysis, and rigorous theory-testing characterized one-half of my days; for the clinical half, I was like an acolyte training for a new priesthood, learning to sense the presence of frightening, invisible forces, buried in patients' monologues.

The trajectory of my subsequent work as a scientist, I believe, stemmed from the initial uneasiness with this divide – that there could be two psychologies, casually tolerated by both camps, so different in how knowledge was acquired – with fundamentally opposed views as to what constituted meaningful data.

In 1958, I joined the psychology faculty at the University of Pittsburgh. In that same year, a book was published that had a profound effect on my future research career: *Psychotherapy by Reciprocal Inhibition*, written by Joseph Wolpe. To understand the book's impact, it is useful to consider the broader cultural context in which it appeared. Indeed, not only the mental health community was in the thrall of psychoanalysis. Analytic theory was a major influence shaping literature and the arts – novels, literary criticism, musical and dramatic theater, Hollywood films – along with everyday cocktail conversation. A plethora of famous artists, scientists, politicians, film and stage actors all underwent analysis. Indeed, Freud was then commonly ranked with Darwin and Karl Marx in breadth of cultural influence on western society.

Wolpe's book was a radical anomaly in this environment. To encapsulate his message: *I tried psychoanalysis: It takes forever, and it doesn't work.* In its place, he proposed comparatively brief treatment protocols based on conditioning procedures founded, surprisingly, on research with animals as carried out by experimental psychologists.

This challenge to orthodoxy was not welcomed by many clinical psychologists, and was bitterly opposed by Wolpe's psychiatric colleagues. For me, however, it was an *aha!* moment. Unlike psychoanalysis and its variants – treatments often interminable, and a priori, with indeterminate goals and aims – *Joseph Wolpe's therapy protocols could be tested by experiment!*

Working closely with a colleague, David Lazovik, we planned a program of laboratory research to evaluate Systematic Desensitization Therapy – Wolpe's method for treating phobic disorders. Our first paper describing an initial pilot study was published in 1960, and we subsequently submitted a grant to the National Institute of Mental Health (NIMH) to support our further investigations.

This first proposal (to study what would later be called a "behavior therapy") received a cautiously positive review. Consistent with the psychoanalytic zeitgeist, however, some reviewers thought the therapy could be dangerously superficial. From the analytic perspective, phobias were just symptoms. This surface fear might well be removed by counterconditioning, but the determining unconscious conflict would remain unresolved, and new, perhaps more dysfunctional symptoms could then appear.

We responded, asserting bravely that we planned to evaluate desensitization in the natural-science context within which it was conceived: That is,
the hypothesis underlying treatment conjectured that phobic fear was
a physiologically determined event. We proposed that objective "fear"
response data could be obtained from three measurement domains: language behavior (e.g., psychometric ratings), overt actions (as escape or
avoidance), and physiological responses (somatic and autonomic).
We would measure participants' reactions, sampling each domain, as
responses were prompted by the phobic stimulus. Desensitization's effectiveness would be supported if we observed a post-treatment pattern of
reduced "fear" across measures – *without emergence of other pathologies.*

The project was funded shortly after the next review meeting, and our
research over the subsequent ten years (1960–1970) strongly supported
desensitization's effectiveness in treating phobia – findings that were
confirmed by the work of other investigators.

As so often happens in research, however, successful outcomes raise
many more questions than they answer. In most cases, for example, the
phobic object could only be presented as an instructed mental image
(e.g., "Alone in the woods, stepping over a log, you see a coiled
snake"). What is an emotional memory image? Can imagery be measured? How does processing an imagined experience change emotional
reactions to the actual fear object? Furthermore, in our treatment studies –
assessing fear ratings, physiological reactivity, and behavior change (physical approach to the fear object) – we were surprised to discover that
these responses changed at different rates, that verbal reports of fear often
failed to co-vary with patients' fear behavior and with their measured
psychophysiology, and that concordance among these response measures
varied widely across participants. Furthermore, although desensitization
and its exposure therapy variants were effective in reducing specific
phobic fears, patients with more complex, co-morbid anxiety disorders
were much less responsive to behavioral interventions.

These findings changed the laboratory's focus. Therapy research would
need to be delayed. Developing and assessing treatments clearly depended
on first making better empirical sense of human emotion: To determine if
phenomenological (everyday) concepts such as "fear" and "anxiety" could
be objectively understood – or productively reconceived – in the terms of
natural science.

The emphasis of our new basic research program was on the psychophysiology of human emotion, exploring the relationship between behavior
and measured bodily responses (heart rate, sweat glands, pupil dilation,
facial muscles, respiration, the startle reflex) and reported emotional
experience, studying reactions to arousing narrative texts, pictures, sounds,

memory imagery, and to objective threats and rewards (e.g., mild electric shocks and monetary gains or losses). As advancing technology permitted, we increasingly added the assessment of functional brain activity to our measurement armamentarium, first with EEG and later with fMRI.

The findings from our research and that of others, linking brain and reflex physiology, strongly support the view that human emotion, in its multiple contexts, is founded on two overlapping, motivational circuits that evolved in the brains of mammals, promoting survival of individuals and their progeny: (a) a defense/protective circuit, prompting attention to and vigilance for threats, and reflexive physiological arousal, preparatory to defensive actions, such as "freezing," avoidance, and escape; and (b) an appetitive circuit that mediates attention to positive cues, and actions that attain nutrients, sexual partners, and other life-sustaining goals.

Guided by the basic emotion research, we began a systematic study of differences in physiological response patterns, wherein anxiety-spectrum patients responded to cues signaling personal "fear" memories. Not surprisingly, all anxious patients reported similarly high levels of "fear" arousal, greater than healthy controls, regardless of their assigned diagnosis (determined by the American Psychiatric Association's *Diagnostic and Statistical Manual* (*DSM*)). Furthermore, patients with a single diagnosis of a specific phobia – since Wolpe's innovation, a disorder successfully treated by exposure – evidenced the expected, hyper-reactive defense reflex pattern. However, over a sustained series of experiments it became clear that many anxiety patients – with greater generalized distress and multiple co-morbid conditions – were not more but, paradoxically, significantly *less* responsive. A pattern slowly emerged of physiological reflex "blunting" that increased with disorder severity and a history of persistent life-stress, but was unrelated to the intensity of reported fear and could not be explained by differences in DSM diagnosis.

Currently, our laboratory is supported by a new NIMH initiative, the Research Domain Criteria (RDoC), that challenges the research community to "develop, for research purposes, new ways of classifying mental disorders based on behavioral dimensions and neurobiological measures." Our new project's immediate aim is to determine, using neural imaging, if the blunted psychophysiological responses of severely disturbed patients reflect disordered brains – a functionally compromised defense circuit. Of course, a successful test would be only one step forward toward the broader goal of developing a biological classification of anxiety patients. And then, even larger questions follow. How do the different brain-based disorders develop? What are the contributions of genetic inheritance and environmental stress? And for future research, what new, better-targeted interventions might then be developed to lessen the distress of an NIMH's reported forty million anxiety patients?

Of course, scientific advances accumulate slowly, dependent on replication and the work of many investigators. As Ivan Pavlov advised young scientists: Prepare for "gradualness, gradualness"; your aims in science may take "two lifetimes." So, not surprisingly, psychology's conceptual divide – which troubled me as a graduate student – has not wholly gone away, and symptom reports alone still define diagnoses. However, the gap has palpably narrowed, and a natural-science conception of emotion and its pathophysiology are now very much in our sights. I believe the work of our laboratory, the efforts of many outstanding graduate students, postdoctoral associates, and collaborating colleagues, has contributed to this development. I've always found the motto of my high school very reassuring: "The best is yet to be."

REFERENCES

Lang, P. J., McTeague, L., & Bradley, M. M. (in press). RDoC, DSM, and the reflex physiology of fear: A biodimensional analysis of the anxiety disorders spectrum. *Psychophysiology*.

Pavlov, I. P. (1936). Bequest of Pavlov (written just before his death; translator P. Kupalov). In Flakeslee, A. F., Discussion. *Science*, *83*, 369–370.

Wolpe, J., (1958). *Psychotherapy by reciprocal inhibition*, Stanford University Press, Stanford, CA.

Section C

Psychotherapy and Behavior Change

94 The Development and Evaluation of Psychological Treatments for Anxiety Disorders

Barlow, David H.

Early in my career I was asked to evaluate a patient who was a very prominent chef at an internationally known resort located about an hour away. One of the perks of his position was a very nice home provided by the resort and located right next door. Despite his extraordinary professional success, his international reputation, and the very comfortable lifestyle that his generous earnings afforded him, he tearfully described an overwhelming problem that was making his life miserable. He reported that he was able to walk the few feet from his home to the kitchen in the resort, but could not venture beyond this area without suffering debilitating anxiety and panic. On his bad days even walking next door became a terrifying ordeal, and he had been imprisoned in his own little world in this way for over ten years. In fact, to get to the hospital where I was located he had to be transported via ambulance while heavily sedated.

It became apparent that this individual was suffering from a severe case of what came to be known in later years as panic disorder and agoraphobia (literally, fear of a crowded area such as a marketplace), a condition in which people experience sudden surges of fear for no apparent reason at unpredictable times, particularly in places where escape is difficult. These unexpected surges of fear are characterized by sharply increased heart rate, blood pressure, muscle tension, and other physical signs in which the body gears up to handle an imminent threat or danger. This set of responses is called the flight/fight reaction. In situations of real danger, this surge in the sympathetic nervous system prepares us to be at our physical best: We are able to see more acutely, run faster, and perform feats of incredible strength. (Newspapers occasionally feature stories of these extraordinary deeds – for example, a 90-pound woman lifting a car off of a trapped child.)

But, if there is actually nothing to fear, this reaction is called a *panic attack*. With nothing dangerous happening, some individuals – those who are susceptible to developing panic disorder – experience the attack as

453

a mysterious jolt out of the blue that they often attribute to a heart attack or some equally terrible bodily affliction, with death soon to follow. Because these panic attacks occur unpredictably, affected individuals soon learn not to venture far from a safe place (or safe person) where help might be available if the panic attack occurs. This pattern of avoidant behavior is called *agoraphobia*. In severe cases, the individual becomes housebound.

But why was the chef engaging in this very irrational behavior, and, more importantly, how could we help him with treatment? I was reminded of an observation made many years ago by a well-known psychologist, O. Hobart Mowrer. He noted in 1950 that common sense holds that normal people and even animals will consider the consequences of their acts: If the net effect is favorable, the actions will be perpetuated; but if it's unfavorable, the actions will be inhibited and abandoned. But with emotional disorders, of which panic disorder is one, actions or behaviors with distinctly unfavorable consequences occur frequently, such as avoidance of things you want and need to do; yet individuals keep doing it, sometimes all their lives. Mowrer called this puzzling state of affairs "the neurotic paradox." Nobody was more aware of the absurdity of the situation than the chef himself who, by the time he came to see us, knew perfectly well from numerous visits to health professionals that there was absolutely nothing to be afraid of, and yet found his life in ruins because of his intense emotions of fear and anxiety. I knew then that understanding and developing treatments for anxiety and related disorders of emotion would become my life's work.

In those days (the 1960s), treatments for mental disorders, including anxiety disorders, were not based on scientific principles, and some of us thought that application of basic principles of psychological science to the clinic might prove fruitful. For fears and phobias, procedures to reduce or "extinguish" anxiety and fear, developed in the laboratories of experimental psychology, involved gradually exposing animals to external fear cues without experiencing any negative consequences. With the chef, we tried out a primitive form of this approach that came to be called "exposure" therapy. Treatment consisted of having him venture as far as he could away from the hospital several times a day, and he would receive enthusiastic praise (from me) for successfully meeting behavioral targets for the day. Although difficult at first, within a week or so he reported with some amazement that he was indeed becoming less fearful and that venturing out was becoming easier. At that point, we began using these procedures on other patients with similar fears and phobias.

While these treatments were certainly more successful than the prevailing long-term psychotherapies, they were not very successful by today's standards. One reason they were primitive was that we had failed to recognize that what triggered massive avoidance and escape was not necessarily external cues in crowded areas or enclosed places, but, rather, the possibility of having another panic attack. In other words, individuals such as the chef developed severe anxiety over the possibility of experiencing their own intense, out-of-control, emotional (fear) reactions.

In the 1980s, my colleague Michelle Craske and I developed a psychological treatment in which individuals with panic disorder were repeatedly exposed to mild versions of the physical sensations associated with their intense fear reactions, such as increased heart rate and dizziness. Based on the process of extinction once again, our patients learned that experiencing these intense physical sensations repeatedly didn't lead to a terrible outcome, such as a heart attack. Of course, their rational self knew this all along, but the emotional brain, where these fear responses originate, tends to override the rational brain in emotional disorders. To assist in strengthening the "rational brain," the patients' basic faulty attributions and appraisals about the dangerousness of these sensations are also identified and challenged. In a number of subsequent studies, we demonstrated that this treatment, a cognitive-behavioral approach, was effective for panic disorder.

My colleagues and I then evaluated the efficacy of this treatment in a number of experiments called "clinical trials." In one large clinical trial, we treated 312 patients with panic disorder at 4 different sites with our psychological treatment or a widely used drug treatment, comparing both to a placebo (sugar) capsule. The experiment was also double-blind, which means that neither the therapists nor the patients knew whether they were getting the actual medication or the placebo (sugar) capsule. We found that, as we expected, both the drug and the psychological treatments were effective, with each better than the placebo. But, much to our surprise, combining the treatments was not any better than the individual treatments. Furthermore, after all treatments were stopped, the psychological treatment was found to be more durable. That is, fewer people relapsed over a period of six months after treatment was stopped, compared with drug treatment. A number of additional clinical trials confirmed the efficacy of this psychological treatment for panic disorder.

At that point, we began examining disorders of emotion more broadly, including all of the anxiety disorders, depression, and other related disorders, such as eating disorders. Based on emerging findings from cognitive science and neuroscience, we found that these disorders were fundamentally more similar than different. We then identified a common set of behavior change principles that could be applied to all emotional disorders. We call this psychological intervention the Unified Protocol for

Transdiagnostic Treatment of Emotional disorders. We conceptualized this intervention as addressing fundamental dimensions that run through all emotional disorders such as "neurotic temperament." This temperament is characterized by frequent and intense experience of unwanted negative emotions, combined with strong reactions of distress or anxiety over experiencing these emotions. In other words, these emotions are perceived as being dangerous and out of the individual's control. Preliminary evaluations of this new transdiagnostic intervention indicate that it is at least as effective as the variety of treatments developed specifically for individual emotional disorders, such as a treatment for panic disorder that differs in many details from a treatment for depression or from a treatment for obsessive-compulsive disorder.

Conclusion

Scientific discoveries about the nature of panic disorder allowed us to develop a specifically tailored psychological treatment based on principles of cognitive and neuroscience. The development of a transdiagnostic treatment holds promise for applicability to a broader range of people with disorders of emotion. Reliance on the slow but inexorable process of science will ensure that our developing treatments will continue to be ever more beneficial to patients suffering from these disorders, and in the future may even allow us to prevent these disorders from developing in the first place.

REFERENCES

Barlow, D. H. (2002). *Anxiety and its disorders: The nature and treatment of anxiety and panic* (2nd edn.). New York: The Guilford Press.

Barlow, D. H., Bullis, J. R., Comer, J. S., & Ametaj, A. A. (2013). Evidence-based psychological treatments: An update and a way forward. In S. Nolen-Hoeksema, T. D. Cannon, & T. Widiger (eds.), *Annual Review of Clinical Psychology* (vol. 9, pp. 1–27). Palo Alto: Annual Reviews.

Barlow, D. H., Sauer-Zavala, S., Carl, J. R., Bullis, J. R., & Ellard, K. K. (2014). The nature, diagnosis, and treatment of neuroticism: Back to the future. *Clinical Psychological Science*, 2(3), 344–365.

Psychosocial Treatment of Children with
Severe Aggressive and Antisocial Behavior

Kazdin, Alan E.

The primary focus of my research has been developing psychological treatments for children who engage in extreme aggressive and antisocial behavior. Such behaviors are relatively prevalent (approximately 9–10 percent of
children in the United States) and are among the most frequent bases for
referring children to treatment (up to 33 percent of cases of children seen in
treatment). The behaviors occur in both boys and girls but are much more
prevalent among boys. In the long term, children with aggressive and antisocial behaviors are at greatly increased risk for mental health problems (e.g.,
psychiatric disorders, substance abuse), physical health problems (e.g., early
death from disease), and criminal behavior (e.g., domestic violence, child
abuse). The problem of aggressive and antisocial behavior is very costly for
society because the children require many social and hospital services, are
often taken to emergency rooms for behaviors that are dangerous or
uncontrollable, are in special classes at school, and are in repeated contact
with the criminal justice system. Until recently, no interventions had been
shown to have impact on the problem – not medication, psychotherapy,
special experiences (e.g., wilderness camps), or special diet.

Contribution and Its Importance

My clinical research has focused on children hospitalized or seen in out-
patient treatment for extremes of these behaviors. The children get into
frequent fights, destroy property, steal, set fires, and run away from home, in
addition to exhibiting many other less severe but still problematic behaviors
such as tantrums, oppositional behavior, and bullying. The constellation of
behaviors constitutes a psychiatric disorder referred to as Conduct Disorder.
As with many other psychiatric disorders (e.g., major depression, autism),
there are varying degrees of severity and impairment.

We have developed two treatments, referred to as parent management
training (PMT) and cognitive problem-solving skills training (PSST)
(please see References at end of chapter). PMT trains parents very

457

concretely in new ways to interact with their children in the home. Parents meet individually with a therapist. The parents learn how to administer antecedents, such as instructions, prompts, or cues on how to perform the behavior; to focus the child on practicing the behavior by gradually reinforcing approximations of the behavior; and on consequences to increase prosocial behaviors by delivering praise and tokens. The therapist uses role-playing of parent–child interactions, repeated practice, modeling of the desired parent behaviors, feedback, and praise. The parents are the ones who actually change the child's behaviors by implementing the techniques they have learned at home.

In PSST, the therapist meets individually with the child. The child engages in a sequence of steps or self-statements designed to help the child look carefully at the demands of the situation, consider what might be alternative positive (rather than aggressive) ways of responding, consider the consequences of different actions, select one of those responses, and actually act out the solution in a role-play situation in the treatment session. As in PMT, modeling by the therapist, role-play of many situations, and repeated practice of easy and then more difficult social situations serve as the basis for the treatment sessions. Over the course of treatment, children have "homework" assignments (called supersolvers) to solve problems using the steps at home, at school, and at any other place where the child exhibits behavior problems.

My contribution has been developing and evaluating these treatments with clinically referred children (two to fourteen years of age) who range in severity from oppositional and defiant behavior to extremely violent and aggressive behavior. We have conducted experiments (randomized controlled clinical trials) to evaluate variations of treatment and their impact. The techniques that comprise PMT also are quite useful in child-rearing to address everyday challenges such as getting children to be ready for school on time, complete homework, or eat vegetables, or to eliminate tantrums and disrespectful behaviors that form "teen attitude." Because of the demand, we expanded our service to provide help to parents with these challenges among children otherwise functioning well in everyday life. We provide our interventions in person at the Yale Parenting Center (http://yaleparentingcenter .yale.edu/) but more often on-line, face-to-face via an encrypted (privacy protected) program that allows our trainers to work individually with parents anywhere in the world where there is access to the Internet.

Impetus for This Work

In a prior job, I was a professor of child psychiatry at a medical school, and as part of that position I was in charge of an in-patient service for children aged five to twelve years old. The children were referred for severe psychiatric problems that required hospitalization; most of the youth were referred for very serious aggressive and antisocial behavior. No in-patient program, group or individual therapy, or medication had been shown to be effective with these children. We tried virtually all reasonable options; occasionally we yielded to parents to try options they viewed as reasonable (e.g., exorcism).

We decided to investigate and develop two treatments: one that could involve parents (PMT), and another treatment (PSST) for instances in which involvement of the parent was not possible (e.g., parent or caretaker was in prison, engaged in prostitution or selling of illicit drugs, was soon to lose custody of the child). We began developing the treatment, testing it with a few clinical cases, making revisions, applying treatment again, and so on, until we believed we had a viable procedure that was feasible and that specified in concrete terms what to do in treatment (e.g., on a session-by-session basis and how to handle obstacles and failure during the course of treatment). We began to study the treatment in controlled research trials, first comparing one of the treatments (PMT, PSST) to the usual hospital care and other commonly used but not well-studied treatments (individual, play-relationship therapy). After a few years, we moved our work from in-patient treatment to an out-patient service. We carried out several outcome studies over a period spanning more than thirty years. We now have two treatments with strong evidence on their behalf. The treatments greatly reduce aggressive and antisocial child behaviors and other symptoms these children often show (e.g., depression, anxiety, hyperactivity) and improve prosocial behavior and functioning at home and at school. Parents and families also change (e.g., reduced stress and depression in the parent, improved family relationships).

Significance of the Idea for Psychological Science and for the World Beyond Academia

The significance of our work derives from several features that address scientific questions, and applications beyond these questions. On the science front, most of the hundreds of psychotherapies in use in clinical practice are not based on empirical evidence that they are effective. Our work, and the work of many other researchers, is based on carefully controlled scientific studies that allow one to analyze facets of treatment, who responds well to treatment, and what can be done to improve effectiveness. This type of work adds greatly to clinical psychological science. In addition, the scientific contribution is reflected in the notion of translational research, i.e., drawing on basic science research and extending that to applications and patient care. For example, PMT draws heavily on human and non-human laboratory research on the nature of learning and factors that facilitate acquisition and retention of behavior.

The work has contributed to everyday life well beyond academia to address real-world issues. First, as noted previously, severe aggressive and antisocial behavior is a debilitating condition with deleterious long-term effects on physical and mental health. We work with children, families, and teachers daily and can see palpable improvements in the children's lives at home, at school, and in the community. Thus, the real-world benefits are evident for the families with whom we work. In addition, the treatments we have developed have much broader generality beyond clinical applications and help parents with normal challenges of child-rearing. Parenting and child-rearing can be less stressful and more effective, and millions of parents could profit from the interventions. Overall, psychological science has produced basic research (e.g., human and non-human animal laboratory studies), translated research to develop treatments under highly controlled conditions, and extended these to clinical applications. Our treatment research is an illustration of the benefits of this process.

Next Steps

Three related steps are necessary to develop what we have learned from our research. First, more work is needed to extend evidence-based treatments to mental health professionals who carry out treatment in clinical practice. It is still the case that many of the psychological techniques routinely in use at clinics, hospitals, and in private practice do not have supportive evidence behind them.

Second, new ways of delivering psychological services, including the use of technology (e.g., Internet, apps, self-help treatments), are needed. Most people (~ 70 percent) in need of psychological services in the United States receive no treatment of any kind. We now have evidence that supports the effectiveness of many different psychological treatments for aggressive and antisocial behaviors and also for many other clinical dysfunctions (e.g., depression, anxiety) in children, adolescents, and adults. Next we need to develop novel ways to deliver them on a large scale to reach the millions of individuals in need of clinical services.

Finally, the techniques we have investigated could help parents in everyday life in concrete ways to develop positive behaviors in their children. Everyday life also includes urgent situations in which effective parenting techniques could help. As an example, in the United States, physical abuse and neglect of children lead to approximately five child deaths every day. Available techniques can help parents be more effective, cope better with the stress of parenting, and develop positive behaviors in their children without resorting to harsh punishment. The critical next step is getting effective parenting techniques to the people who could benefit from their use.

REFERENCES

Kazdin, A. E. (2009). *Parent management training: Treatment for oppositional, aggressive, and antisocial behavior in children and adolescents.* New York: Oxford University Press.

Kazdin, A. E. (2010). Problem-solving skills training and parent management training for Oppositional Defiant Disorder and Conduct Disorder. In J. R. Weisz & A. E. Kazdin (eds.), *Evidence-based psychotherapies for children and adolescents* (2nd edn., pp. 211–226). New York: Guilford Press.

Kazdin, A. E., & Rotella, C. (2008). *The Kazdin Method for parenting the defiant child: With no pills, no therapy, no contest of wills.* Boston: Houghton Mifflin Harcourt.

Pennebaker, James W.

When people are asked to write about emotional upheavals for as little as fifteen minutes a day for three days, their physical and mental health often improves. Not a particularly shocking finding. But in 1986, when the first expressive writing study was published, the idea caused quite a stir.

The discovery of expressive writing was a mix of chance, dead ends, and the fitting together of a glorious puzzle. After graduate school, most of my research focused on the psychology of physical symptoms. When, how, and why did people notice symptoms and sensations? Although most studies were lab experiments, I was interested in the ways people reported and acted on their symptoms in the real world. Around this time, a student told me about her roommate, who was secretly gorging and purging large amounts of food almost every day. Later, other undergraduates admitted they were doing the same thing. There was virtually nothing in the research literature about bulimia at the time. Why not pass out a questionnaire to several hundred students to get a sense of its incidence and correlates?

Working with a small group of undergraduates, we devised a lengthy questionnaire that asked about eating behaviors, food preferences, and family eating practices. We threw in some random questions, asking about things such as how they got along with their parents, their health problems and behaviors, and "Prior to the age of 17, did you ever have a traumatic sexual experience?" Why did we include the sexual trauma question? No reason. It just sounded interesting.

The questionnaire went out to 800 undergraduates. Although we didn't find much about eating disorders, one powerful and unexpected finding emerged: People who claimed to have experienced a sexual trauma were more likely to have every health problem we asked about. The same pattern emerged on a large survey I conducted with the

Preparation of this chapter was aided by funding from the National Science Foundation (IIS-1344257) and the Army Research Institute (W5J9CQ12C0043).

magazine *Psychology Today* a few months later. Both women and men who said they had experienced a sexual trauma were twice as likely to have been hospitalized in the previous year for any cause. They also reported that they were more likely to have been diagnosed with cancer, high blood pressure, ulcers, colds, flus, and almost every other disease we asked about.

What was it about a sexual trauma that resulted in so many health problems? More surveys and personal interviews revealed an answer: secrets. People who were keeping major life secrets had far more health problems than people who weren't. Most who reported sexual traumas said they hadn't told others about them. Later studies found that the real culprit was the secret itself. Any major upheaval – sexual or otherwise – that was actively concealed increased the risk of illness. Having to hide major secrets from friends and family was highly stressful and ultimately toxic.

The sexual trauma and secrets findings took me in completely new directions. I started talking with therapists about secrets and disclosure. I spoke at length with FBI polygraphers, priests, and preachers about confession and health. As I read about the nonspecific effects of all psychotherapies, the roles of physicians in the nineteenth century, and even healing rituals in tribal cultures, it became clear that sharing dark secrets with others was a component of healing.

Could this effect be replicated in the lab? If keeping secrets is bad for people, can disclosing them boost health? I toyed with the idea of having students disclose deeply personal upheavals to therapists, clinical graduate students, or other students. Doing so would be too expensive, too unwieldy, and too risky. How would the listeners react? Would people actually disclose to a total stranger?

Experiences from my own life helped guide my answer. Years earlier, my wife and I had undergone a particularly tumultuous time in our relationship. It was one of those turning points that touch most of us. After another painful talk, I went to another room and started writing. I probably wrote for an hour working through issues we had been dealing with. By the end, the clouds parted, and I understood myself and our relationship better than I ever had. We soon patched things up and moved forward with our lives. (We just celebrated our forty-third wedding anniversary.)

Another transformative event shaped my thinking. As I was putting all of these ideas together, I was blindsided by being turned down for tenure. It was a crushing and humiliating experience. Within a week of the news, I began to write – not a lot, but enough to begin putting things in perspective. As with the conflict with my wife, I did not feel comfortable talking about these emotional issues with friends or a therapist. Writing about them was more satisfying and better suited my temperament.

A few months later, I had landed another academic position at Southern Methodist University (SMU). By then, I concluded that writing about emotional upheavals might bring about health improvements in ways similar to therapy. Did I have a good theory? No. I had something better: a good hunch.

SMU was a good match. My first of many remarkable master's students, Sandy Beall, was efficient and motivated. In our first meeting, we settled on an expressive writing study. The study involved recruiting about forty-eight students who would write for four consecutive days, for fifteen minutes each day, about either the most traumatic experience of their life – ideally one that they had kept secret – or one of three control writing topics.

Some of the small decisions about the study were just lucky or were guided by factors beyond our control. Why four days? It seemed to me that the more people wrote, the better. Because we were going to use students from Introductory Psychology, there was a five-hour experimental requirement. If students were to fill out questionnaires and write multiple times in the lab, four writing days would be the upper limit. Why fifteen minutes? We could only get about eight rooms in the building, between 5–10 PM, for four nights and, if forty-eight students were going to be run in the same week, one at a time, that would allow only fifteen minutes per person.

You work with what you have.

Perhaps the luckiest part of the experiment was the university itself. SMU was a private school where most students were from outside the state. The Student Health Center was on campus next door to the freshman dormitories. I later learned that students are most likely to go to a campus health center if they are far away from home and if the center is close by. In fact, SMU students visited the health center at rates two to three times higher than most state universities.

The writing study worked. Those asked to write about their thoughts and feelings about traumatic experiences subsequently had half the illness visits compared with those in the control condition. Looking back, I now realize how lucky we were to find the effects we did. There have now been more than 300 replication attempts, and the common wisdom is that the true effect size is modest, $d = 0.16$. Power analyses would tell us that we should have run at least 80 people per condition instead of 12.

In the years that followed, my students, colleagues, and I replicated the expressive writing findings with different outcome measures, including immune markers and college grades. Other researchers found health improvements with people suffering from chronic illness and mental disorders. Particularly satisfying has been watching how expressive writing has seeped into clinical practice and the general population.

A side benefit of the expressive writing discovery has been my research on natural language. Because I was initially fixated on the underlying mechanisms that drove expressive writing, I looked for clues in people's writing samples. Discouraged by the results of human raters, I developed a text analysis program, Linguistic Inquiry and Word Count, or LIWC, that provided a means of assessing the ways in which participants in our writing studies used words. The LIWC approach ultimately expanded to the study of everyday language and basic social and personality processes.

If you are a student reading this, there are a few lessons that may be helpful as you start a career:

- Keep an open mind to new ideas. Don't spend all of your time talking to colleagues in your own area. Talk with everyday people, practitioners, and scientists of different stripes to get a better handle on the topics you study.
- Don't buy the dogma that all great research is hypothesis driven. Theories are cheap. Use them to guide your work. If an important and reliable finding undermines your theory, dump the theory and devise a new one. This is what great science has always been.
- Expect rejection and failure. It comes with the territory. If you don't have papers and grants rejected, you aren't challenging the conventional wisdom. Develop a thick skin.
- Celebrate living in a wildly complicated world. For those who are curious about how the world works, it is a wonderful time to be alive.

REFERENCES

Pennebaker, J. W. (2011). *The secret life of pronouns: What our words say about us.* New York: Bloomsbury.
Pennebaker, J. W., & Smyth, J. M. (2016). *Opening up: The healing power of expressive writing.* New York: Guilford.

97 Staging: A Revolution in Changing Health Risk Behaviors

Prochaska, James O.

Prior to our discovery of the stages of behavior change, most research and treatments for health risk behaviors, such as smoking, alcohol abuse, and unhealthy diets, were based on an action model. Behavior change was seen as an event when individuals stopped smoking, drinking, or unhealthy eating. Interviews with smokers who quit on their own taught us a new model: Behavior change is viewed as a process that unfolds over time and involves progress thorough six stages of change. The first stage we labeled *Precontemplation*, because at-risk individuals, such as smokers, are not intending to quit in the foreseeable future. They underestimate the pros or benefits of quitting and overestimate the cons or costs. They make up about 40 percent of smokers in the United States, and historically were excluded because the available science and practice did not know how to help them progress. We now know that across more than fifty risk behaviors progress from precontemplation to *action*, requires individuals to increase their awareness and appreciation of the multitude of pros of changing.

Once individuals progress to the *Contemplation* stage, they intend to take action in the next six months. But they have deep doubts about whether the efforts to change are worth it. Their pros and cons of changing are essentially equal. Their rule of thumb is, "When in doubt, don't act!" The second principle of progress is to lower the cons. If withdrawal from smoking is a big barrier, treatment can provide nicotine patches that can reduce this con.

Individuals who progress to the *Preparation* stage are ready to take action within the next month. They are convinced the pros outweigh the cons but are afraid that when they act, they may fail. They need to learn that just making the decision to act is not enough. They have to apply other principles, such as being prepared for their biggest risks for relapse. How will they cope with stress or distress? Who will they turn to for help and support, which is one of the best buffers for stress? What substitutes, such as chewing gum, or taking deep breaths to relax, will they use when tempted to smoke? These individuals are ready for action-oriented programs but make up only 20 percent of smokers.

The *Action* stage is the first six months of quitting, a period that has the highest risk for relapse. Individuals need to think of action as the behavioral equivalent of life-saving surgery. They need to let others know they will need more support and more reinforcement, that they may not be at their emotional best, and they need to make quitting a top priority.

The *Maintenance* stage begins after six months and may last for five years – or, in some cases, a lifetime. In this stage, individuals don't have to work nearly as hard to prevent relapse. But, they have to be especially prepared for times of distress. So what is their relapse prevention plan? They can talk, walk, or use meditation as strategies for coping with stress.

Termination is the stage in which individuals have zero temptation to relapse and 100 percent confidence or self-efficacy that they will not go back to smoking or to drinking, even if they are anxious, lonely, or depressed. Some believe that with severe addictions it is a lifetime of recovery; others believe some former addicts can recover.

The construct of stages provides a framework for integrating change principles and processes from across different theories. Increasing awareness was first emphasized by Freud and is applied in Precontemplation to increase readiness and reduce resistance to change. Reinforcement was emphasized by Skinner and is used most in Action to reward progress in the face of temptations to relapse. We labeled our theory the Transtheoretical Model (TTM), because it integrates stages with processes of change from across different theories.

TTM was quickly recognized as a treatment paradigm for entire populations, and not just the select individuals ready to take immediate action. A population approach to health care calls for applied programs to be proactive and reach out to engage individuals in behavior change rather than wait passively for clients to call. Further, populations not ready to take action cannot be expected to come to clinics. We needed to create home or worksite interventions that provided interactive and individualized treatments. TTM inspired the first use of digital health interventions that guide participants through the stages with low cost and easy access. These innovations provide psychology a platform that combines the best of a clinical model (namely, individualized and interactive treatments) with the best of a public health model (namely, population-based interventions).

These complex innovations grew out of very simple scientific strategies. Stages were discovered through interviews with a sample of former smokers who quit on their own. Carlo DiClemente (a former student and cofounder of TTM) and I asked how often they applied each of ten change processes. Their answer was, "That depends on when you are talking about. I used one process [e.g., increasing awareness] quite a bit early on, but later I used other processes [e.g., reinforcement] most after quitting." Listening with the third ear of clinicians, these self-quitters were teaching us the stages of change.

With a much larger sample, we assessed each participant's stage and processes of change at baseline and followed them across time. In this initial analysis, done at one point in time (a cross-sectional analysis), we confirmed the systematic relationships between stages and processes predicted from our interviews. While students are often taught that cross-sectional studies produce low-impact research, our cross-sectional study was the second most cited article out of nearly 10,000 articles on tobacco. The first most cited article was our conceptual paper that included our initial discoveries on stages and processes.

As a student I learned that science is the search for truths, no holds barred. I also learned that constructs drive most behavior and behavior change – constructs such as stages and processes. The message is: your creative ideas matter most. Use the best methods your resources can support. But, recognize that like the stages and processes, big ideas can be supported by small and simple studies. Bigger studies can follow as your innovative ideas generate more resources.

After publishing descriptive cross-sectional studies, I proposed a bigger and riskier project, requiring more resources, for a randomized clinical trial testing three TTM treatments. Rather than a no-treatment control group, our riskier comparison group was the best home-based action and maintenance smoking cessation manual available. Our TTM treatments included: a stage-based cessation manual; this manual plus a computer driven treatment that matched expert guidance for processes at each stage; the manual, plus three computer guides and four proactive TTM counselor calls.

Our proposal responded to a Request for Proposals (RFP) for self-help cessation programs. Colleagues funded by this RFP said it was written for me and that our research design was elegant. But the primary reviewer concluded I was trying to leap ahead of the field, and gave the worst score we had ever received. Fortunately, a friend at the National Institutes for Health confided that I received a biased review but there was nothing I could do. He urged me to submit my proposal, with no revisions, to the Behavior Medicine Review Group, which was known as a killer committee. My proposal received the best score this committee had ever given. The message is that even if a reviewer doesn't like your big idea, you still may be right, and you have the right to test your ideas with the best methods available.

We were funded and our results were innovative and disruptive. We predicted that the computers plus counselors would produce the best outcomes; however, it was the computers alone that did best. Our counselors got depressed: our computers told them to seek social support. And this trial launched bigger and riskier studies driven primarily by digital technologies on single and multiple risk behaviors. Almost all of these trials produced high-impact outcomes, and we kept raising the bar with a broader range of populations and problems.

The next bar we hope to surpass is higher impact interventions for overweight and obese populations. A student and I reviewed the literature and were dismayed to find that there were practically no baseline predictors of successful weight loss across a broad range of theories, treatments, and samples. If you can't predict outcomes, how can you control outcomes?

In our single study to date, we found that only one of our best predictors of long-term weight loss was based on preventing disease. Other predictors included stage of change for exercise, diet, and emotional eating. The remaining predictors were related to multiple domains of well-being, such as happiness, respect, relationships to family, and functioning at home and work. My assumption is that our programs, and most of the field, have relied on health constructs as the biggest drivers for reducing risks. A second assumption is that multiple domains of well-being, such as happiness, relatedness, and thriving, can drive breakthrough outcomes.

Fortunately, we did a study with 4,000 participants from 39 states using computer-tailored interventions (CTIs) delivered by telephone counselors or online programs. The populations averaged 4 risk behaviors and 4 chronic conditions (e.g., diabetes), with 70 percent overweight or obese and the majority suffering or struggling rather than thriving. Compared to controls, our TTM treatments changed multiple behaviors (e.g., exercise, stress management, and diet) and enhanced multiple domains of well-being, including happiness, joy, and social relatedness. Most impressive was that our treatments produced a majority who went from suffering or struggling to thriving. This study was not about weight loss, but the results make us optimistic that a well-being-based weight program may produce unprecedented impacts.

REFERENCES

Prochaska, J. O., Norcross, J. C., & DiClemente, C. C. (1994). *Changing for good.* New York: Harper Collins.

Section D

Health and Positive Psychology

98   Psychological Origins of Cardiovascular Disease

Matthews, Karen

I had the good fortune of beginning graduate school when my major professor, David Glass, began his theoretical work on the Type A behavior pattern as a coping style aimed at maintaining control over stressful circumstances. Two cardiologists, Meyer Friedman and Ray Rosenman, described the Type A pattern as a constellation of characteristics: competitiveness, excessive achievement striving, time urgency, hypervigilance, and easily angered and hostile. They demonstrated that initially healthy men classified as Type A were at higher risk for subsequent coronary heart disease (CHD) compared to non-Type As (called Type Bs). As one who had vacillated between becoming a physician versus becoming a psychologist, I thought that investigating Type A behavior would be an optimal way to combine my interests in both psychology and health. Little did I realize at the time that a focus on Type A would launch my own career in investigating more broadly the psychological underpinnings of risk for cardiovascular disease (CVD). My primary research questions were two-fold: Who is at psychological risk for CVD? How does psychological risk for CVD develop over the life span? Before I describe how we addressed those questions, I briefly describe cardiovascular diseases, and I conclude by describing next steps for these research questions.

Cardiovascular Disease

Cardiovascular disease (CVD) refers to a number of diseases of the heart and circulation. Underlying many types of CVD is atherosclerosis, the accumulation of plaque in the arterial wall. Plaque is composed of fat, cholesterol, and other substances. Over time, the build-up of plaque and potential for rupture can partially or completely block blood flow to tissues, resulting in ischemia (i.e., inadequate blood supply) and tissue death. Depending on which arteries are blocked by plaque, different conditions occur. Heart attacks and chest pain (angina) result from

473

inadequate blood flow to the coronary arteries, stroke from inadequate blood flow to carotid arteries, and peripheral artery disease from inadequate blood flow to the arteries in the legs. Atherosclerosis develops slowly over the life-span, beginning in adolescence and young adulthood and accelerating in women after the menopause and in men in midlife. These facts suggest that investigations of psychological risk for CVD should take a life-span approach.

Who Is at Psychological Risk for CVD?

I began my research by asking a simple question. Given that the Type A behavior pattern is a constellation of characteristics, are some more important than others in conferring CVD risk? To investigate this question, David Glass and I were provided Type A interview data from men who were initially healthy but subsequently developed CVD and age-matched men who stayed CVD-free. We compared the men's answers in terms of content and style of answering the questions. For example, when asked if they felt a sense of time urgency, those who said "yes, most of the time" would be given a higher rating and their style of their response would be noted if they were quick and emphatic in their answers. To our surprise, the men who had CVD did *not* report that they were always punctual or enjoyed competition at work, relative to healthy controls. Rather, they reported being irritated waiting in lines, got angry frequently, and directed anger outward compared to healthy controls. Perhaps more important, their style of responding was rated overall as being relatively more vigorous and emphatic, and having a higher potential for hostility. We replicated the importance of overall hostility in a follow-up of men at high risk for CVD who were enrolled in the Multiple Risk Factor Intervention Trial. In that study, we showed that clinical ratings of potential for hostility, based on interview responses, predicted CVD mortality across sixteen years. These observations led us and other investigators to focus on angry affect and hostile attitudes as likely risk factors for CVD.

Even well-conducted longitudinal studies of risk factors for CVD morbidity and mortality have some disadvantages. Many individuals have underlying atherosclerosis but no symptoms indicative of ischemia, and some with debilitating chest pain have little evidence of plaque blockage in the coronary arteries, especially among women. Thus, only examining predictors of CVD morbidity and mortality may not estimate accurately the association of a psychological variable with CVD risk. Given our interest in the development of CVD risk across the life span, we began a series of studies of individuals without diagnosed CVD or stroke and we measured indices of subclinical CVD – that is, atherosclerosis in the coronary and carotid arteries. Our investigations, as well as studies by others, identified that negative cognitions (hostile, mistrustful attitudes, and pessimism) and negative emotions (anxiety, depression, and anger) were related to risk for subclinical CVD disease in men and women. These relationships were obtained well before the usual onset of clinical events. For example, in our study of healthy premenopausal women in their forties, those with a history of at least two episodes of major depression were more likely to have plaque in their carotid arteries and calcification in the coronary arteries and aorta than those without history. In the aggregate, the work on risk for subclinical CVD supports the utility of examining predictors of CVD risk at earlier stages in the life span. The answer to who is at risk for CVD has moved beyond Type A to include hostility, anger, and other negative emotions and cognitions.

How Does Psychological Risk for CVD Develop over the Life Span?

Although the initial concept of Type A was developed based on observations of middle- and upper-middle-class men, it is well known that individuals who are classified as lower in socioeconomic status (SES) based on income, education, and occupational prestige are at greater risk for CVD. Perhaps surprising is that being raised in low-SES families as a child is a strong predictor of CVD in adulthood, even in some analyses adjusting statistically for adult SES. Greater psychological stress and lower social support, as well as greater negative emotions, are correlated with lower SES. Thus, a comprehensive perspective regarding who is at elevated risk for CVD must consider psychological risk in the context of connections among SES, the social environment, and individual characteristics over the life span.

With Linda Gallo and Edith Chen, I have evolved life-span models that incorporate low-SES environments in order to understand pathways to CVD. Low-SES children are thought to grow up in more stressful and unpredictable environments, which may lead to developing a pattern of perceiving the world as a threatening place requiring heightened vigilance. If these experiences occur repeatedly, low-SES children may become pessimistic about their future, chronically anxious, and emotionally reactive, with the resultant physiological cost and the failure to develop a set of psychosocial resources (labeled "reserve capacity") to combat adversity. Reserve capacity is thought to be like a bank account, where environmental demands due to low SES can deplete resources and also prevent having the types of experiences that allow one to "add" to the account.

I have used the life-span model as a framework to guide hypothesis testing of aspects of the model rather than to confirm or reject the full model. Our studies have typically recruited samples of adolescents numbering 200–250, both Caucasian and African American, and followed them over several years. We measure psychosocial characteristics, stress, and biological parameters, including lipids, glucose, insulin, ambulatory blood pressure, sleep, and, in one study, subclinical CVD. We have reported that many of the hypothesized connections do occur and are similar to relationships observed in adult samples. For example, lower SES adolescents experience more chronic, ongoing stressors and also have elevated ambulatory blood pressure throughout the day. In addition, lower SES adolescents interpret ambiguous situations more negatively and have higher indices of subclinical disease. Moreover, reserve capacity (as reflected in positive psychosocial resources) is related to lower risk for the metabolic syndrome, defined as a composite clinical condition of high blood pressure, adverse levels of lipids and glucose, and large waist circumference. In most cases, our results are similar for Caucasians and African Americans. Our longitudinal work among adolescents and young adults thus far has not emphasized specific features of the family environment, namely conflict, expression of emotions, and parenting style. This brings us to the final question.

What Are the Next Steps in Understanding Psychological Underpinnings of CVD Risk?

Developmental psychology has a long history of identifying family characteristics and processes that lead children and adolescents to have adverse stress responses and poor mental health, including psychopathology and substance abuse. Investigators are expanding the outcomes of interest to precursors or indices of poor physical health, including those related to CVD risk. Ongoing efforts are mining data from longitudinal studies on family, school, and neighborhood environments and individual attributes, and collecting new data on physical health to address the early psychosocial underpinnings of cardiovascular risk in adulthood. Our own current studies address whether environmental and individual characteristics measured repeatedly in childhood and adolescence are associated with cardiovascular risk factors, sleep, and reactivity to stress among adults of different ethnic/racial groups. With these data, we hope to (a) disentangle the effects of SES and race/ethnicity on CVD risk; (b) identify the environmental characteristics that are health-damaging and the protective factors that are health-promoting; and (c) whether the relationships vary by developmental stage or race/ethnicity. Together with evidence from other investigations, our goal is to refine our understanding of the psychological origins of CVD based on detailed, longitudinal data. The next step will be to apply the knowledge base from the longitudinal studies to develop prevention programs that will improve the cardiovascular health of children and adolescence into the adult years – an important step that I hope our research will facilitate.

REFERENCES

Matthews, K. A. (2005). Psychological perspectives on the development of coronary heart disease. *American Psychologist, 60,* 783–796.

Matthews, K. A., & Gallo L. C. (2011). Psychological perspectives on pathways linking socioeconomic status and physical health. *Annual Review of Psychology, 62,* 501–530.

99   How Positive Psychology Happened and Where It Is Going

Seligman, Martin

How It Happened

"You're in deep shit, Marty," confided Ron Levant to me over a double scotch shortly after I had bombed in my attempt to persuade CAPP of my bright idea. CAPP was the organization of independent therapists that had controlled the 160,000-member American Psychological Association (APA) for two decades, and they were none too happy about my surprise election – by the largest margin in memory – to the Presidency of APA. He's a wolf in sheep's clothing, they rightly believed.

APA presidents are supposed to have an initiative and, having worked on the prevention and treatment of depression and helplessness for two decades, I thought mine could be "evidence-based treatment and prevention." So I went to my friend, Steve Hyman, the director of NIMH. He was thrilled and told me he would chip in $40 million dollars if I could get APA working on evidence-based treatment.

So I told CAPP about my plan and about NIMH's willingness. I felt the room get chillier and chillier. I rattled on. Finally, the chair of CAPP memorably said, "What if the evidence doesn't come out in our favor?"

I had made at least one friend in the ruling circles of APA – Ray Fowler, the long-serving and long-suffering CEO – and I limped my way to his office for some fatherly advice.

"Marty," he opined, "you are trying to be a transactional president. But you cannot out-transact these people. They are the masters of process and have more sitting power in their little fingers than your bottom could ever accumulate. You have to be a transformational leader."

And so I proposed that Psychology turn its scientific and practice attention away from pathology and victimology and more toward what makes life worth living: positive emotion, positive character, and positive institutions. I never looked back and this became my mission for the next fifteen years. The endeavor was generously backed by the Templeton Foundation and by Atlantic Philanthropies, and, to my surprise, it caught on.

Some metrics of its catching on and making a difference from 1998–2015:

- Funding. From zero to a total of at least $200 million.
- Courses: From none to hundreds and in almost every university in the world.
- Science: From a handful to thousands of refereed articles on well-being, meaning, positive emotion, good relationships, and life satisfaction. Dozens of monographs, several textbooks, and scores of science-based trade books on well-being.
- Interventions: A dozen random-assignment placebo-controlled validated interventions to build well-being.
- Practitioners: Thousands of practitioners worldwide using positive psychology in the consulting room, the class room, the military, and the board room.
- Associations: The International Positive Psychology Association – the Chinese, Indian, Canadian, Colombian, Mexican, Brazilian, South African, European, Austrian, Australian, Danish, Czech, and Polish, to name a few.
- Graduate degrees: Masters of Applied Positive Psychology at Penn, East London, Chile, and Melbourne. Doctorate in Positive Psychology at Claremont.
- Spin-off Sciences: Positive Education, Positive Neuroscience, Positive Health.

Where Is Positive Psychology Headed Now?

After about a decade of working on PERMA (Positive emotions, Engagement, Relationships, Meaning, and Accomplishment), I sensed that something deeper than the mere neglect of the positive was missing from psychology-as-usual.

What troubles people – what we are sad or anxious or angry about – is for the most part in the past or in the present. What we desire, in contrast, is more often in the future. A psychology that devotes itself to troubles – psychology-as-usual – can get away with an epistemology that emphasizes the past and the present and that regards the future as wholly derived from the past and present. Hence psychology's 120-year obsession with memory (the past) and perception (the present), and the absence of serious work on such constructs as expectation and planning. Hence the appeal of a naïve hard determinism in which behavior in the future is frog-marched by past history in combination with genes and present stimuli.

Psychology can do better than this, and with Roy Baumeister, Peter Railton, and Chandra Sripada, and backed by the Templeton Foundation, we began to work on *prospection*, the idea that we are *homo prospectus* not *homo sapiens*. What our species is really good at is looking into the future. Once you take this name seriously, what follows is much more than semantic. It promotes prospection to the front and center of a new psychological science. The future – and particularly cognition about the future – is very much a back-burner issue in psychology currently and has been so for more than a century. The canonical human being *homo psychologicus* is a prisoner of the past and the present. Psychoanalysis, Behaviorism, and even most of Cognitive Psychology embody this deterministic premise. But their results – in terms of predicting future behavior – have been less than impressive; some would say they have been a failure.

We view human action as drawn by the future. Humans metabolize the past to create the future, *but we are not driven* by the past. We suspect there are many topics opaque to a past/present framework that prospection breaks wide open: free will, vision, consciousness, morality, intuition, character, emotion, creativity, social intelligence, and psychopathology.

Here are the questions we are pursuing now:

What if vision is not the registration of what is present, but a hallucination of the future?

What if memory is not a file drawer of photographs, but a hope chest of possibilities?

What if emotion is not agitation from the now, but guidance for the future?

What if happiness is not the report of a current state, but the prediction of how things are going to go?

What if morality is not evaluation of the present action, but the prediction of character and its thrust into the future?

What if knowing a person is not about the last crossroad they faced, but what they will do at the next crossroad?

What if the mind is not a storehouse of knowledge, but an engine of prediction?

Taylor, Shelley E.

A favorite story of mine concerns a child riding on her father's shoulders while out on a walk, when they encounter a friend. "My, how you've grown," says the friend. "Not all of this is me," responds the little girl. Writing about one's "most important scientific contribution" is like this story, in the sense that all science is collaborative. Consequently, many other people are implicated in these comments, and others may remember things quite differently. Nonetheless, that said, I believe my most important scientific contribution has been nurturing and giving structure to new scientific fields, specifically three now-active areas of research.

The first field is health psychology. In 1975, Judith Rodin (then a Yale professor) asked me if I would write a paper for the West Coast Cancer Foundation on what psychology has to teach us about breast cancer and its management. I told her it would be a pretty short paper, as there was not much literature on the topic. She urged me to take it on anyway, and so Smadar Levin (a graduate student at Harvard who was also a breast cancer patient) and I wrote the paper, which ultimately was nearly 100 pages long.

That experience whetted my appetite for bringing health and psychology together. I began by writing a textbook to try to shape the field, borrowing heavily from what were called, at the time, medical sociology and medical anthropology, as well as related fields. It took a while to get the book published, because there was no obvious market for it. Eventually, a very enthusiastic editor at Random House, Judith Rothman, accepted it, calling it a chicken–egg book: The book will help create the field; the field will adopt the book. I am grateful to her for her encouragement, for her insight, and, consequently, for putting my children through college.

The field began to come together through the separate efforts of several groups, some of which were unknown to each other. The time was right. The National Heart, Lung, and Blood Institute was beginning to fund behavioral medicine grants. A group at UCSF, under the leadership of George Stone, published the first collection of readings in the field.

Clinical psychology graduate students were beginning to find jobs in medical settings that went beyond therapy and psychological testing. Research programs began to spring up. My own empirical contributions focused primarily on psychosocial resources and their benefits for coping with cancer. Later, with Margaret Kemeny, we showed how such resources not only assist coping with HIV infection, but also affect the course of disease.

At present, the field is enormous, with its own division at APA and many scholarly groups around the country and around the world. I am happy to have been a part of health psychology's early history and to have had a role in training its early scholars and shaping its future.

The second field in which I had an early nurturing role is social cognition. When Susan Fiske and I set out in the early 1980s to write a book that would define what is now a vibrant cross-disciplinary field, there was only a set of loosely woven threads, including attribution theory, person perception, social inference, and social schemas, among other topics. Susan had joined the faculty at Carnegie-Mellon University, and her colleague, Chuck Kiesler, pushed us to do the book. (It is no surprise that Chuck's field of expertise was persuasion.) Susan took the lead, and together we crafted an outline that Addison Wesley assured us would have high visibility and make lots of money. Our royalties turned out to be a meager 10 percent of what had been projected, but, in the spirit of turning lemons into lemonade, it also contributed to my empirical work on the benefits of positive illusions. That book has now come out in several iterations, as it has incorporated the newer work of the past thirty-five years, especially social cognitive neuroscience. The impact of social cognition has been felt throughout psychology as cognitive perspectives have been incorporated in every sub-discipline. Social cognition also helped shape the highly impactful field of behavioral economics, so much so that some leading economists call themselves psychologists as much as economists (or, at least, they ought to).

Social cognition began with liberal borrowing from cognitive psychology, but slowly the social and affective underpinnings of social thinking and behavior began to be integrated as well. As more became known about how the brain processes social information, fMRI and related technologies became tools of the field, and biological perspectives were integrated into social cognition. These developments helped to shape the third field whose development I have had the privilege of nurturing.

That field is social neuroscience. In the early 1990s, I became intrigued by the biological underpinnings of social phenomena. This curiosity was fueled by participation in the MacArthur network on Socioeconomic Status and Health, under the direction of Nancy Adler. The members of that group, especially Bruce McEwen and Karen Matthews, were far more biologically sophisticated than I was, and that spurred me to become more knowledgeable. My lab and I focused especially on the neuroendocrine underpinnings of social behavior. We studied the psychosocial and biological costs of stress, especially effects on immune and hypothalamic adrenocortical (HPA) axis functioning. We considered how the compromised functioning of these systems, especially early in life, might portend future physical and mental health disorders. We developed a theory termed "tend and befriend," which maintains that hormones (including oxytocin and vasopressin) and opioid functioning underpin social responses to stress, especially tending (the protection and care of offspring during times of stress) and befriending (namely, turning to others for social support). This theory was not intended to replace the classic fight-or-flight model of responses to stress, but, rather, point to how the general arousal caused by stress is channeled into socially protective group behaviors, especially among women.

Social neuroscience eventually morphed into social cognitive neuroscience, which focuses on brain pathways implicated in social psychological phenomena. I was a late arrival to the brain party, but having already done a lot of neuroendocrine work, I was an enthusiastic, well-lubricated latecomer. Our work has focused on changes in the aging brain that may contribute to vulnerability to deception among older adults.

Our focus on neuroendocrine pathways has, I think, benefitted the field in two primary ways. First, it has helped link social neuroscience directly to health psychology, and, as a result, many social neuroscientists maintain a strong presence in both fields. (Naomi Eisenberger is a good example of a scholar who has made exceptional contributions to both fields.) The second benefit has been to foster a perspective that links macro- and micro-levels of analysis. By linking data within participants, beginning with their SES and family background, to psychosocial resources (such as social support) to individual resources (such as optimism and personal control), and to brain and neuroendocrine responses in a stress paradigm, we are able to create a biopsychosocial portrait of a person that has implications for their mental and physical health across the life-span.

At one time, bringing biological perspectives into psychology was regarded as reductionistic, diminishing psychological phenomena to firing neurons, with no brain, heart, or soul. The biobehavioral integration we currently see, which is fostered by both health psychology and social neuroscience, acknowledges and celebrates the fact that responses to life's circumstances occur at all interacting levels of the organism, from cells to social status.

When I first decided to become a scientific researcher, I had hoped to find a big picture – an answer to questions of how people become who they are and why they behave as they do. The first dozen or so years of my career provided modest answers, but not the big ones. But as these fields – social cognition, health psychology, and social neuroscience – have grown and attracted many researchers, each of whom brings some puzzle pieces to the table, a broad vision has taken shape.

The integrative biobehavioral vision that has emerged in my work and that of others has helped me transition to a new phase in my career. It involves fostering the integrative research of others, designed to elucidate and improve social and living conditions. I was originally attracted to psychology because of its focus on racial, gender, and social inequalities. At this advanced stage in my career, I can return in important ways to those roots. By serving on multiple boards, including the Russell Sage Foundation, the Annual Review of Psychology, the American Academy of Political and Social Science, and DBASSE (Division of Behavioral and Social Science and Education) in the National Academy of Sciences, I try to foster, and fight for, the integrative research I value so highly, and to contribute in a small way to reducing social inequalities and improving mental and physical health.

REFERENCES

Fiske, S. T., & Taylor, S. E. (2013). *Social cognition: From brains to culture* (2nd edn.). Beverly Hills: Sage Publishers.

Taylor, S. E. (2002). *The tending instinct: How nurturing is essential to who we are and how we live*. New York: Holt.

Taylor, S. E. (2015). *Health psychology* (9th edn.). New York: McGraw-Hill.

Part VIII

Conclusion

101 Becoming an Eminent Researcher in Psychological Science

Sternberg, Robert J.

If you will agree that, by virtue of their objectively defined eminence, the contributors to this volume qualify as eminent, then you might ask what characteristics *you* would need to develop to become an eminent researcher like they are. I have reviewed the contributions in this book and find that the contributors, collectively, show the characteristics that theories of creativity identify as critical for doing creative work. What are some of these characteristics?

- **Hard work.** When you read the essays, you find that *all* of the scientists have at least one thing in common: They have worked incredibly hard. There are lots of smart people in this world – people with elevated test scores, high grades, clever ideas. But without hard work, you just can't get on a list of top researchers.
- **Willingness to formulate an extended program of research.** In academia, there are plenty of "one-shot" wonders – scientists who have one great idea and then are never able to get past it. Although most of the investigators in this book have written about their best – or, at least, favorite – idea, in no case did they just do one big study and then call it a day. All of the investigators pursued their big idea(s) through extended investigations, testing the ideas, comparing the ideas to opposing ideas, revising the ideas as needed. They all were in the research enterprise as a marathon, not as a sprint.
- **Willingness to set their own, often idiosyncratic paths.** Some investigators began their key research with their doctoral advisors. Others set out on paths entirely different from those of their advisors. But none of the contributors just took someone else's idea and pursued it. However they may have started out, they eventually forged their own path, moving forward (or sometimes sideways) along whatever paths they or their advisors may have started on.
- **Willingness to surmount obstacles.** There is quite a bit of variation in the described level of obstacles the investigators met. Some speak of obstacles strewn all along the paths they followed; others hardly

mention obstacles at all. But you cannot achieve greatness without setbacks, including major ones: critical grant proposals turned down, major articles rejected, failed colloquia, conflicts with collaborators. The great investigators persist in the face of difficulties that would lead others simply to give up.

- **Above-average analytical intelligence.** To be a great scientist, you do not have to be an IQ maven. But you probably need to have above-average intelligence to be highly successful. Intelligence is something you can develop, up to a point. Schooling is one of the best ways to develop it; applying yourself to any challenging intellectual task, in school or outside, is another.

- **Intellectual curiosity.** A theme that comes out again and again is that the investigators were driven not primarily by awards or promotions or "publish or perish" or really any extrinsic motivators – they were driven by their intense intellectual curiosity to understand and even "conquer" certain psychological phenomena. They worked hard because they wanted to learn, not just because they wanted to achieve the trappings of success.

- **Openness to new experiences.** The investigators in this volume show themselves to be "intellectual opportunists." They see an opportunity to learn something new, to do something new, to try out a new technique, and they grab that opportunity. They are not investigators who just settle on a fixed idea or set of ideas and then stay with the same agenda throughout their careers. Rather, their intellectual agendas evolve as they do. Importantly, they do not let their expertise get in the way of creating. They do not just have one success, bask in it, and then continue to do the same old same old throughout their careers.

- **Intellectual honesty.** You can fake your way to the first level of fame and maybe even the second, but, at least today, you can't fake your way to the top in psychological science. Along with professional visibility comes increased scrutiny, and the more visible you become, the more you and your work are scrutinized. If you can't pass the scrutiny, you become stuck on the ladder of fame – or, worse, fall quickly from it and come crashing down. As in the children's game of Chutes and Ladders, for every ladder, there is a chute waiting to catch those who are not wary of how quickly they can fall.

- **Intellectual courage.** Very few scientists who make it to the top simply buy into existing paradigms and extend those paradigms. Much more often, they invent their own paradigms, or at least substantially transform existing paradigms. To set out in these new directions takes courage. When you "defy the crowd," you make people nervous. Scientists all love creativity, except when it threatens them personally.

Colleagues often view as threats scientists who up-end the existing order.

- **Collaborative skills.** Although our focus in this volume is on individual contributions, a common theme in the chapters is the extent to which collaboration has propelled individuals in their careers. If you can't work with others, you lose the great benefits of those collaborations. It is worth noting that this volume contains chapters by mentors and their students – that is, success often passes between generations from mentor to advisee and on to the next generation of advisees. Therefore, find great mentors and collaborators!

- **Willingness to take intellectual risks.** None of the contributors to this volume are scientists who, throughout their careers, have chosen to "play it safe." They all took great intellectual risks, sometimes pursuing ideas that many of their colleagues would have viewed as hare-brained or foolish. You can become a mid-level researcher by playing it safe; you can't reach the top that way.

- **Taste in scientific problems.** It is sometimes said that "there is no accounting for taste," and it truly is hard to understand why some people develop better scientific taste than others; role models would seem to play a large role. But great scientists recognize important problems and can distinguish them from less important ones. Being in an environment that appreciates big and important problems certain helps. Although most of the emphasis in a graduate education is on problem solving, in the end, the greatest scientists are first and foremost those who find important problems to solve.

- **Finding what you love to do.** Great scientists love their work. You can see it as a subtext in each and every account in this book, and Howard Gardner, a contributor to this volume, has found that essentially all of the most creative people he studied reveled in their work. Excitement about your work does not guarantee you will reach the top, but it is hard to get there without it.

- **Communication and persuasion skills.** Most, although certainly not all, great psychological scientists are excellent communicators. They have to be. Creative work does not explain or sell itself; the scientist has to explain his or her work and then convince people that the work is important. Without strong communication skills, it is easy to become a frustrated scientist, because while you may be doing great work, you are likely to have trouble persuading people that it is great.

- **Tolerance of ambiguity.** When one commences one's scientific career, one hopes that one will design conclusive studies that, at best, prove one's hypotheses to be correct, and, at worst, show them to be wrong. Then one will know whether to keep going with an idea or to call it quits. In reality, such conclusive results rarely occur. Most studies yield ambiguous results, even if the ambiguity is not apparent at first. After one submits an article for peer review, one often discovers that referees see in one's results ambiguities that one did not detect oneself. To keep going, one needs to learn to tolerate ambiguity and to live with the fact that there is very little – if anything – in psychological science that can be shown to be true for all people under all circumstances.

- **Self-efficacy.** Self-efficacy is basically your belief in your own competence for your work and your ability to increase this competence with effort. There will be many times in most people's careers when one senses that others are losing confidence in one. It may be that one has had some rejected papers or grant proposals, or that one has had a string of failed experiments. It may be that one has become distracted by external life events. Everyone has challenging periods in life. The truly successful scientists are the ones who keep believing they can succeed, even in the face of such difficult times.

- **Know your strengths and weaknesses.** No one is good at everything. But virtually everyone is good at some things. The contributors to this volume all succeeded at a very high level, but in entirely different ways. Some were quantitatively oriented, others biologically oriented; some more theoretical in their approach, others more straight empirical. There is no one "right" way to do research: You need to find approaches as well as topics that work for you individually.

- **Niche-picking.** As Teresa Amabile points out in her chapter in this volume, people's creativity depends heavily on the environment they are in. If an environment discourages creativity, it is difficult to take the risks involved in being creative. Therefore, you want to do whatever you can to find an environment in which to work – and live – that encourages and rewards creativity and lets you follow your dreams. Many institutional environments advertise that they do so – that's not enough. Make *sure* they do.

- **Luck.** We're ending with luck for a reason. When all is said and done, luck plays a much greater part in success than any of us would like to admit. Were you born in a country or region of a country where you have even a reasonable chance of becoming educated? Did your parents support your education, or could they even afford to get you educated? Did you find good mentors? Did you take one or more courses in psychology that turned you on to the field? The list goes on. To some extent, you can make your own good luck by seizing opportunities when they are presented to you. But realistically, some people are never presented with the opportunities that can lead them to become star researchers.

We all are malleable. If you think you can develop these characteristics within yourself, you are on your way, if not to becoming one of the top psychological scientists, then at least toward becoming a distinguished psychological scientist who can take great pride in his or her accomplishments.

REFERENCES

Amabile, T. M. (1996). *Creativity in context*. Boulder: Westview.

Gardner, H. (2011). *Creating minds*. New York: Basic.

Kaufman, J. C., & Sternberg, R. J. (eds.) (2010). *Cambridge handbook of creativity*. New York: Cambridge University Press.

Simonton, D. K. (2002). *Great psychologists and their times: Insights into psychology's history*. Washington, D.C.: American Psychological Association.

Sternberg, R. J., & Lubart, T. I. (1995). *Defying the crowd: Cultivating creativity in a culture of conformity*. New York: Free Press.

Afterword: Doing Psychology 24×7 and Why It Matters

Cantor, Nancy

Careers, like much of life, are funny things, rarely following a linear, predictable course, but often carrying forward a theme expressed in a multitude of ways. I started my "career" as a psychologist as a child riding the New York City subways back and forth to school, soaking in the energy and vibrancy of the diversity in the faces in those crowded cars, always wondering what each person's story was and where they were going, what they believed in and how they and I would all get along and make it to our destinations, being so different both on the surface and surely beneath it.

That theme – the complexity and diversity of individuals and the challenge and opportunity for us to travel together – still fascinates me. It motivated me as a student and then a faculty member to pursue both laboratory and field research in social and personality psychology, but always with an interest in the "real world," and how what we did in academia could make life better beyond it. And I haven't been disappointed, even if there is much more to do.

As the range of the essays in this remarkable volume attest, psychological science has unpacked everything from the plasticity of the brain to the toughest questions of human aggression and violence, and there is still so much more that we can learn about why human beings sometimes do and often don't live up to our potential as "social animals," as Elliot Aronson so compellingly labelled us.

Now as a university chancellor, so many years after I first read *The Social Animal* and thought back to those faces on the NYC subway, colleagues and friends often ask me why I gave up psychology for academic leadership (as a chair, dean, provost, and then chancellor). And, frankly, I look at them as if they are crazy and say "What? I do psychology 24x7 in this job" – and that is the beauty and power of psychological science. It is everywhere and it matters.

I do psychology when I think about how to recognize talent in the children in our communities who are often left out of the "race to the top," especially those whose "intelligence" and "creativity" might not be captured by narrow indicators on standardized tests used for selecting who gets the chance to excel in life that education affords. I think then of the groundbreaking work of Sternberg, Gardner, Amabile, Salovey, and others in this volume, which leads us to stretch our imaginations about what it means to be "smart" on so many dimensions. And I wonder how to convince us all to look for the students whose range of intelligence is shrouded by the curtain that poverty and poorly performing schools inevitably brings down.

As a university leader and community-engaged citizen in Newark, New Jersey, where my university is located, I see both the talent and the curtains that come down on it, and I know that we can't build a thriving nation without that talent being able to enter the race to excellence. Heartfelt words, however, won't suffice to motivate the kinds of investment in our future talent pool that needs to happen. We need to use psychological science to remind people that some children start life as if already on third base, and as much as we want them to keep on running, there are others too that might well thrive if we just looked hard enough below the surface.

I do psychology when I think of the positive effect that a "growth mindset," as described by Carol Dweck, would have in motivating and supporting the educational race for those children. At the same time, I ponder the risks they face of under-performing due to stereotype threat, which as Claude Steele so forcefully reminds us is ubiquitous in this highly charged landscape of implicit biases about race, gender, sexuality, class, and other dimensions of difference engrained in our social-cognitive maps of the world. We can't take for granted that uncovering talent is enough; we have to keep using psychology to overcome the obstacles along each person's pathway to growth and achievement.

I do psychology when the amazingly diverse students of my university, where there is no predominant racial or ethnic group and many students are the first in their families to go to college, ask how we can better leverage that diversity. How do we build a maximally inclusive community where solidarity with one's "own kind" need not preclude connectedness to the "other"? I think immediately of the grand tradition of research on group dynamics, inter-group contact, culture, and conflict resolution, as Morton Deutsch and Harry Triandis exemplify.

I do psychology when I act like a defensive pessimist – a concept that Julie Norem and I coined many years ago to describe the tendency of some high-achieving individuals to set low expectations in the face of challenges, only to work like the dickens to proactively make sure that good outcomes happen. It is easy to think like a defensive pessimist, to anticipate that the human tendency toward diffusion of responsibility – "oh, someone else will handle that emergency" – will overcome the care that we should naturally show for others, even strangers, and then to be moved by the compassion that sometimes surfaces in this very stressed and strife-filled world, as Susan Fiske reminds us.

The study of complex human social behavior – social cognition, intelligence, group dynamics, social development, personality, even brain and behavior relationships and the effects of stress on mood, performance, and health – matters to virtually every interaction we have in the world: to how we get along in the workplace, in relationships, with friends and with strangers, and to our ability to think creatively, to set goals, to weather crises, and to grab opportunities, as all of the essays in this volume so pointedly remind us. For me, the links between how individuals understand themselves and their world, and their scripts and strategies for adapting to it, on the one hand – John Kihlstrom and I called it social intelligence – and the challenges that we seem to have in this world in living together, in supporting each other, in relating to people with different life experiences, in building a just, peaceful, and socially connected society, on the other hand, are so profoundly important to unpack that we can't possibly progress without doing psychology 24/7, each and every one of us.

So, like the curious young girl on the subway, the committed (if somewhat defensively pessimistic) student and then scholar, and now the civically engaged university leader, I'm still watching and wondering, and trying to do my part in smoothing the trip for the next diverse generation of citizens, professionals, and leaders. To do that, I need psychology 24/7, and it matters. If you've read this book, you know how much it matters, and how much psychology can change the world for the better.

REFERENCES

Cantor, N., & Kihlstrom, J. F. (1987). *Personality and social intelligence*. Englewood Cliffs: Prentice-Hall.

Norem, J., & Cantor, N. (1986). Defensive pessimism: "Harnessing" anxiety as motivation. *Journal of Personality and Social Psychology, 51*(6), 1208–1217.

Steele, C. M. (2010). *Whistling Vivaldi: How stereotypes affect us and what we can do*. New York: W.W. Norton & Company.

Index